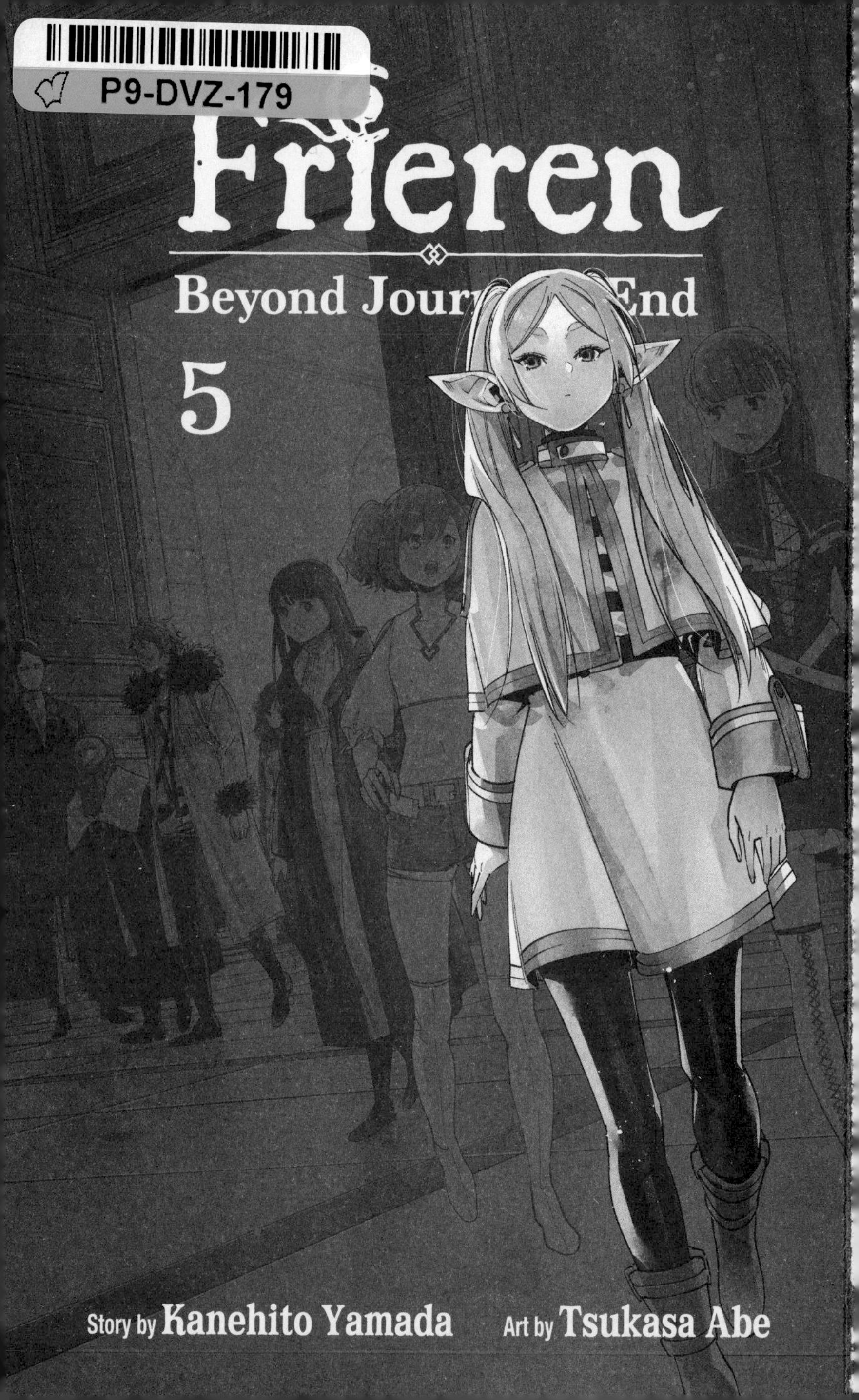
Frieren
Beyond Jour End
5
Story by Kanehito Yamada
Art by Tsukasa Abe

CONTENTS

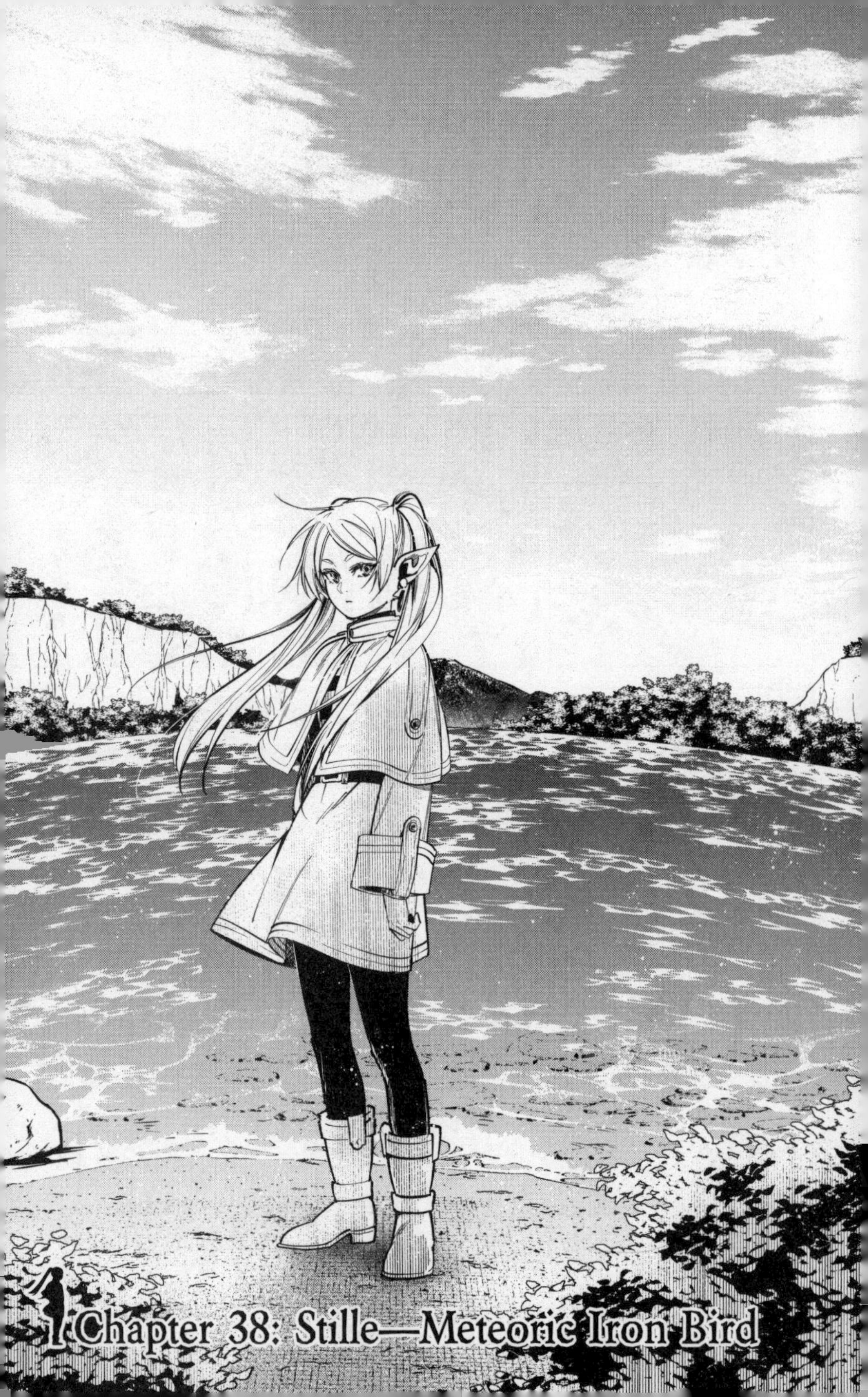
Chapter 38: Stille—Meteoric Iron Bird

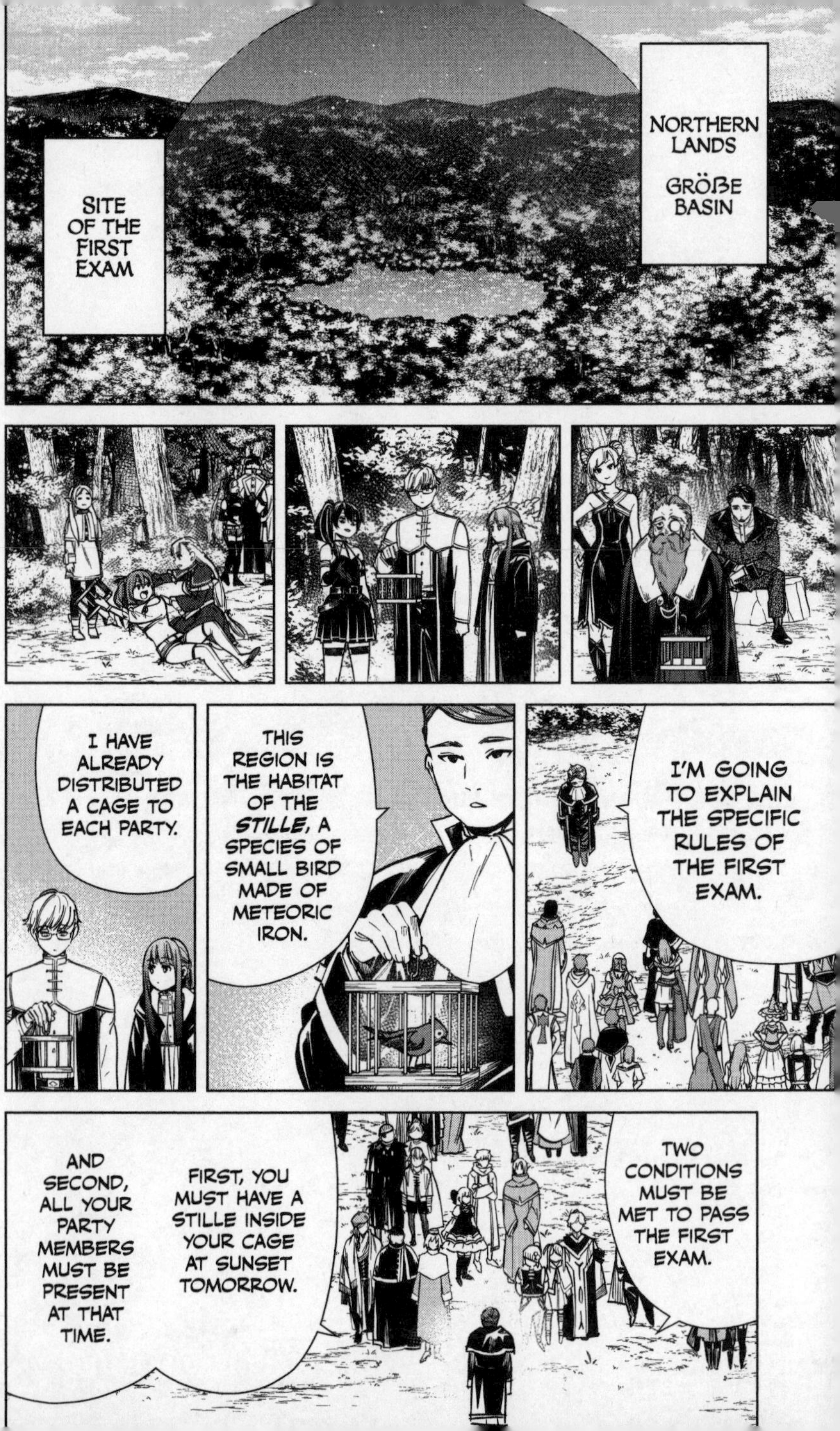
NORTHERN LANDS
GRÖßE BASIN
SITE OF THE FIRST EXAM
I'M GOING TO EXPLAIN THE SPECIFIC RULES OF THE FIRST EXAM.
THIS REGION IS THE HABITAT OF THE *STILLE*, A SPECIES OF SMALL BIRD MADE OF METEORIC IRON.
I HAVE ALREADY DISTRIBUTED A CAGE TO EACH PARTY.
TWO CONDITIONS MUST BE MET TO PASS THE FIRST EXAM.
FIRST, YOU MUST HAVE A STILLE INSIDE YOUR CAGE AT SUNSET TOMORROW.
AND SECOND, ALL YOUR PARTY MEMBERS MUST BE PRESENT AT THAT TIME.

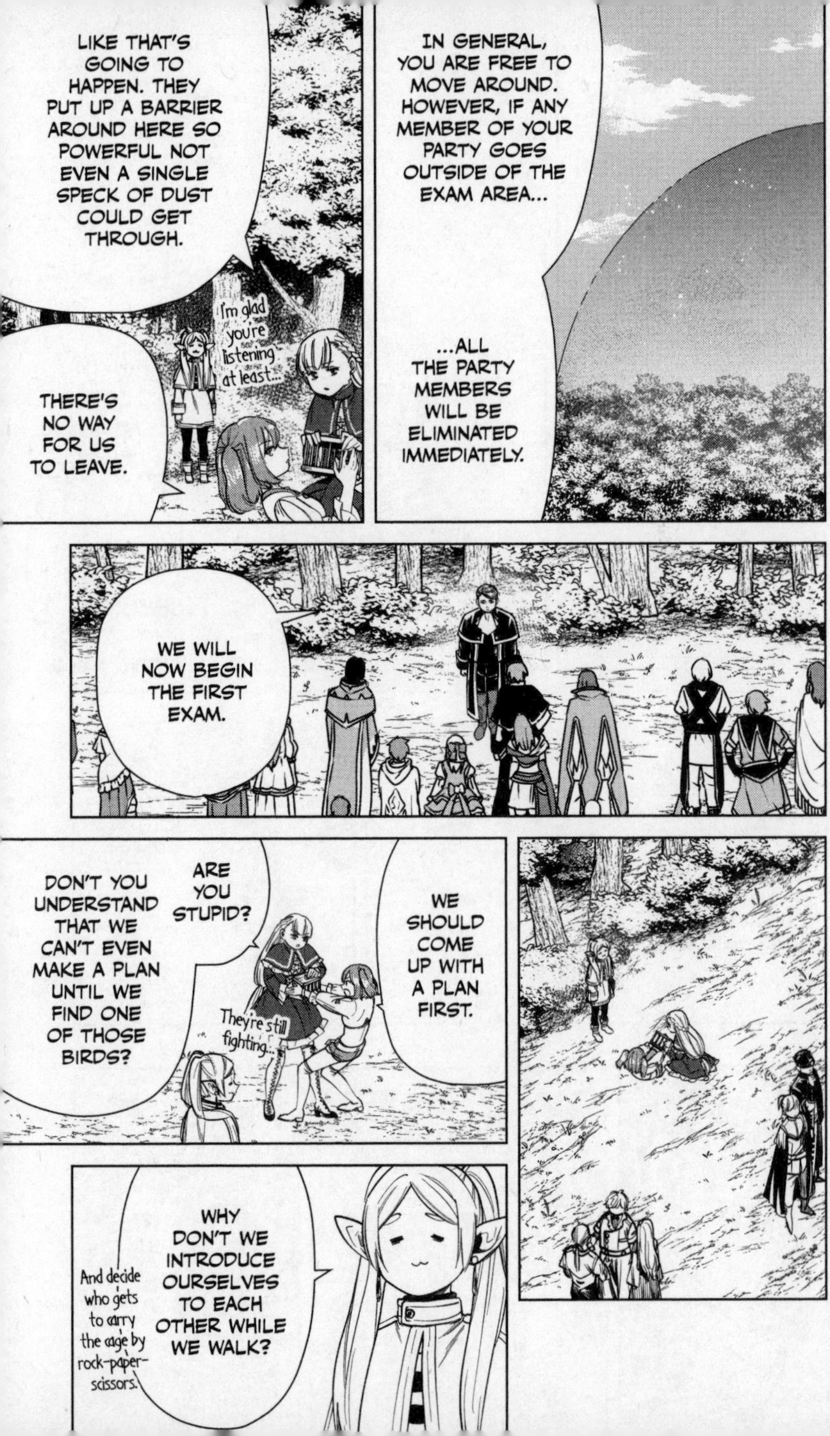
IN GENERAL, YOU ARE FREE TO MOVE AROUND. HOWEVER, IF ANY MEMBER OF YOUR PARTY GOES OUTSIDE OF THE EXAM AREA...
...ALL THE PARTY MEMBERS WILL BE ELIMINATED IMMEDIATELY.
LIKE THAT'S GOING TO HAPPEN. THEY PUT UP A BARRIER AROUND HERE SO POWERFUL NOT EVEN A SINGLE SPECK OF DUST COULD GET THROUGH.
I'm glad you're listening at least...
THERE'S NO WAY FOR US TO LEAVE.
WE WILL NOW BEGIN THE FIRST EXAM.
WE SHOULD COME UP WITH A PLAN FIRST.
ARE YOU STUPID?
DON'T YOU UNDERSTAND THAT WE CAN'T EVEN MAKE A PLAN UNTIL WE FIND ONE OF THOSE BIRDS?
They're still fighting...
WHY DON'T WE INTRODUCE OURSELVES TO EACH OTHER WHILE WE WALK?
And decide who gets to carry the cage by rock-paper-scissors.

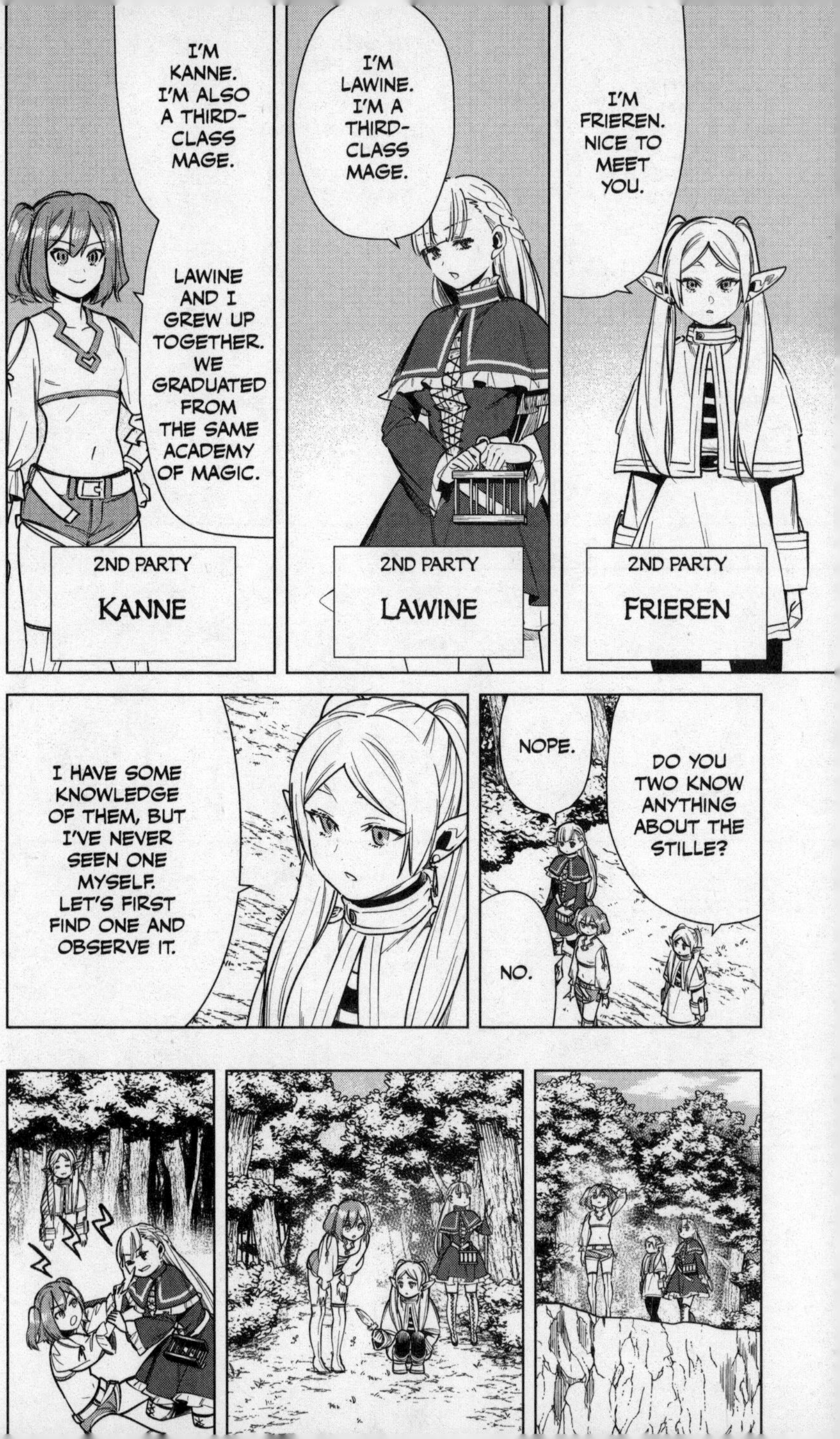
I'M FRIEREN. NICE TO MEET YOU.
2ND PARTY
FRIEREN
I'M LAWINE. I'M A THIRD-CLASS MAGE.
2ND PARTY
LAWINE
I'M KANNE. I'M ALSO A THIRD-CLASS MAGE.
LAWINE AND I GREW UP TOGETHER. WE GRADUATED FROM THE SAME ACADEMY OF MAGIC.
2ND PARTY
KANNE
DO YOU TWO KNOW ANYTHING ABOUT THE STILLE?
NOPE.
NO.
I HAVE SOME KNOWLEDGE OF THEM, BUT I'VE NEVER SEEN ONE MYSELF. LET'S FIRST FIND ONE AND OBSERVE IT.

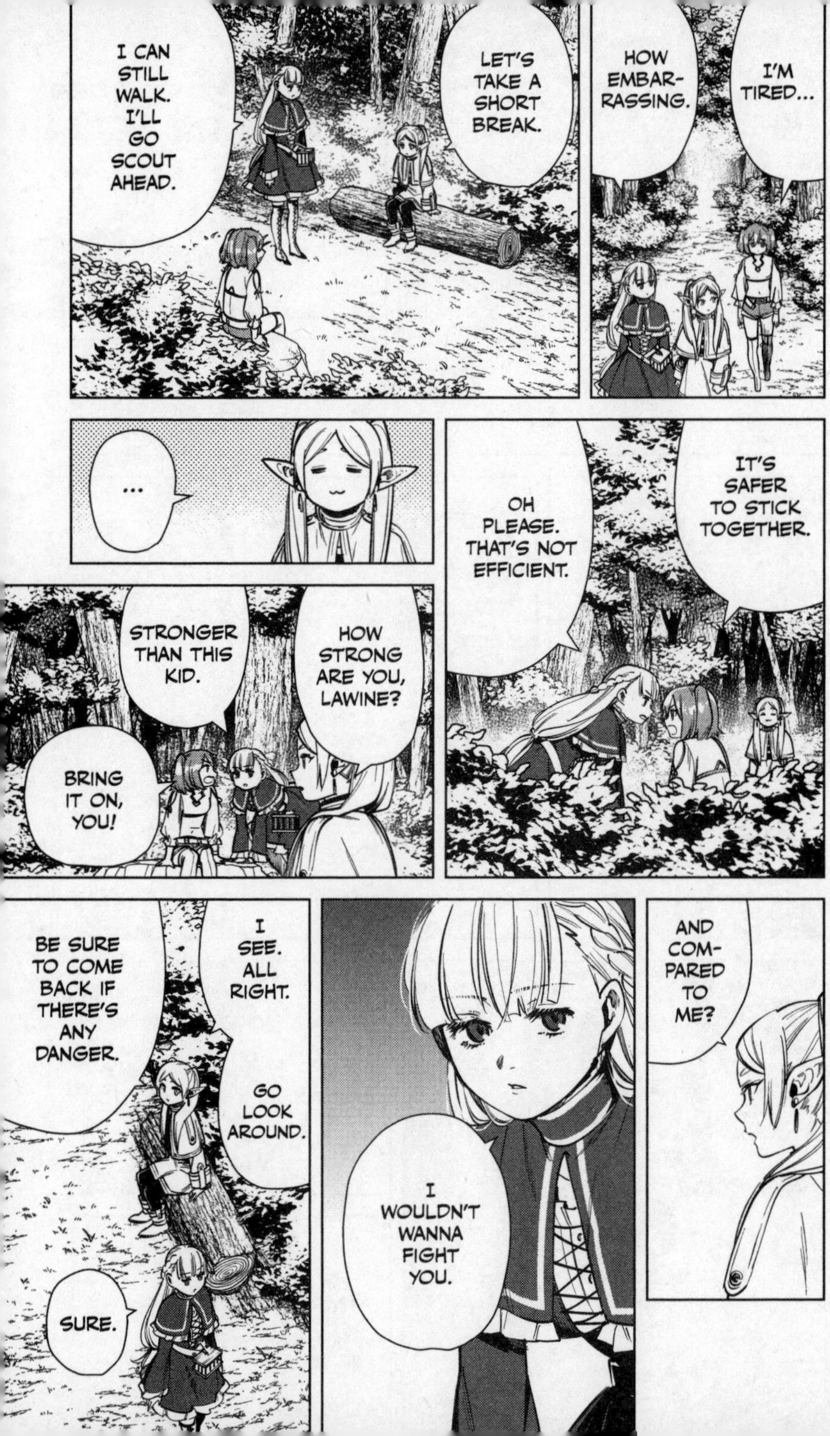

I'M TIRED...
HOW EMBARRASSING.
LET'S TAKE A SHORT BREAK.
I CAN STILL WALK. I'LL GO SCOUT AHEAD.
IT'S SAFER TO STICK TOGETHER.
OH PLEASE. THAT'S NOT EFFICIENT.
...
HOW STRONG ARE YOU, LAWINE?
STRONGER THAN THIS KID.
BRING IT ON, YOU!
AND COMPARED TO ME?
I WOULDN'T WANNA FIGHT YOU.
I SEE. ALL RIGHT.
BE SURE TO COME BACK IF THERE'S ANY DANGER.
GO LOOK AROUND.
SURE.

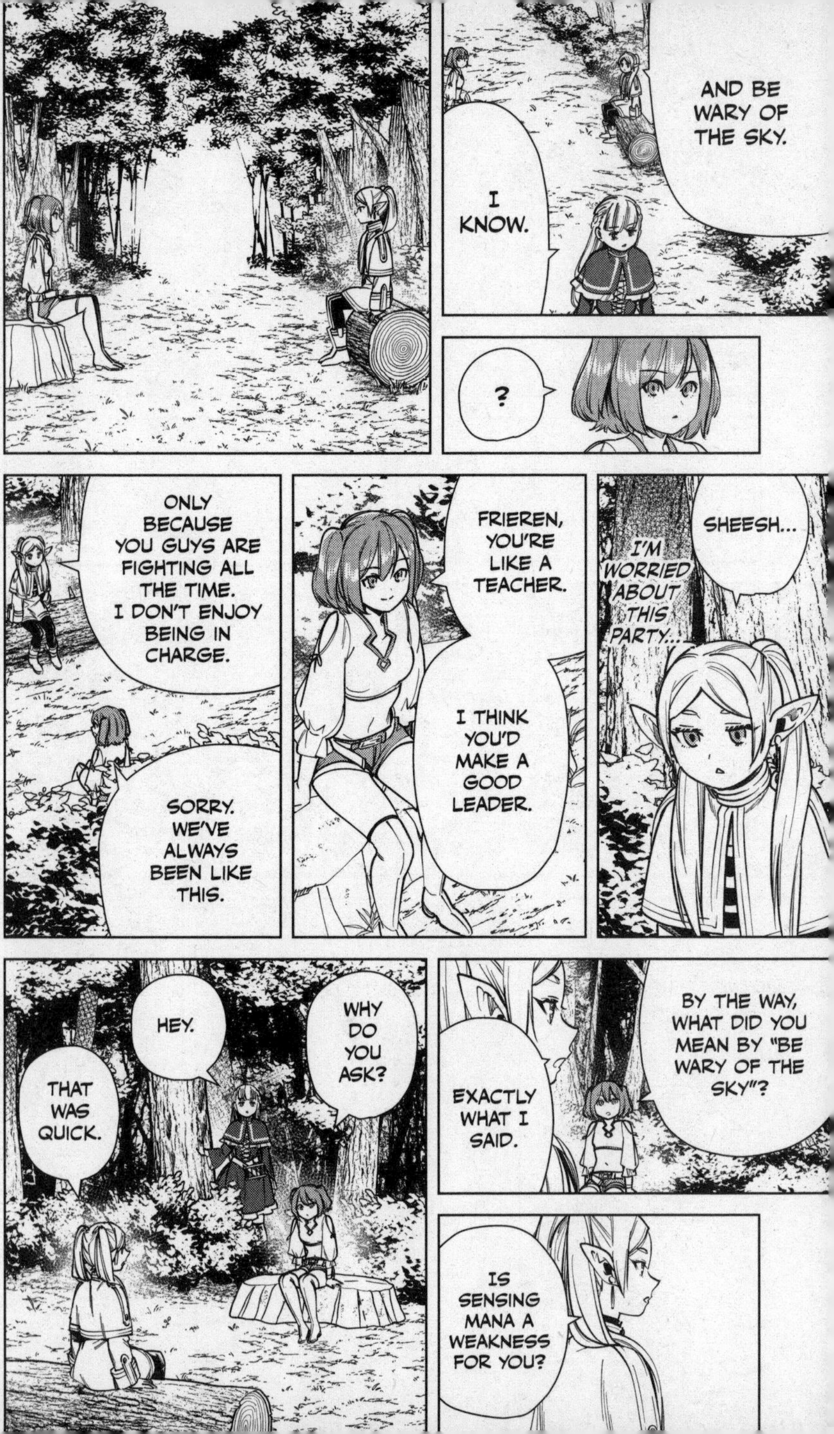
AND BE WARY OF THE SKY.
I KNOW.
?
SHEESH...
I'M WORRIED ABOUT THIS PARTY...
FRIEREN, YOU'RE LIKE A TEACHER.
I THINK YOU'D MAKE A GOOD LEADER.
ONLY BECAUSE YOU GUYS ARE FIGHTING ALL THE TIME. I DON'T ENJOY BEING IN CHARGE.
SORRY. WE'VE ALWAYS BEEN LIKE THIS.
BY THE WAY, WHAT DID YOU MEAN BY "BE WARY OF THE SKY"?
EXACTLY WHAT I SAID.
IS SENSING MANA A WEAKNESS FOR YOU?
WHY DO YOU ASK?
HEY.
THAT WAS QUICK.

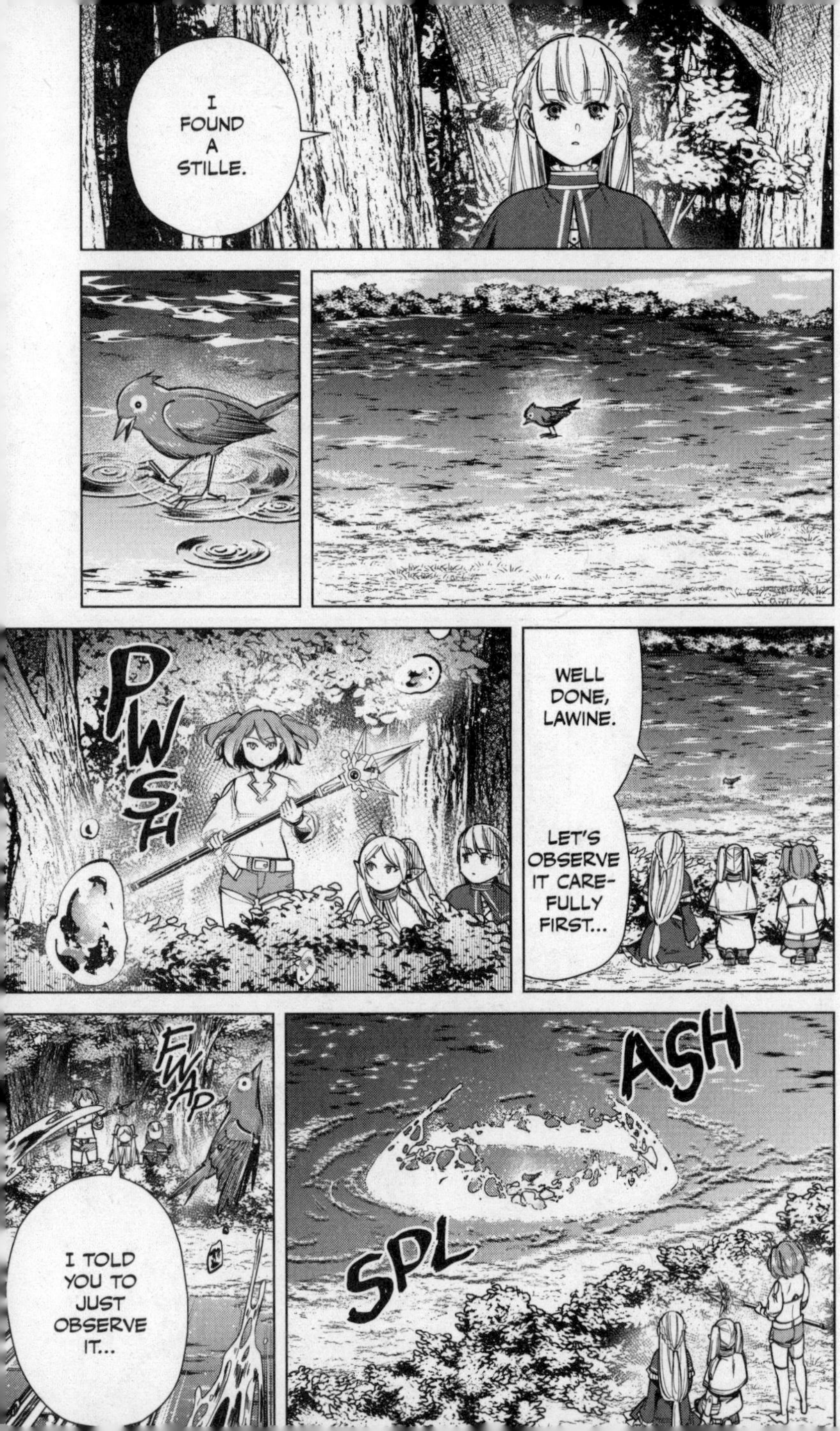
I FOUND A STILLE.
WELL DONE, LAWINE.
LET'S OBSERVE IT CARE-FULLY FIRST...
PWSH
ASH
SPL
FWAP
I TOLD YOU TO JUST OBSERVE IT...

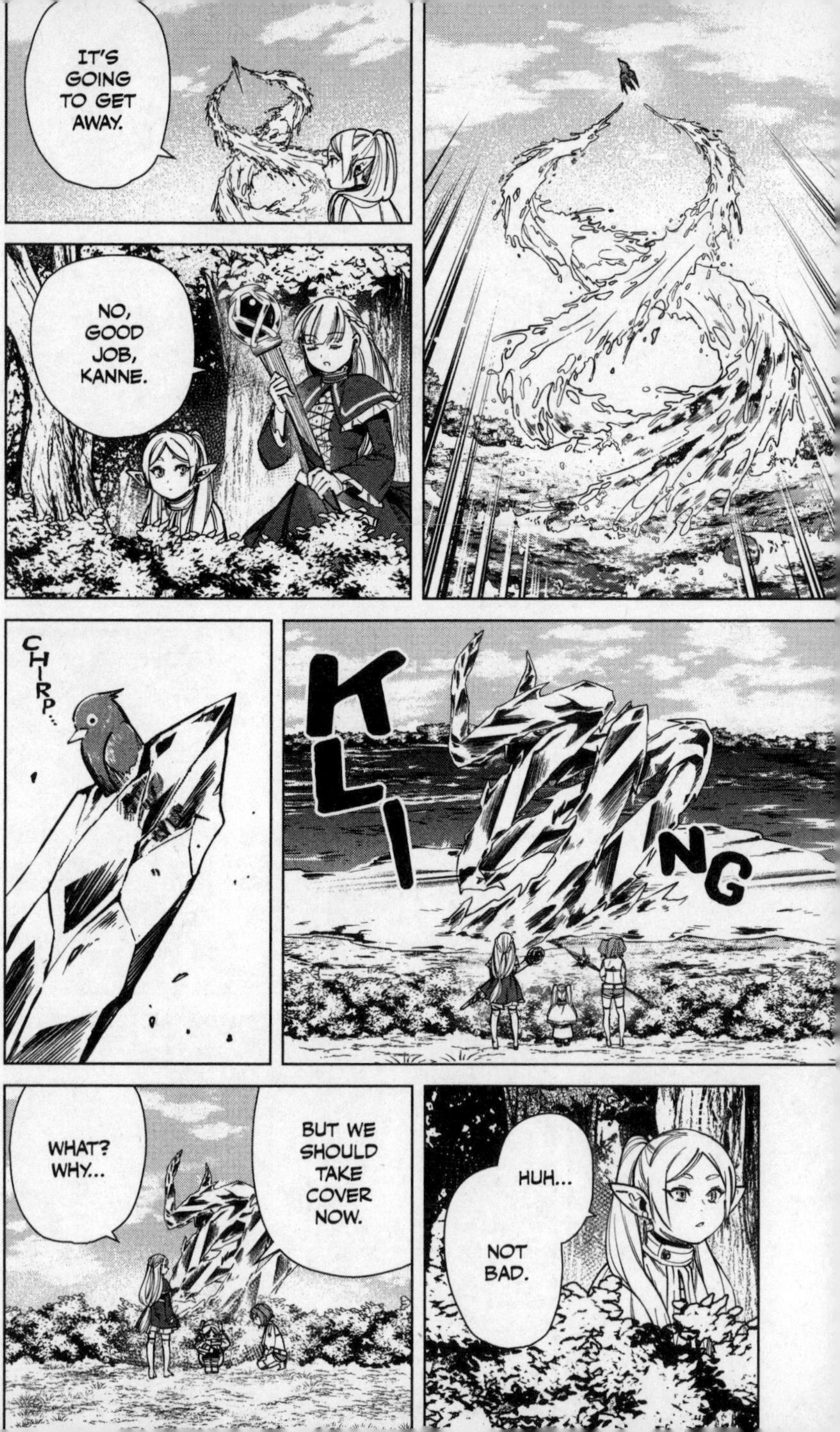
IT'S GOING TO GET AWAY.
NO, GOOD JOB, KANNE.
KLIIING
CHIRP...
HUH...
NOT BAD.
BUT WE SHOULD TAKE COVER NOW.
WHAT? WHY...

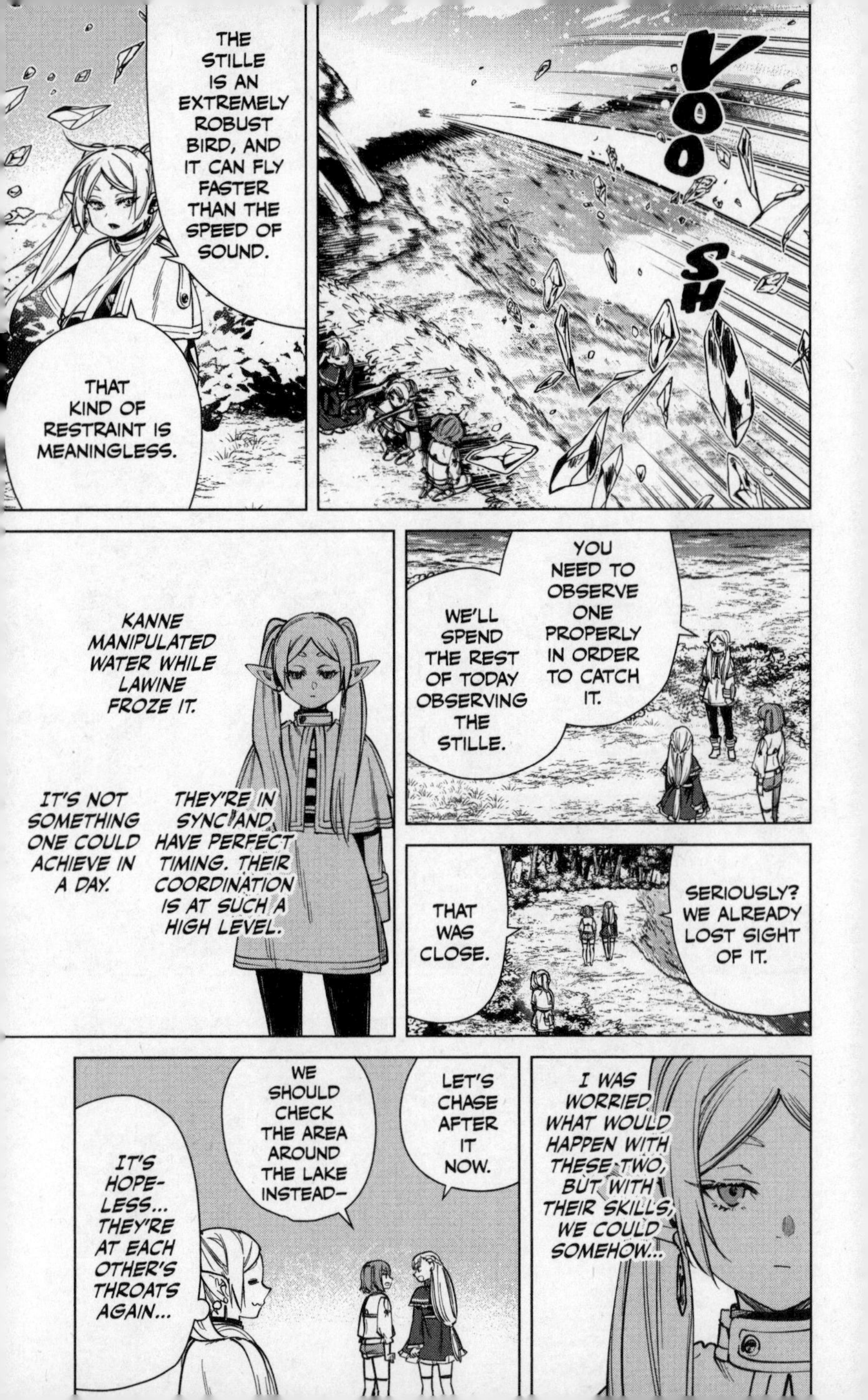
VOOOSH
THE STILLE IS AN EXTREMELY ROBUST BIRD, AND IT CAN FLY FASTER THAN THE SPEED OF SOUND.
THAT KIND OF RESTRAINT IS MEANINGLESS.
YOU NEED TO OBSERVE ONE PROPERLY IN ORDER TO CATCH IT.
WE'LL SPEND THE REST OF TODAY OBSERVING THE STILLE.
SERIOUSLY? WE ALREADY LOST SIGHT OF IT.
THAT WAS CLOSE.
KANNE MANIPULATED WATER WHILE LAWINE FROZE IT.
THEY'RE IN SYNC AND HAVE PERFECT TIMING. THEIR COORDINATION IS AT SUCH A HIGH LEVEL.
IT'S NOT SOMETHING ONE COULD ACHIEVE IN A DAY.
I WAS WORRIED WHAT WOULD HAPPEN WITH THESE TWO, BUT WITH THEIR SKILLS, WE COULD SOMEHOW...
LET'S CHASE AFTER IT NOW.
WE SHOULD CHECK THE AREA AROUND THE LAKE INSTEAD—
IT'S HOPE-LESS... THEY'RE AT EACH OTHER'S THROATS AGAIN...

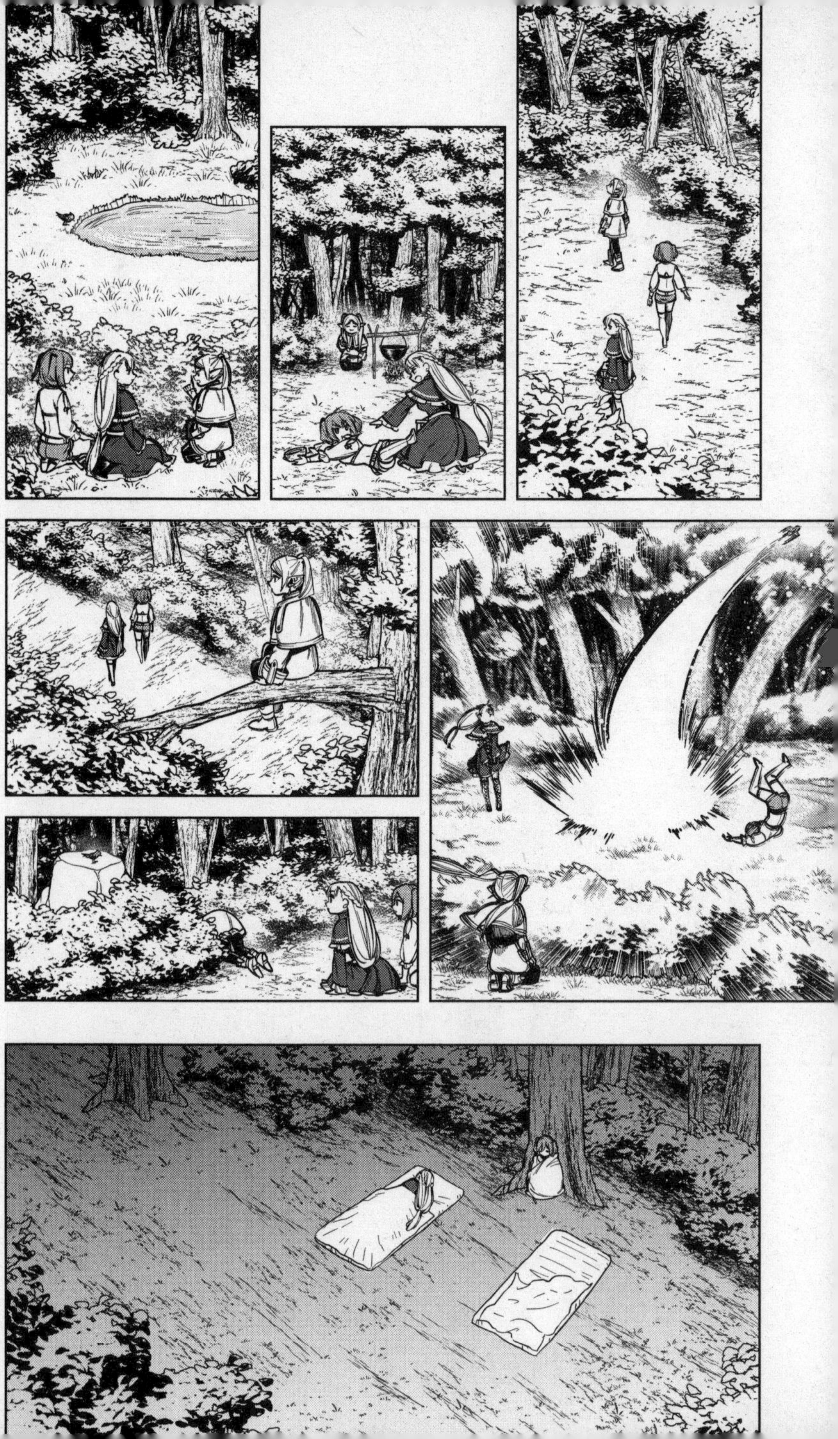

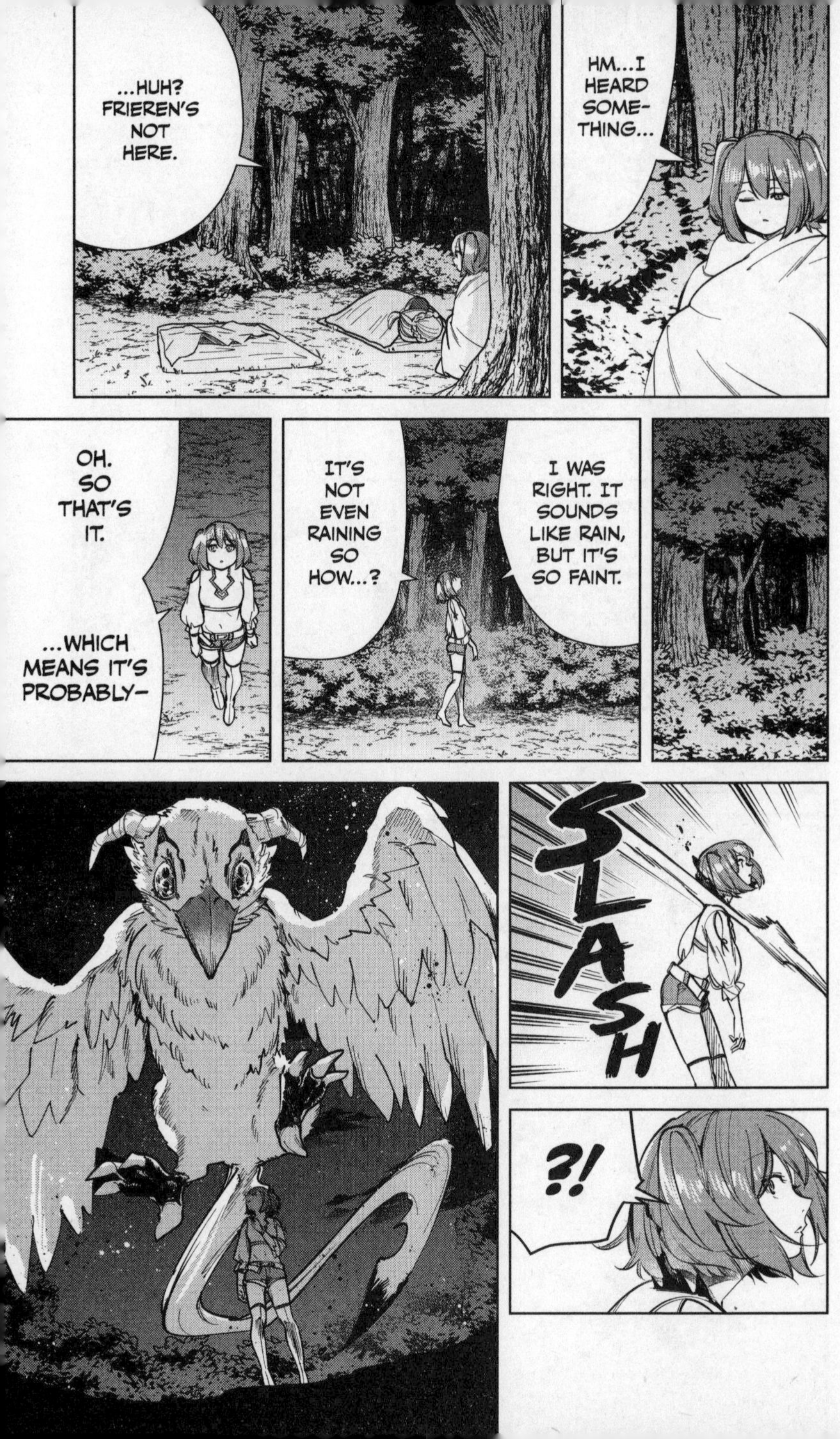
HM...I HEARD SOME-THING...
...HUH? FRIEREN'S NOT HERE.
I WAS RIGHT. IT SOUNDS LIKE RAIN, BUT IT'S SO FAINT.
IT'S NOT EVEN RAINING SO HOW...?
OH. SO THAT'S IT.
...WHICH MEANS IT'S PROBABLY–
SLASH
?!

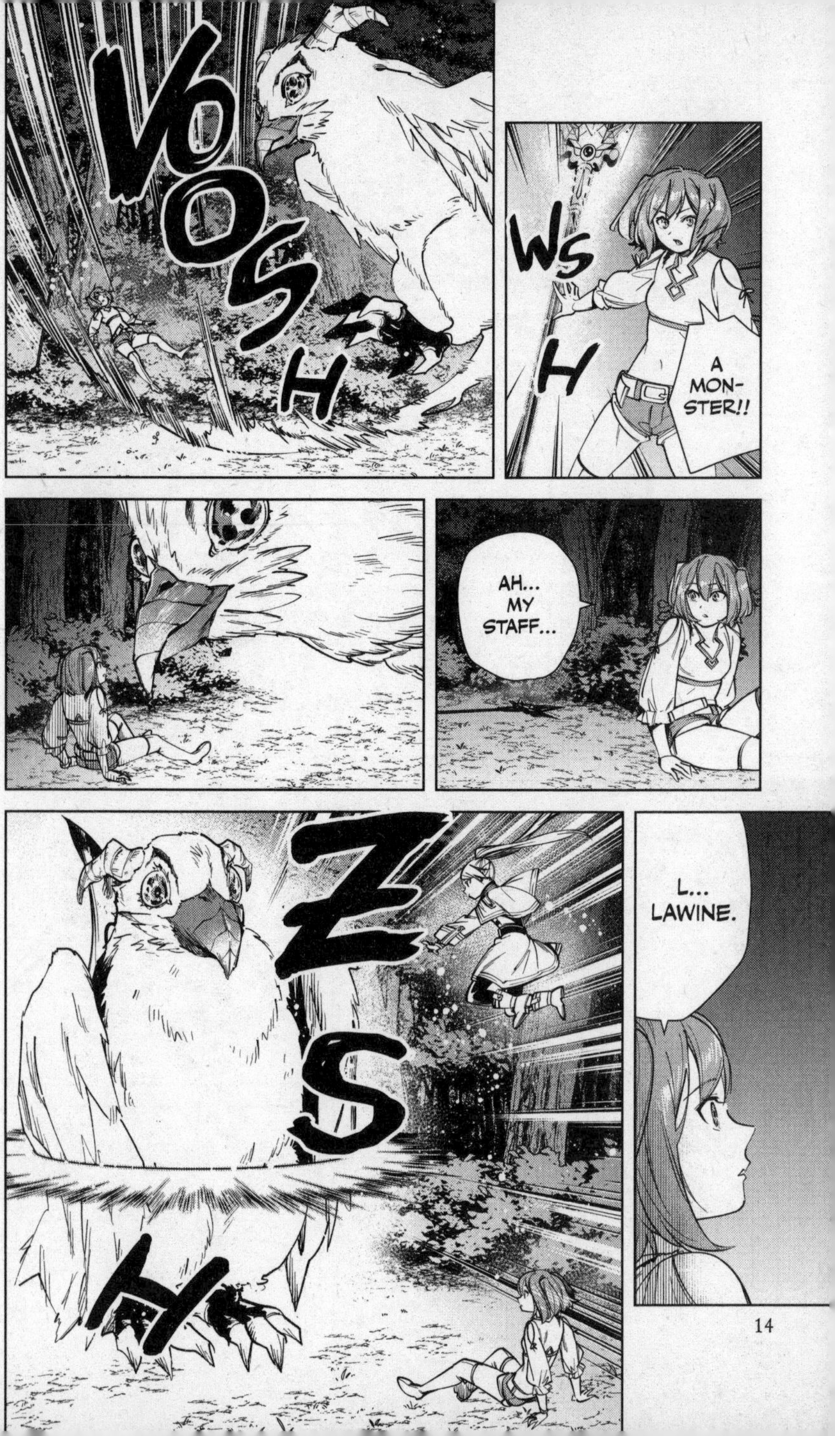
WSH
A MON-STER!!
VOOSH
AH... MY STAFF...
L... LAWINE.
ZSSH

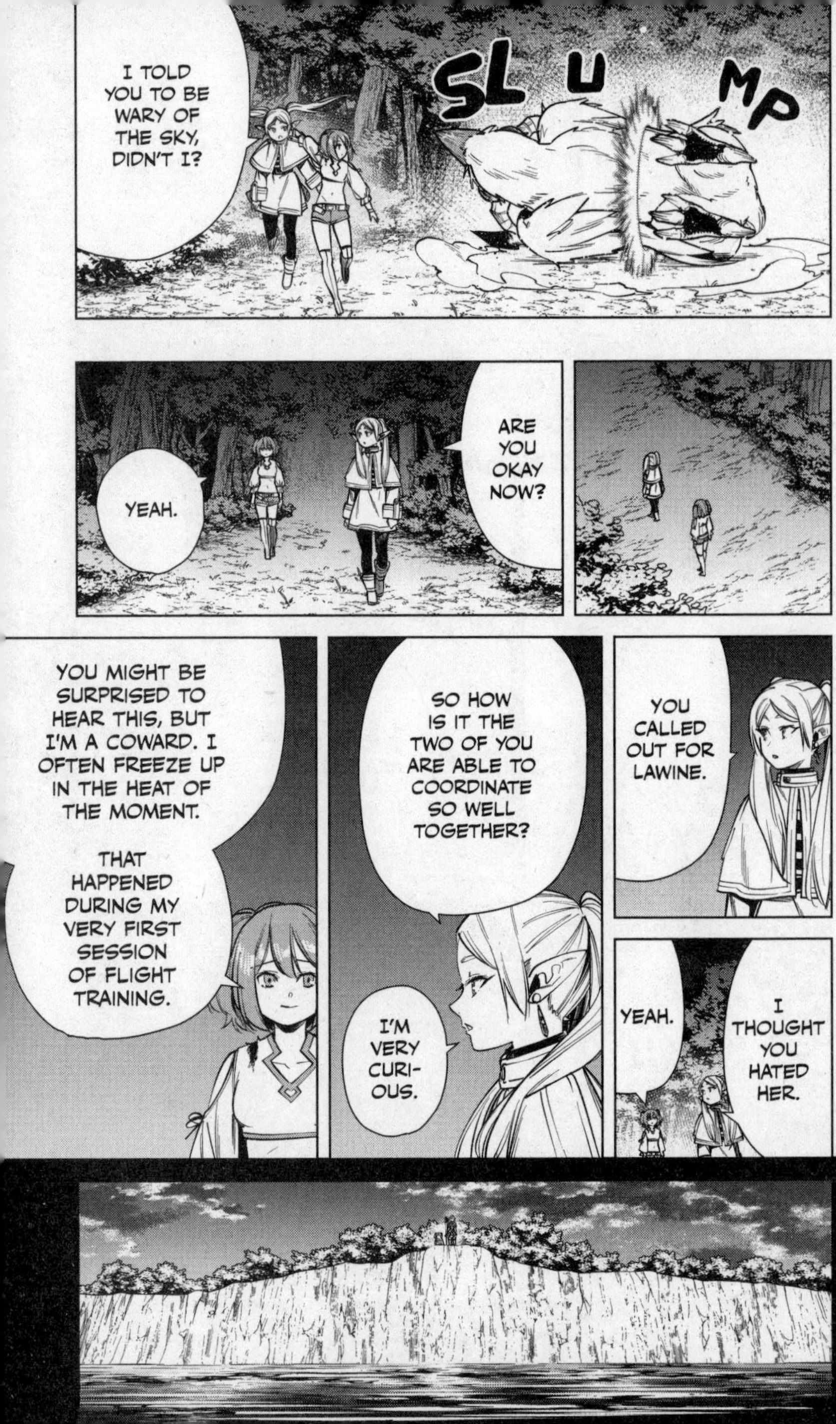
SLUMP
I TOLD YOU TO BE WARY OF THE SKY, DIDN'T I?
ARE YOU OKAY NOW?
YEAH.
YOU CALLED OUT FOR LAWINE.
I THOUGHT YOU HATED HER.
YEAH.
SO HOW IS IT THE TWO OF YOU ARE ABLE TO COORDINATE SO WELL TOGETHER?
I'M VERY CURI-OUS.
YOU MIGHT BE SURPRISED TO HEAR THIS, BUT I'M A COWARD. I OFTEN FREEZE UP IN THE HEAT OF THE MOMENT.
THAT HAPPENED DURING MY VERY FIRST SESSION OF FLIGHT TRAINING.

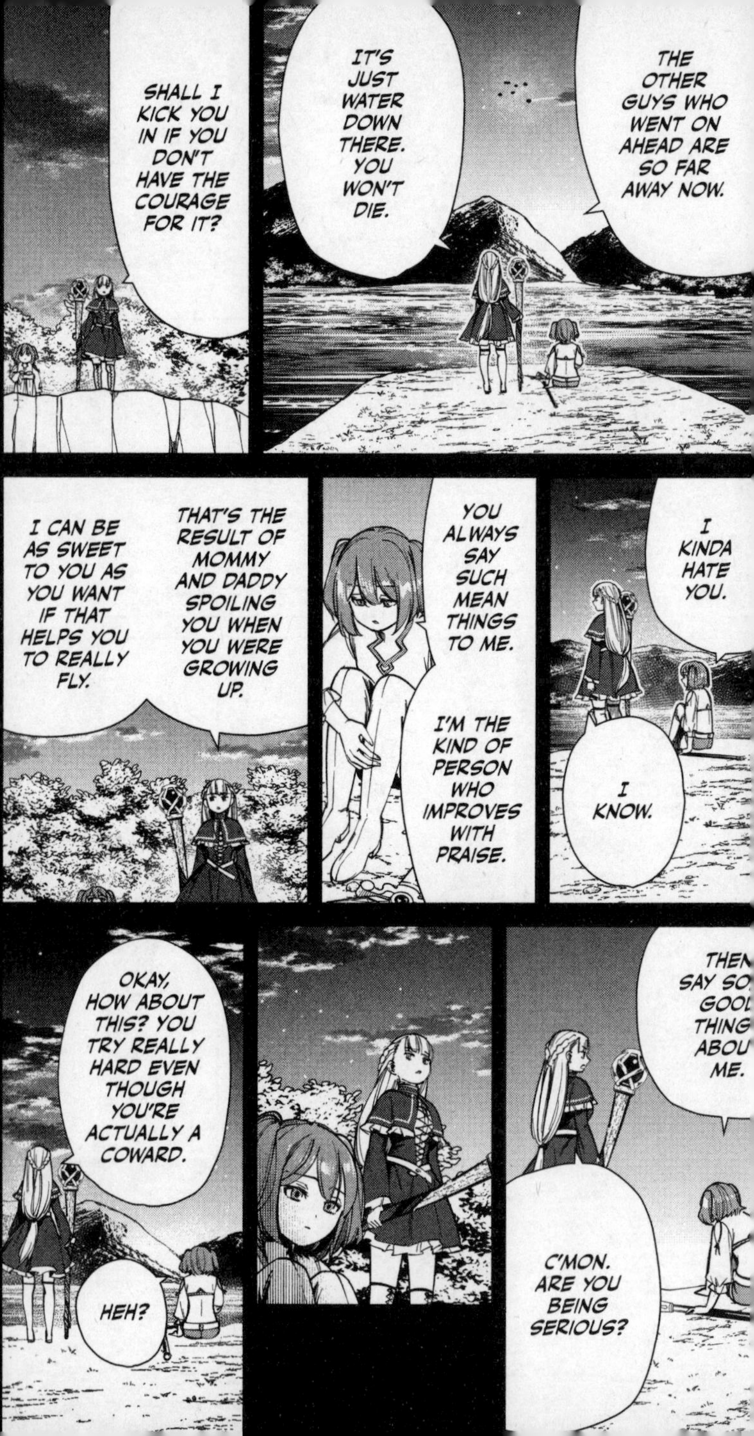
THE OTHER GUYS WHO WENT ON AHEAD ARE SO FAR AWAY NOW.
IT'S JUST WATER DOWN THERE. YOU WON'T DIE.
SHALL I KICK YOU IN IF YOU DON'T HAVE THE COURAGE FOR IT?
I KINDA HATE YOU.
I KNOW.
YOU ALWAYS SAY SUCH MEAN THINGS TO ME.
I'M THE KIND OF PERSON WHO IMPROVES WITH PRAISE.
THAT'S THE RESULT OF MOMMY AND DADDY SPOILING YOU WHEN YOU WERE GROWING UP.
I CAN BE AS SWEET TO YOU AS YOU WANT IF THAT HELPS YOU TO REALLY FLY.
THEN SAY SO GOOD THING ABOU ME.
C'MON. ARE YOU BEING SERIOUS?
OKAY, HOW ABOUT THIS? YOU TRY REALLY HARD EVEN THOUGH YOU'RE ACTUALLY A COWARD.
HEH?

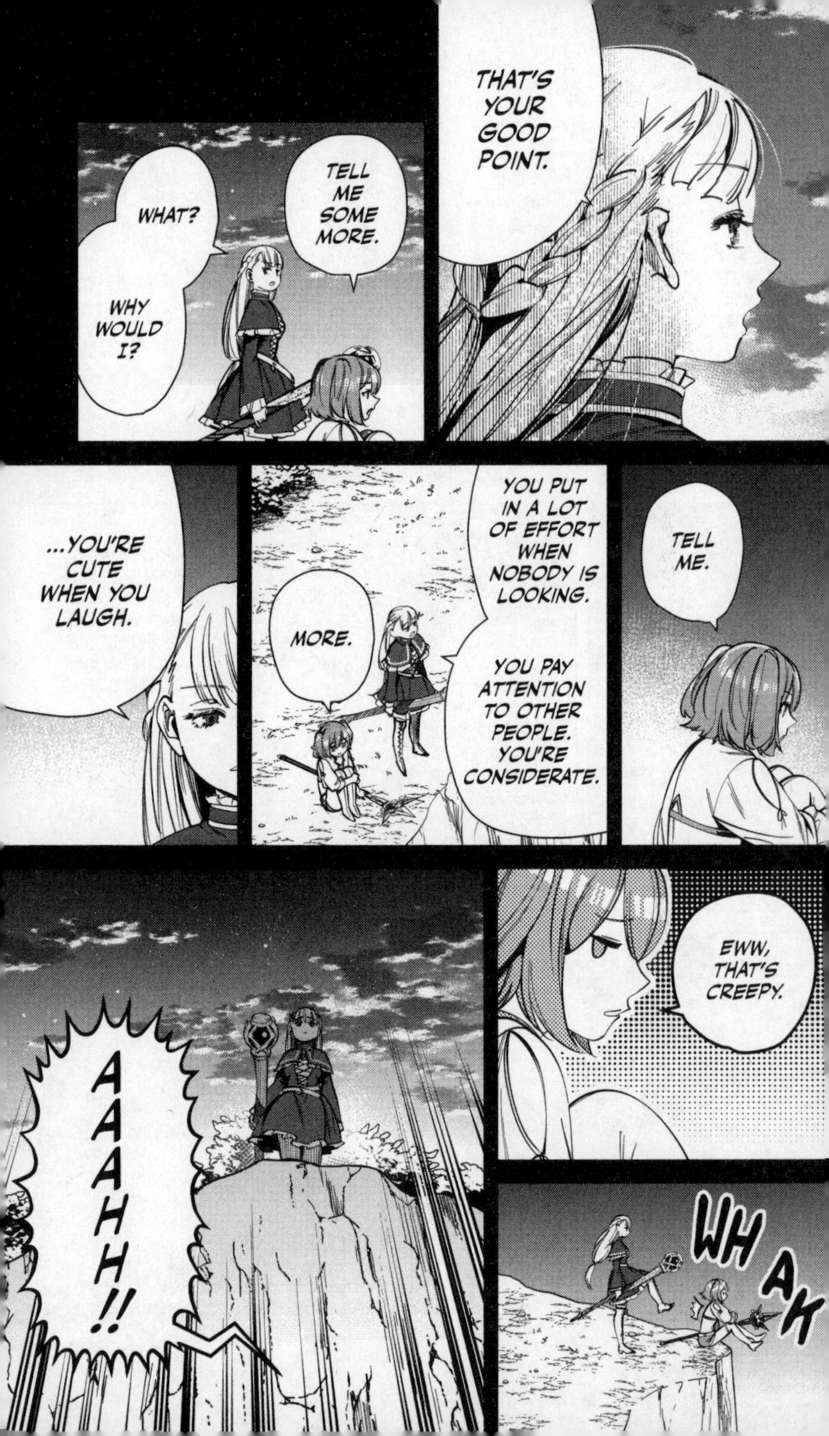
THAT'S YOUR GOOD POINT.
TELL ME SOME MORE.
WHAT?
WHY WOULD I?
TELL ME.
YOU PUT IN A LOT OF EFFORT WHEN NOBODY IS LOOKING.
YOU PAY ATTENTION TO OTHER PEOPLE. YOU'RE CONSIDERATE.
MORE.
...YOU'RE CUTE WHEN YOU LAUGH.
EWW, THAT'S CREEPY.
WHAK
AAAAHH!!

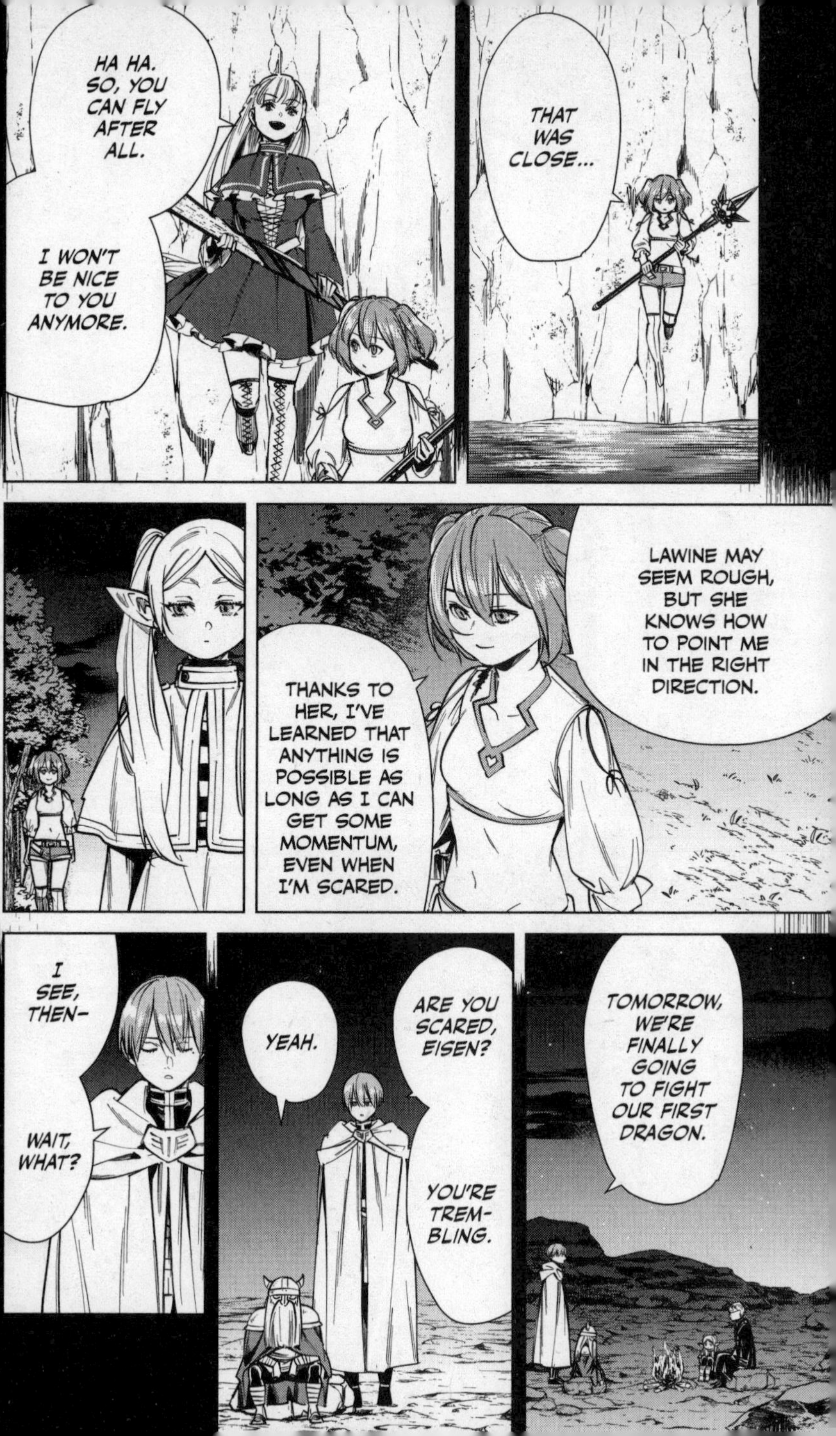
THAT WAS CLOSE...
HA HA. SO, YOU CAN FLY AFTER ALL.
I WON'T BE NICE TO YOU ANYMORE.
LAWINE MAY SEEM ROUGH, BUT SHE KNOWS HOW TO POINT ME IN THE RIGHT DIRECTION.
THANKS TO HER, I'VE LEARNED THAT ANYTHING IS POSSIBLE AS LONG AS I CAN GET SOME MOMENTUM, EVEN WHEN I'M SCARED.
TOMORROW, WE'RE FINALLY GOING TO FIGHT OUR FIRST DRAGON.
ARE YOU SCARED, EISEN?
YEAH.
YOU'RE TREMBLING.
I SEE, THEN-
WAIT, WHAT?

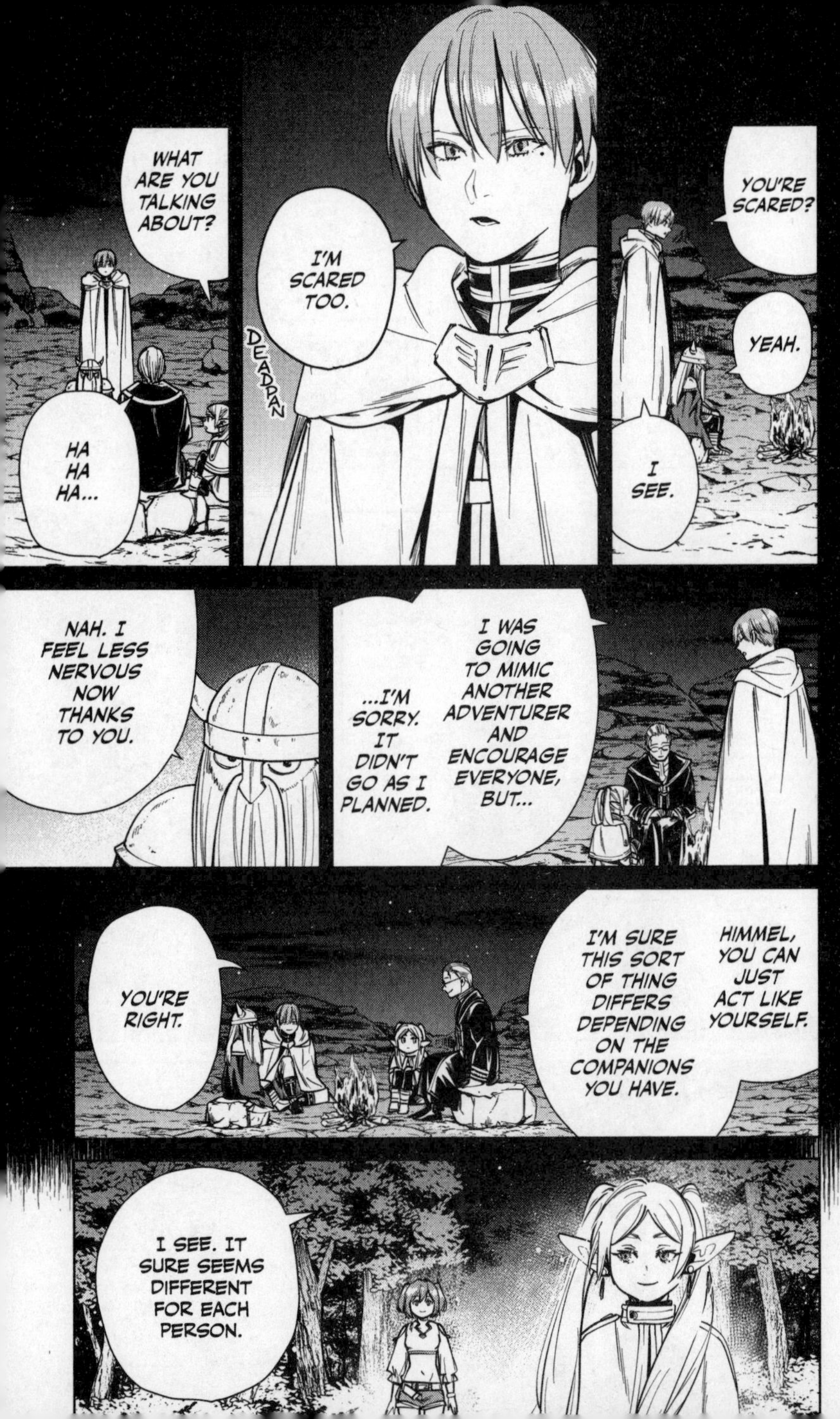
YOU'RE SCARED?
YEAH.
I SEE.
I'M SCARED TOO.
DEADPAN
WHAT ARE YOU TALKING ABOUT?
HA HA HA...
I WAS GOING TO MIMIC ANOTHER ADVENTURER AND ENCOURAGE EVERYONE, BUT...
...I'M SORRY. IT DIDN'T GO AS I PLANNED.
NAH. I FEEL LESS NERVOUS NOW THANKS TO YOU.
HIMMEL, YOU CAN JUST ACT LIKE YOURSELF.
I'M SURE THIS SORT OF THING DIFFERS DEPENDING ON THE COMPANIONS YOU HAVE.
YOU'RE RIGHT.
I SEE. IT SURE SEEMS DIFFERENT FOR EACH PERSON.

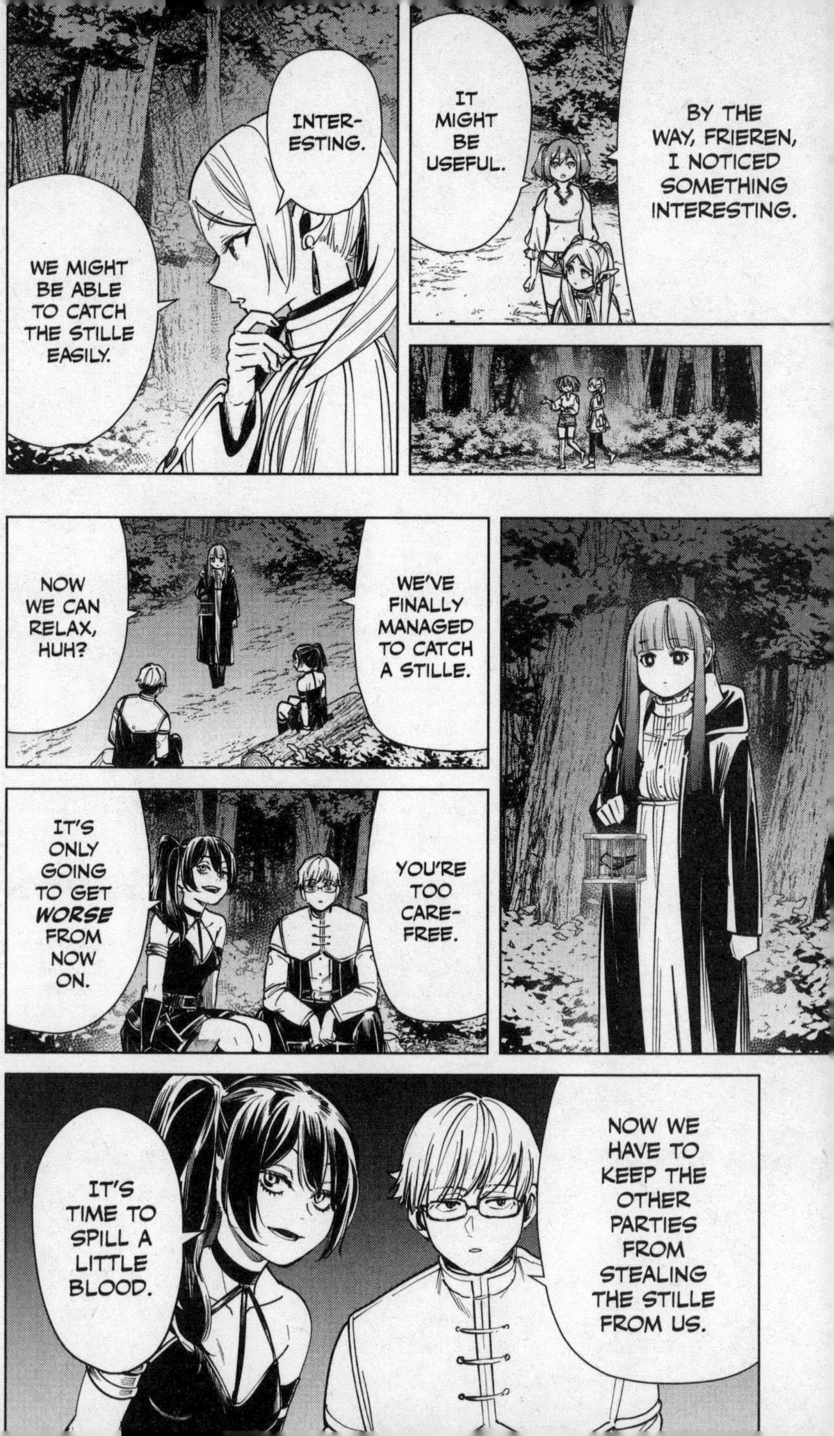
BY THE WAY, FRIEREN, I NOTICED SOMETHING INTERESTING.
IT MIGHT BE USEFUL.
INTER-ESTING.
WE MIGHT BE ABLE TO CATCH THE STILLE EASILY.
WE'VE FINALLY MANAGED TO CATCH A STILLE.
NOW WE CAN RELAX, HUH?
YOU'RE TOO CARE-FREE.
IT'S ONLY GOING TO GET *WORSE* FROM NOW ON.
NOW WE HAVE TO KEEP THE OTHER PARTIES FROM STEALING THE STILLE FROM US.
IT'S TIME TO SPILL A LITTLE BLOOD.

Chapter 39: Commence Capture Strategy

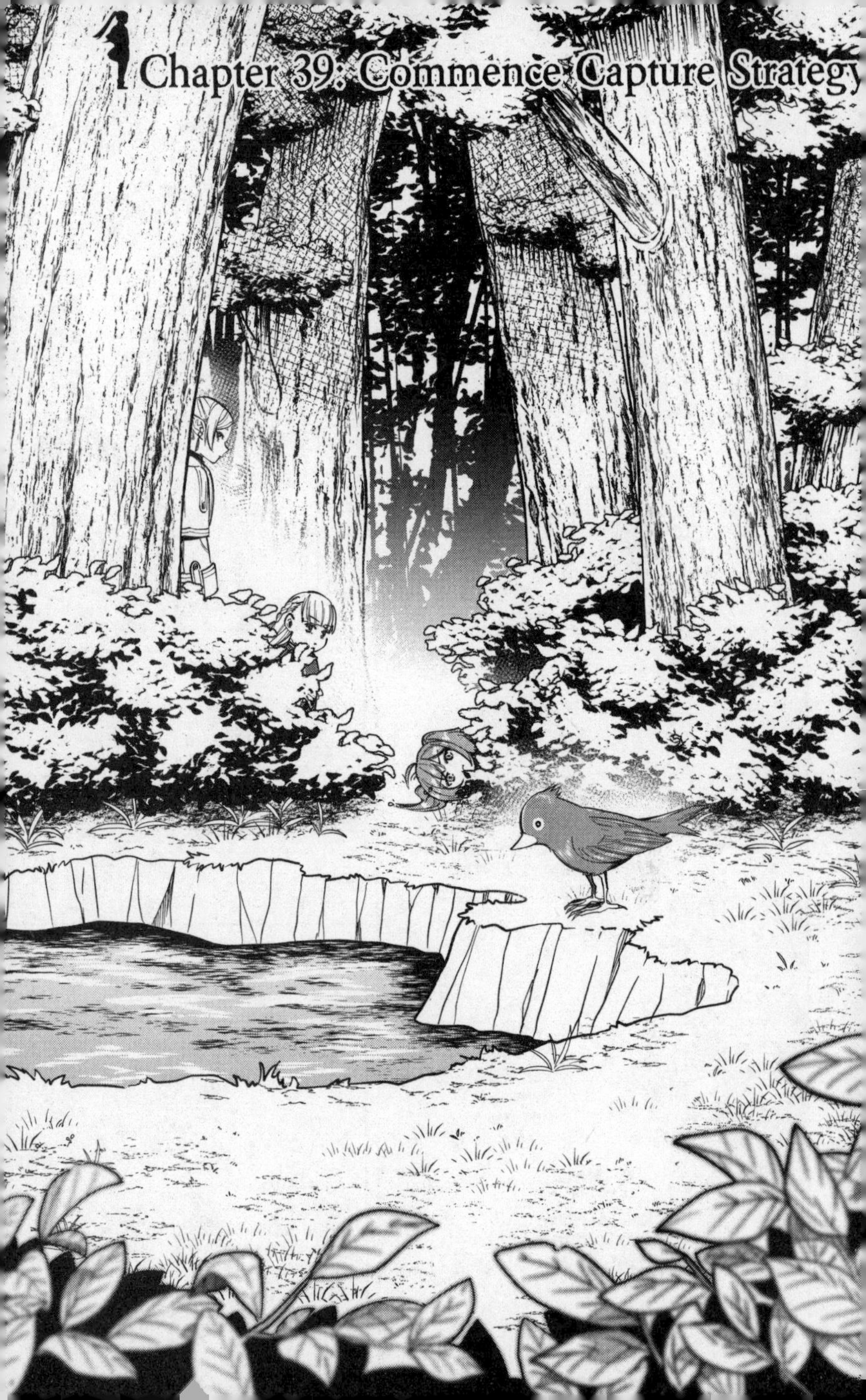

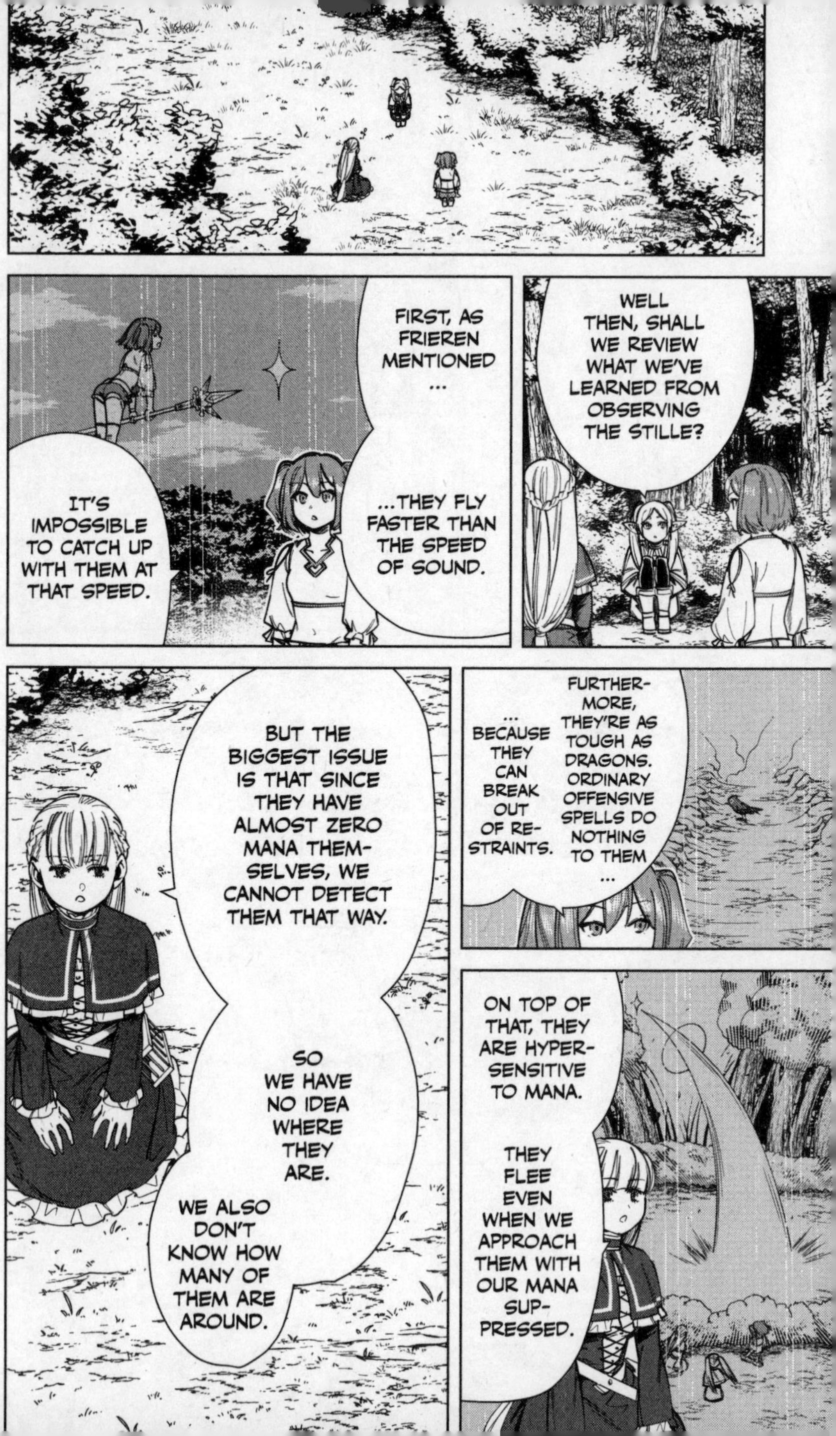
WELL THEN, SHALL WE REVIEW WHAT WE'VE LEARNED FROM OBSERVING THE STILLE?
FIRST, AS FRIEREN MENTIONED ...
...THEY FLY FASTER THAN THE SPEED OF SOUND.
IT'S IMPOSSIBLE TO CATCH UP WITH THEM AT THAT SPEED.
FURTHERMORE, THEY'RE AS TOUGH AS DRAGONS. ORDINARY OFFENSIVE SPELLS DO NOTHING TO THEM ...
... BECAUSE THEY CAN BREAK OUT OF RESTRAINTS.
ON TOP OF THAT, THEY ARE HYPERSENSITIVE TO MANA.
THEY FLEE EVEN WHEN WE APPROACH THEM WITH OUR MANA SUPPRESSED.
BUT THE BIGGEST ISSUE IS THAT SINCE THEY HAVE ALMOST ZERO MANA THEMSELVES, WE CANNOT DETECT THEM THAT WAY.
SO WE HAVE NO IDEA WHERE THEY ARE.
WE ALSO DON'T KNOW HOW MANY OF THEM ARE AROUND.

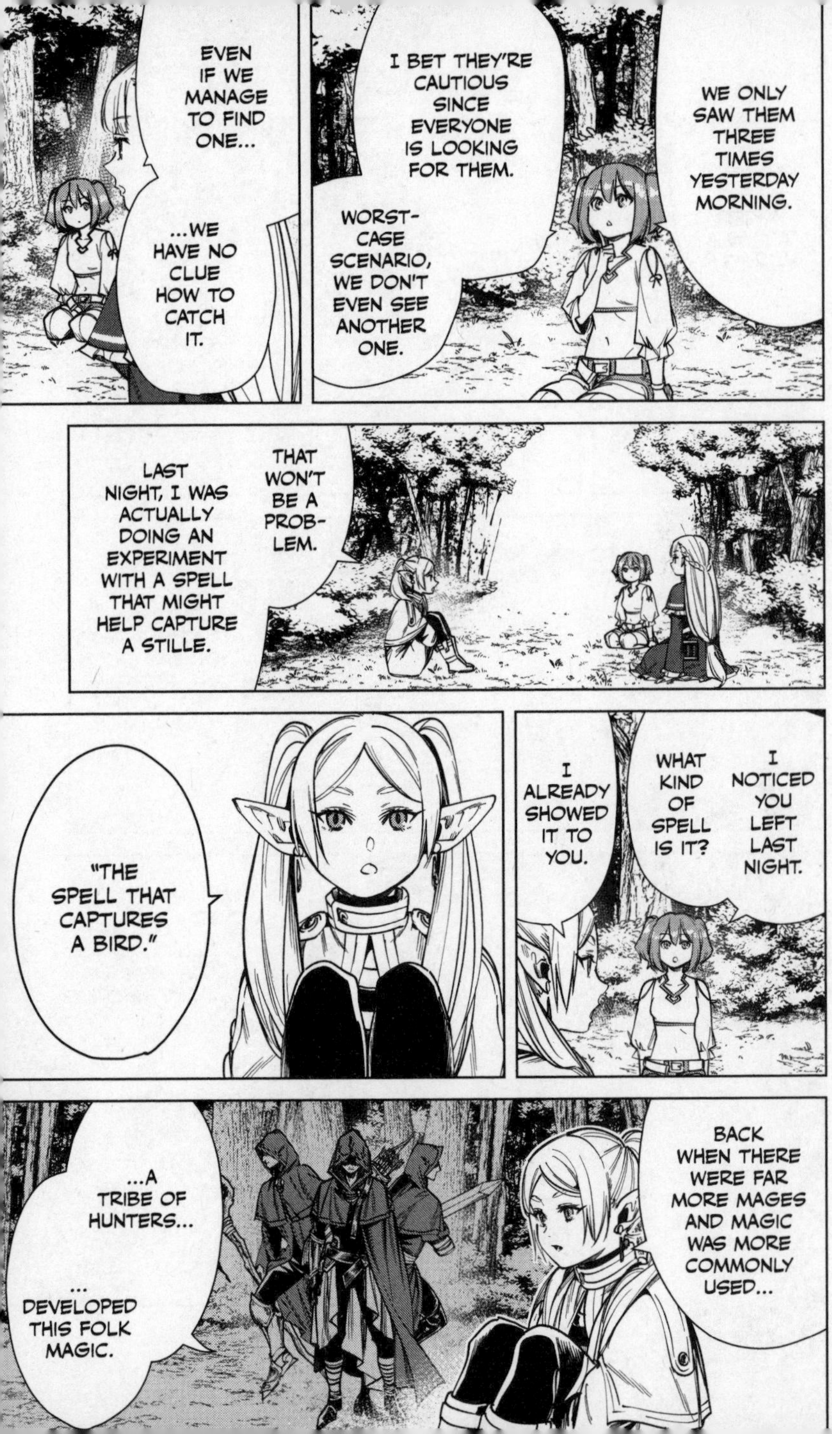
WE ONLY SAW THEM THREE TIMES YESTERDAY MORNING.
I BET THEY'RE CAUTIOUS SINCE EVERYONE IS LOOKING FOR THEM.
WORST-CASE SCENARIO, WE DON'T EVEN SEE ANOTHER ONE.
EVEN IF WE MANAGE TO FIND ONE...
...WE HAVE NO CLUE HOW TO CATCH IT.
THAT WON'T BE A PROBLEM.
LAST NIGHT, I WAS ACTUALLY DOING AN EXPERIMENT WITH A SPELL THAT MIGHT HELP CAPTURE A STILLE.
I NOTICED YOU LEFT LAST NIGHT.
WHAT KIND OF SPELL IS IT?
I ALREADY SHOWED IT TO YOU.
"THE SPELL THAT CAPTURES A BIRD."
BACK WHEN THERE WERE FAR MORE MAGES AND MAGIC WAS MORE COMMONLY USED...
...A TRIBE OF HUNTERS...
...DEVELOPED THIS FOLK MAGIC.

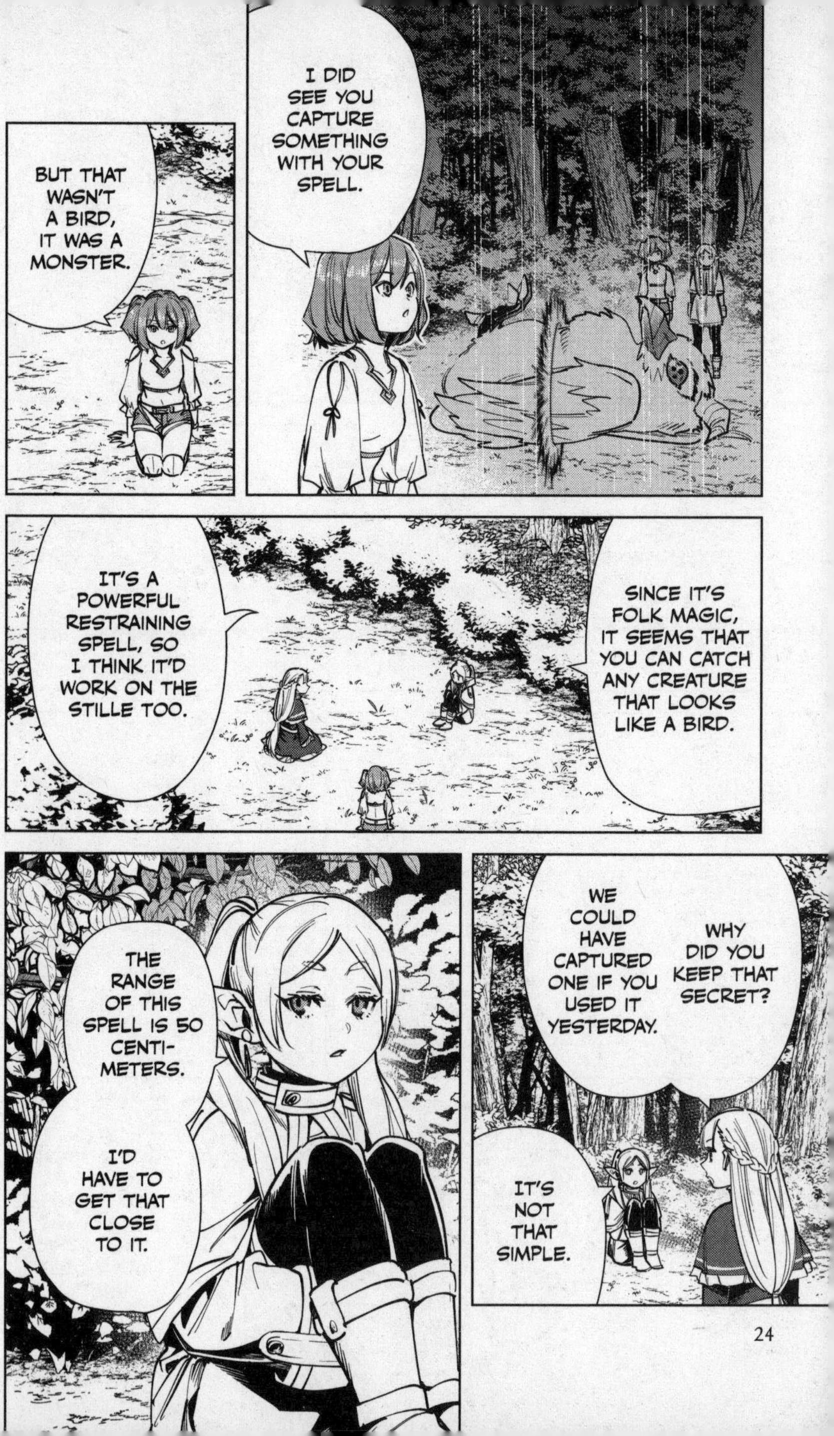
I DID SEE YOU CAPTURE SOMETHING WITH YOUR SPELL.
BUT THAT WASN'T A BIRD, IT WAS A MONSTER.
SINCE IT'S FOLK MAGIC, IT SEEMS THAT YOU CAN CATCH ANY CREATURE THAT LOOKS LIKE A BIRD.
IT'S A POWERFUL RESTRAINING SPELL, SO I THINK IT'D WORK ON THE STILLE TOO.
WHY DID YOU KEEP THAT SECRET?
WE COULD HAVE CAPTURED ONE IF YOU USED IT YESTERDAY.
IT'S NOT THAT SIMPLE.
THE RANGE OF THIS SPELL IS 50 CENTI-METERS.
I'D HAVE TO GET THAT CLOSE TO IT.

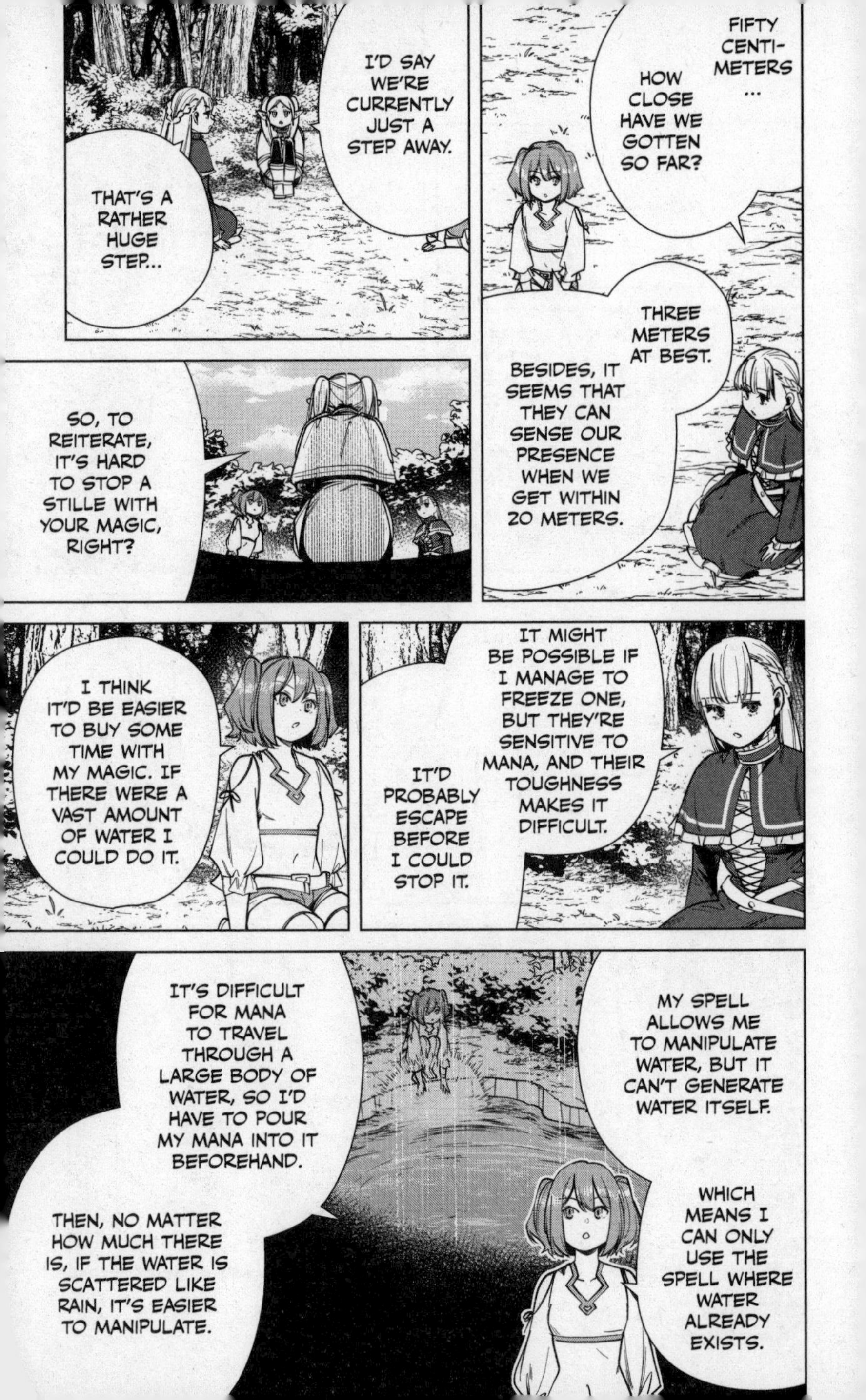
HOW CLOSE HAVE WE GOTTEN SO FAR?
FIFTY CENTIMETERS...
THREE METERS AT BEST.
BESIDES, IT SEEMS THAT THEY CAN SENSE OUR PRESENCE WHEN WE GET WITHIN 20 METERS.
I'D SAY WE'RE CURRENTLY JUST A STEP AWAY.
THAT'S A RATHER HUGE STEP...
SO, TO REITERATE, IT'S HARD TO STOP A STILLE WITH YOUR MAGIC, RIGHT?
IT MIGHT BE POSSIBLE IF I MANAGE TO FREEZE ONE, BUT THEY'RE SENSITIVE TO MANA, AND THEIR TOUGHNESS MAKES IT DIFFICULT.
IT'D PROBABLY ESCAPE BEFORE I COULD STOP IT.
I THINK IT'D BE EASIER TO BUY SOME TIME WITH MY MAGIC. IF THERE WERE A VAST AMOUNT OF WATER I COULD DO IT.
MY SPELL ALLOWS ME TO MANIPULATE WATER, BUT IT CAN'T GENERATE WATER ITSELF.
WHICH MEANS I CAN ONLY USE THE SPELL WHERE WATER ALREADY EXISTS.
IT'S DIFFICULT FOR MANA TO TRAVEL THROUGH A LARGE BODY OF WATER, SO I'D HAVE TO POUR MY MANA INTO IT BEFOREHAND.
THEN, NO MATTER HOW MUCH THERE IS, IF THE WATER IS SCATTERED LIKE RAIN, IT'S EASIER TO MANIPULATE.

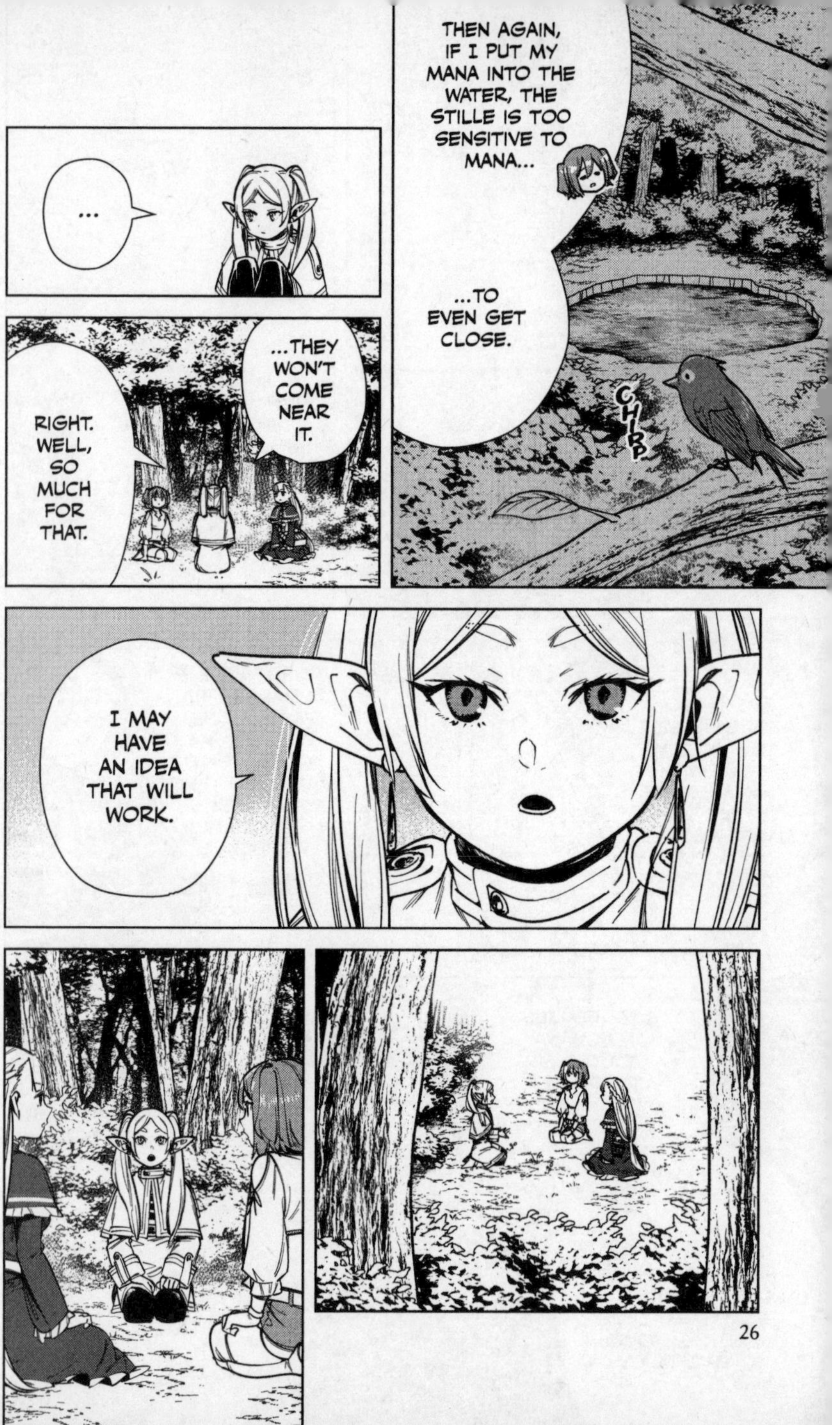
THEN AGAIN, IF I PUT MY MANA INTO THE WATER, THE STILLE IS TOO SENSITIVE TO MANA...
...TO EVEN GET CLOSE.
CHIRP
...
...THEY WON'T COME NEAR IT.
RIGHT. WELL, SO MUCH FOR THAT.
I MAY HAVE AN IDEA THAT WILL WORK.

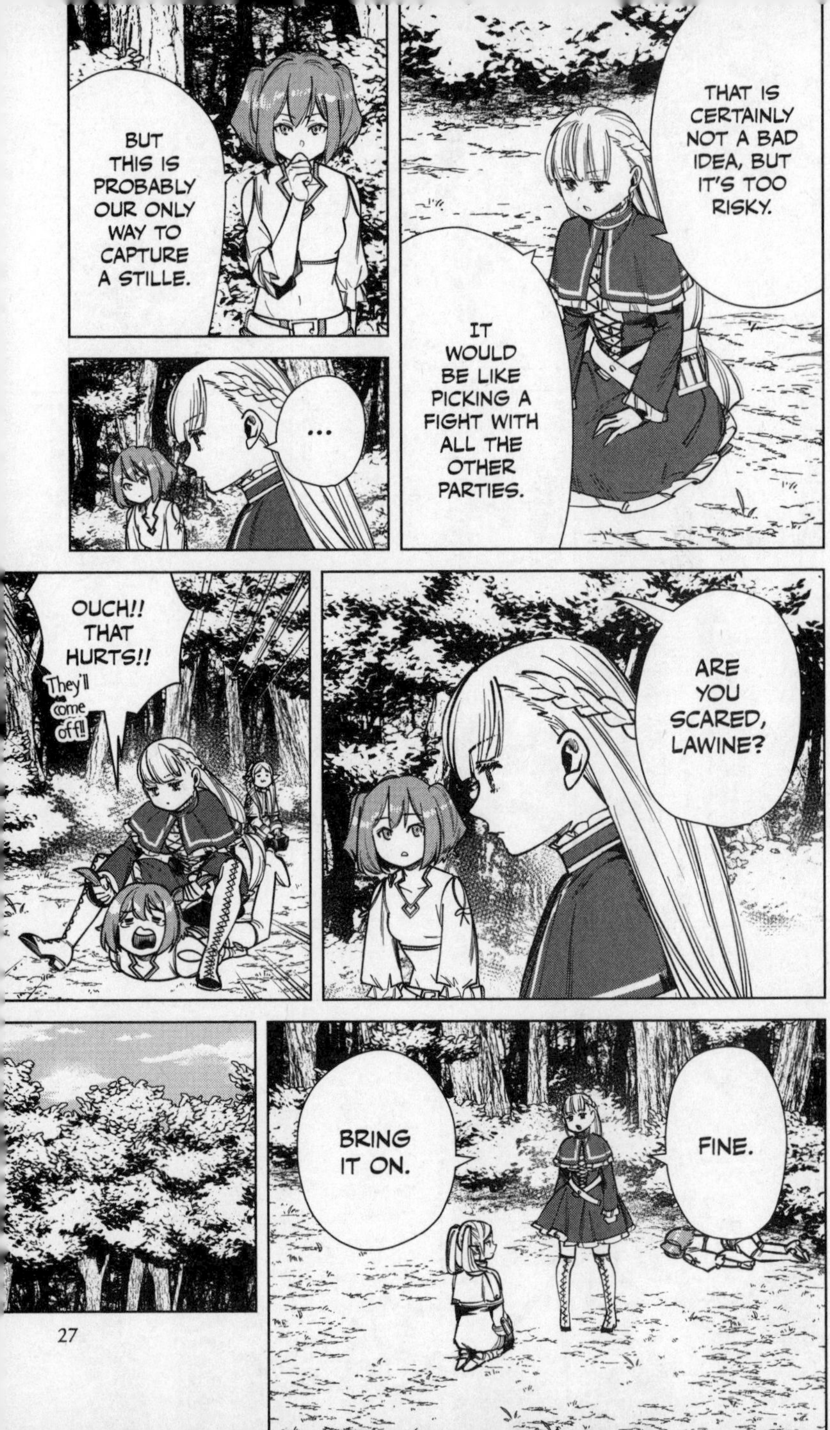
THAT IS CERTAINLY NOT A BAD IDEA, BUT IT'S TOO RISKY.
IT WOULD BE LIKE PICKING A FIGHT WITH ALL THE OTHER PARTIES.
BUT THIS IS PROBABLY OUR ONLY WAY TO CAPTURE A STILLE.
...
ARE YOU SCARED, LAWINE?
OUCH!! THAT HURTS!!
They'll come off!!
FINE.
BRING IT ON.

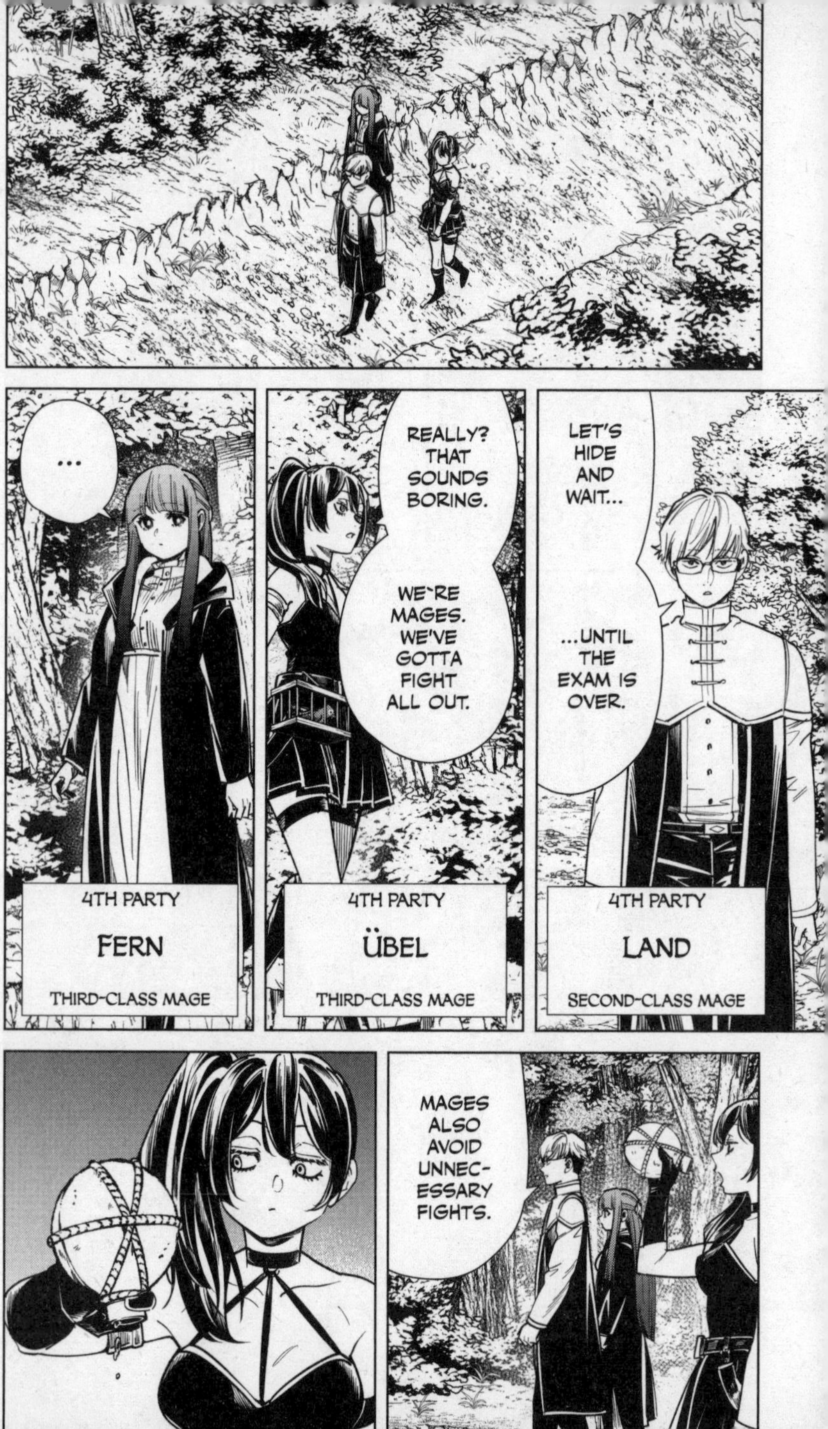
LET'S HIDE AND WAIT...
...UNTIL THE EXAM IS OVER.
4TH PARTY
LAND
SECOND-CLASS MAGE
REALLY? THAT SOUNDS BORING.
WE'RE MAGES. WE'VE GOTTA FIGHT ALL OUT.
4TH PARTY
ÜBEL
THIRD-CLASS MAGE
...
4TH PARTY
FERN
THIRD-CLASS MAGE
MAGES ALSO AVOID UNNEC-ESSARY FIGHTS.

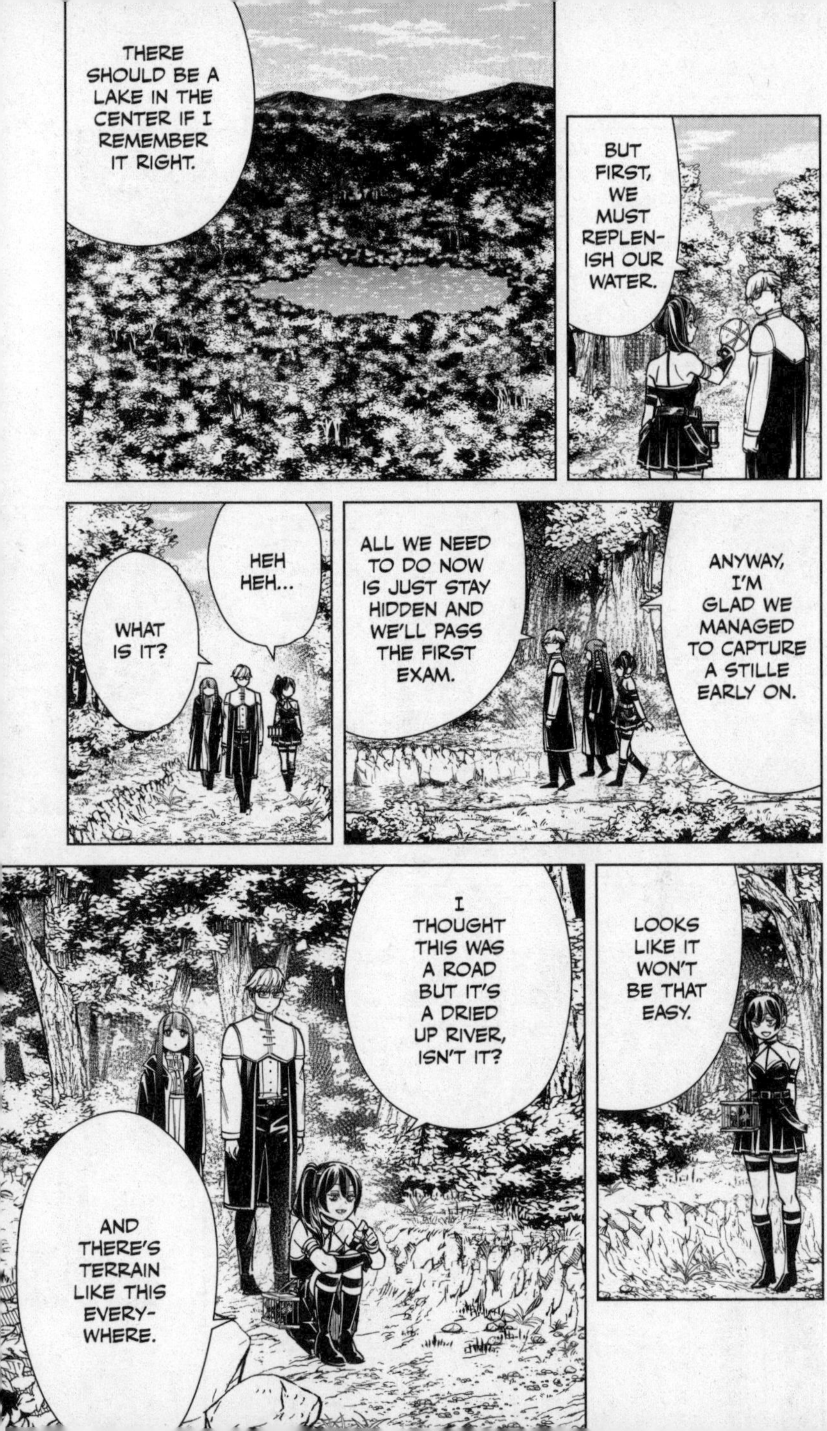
BUT FIRST, WE MUST REPLEN-ISH OUR WATER.
THERE SHOULD BE A LAKE IN THE CENTER IF I REMEMBER IT RIGHT.
ANYWAY, I'M GLAD WE MANAGED TO CAPTURE A STILLE EARLY ON.
ALL WE NEED TO DO NOW IS JUST STAY HIDDEN AND WE'LL PASS THE FIRST EXAM.
HEH HEH...
WHAT IS IT?
LOOKS LIKE IT WON'T BE THAT EASY.
I THOUGHT THIS WAS A ROAD BUT IT'S A DRIED UP RIVER, ISN'T IT?
AND THERE'S TERRAIN LIKE THIS EVERY-WHERE.

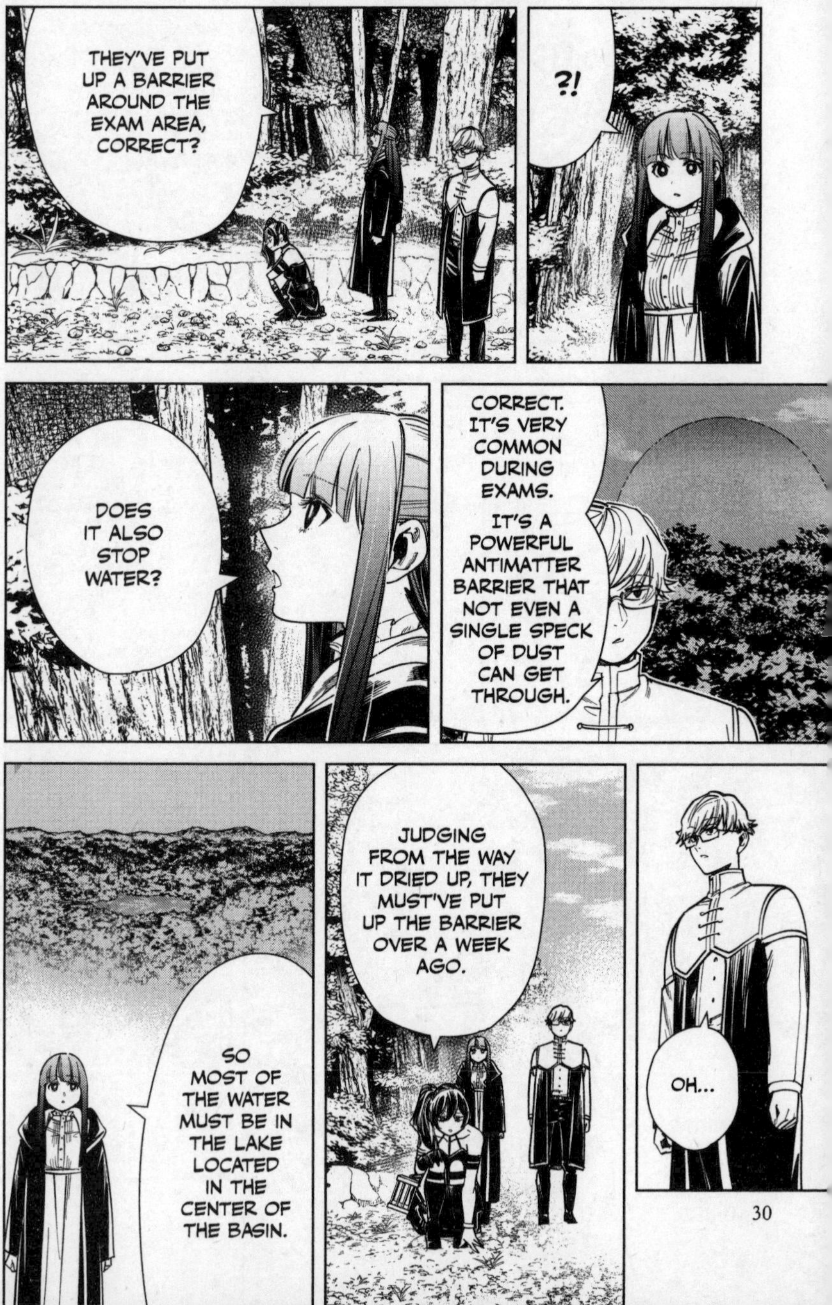
?!
THEY'VE PUT UP A BARRIER AROUND THE EXAM AREA, CORRECT?
CORRECT. IT'S VERY COMMON DURING EXAMS.
IT'S A POWERFUL ANTIMATTER BARRIER THAT NOT EVEN A SINGLE SPECK OF DUST CAN GET THROUGH.
DOES IT ALSO STOP WATER?
OH...
JUDGING FROM THE WAY IT DRIED UP, THEY MUST'VE PUT UP THE BARRIER OVER A WEEK AGO.
SO MOST OF THE WATER MUST BE IN THE LAKE LOCATED IN THE CENTER OF THE BASIN.

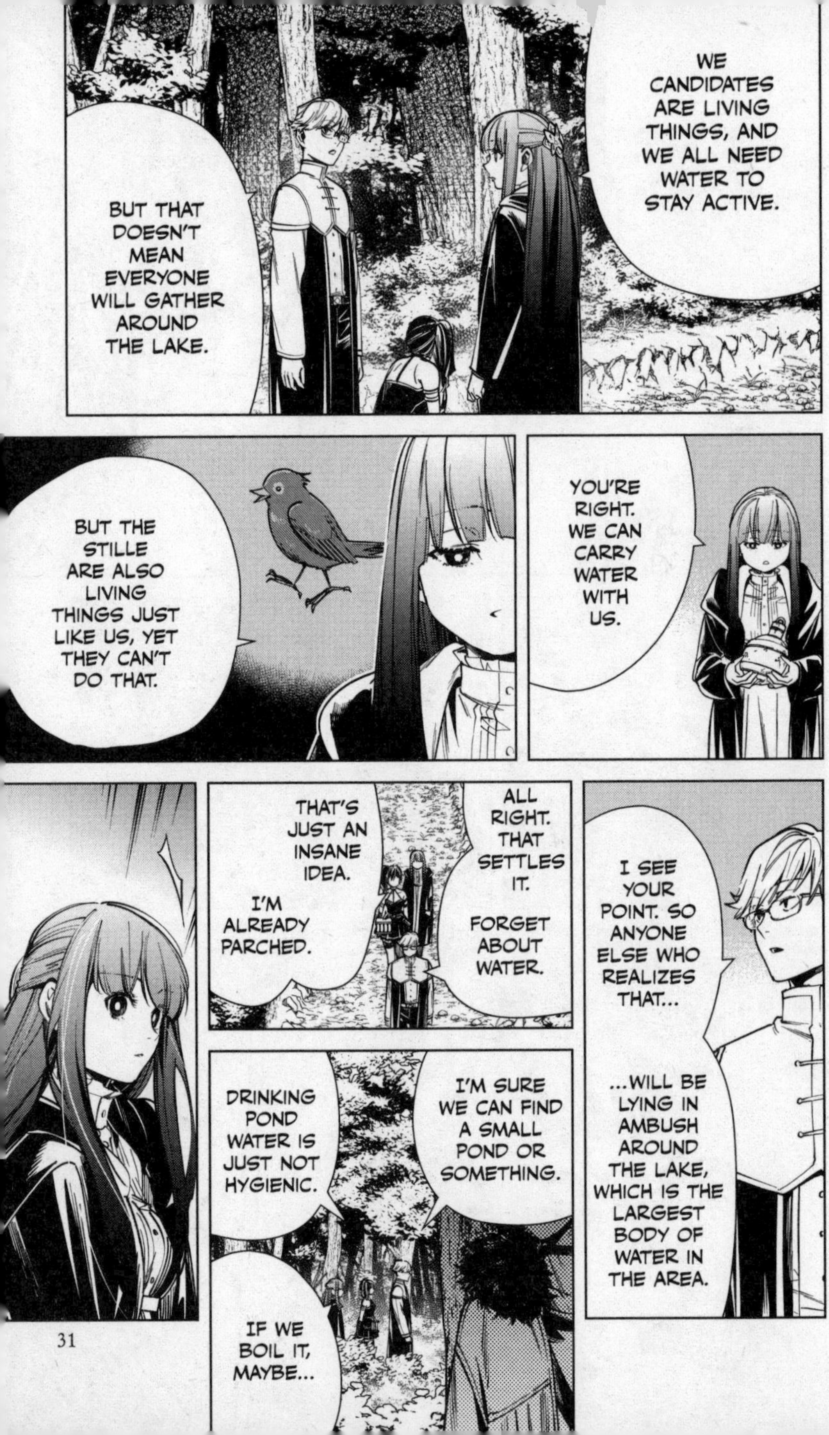
WE CANDIDATES ARE LIVING THINGS, AND WE ALL NEED WATER TO STAY ACTIVE.
BUT THAT DOESN'T MEAN EVERYONE WILL GATHER AROUND THE LAKE.
YOU'RE RIGHT. WE CAN CARRY WATER WITH US.
BUT THE STILLE ARE ALSO LIVING THINGS JUST LIKE US, YET THEY CAN'T DO THAT.
I SEE YOUR POINT. SO ANYONE ELSE WHO REALIZES THAT...
...WILL BE LYING IN AMBUSH AROUND THE LAKE, WHICH IS THE LARGEST BODY OF WATER IN THE AREA.
ALL RIGHT. THAT SETTLES IT.
FORGET ABOUT WATER.
THAT'S JUST AN INSANE IDEA.
I'M ALREADY PARCHED.
I'M SURE WE CAN FIND A SMALL POND OR SOMETHING.
DRINKING POND WATER IS JUST NOT HYGIENIC.
IF WE BOIL IT, MAYBE...

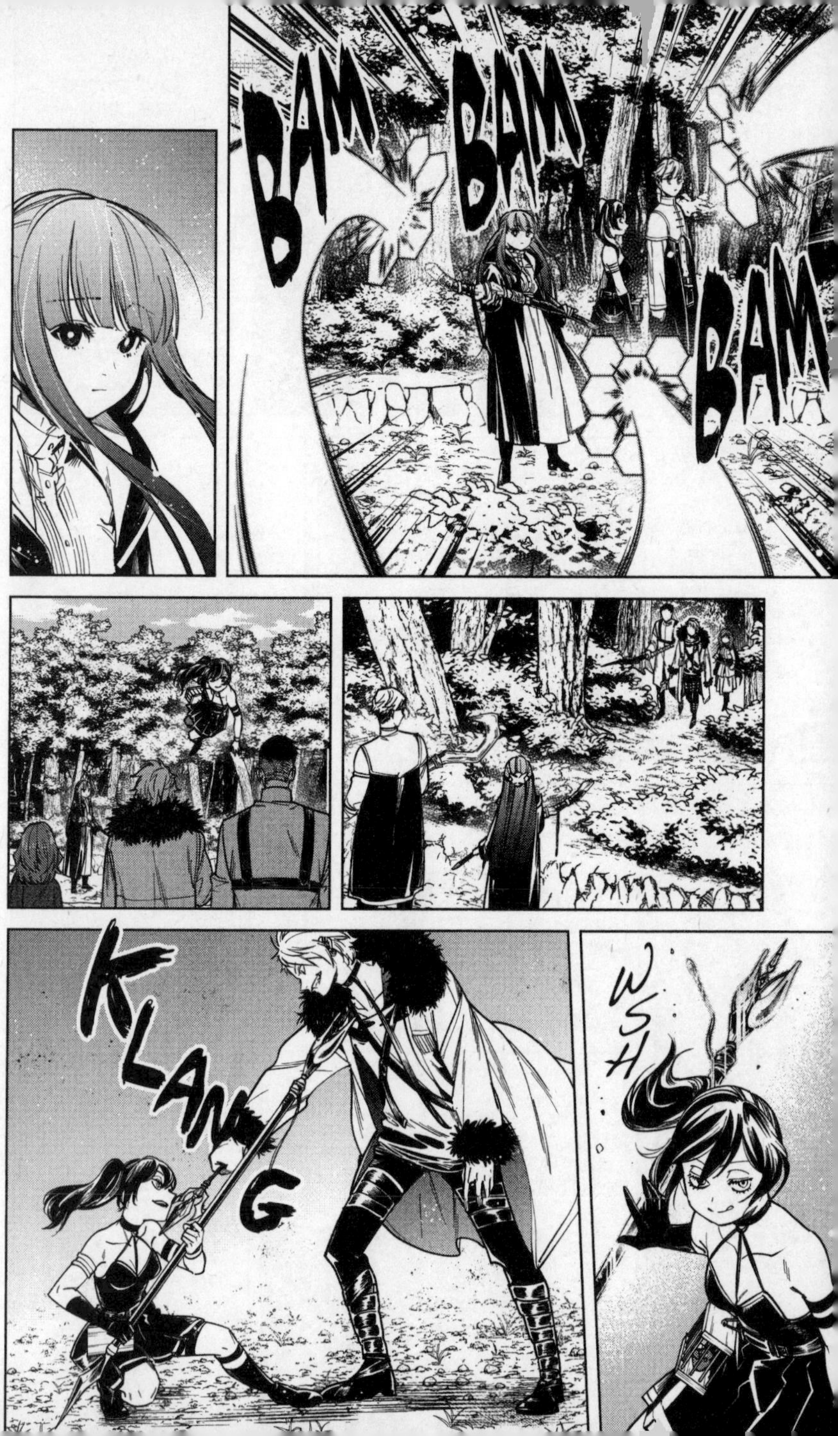
BAM
BAM
BAM
WSH
KLANG

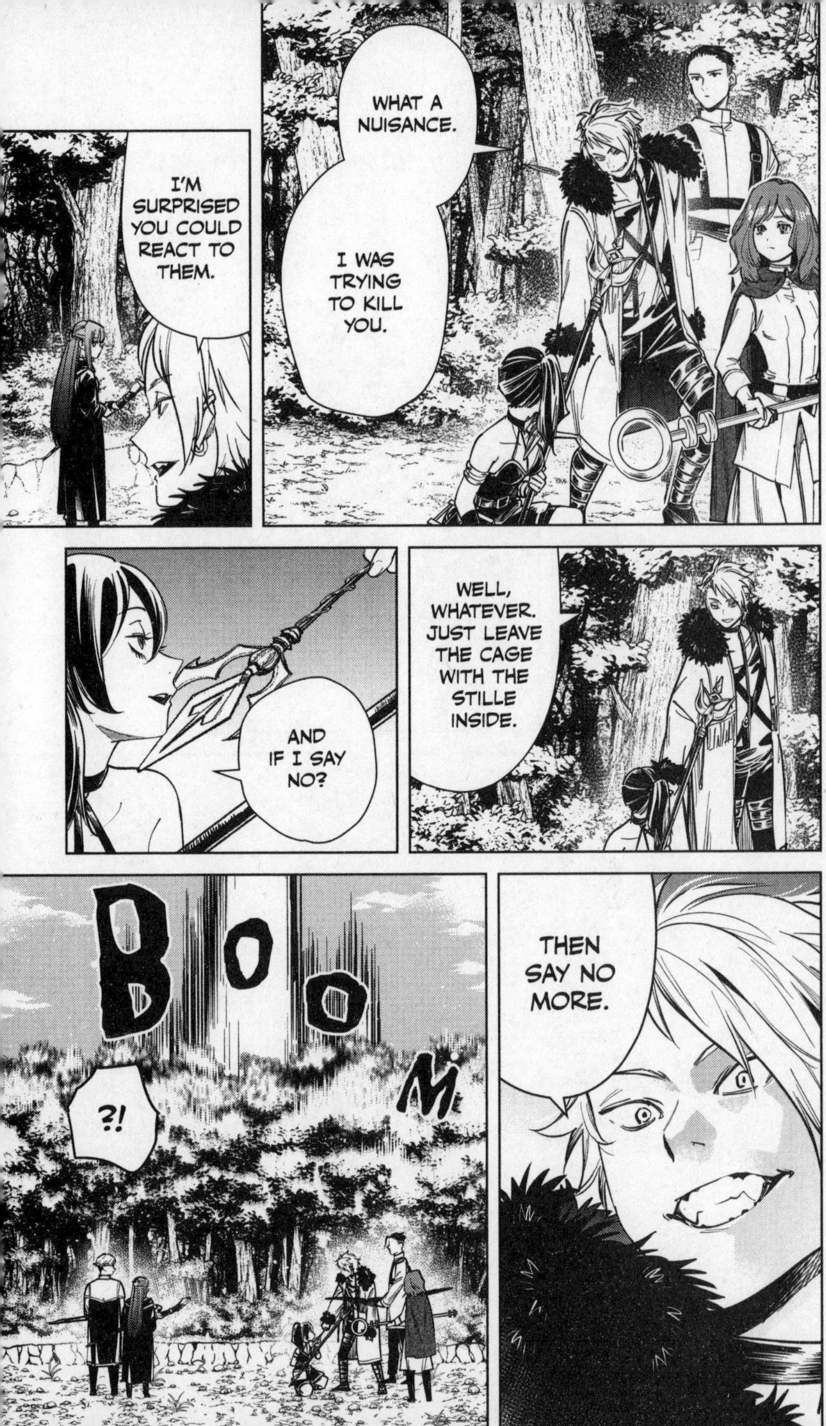
WHAT A NUISANCE.
I WAS TRYING TO KILL YOU.
I'M SURPRISED YOU COULD REACT TO THEM.
WELL, WHATEVER. JUST LEAVE THE CAGE WITH THE STILLE INSIDE.
AND IF I SAY NO?
THEN SAY NO MORE.
BOOM
?!

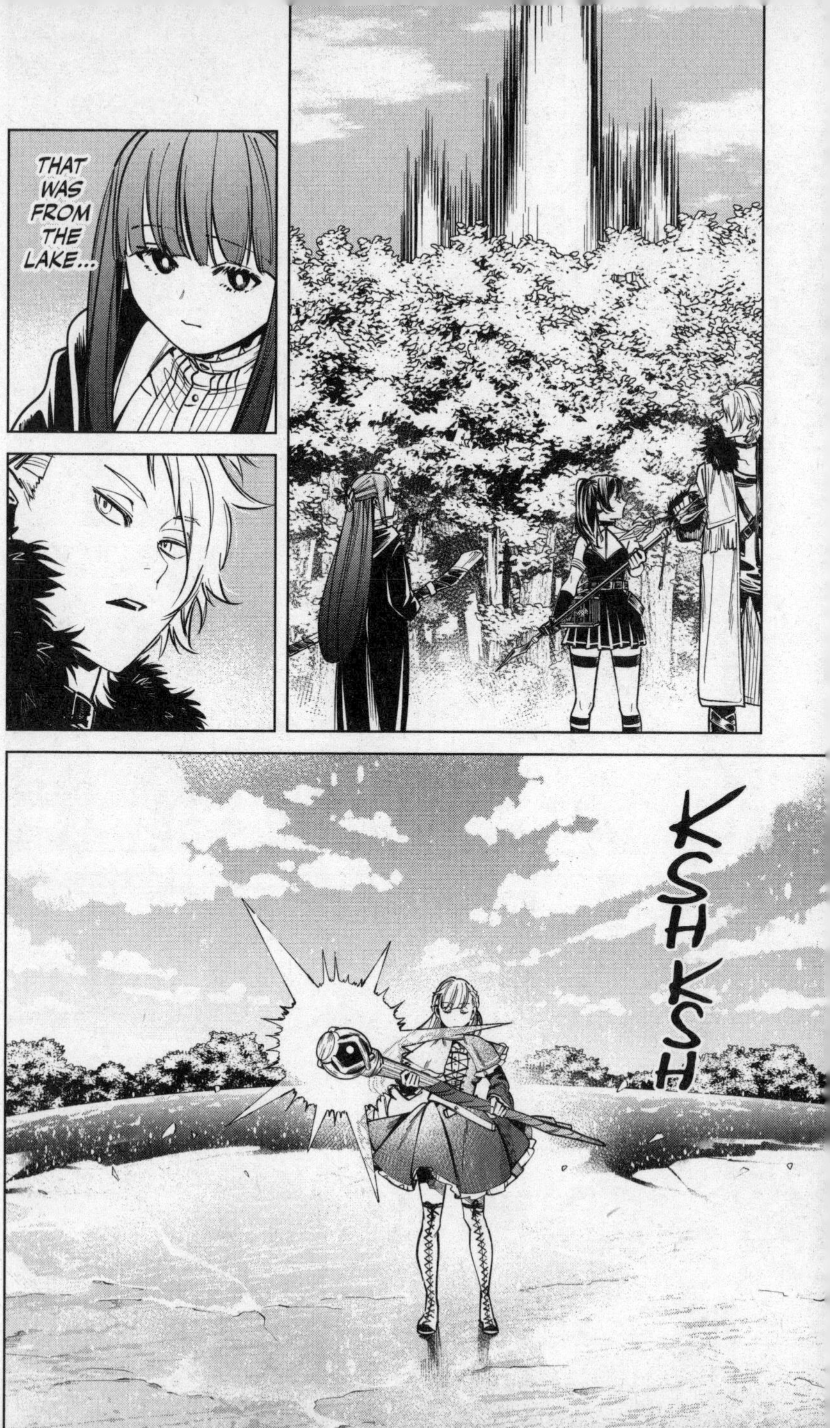
THAT WAS FROM THE LAKE...
KSH KSH

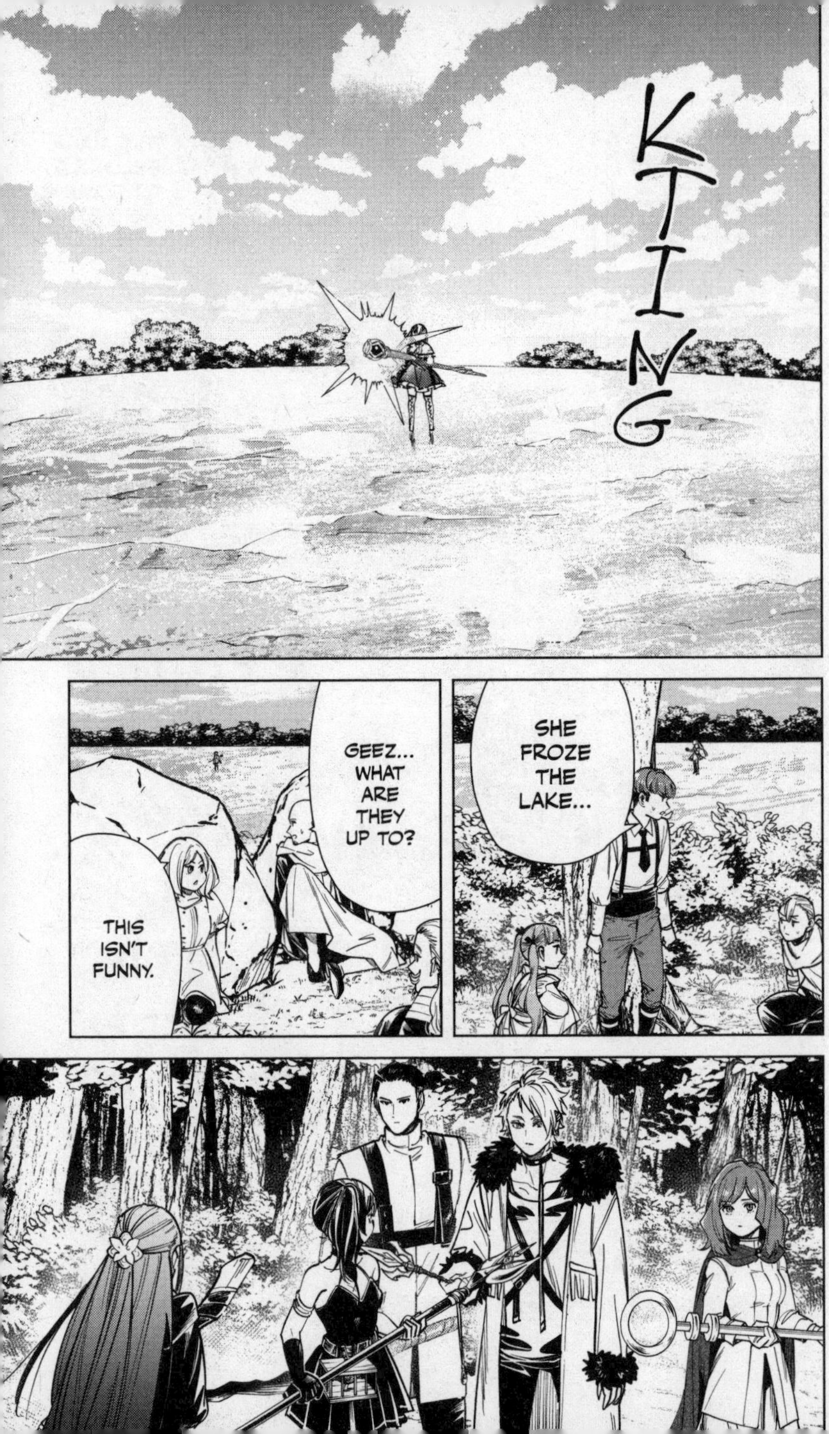
KTING
SHE FROZE THE LAKE...
GEEZ... WHAT ARE THEY UP TO?
THIS ISN'T FUNNY.

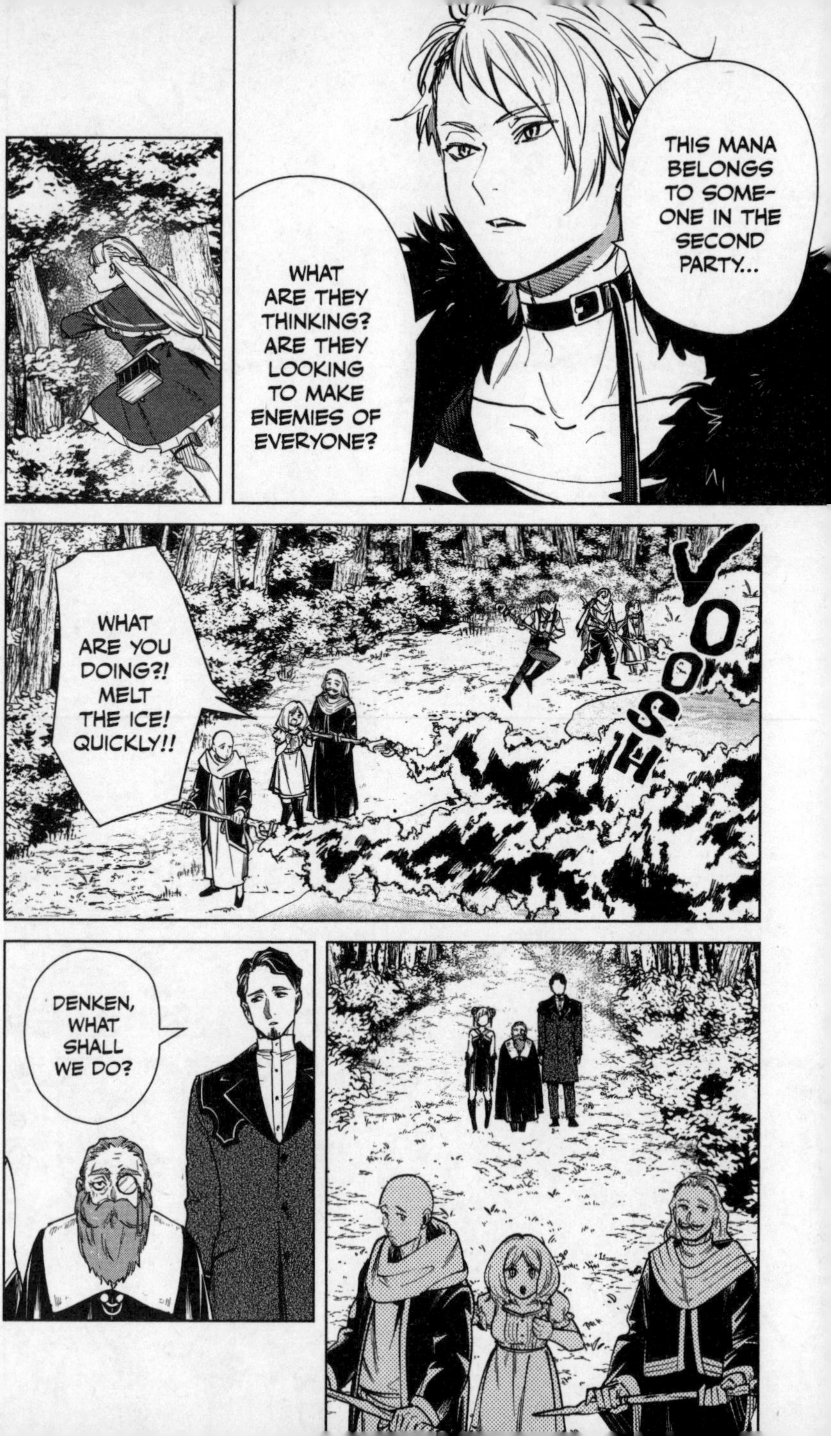
THIS MANA BELONGS TO SOME-ONE IN THE SECOND PARTY...
WHAT ARE THEY THINKING? ARE THEY LOOKING TO MAKE ENEMIES OF EVERYONE?
VOOSH
WHAT ARE YOU DOING?! MELT THE ICE! QUICKLY!!
DENKEN, WHAT SHALL WE DO?

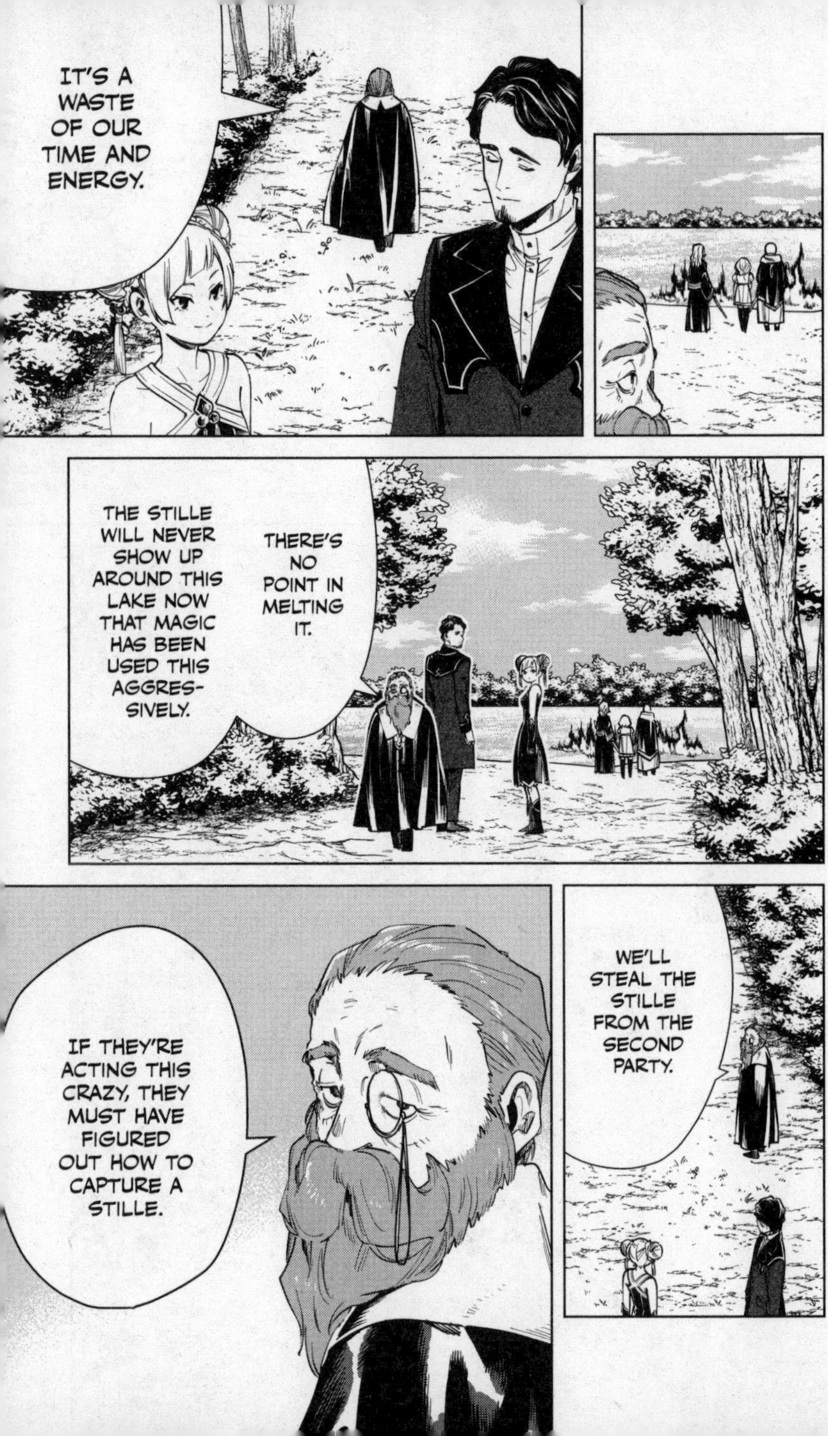
IT'S A WASTE OF OUR TIME AND ENERGY.
THERE'S NO POINT IN MELTING IT.
THE STILLE WILL NEVER SHOW UP AROUND THIS LAKE NOW THAT MAGIC HAS BEEN USED THIS AGGRES-SIVELY.
WE'LL STEAL THE STILLE FROM THE SECOND PARTY.
IF THEY'RE ACTING THIS CRAZY, THEY MUST HAVE FIGURED OUT HOW TO CAPTURE A STILLE.

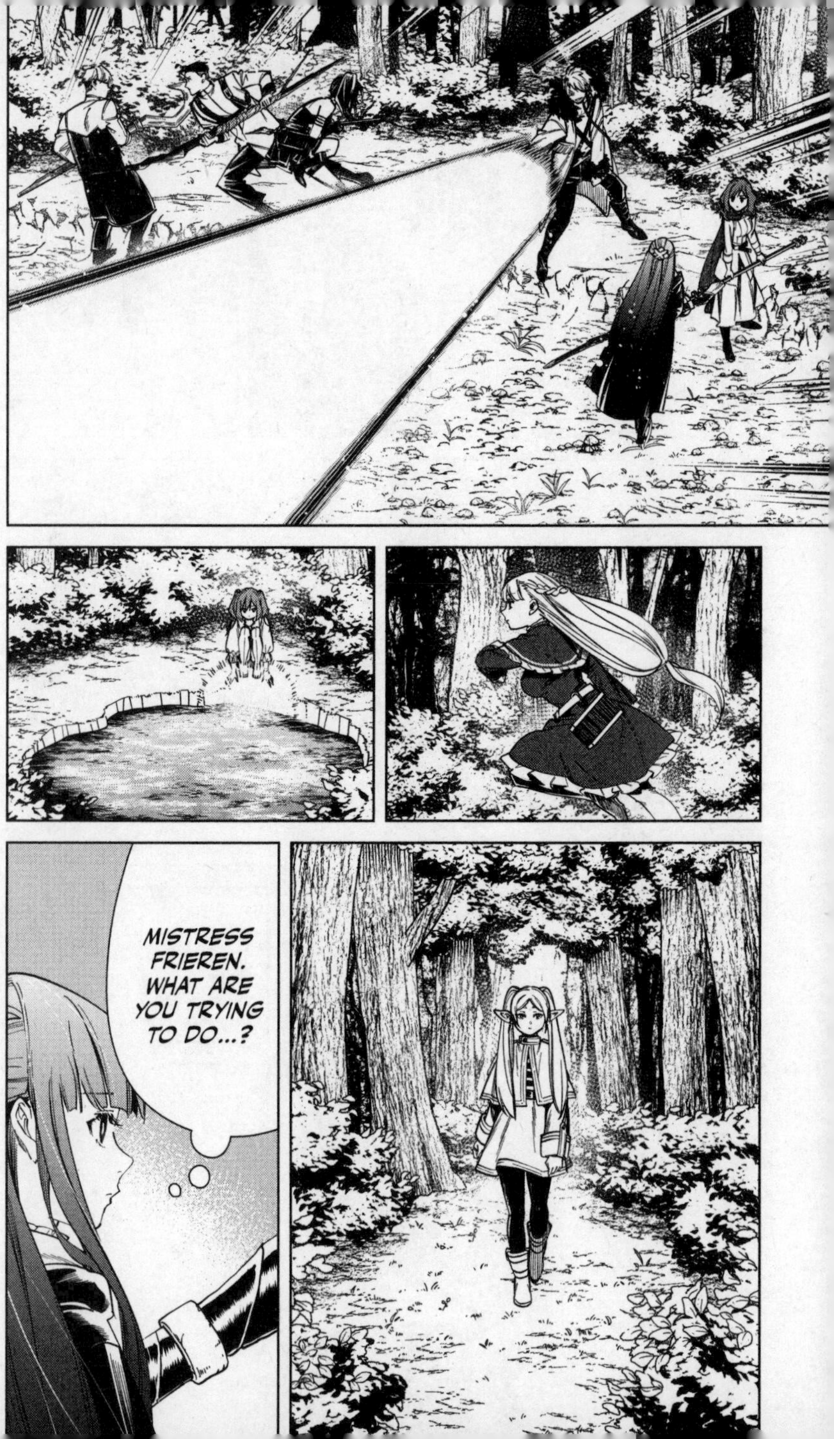
MISTRESS FRIEREN. WHAT ARE YOU TRYING TO DO...?

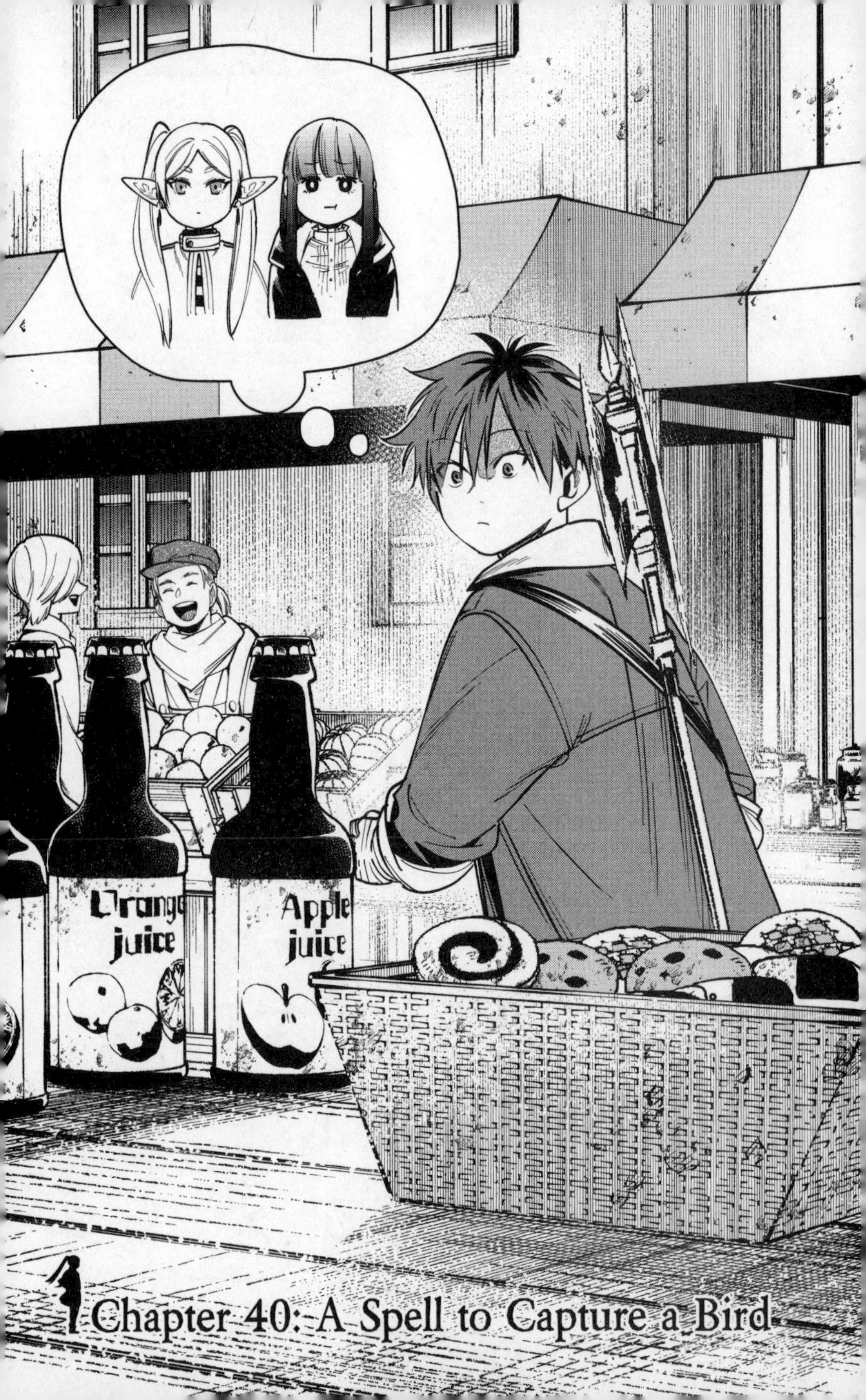
Orange juice
Apple juice

Chapter 40: A Spell to Capture a Bird

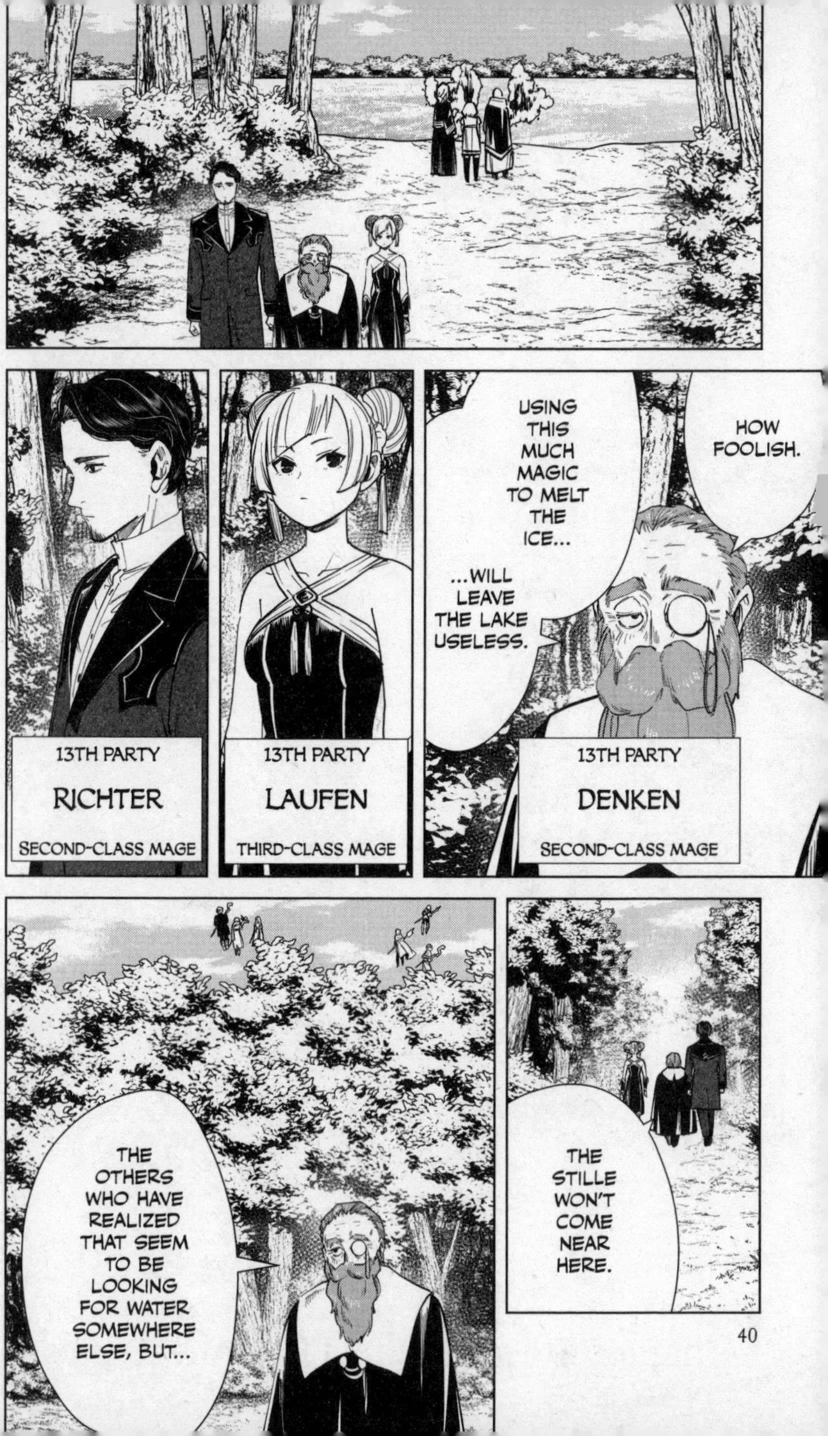
HOW FOOLISH.
USING THIS MUCH MAGIC TO MELT THE ICE...
...WILL LEAVE THE LAKE USELESS.
13TH PARTY
DENKEN
SECOND-CLASS MAGE
13TH PARTY
LAUFEN
THIRD-CLASS MAGE
13TH PARTY
RICHTER
SECOND-CLASS MAGE
THE STILLE WON'T COME NEAR HERE.
THE OTHERS WHO HAVE REALIZED THAT SEEM TO BE LOOKING FOR WATER SOMEWHERE ELSE, BUT...

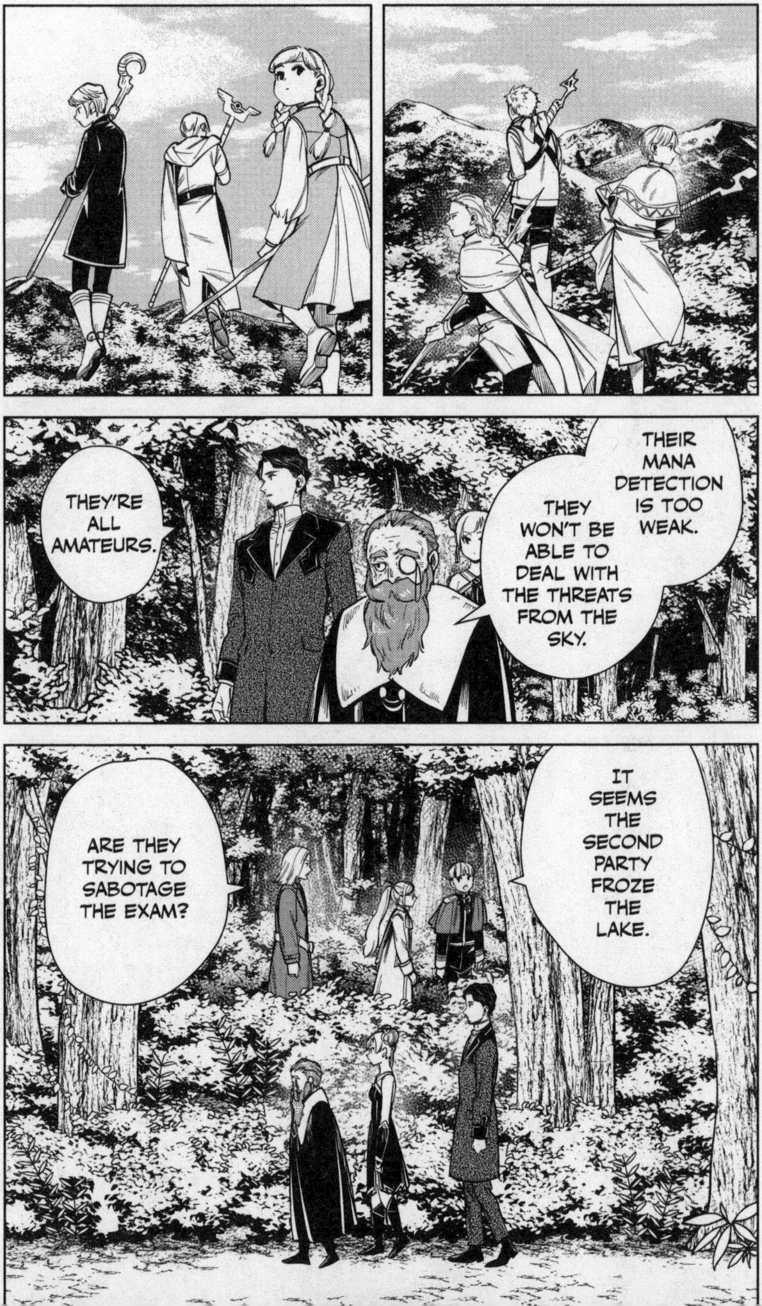
THEIR MANA DETECTION IS TOO WEAK.
THEY WON'T BE ABLE TO DEAL WITH THE THREATS FROM THE SKY.
THEY'RE ALL AMATEURS.
IT SEEMS THE SECOND PARTY FROZE THE LAKE.
ARE THEY TRYING TO SABOTAGE THE EXAM?

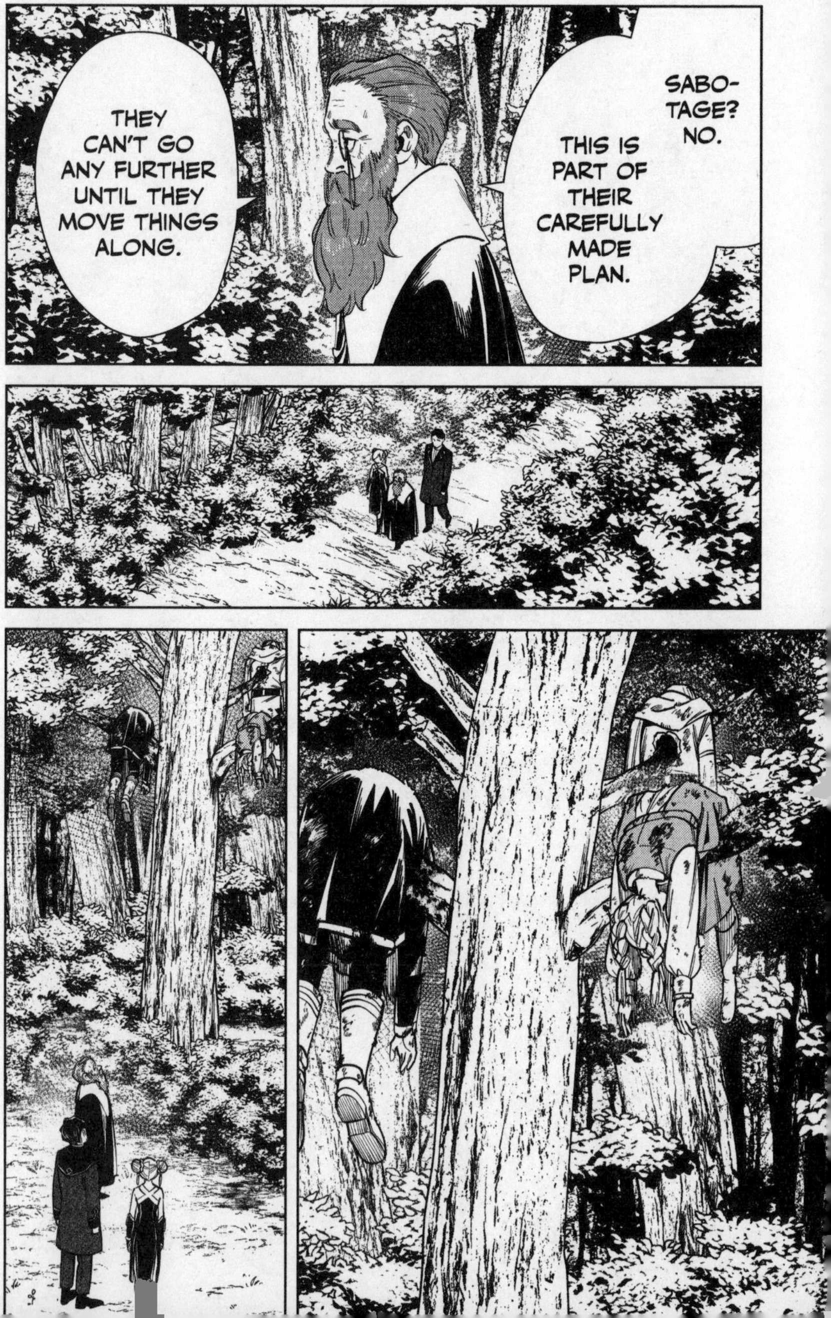
SABO-TAGE? NO.
THIS IS PART OF THEIR CAREFULLY MADE PLAN.
THEY CAN'T GO ANY FURTHER UNTIL THEY MOVE THINGS ALONG.

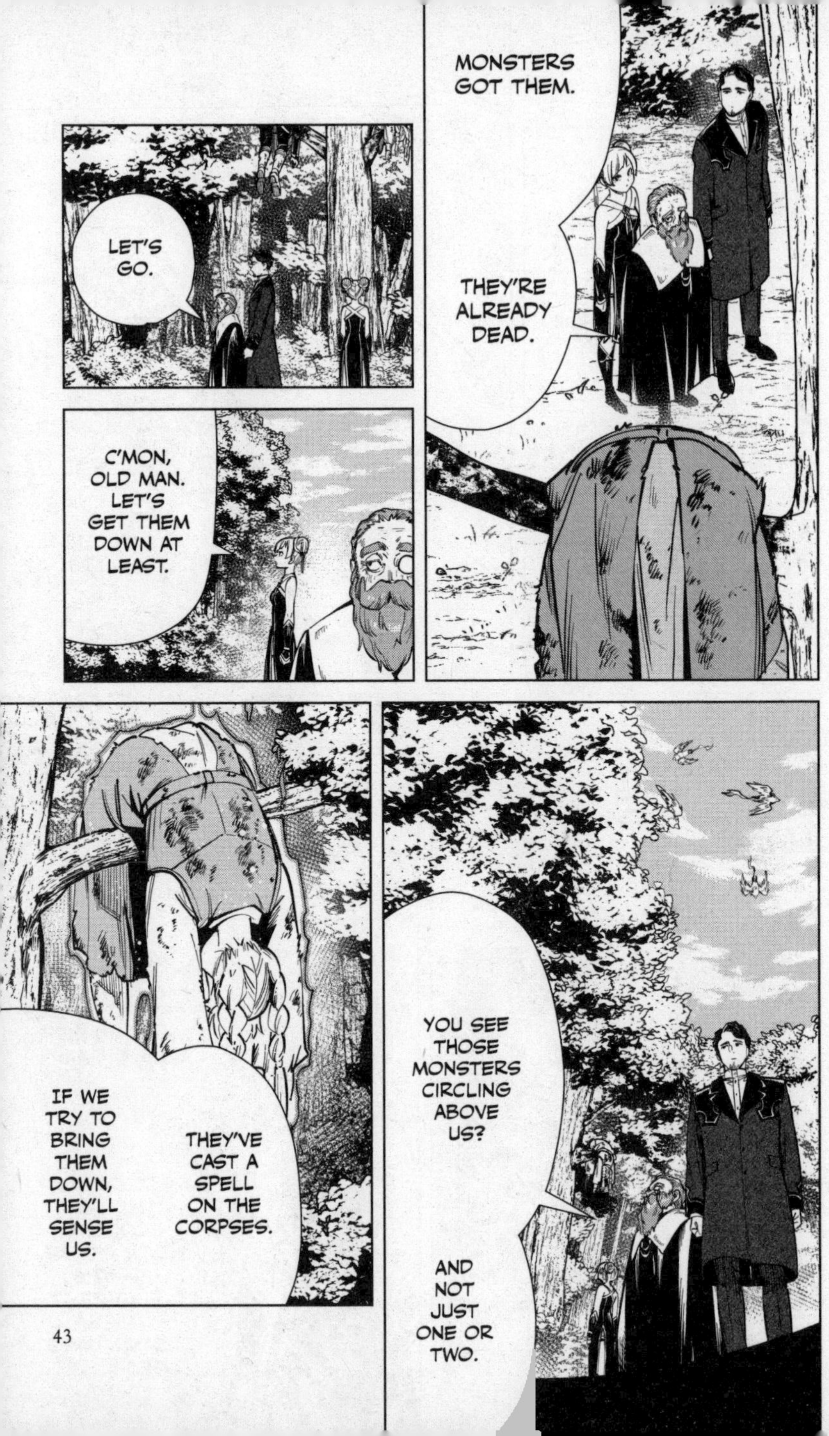
MONSTERS GOT THEM.
THEY'RE ALREADY DEAD.
LET'S GO.
C'MON, OLD MAN. LET'S GET THEM DOWN AT LEAST.
YOU SEE THOSE MONSTERS CIRCLING ABOVE US?
AND NOT JUST ONE OR TWO.
THEY'VE CAST A SPELL ON THE CORPSES.
IF WE TRY TO BRING THEM DOWN, THEY'LL SENSE US.

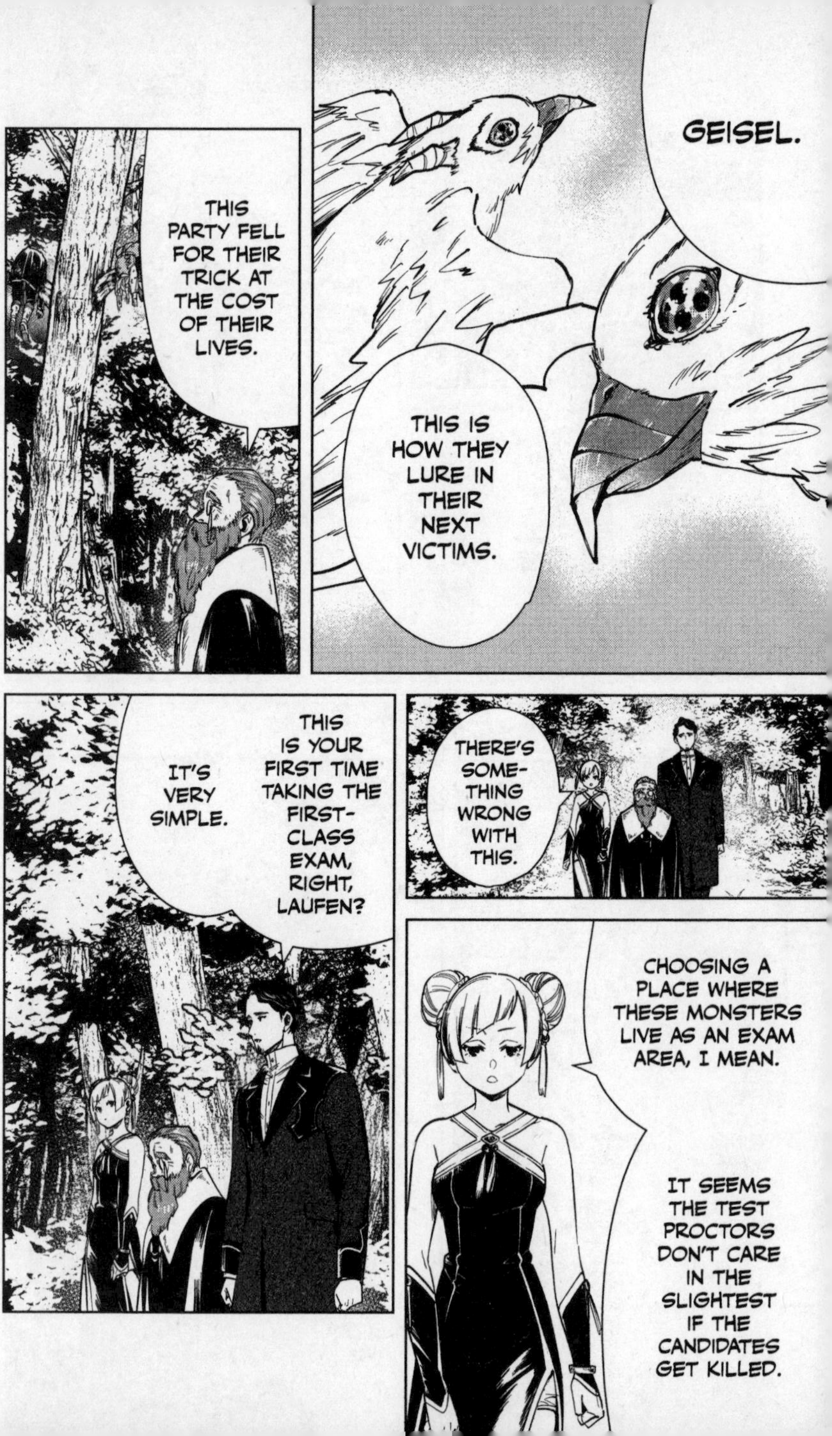
GEISEL.
THIS IS HOW THEY LURE IN THEIR NEXT VICTIMS.
THIS PARTY FELL FOR THEIR TRICK AT THE COST OF THEIR LIVES.
THERE'S SOME-THING WRONG WITH THIS.
CHOOSING A PLACE WHERE THESE MONSTERS LIVE AS AN EXAM AREA, I MEAN.
IT SEEMS THE TEST PROCTORS DON'T CARE IN THE SLIGHTEST IF THE CANDIDATES GET KILLED.
THIS IS YOUR FIRST TIME TAKING THE FIRST-CLASS EXAM, RIGHT, LAUFEN?
IT'S VERY SIMPLE.

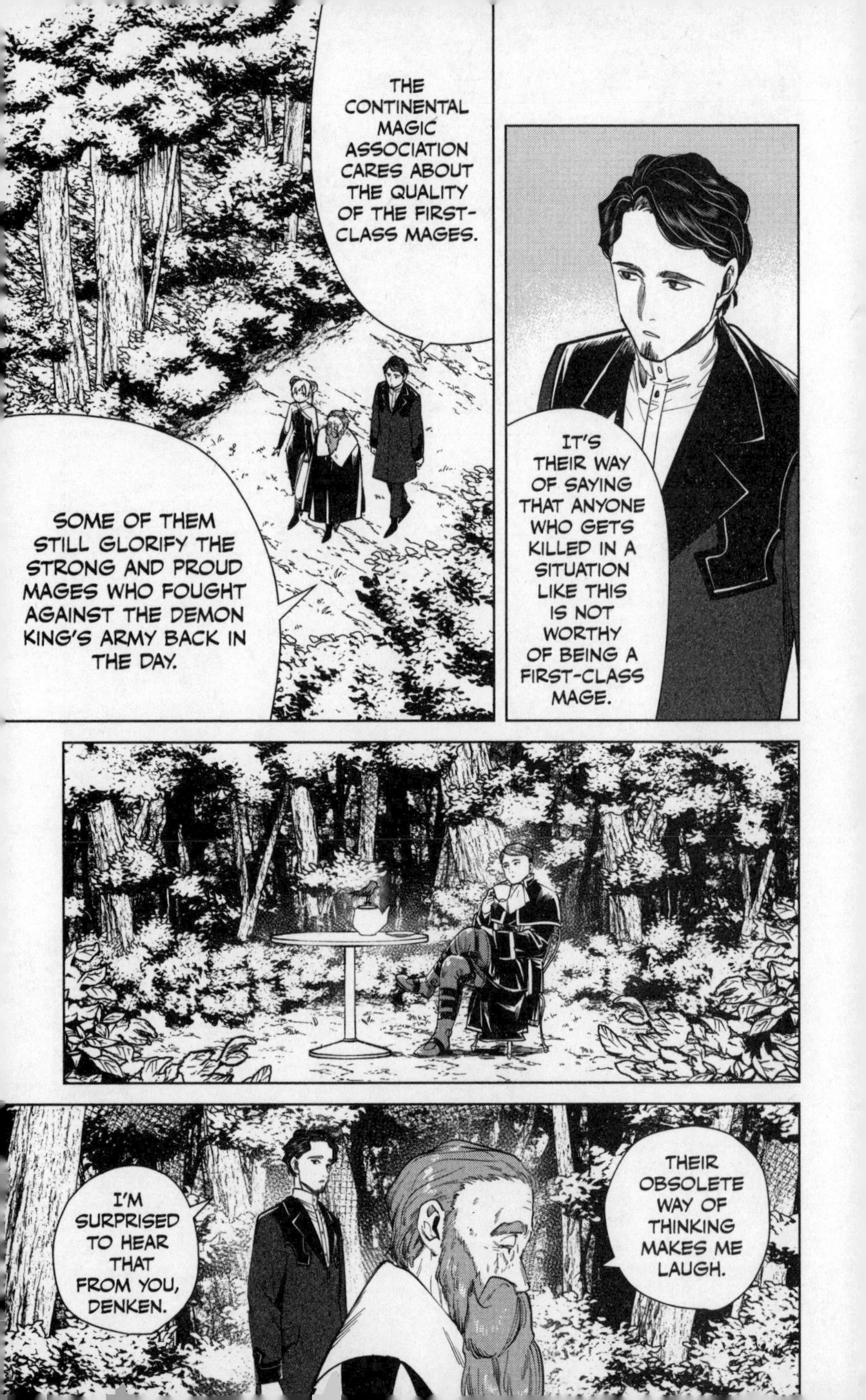
THE CONTINENTAL MAGIC ASSOCIATION CARES ABOUT THE QUALITY OF THE FIRST-CLASS MAGES.
IT'S THEIR WAY OF SAYING THAT ANYONE WHO GETS KILLED IN A SITUATION LIKE THIS IS NOT WORTHY OF BEING A FIRST-CLASS MAGE.
SOME OF THEM STILL GLORIFY THE STRONG AND PROUD MAGES WHO FOUGHT AGAINST THE DEMON KING'S ARMY BACK IN THE DAY.
THEIR OBSOLETE WAY OF THINKING MAKES ME LAUGH.
I'M SURPRISED TO HEAR THAT FROM YOU, DENKEN.

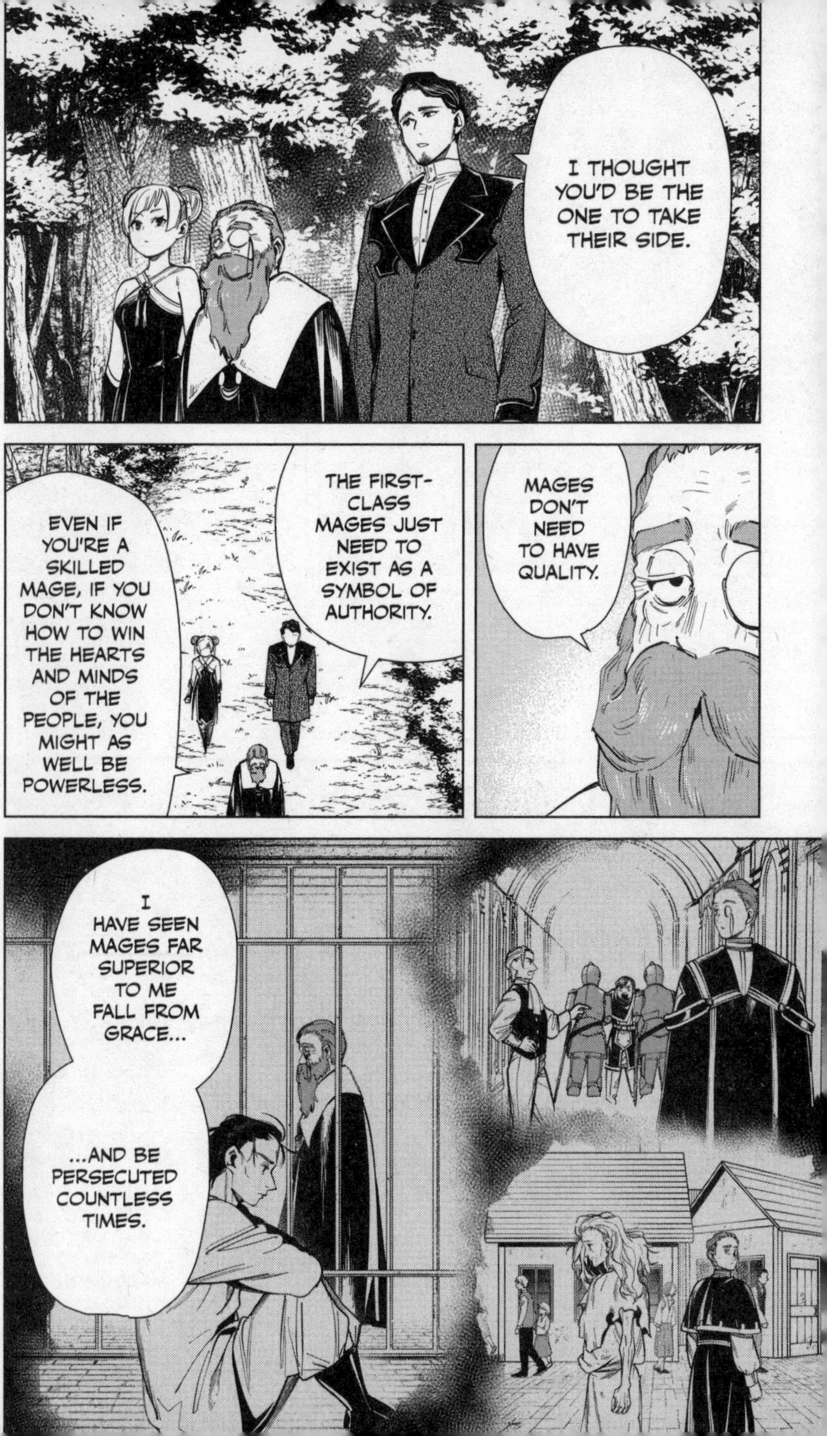
I THOUGHT YOU'D BE THE ONE TO TAKE THEIR SIDE.
MAGES DON'T NEED TO HAVE QUALITY.
THE FIRST-CLASS MAGES JUST NEED TO EXIST AS A SYMBOL OF AUTHORITY.
EVEN IF YOU'RE A SKILLED MAGE, IF YOU DON'T KNOW HOW TO WIN THE HEARTS AND MINDS OF THE PEOPLE, YOU MIGHT AS WELL BE POWERLESS.
I HAVE SEEN MAGES FAR SUPERIOR TO ME FALL FROM GRACE...
...AND BE PERSECUTED COUNTLESS TIMES.

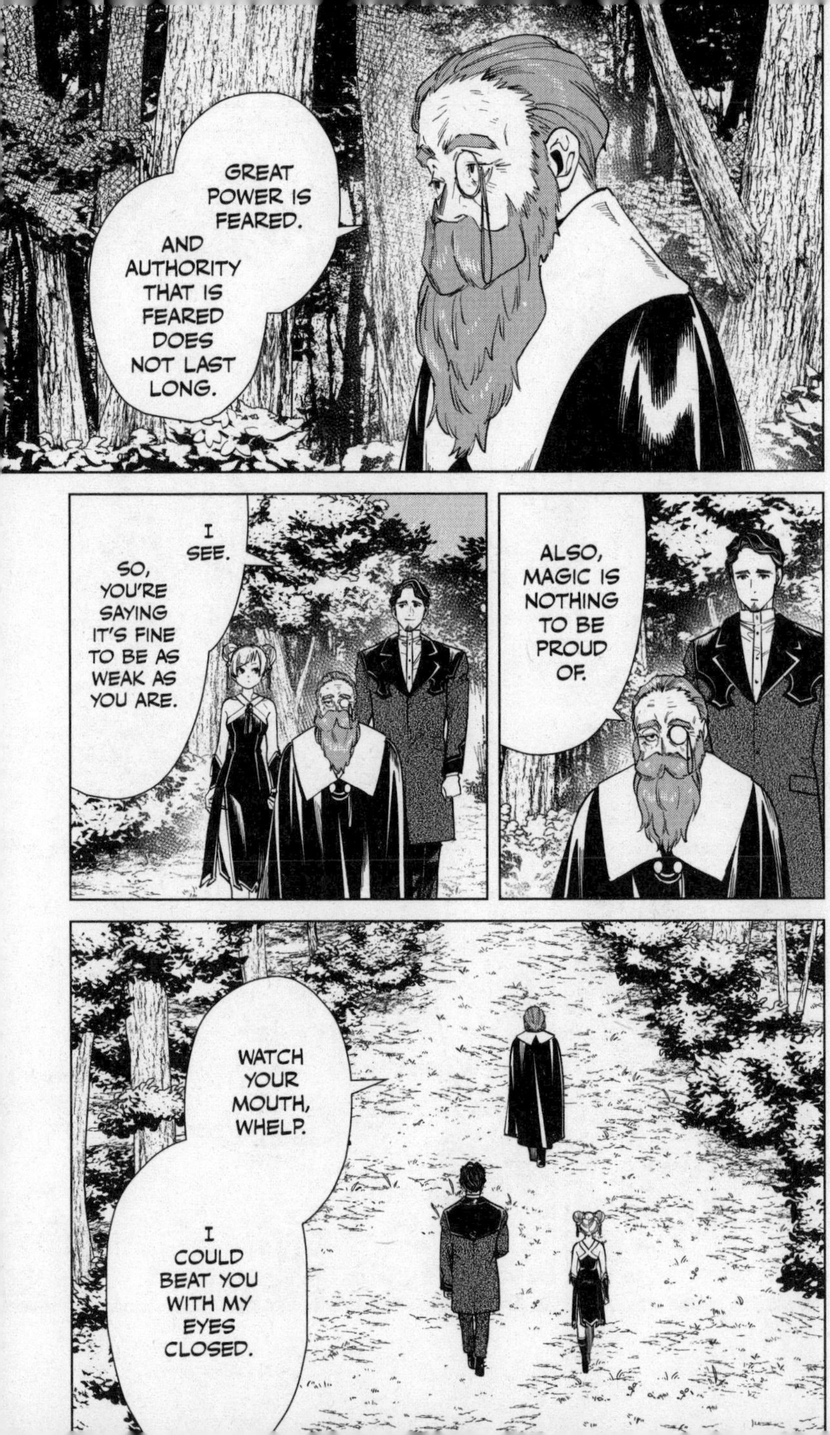
GREAT POWER IS FEARED.
AND AUTHORITY THAT IS FEARED DOES NOT LAST LONG.
ALSO, MAGIC IS NOTHING TO BE PROUD OF.
I SEE.
SO, YOU'RE SAYING IT'S FINE TO BE AS WEAK AS YOU ARE.
WATCH YOUR MOUTH, WHELP.
I COULD BEAT YOU WITH MY EYES CLOSED.

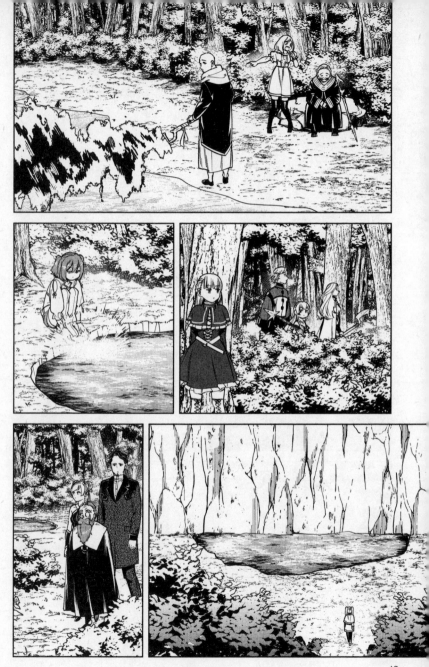

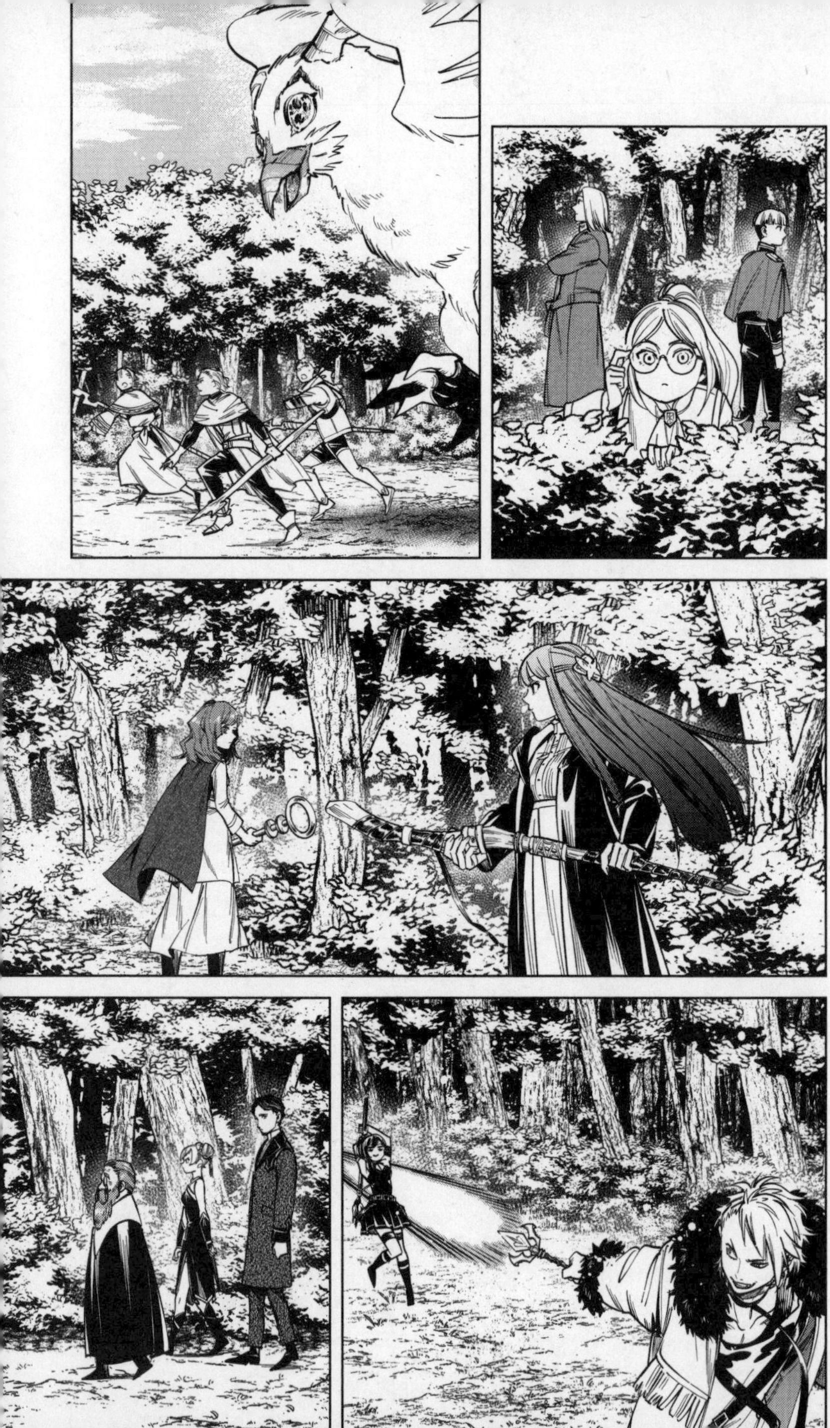

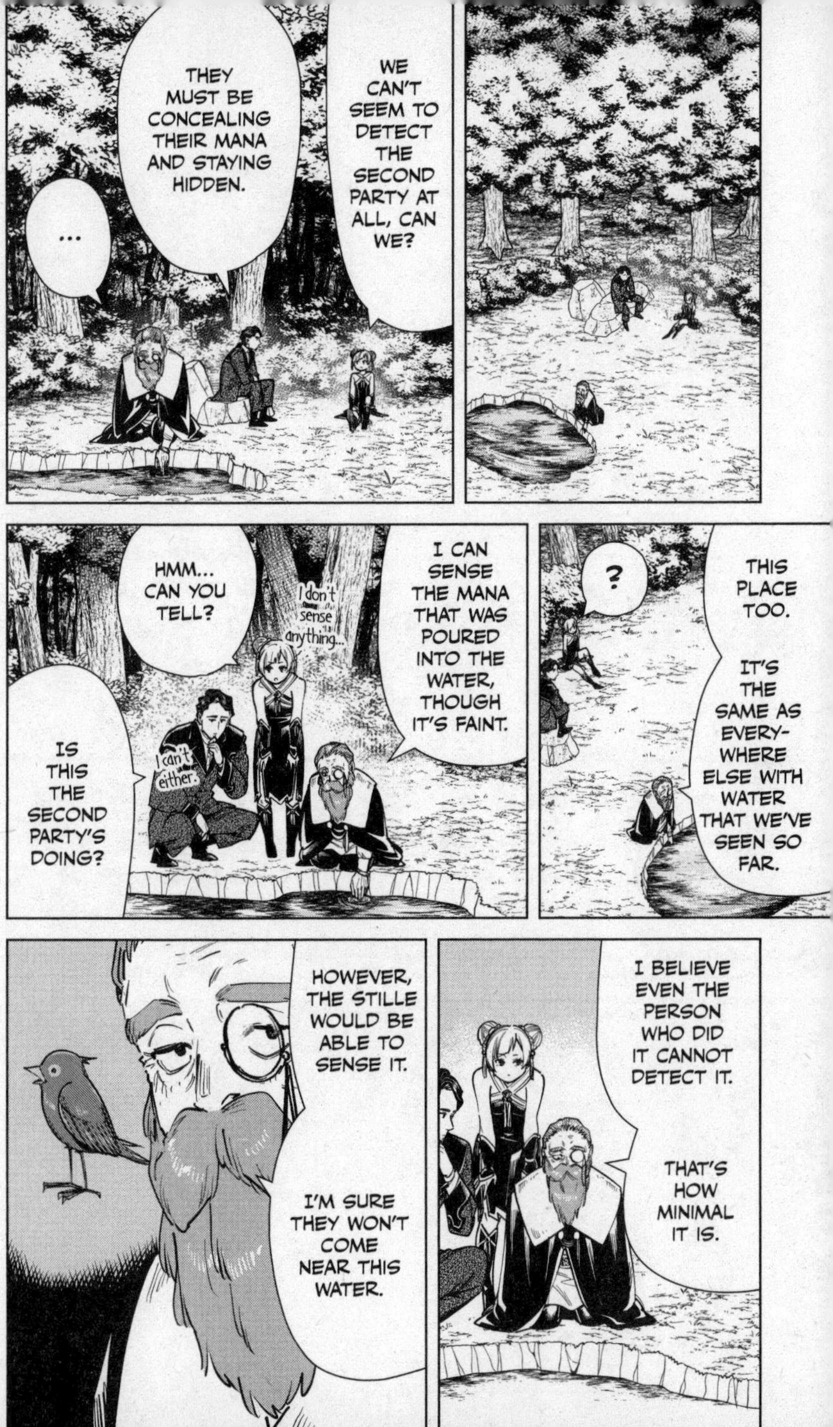
WE CAN'T SEEM TO DETECT THE SECOND PARTY AT ALL, CAN WE?
THEY MUST BE CONCEALING THEIR MANA AND STAYING HIDDEN.
...
THIS PLACE TOO. IT'S THE SAME AS EVERY-WHERE ELSE WITH WATER THAT WE'VE SEEN SO FAR.
?
I CAN SENSE THE MANA THAT WAS POURED INTO THE WATER, THOUGH IT'S FAINT.
HMM... CAN YOU TELL?
I don't sense anything...
I can't either.
IS THIS THE SECOND PARTY'S DOING?
I BELIEVE EVEN THE PERSON WHO DID IT CANNOT DETECT IT.
THAT'S HOW MINIMAL IT IS.
HOWEVER, THE STILLE WOULD BE ABLE TO SENSE IT.
I'M SURE THEY WON'T COME NEAR THIS WATER.

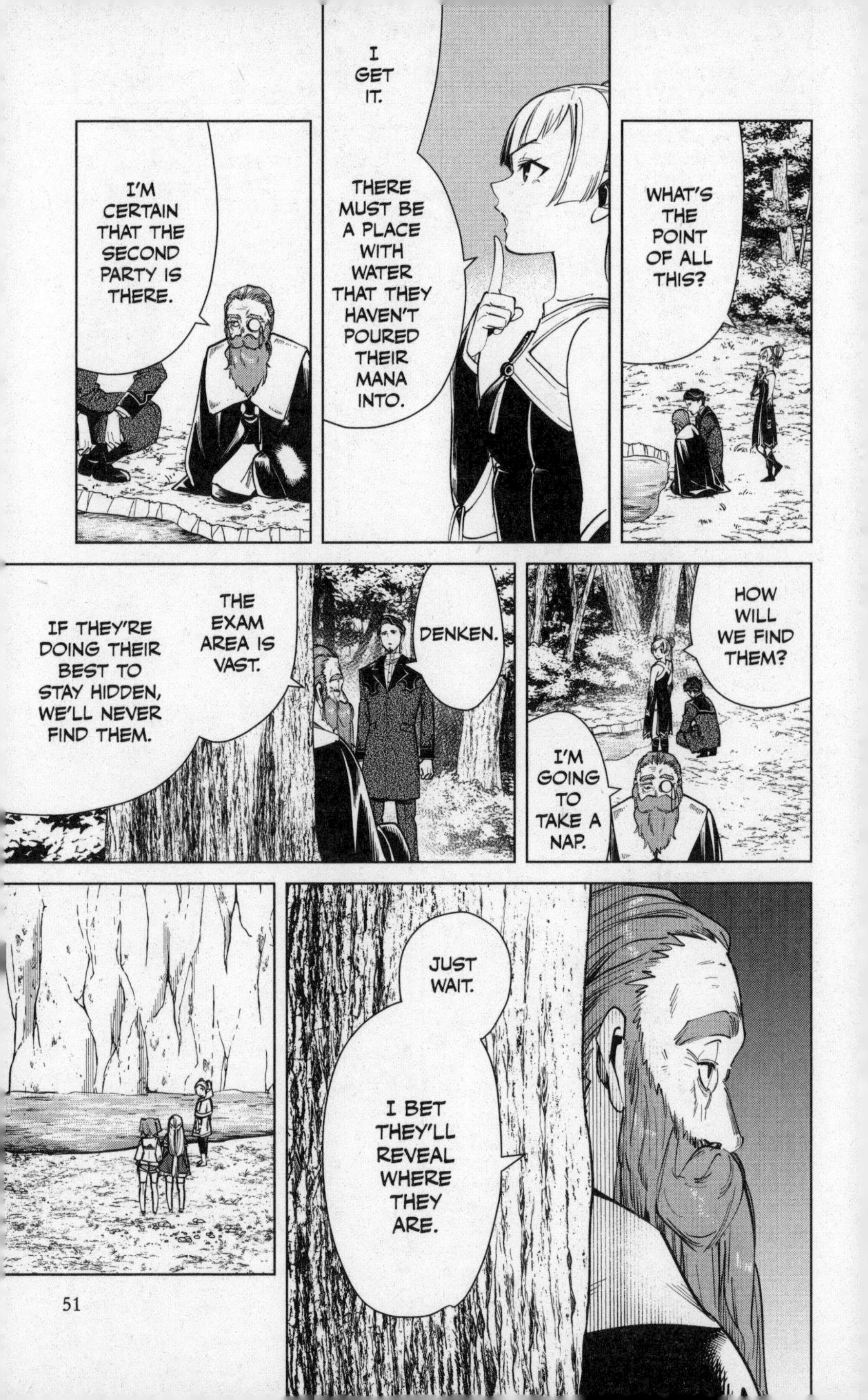
WHAT'S THE POINT OF ALL THIS?
I GET IT.
THERE MUST BE A PLACE WITH WATER THAT THEY HAVEN'T POURED THEIR MANA INTO.
I'M CERTAIN THAT THE SECOND PARTY IS THERE.
HOW WILL WE FIND THEM?
I'M GOING TO TAKE A NAP.
DENKEN.
THE EXAM AREA IS VAST.
IF THEY'RE DOING THEIR BEST TO STAY HIDDEN, WE'LL NEVER FIND THEM.
JUST WAIT.
I BET THEY'LL REVEAL WHERE THEY ARE.

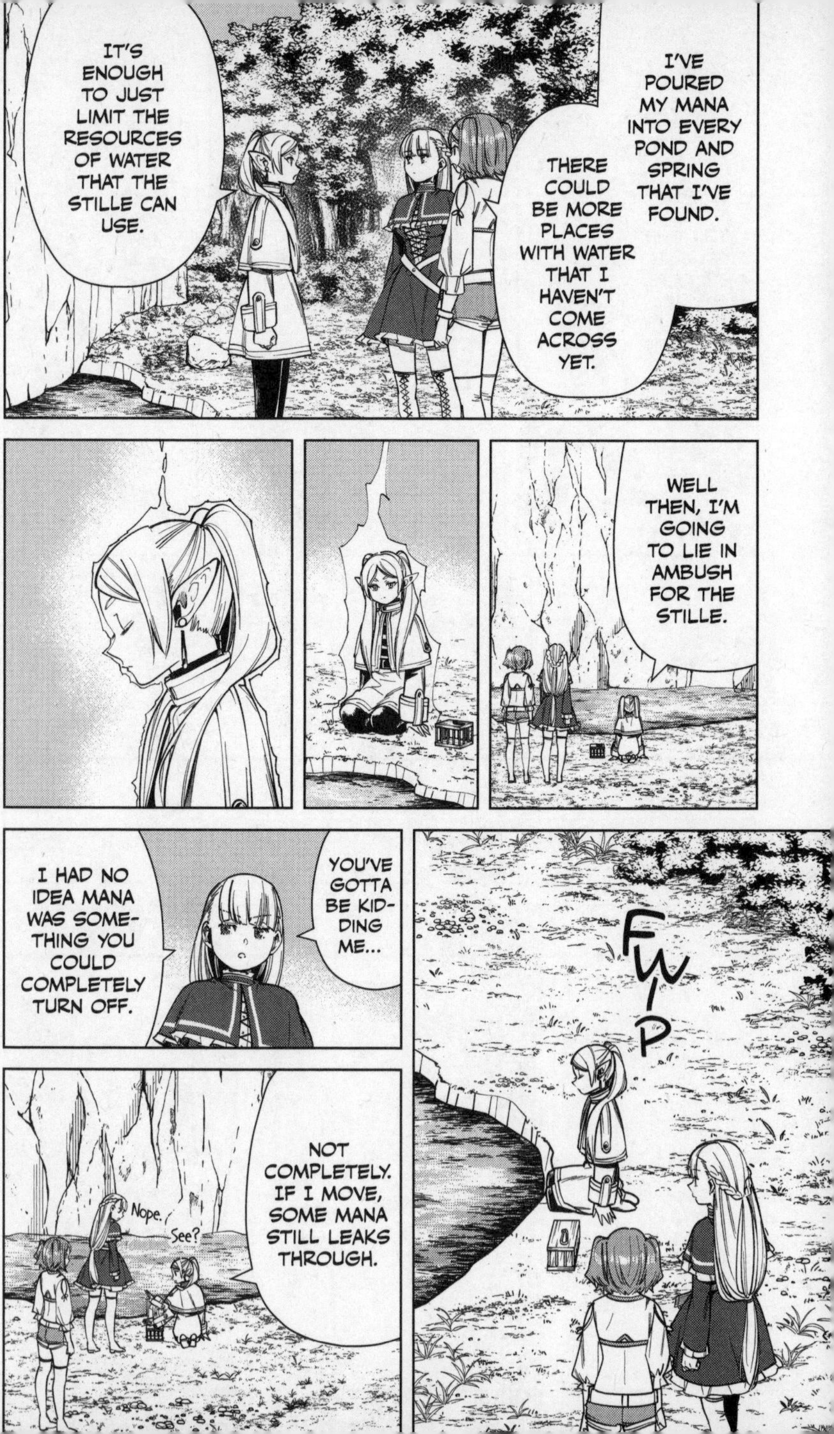
I'VE POURED MY MANA INTO EVERY POND AND SPRING THAT I'VE FOUND.
THERE COULD BE MORE PLACES WITH WATER THAT I HAVEN'T COME ACROSS YET.
IT'S ENOUGH TO JUST LIMIT THE RESOURCES OF WATER THAT THE STILLE CAN USE.
WELL THEN, I'M GOING TO LIE IN AMBUSH FOR THE STILLE.
FWIP
YOU'VE GOTTA BE KID-DING ME...
I HAD NO IDEA MANA WAS SOME-THING YOU COULD COMPLETELY TURN OFF.
NOT COMPLETELY. IF I MOVE, SOME MANA STILL LEAKS THROUGH.
See?
Nope.

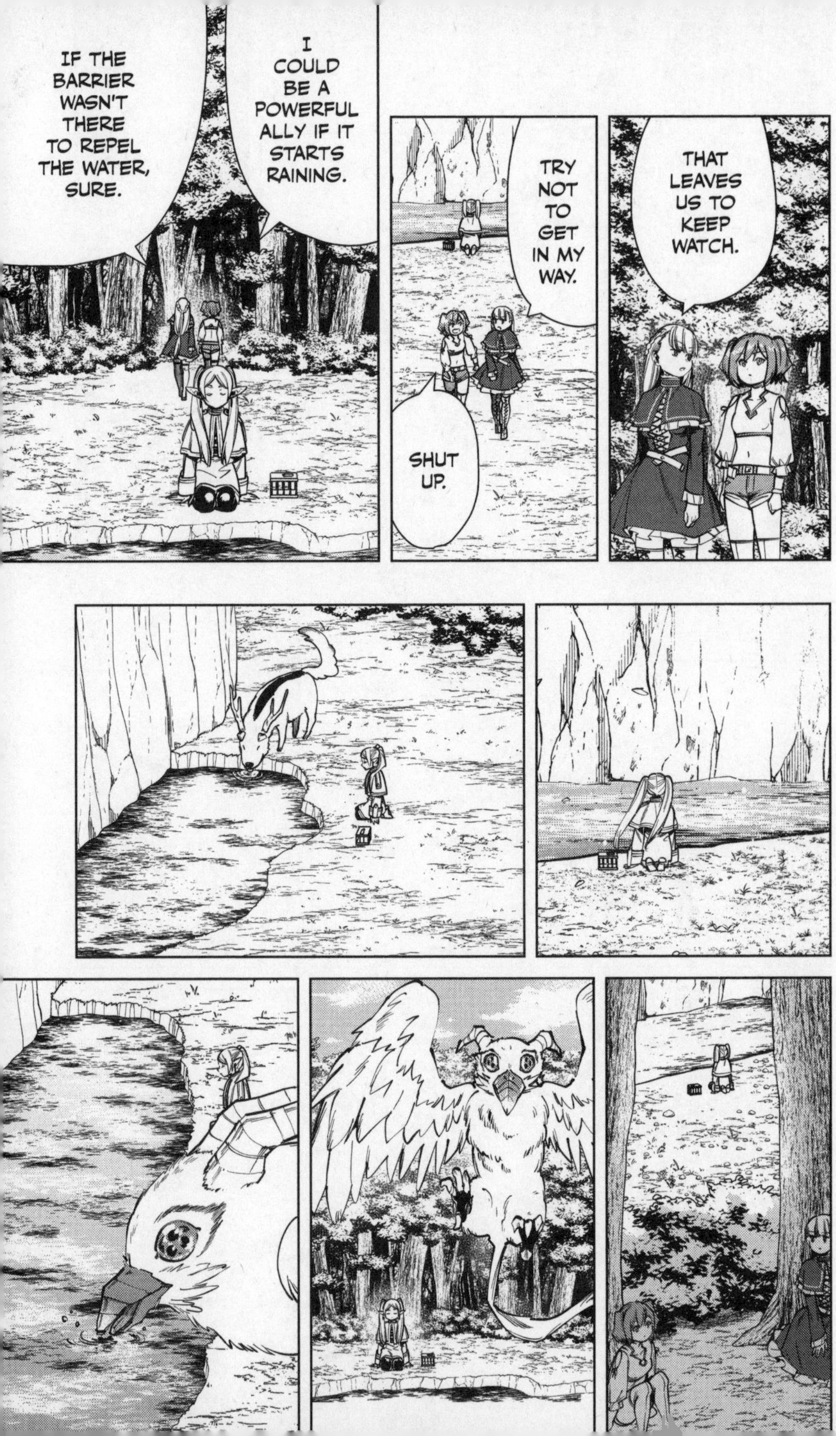
THAT LEAVES US TO KEEP WATCH.
TRY NOT TO GET IN MY WAY.
SHUT UP.
I COULD BE A POWERFUL ALLY IF IT STARTS RAINING.
IF THE BARRIER WASN'T THERE TO REPEL THE WATER, SURE.

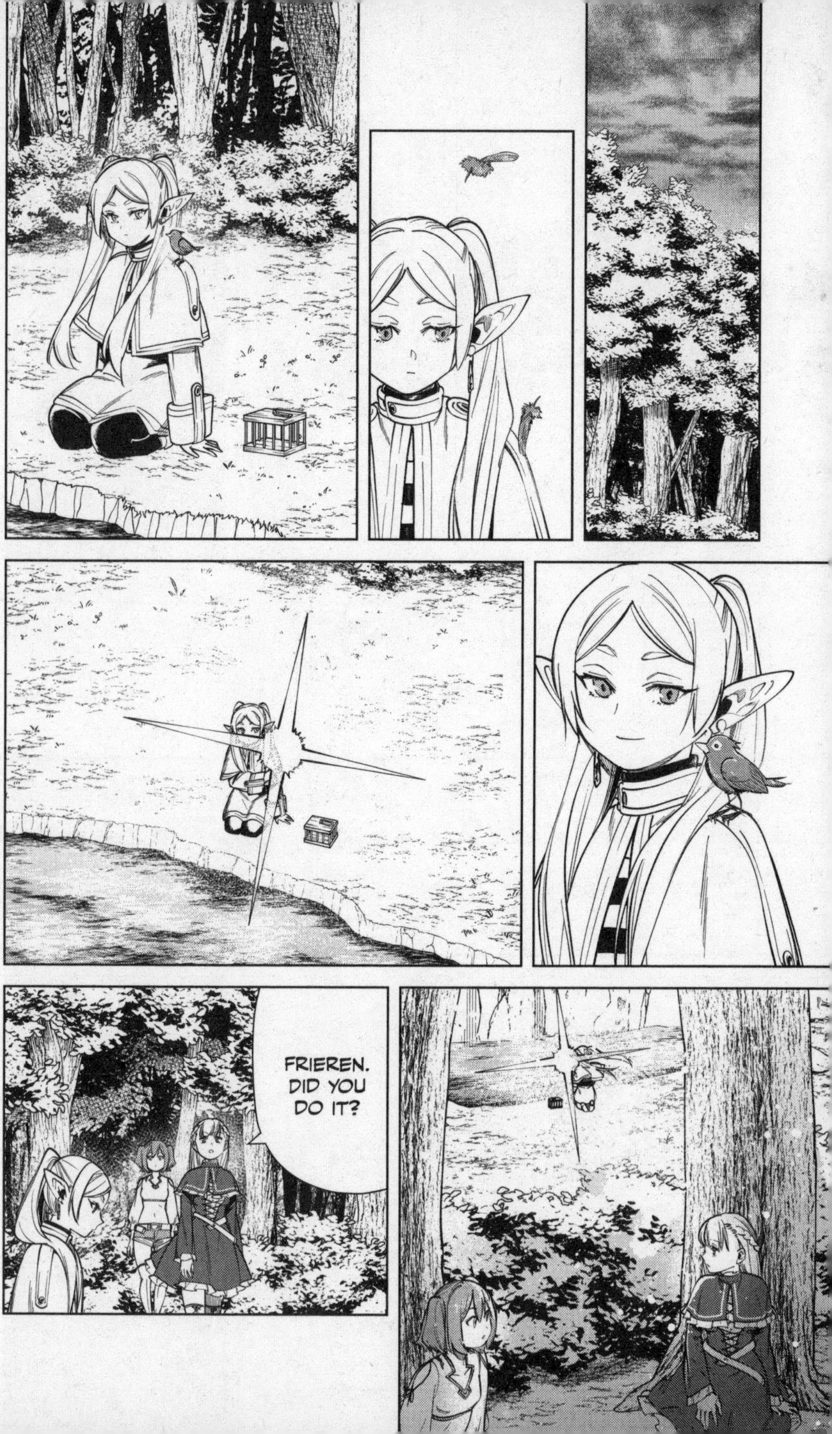
FRIEREN. DID YOU DO IT?

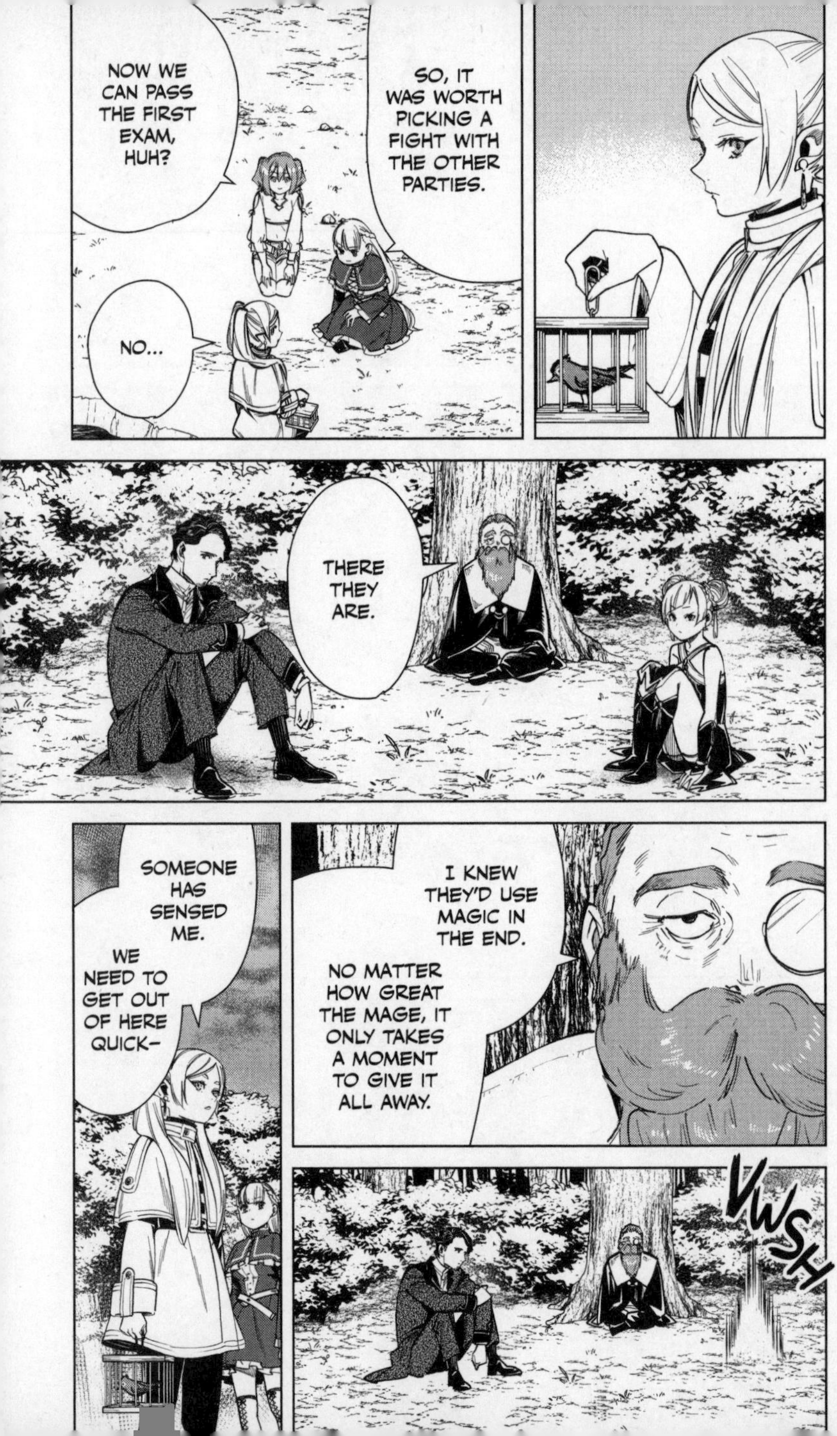
SO, IT WAS WORTH PICKING A FIGHT WITH THE OTHER PARTIES.
NOW WE CAN PASS THE FIRST EXAM, HUH?
NO...
THERE THEY ARE.
I KNEW THEY'D USE MAGIC IN THE END.
NO MATTER HOW GREAT THE MAGE, IT ONLY TAKES A MOMENT TO GIVE IT ALL AWAY.
VWSH
SOMEONE HAS SENSED ME.
WE NEED TO GET OUT OF HERE QUICK-

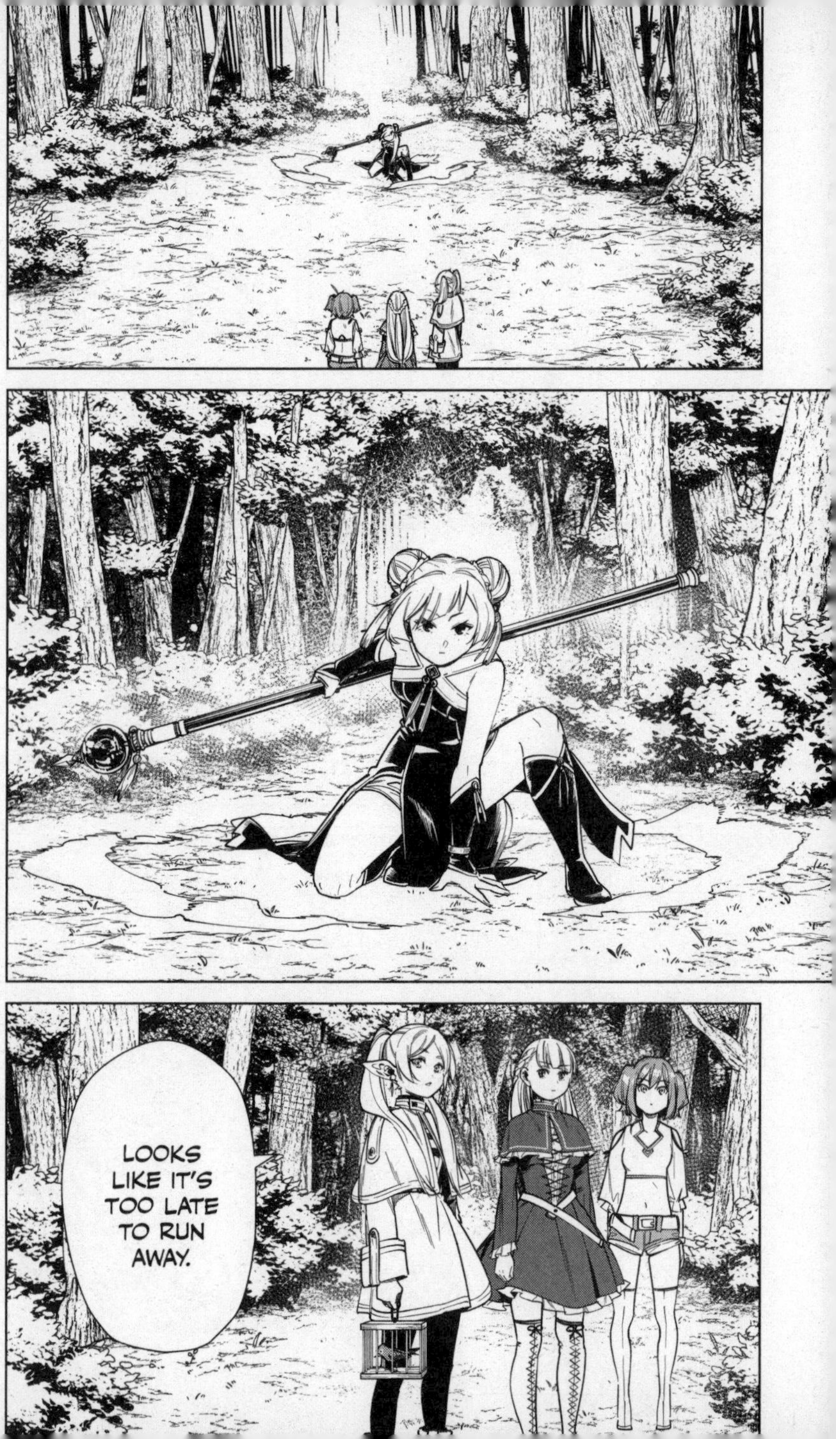
LOOKS LIKE IT'S TOO LATE TO RUN AWAY.

Chapter 41: Time for Resolve

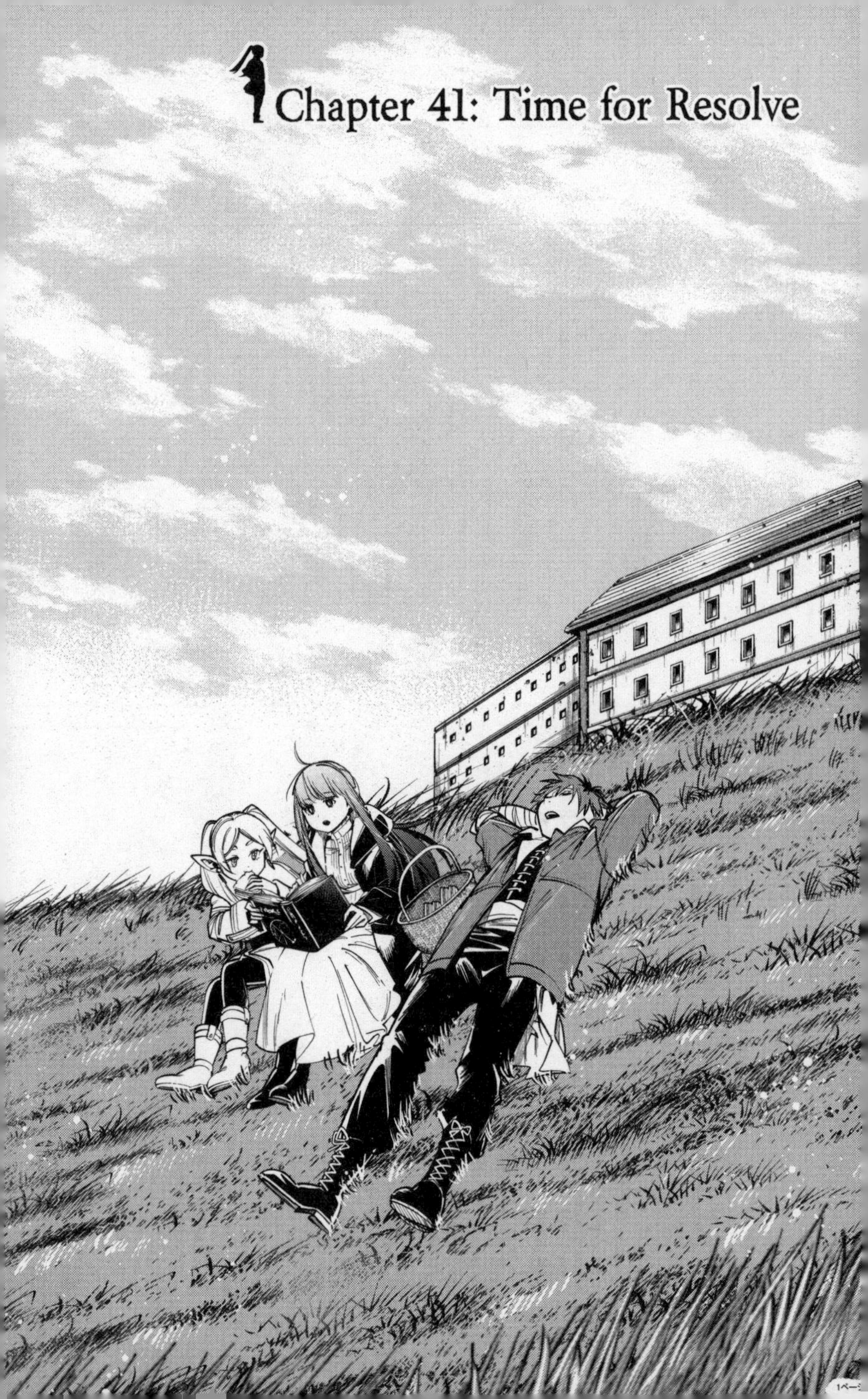

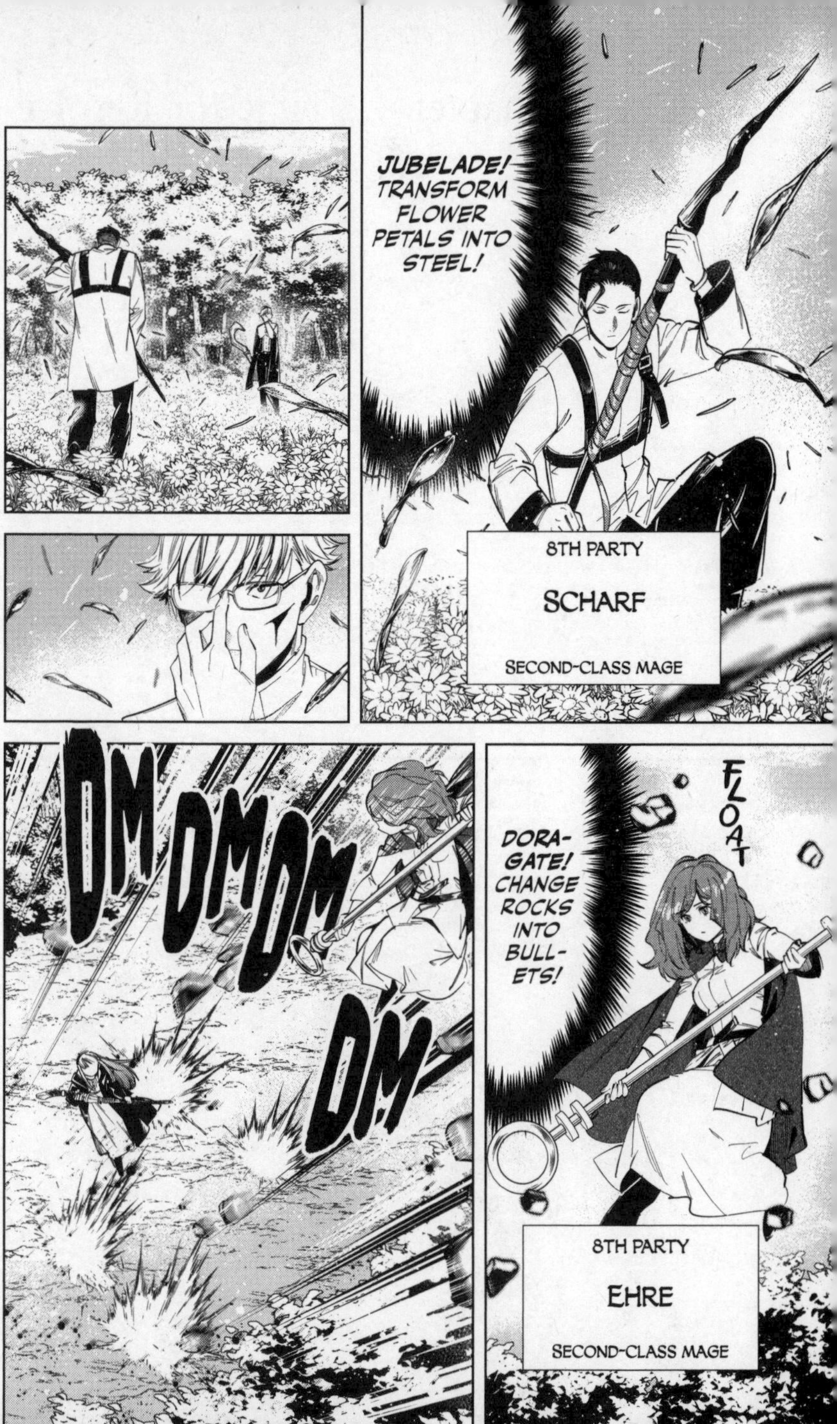
JUBELADE! TRANSFORM FLOWER PETALS INTO STEEL!
8TH PARTY
SCHARF
SECOND-CLASS MAGE
FLOAT
DORA-GATE! CHANGE ROCKS INTO BULL-ETS!
8TH PARTY
EHRE
SECOND-CLASS MAGE
DM DM DM DM
DM

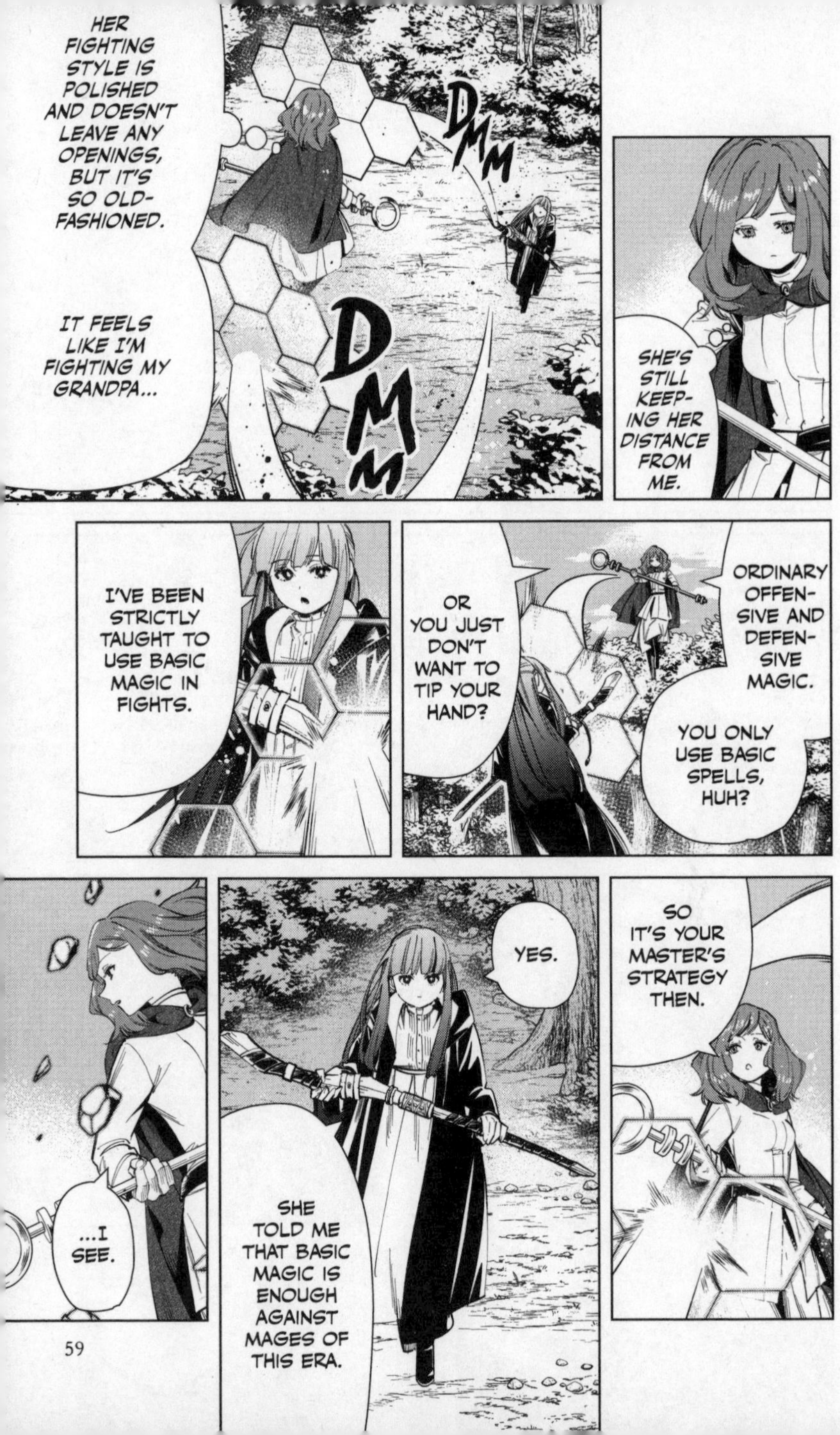
SHE'S STILL KEEP-ING HER DISTANCE FROM ME.
HER FIGHTING STYLE IS POLISHED AND DOESN'T LEAVE ANY OPENINGS, BUT IT'S SO OLD-FASHIONED.
DMM
DMM
IT FEELS LIKE I'M FIGHTING MY GRANDPA...
ORDINARY OFFEN-SIVE AND DEFEN-SIVE MAGIC.
YOU ONLY USE BASIC SPELLS, HUH?
OR YOU JUST DON'T WANT TO TIP YOUR HAND?
I'VE BEEN STRICTLY TAUGHT TO USE BASIC MAGIC IN FIGHTS.
SO IT'S YOUR MASTER'S STRATEGY THEN.
YES.
SHE TOLD ME THAT BASIC MAGIC IS ENOUGH AGAINST MAGES OF THIS ERA.
...I SEE.

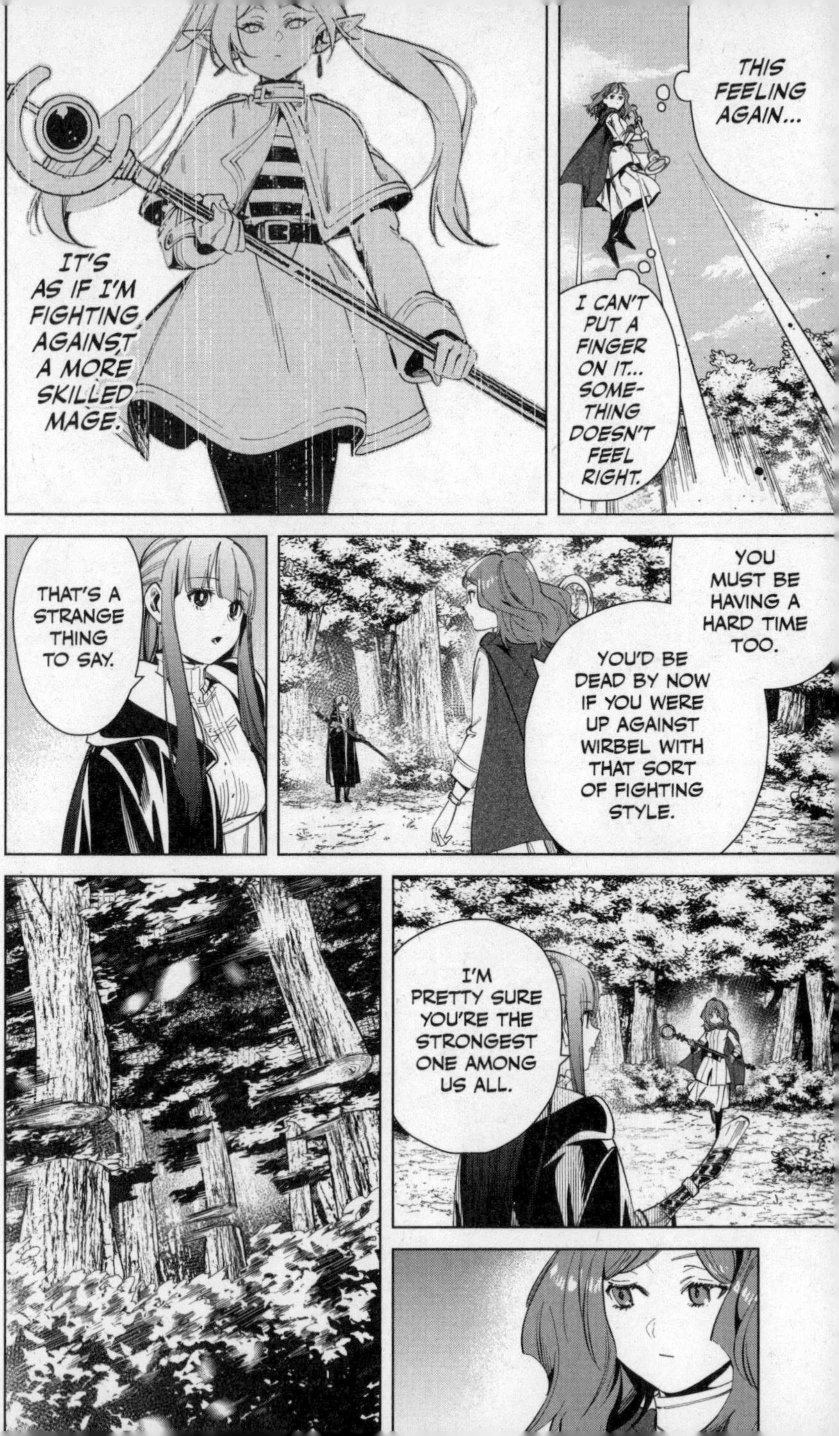
THIS FEELING AGAIN...
I CAN'T PUT A FINGER ON IT... SOMETHING DOESN'T FEEL RIGHT.
IT'S AS IF I'M FIGHTING AGAINST A MORE SKILLED MAGE.
YOU MUST BE HAVING A HARD TIME TOO.
YOU'D BE DEAD BY NOW IF YOU WERE UP AGAINST WIRBEL WITH THAT SORT OF FIGHTING STYLE.
THAT'S A STRANGE THING TO SAY.
I'M PRETTY SURE YOU'RE THE STRONGEST ONE AMONG US ALL.

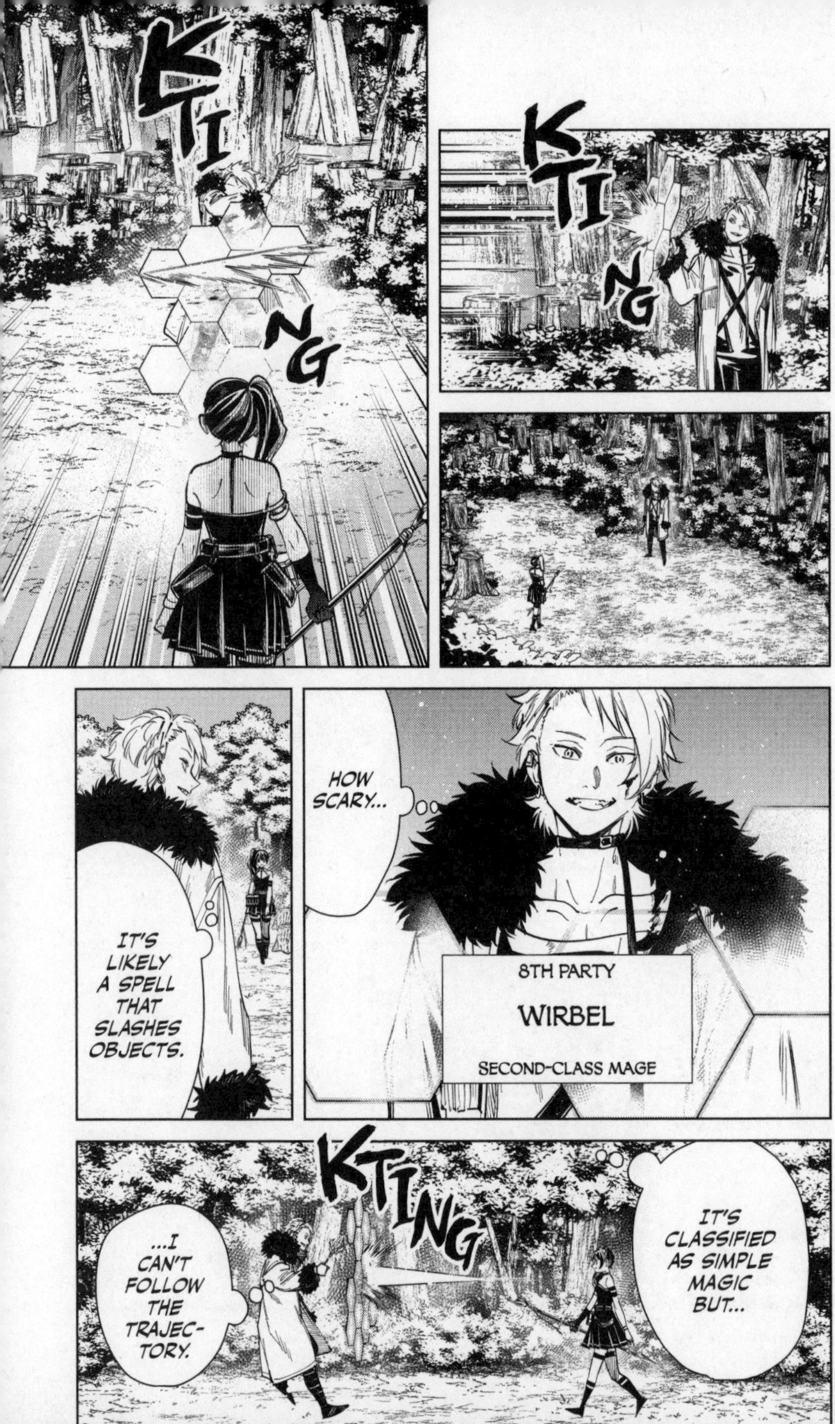
KTING
KTING
HOW SCARY...
8TH PARTY
WIRBEL
SECOND-CLASS MAGE
IT'S LIKELY A SPELL THAT SLASHES OBJECTS.
KTING
IT'S CLASSIFIED AS SIMPLE MAGIC BUT...
...I CAN'T FOLLOW THE TRAJEC-TORY.

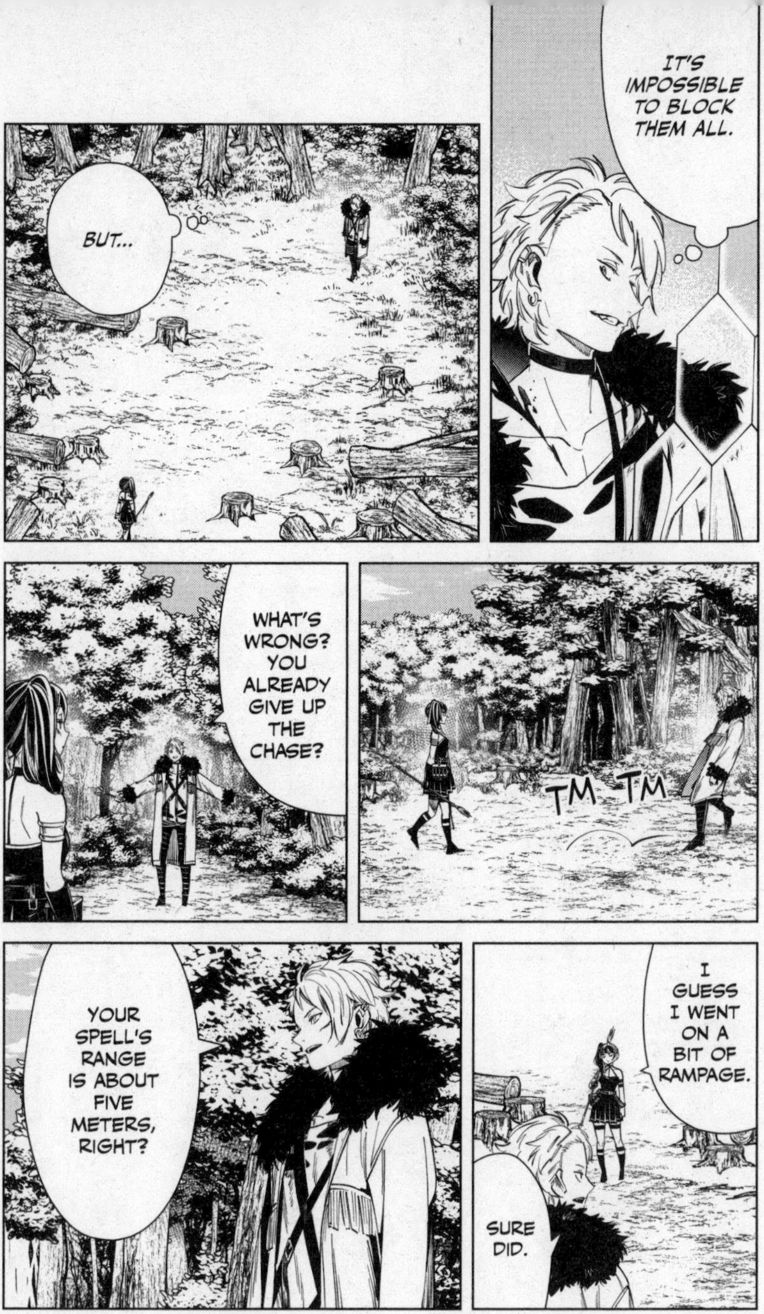
IT'S IMPOSSIBLE TO BLOCK THEM ALL.
BUT...
TM TM
WHAT'S WRONG? YOU ALREADY GIVE UP THE CHASE?
I GUESS I WENT ON A BIT OF RAMPAGE.
SURE DID.
YOUR SPELL'S RANGE IS ABOUT FIVE METERS, RIGHT?

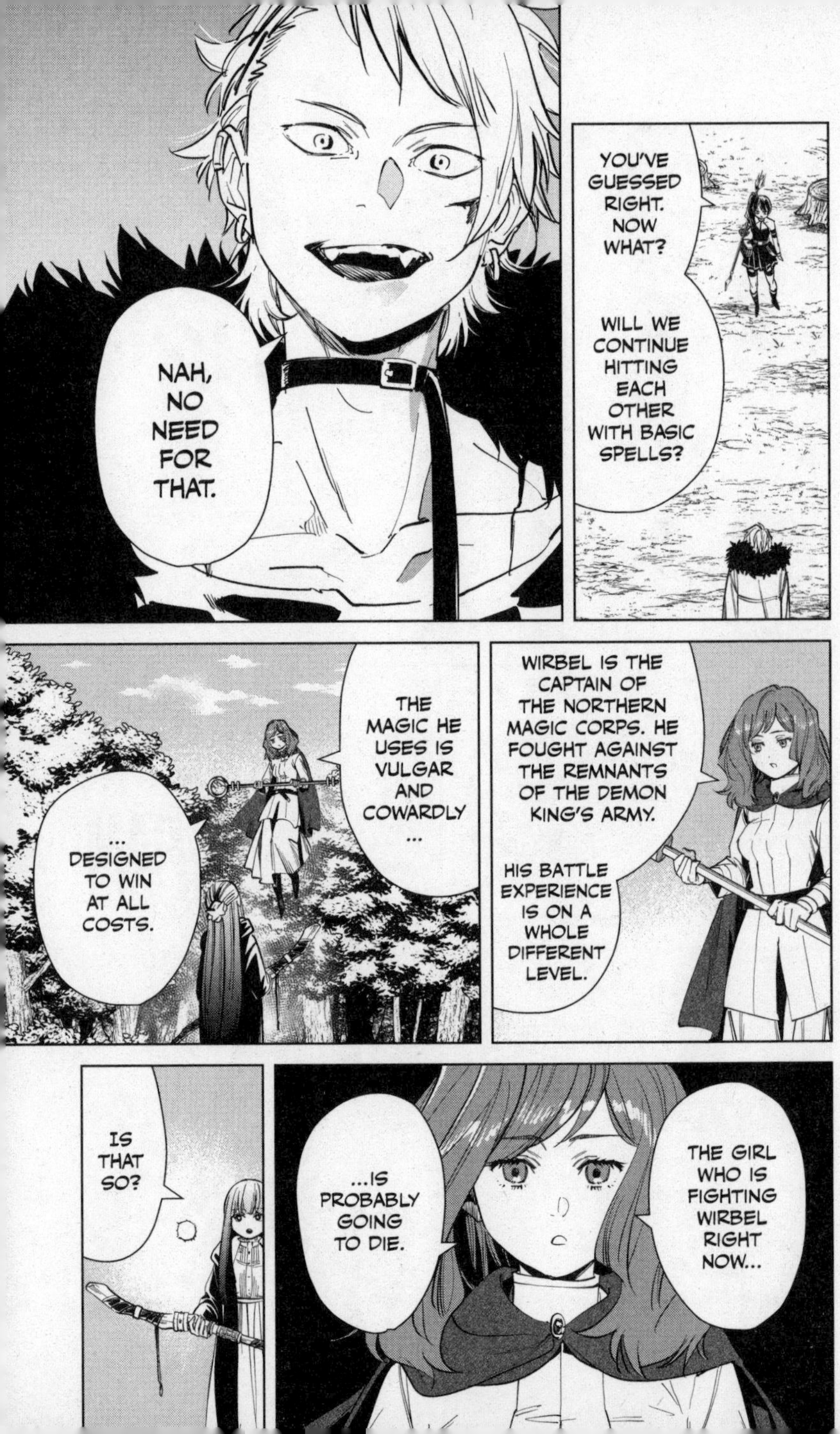
YOU'VE GUESSED RIGHT. NOW WHAT?
WILL WE CONTINUE HITTING EACH OTHER WITH BASIC SPELLS?
NAH, NO NEED FOR THAT.
WIRBEL IS THE CAPTAIN OF THE NORTHERN MAGIC CORPS. HE FOUGHT AGAINST THE REMNANTS OF THE DEMON KING'S ARMY.
HIS BATTLE EXPERIENCE IS ON A WHOLE DIFFERENT LEVEL.
THE MAGIC HE USES IS VULGAR AND COWARDLY ...
... DESIGNED TO WIN AT ALL COSTS.
THE GIRL WHO IS FIGHTING WIRBEL RIGHT NOW...
...IS PROBABLY GOING TO DIE.
IS THAT SO?

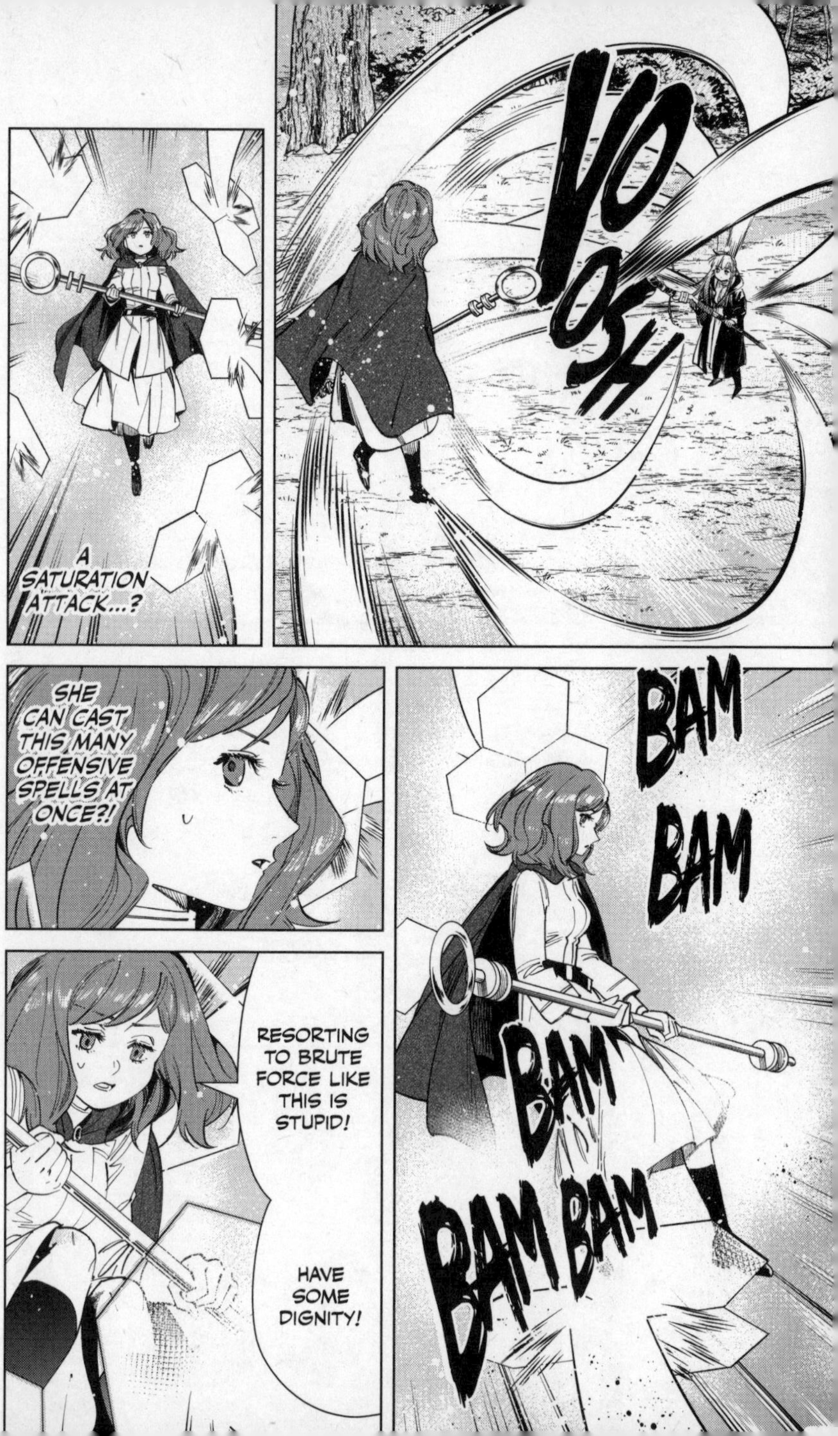
VOOSH
A SATURATION ATTACK...?
BAM BAM BAM BAM BAM
SHE CAN CAST THIS MANY OFFENSIVE SPELLS AT ONCE?!
RESORTING TO BRUTE FORCE LIKE THIS IS STUPID!
HAVE SOME DIGNITY!

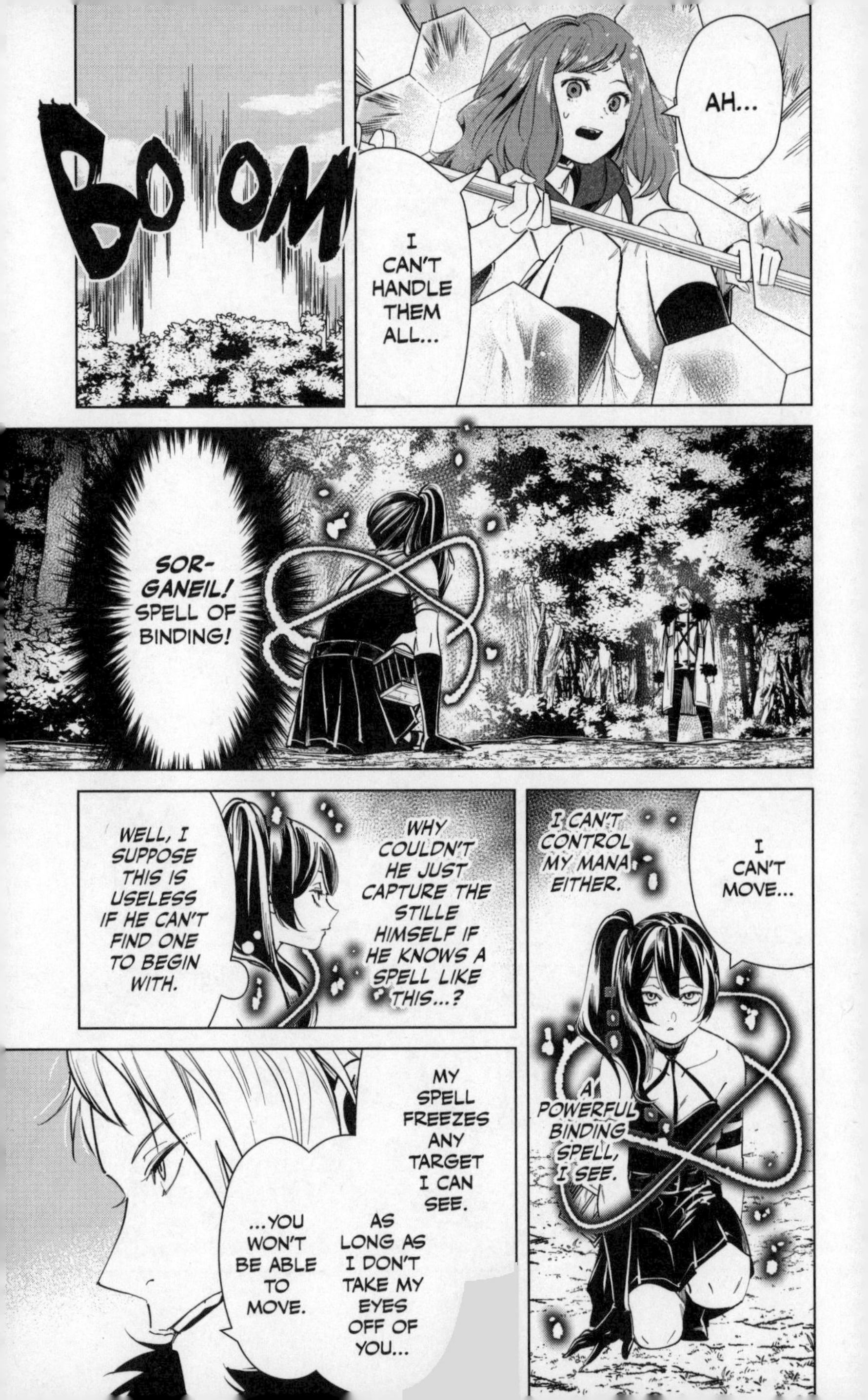
AH...
I CAN'T HANDLE THEM ALL...
BOOM
SOR-GANEIL! SPELL OF BINDING!
I CAN'T MOVE...
I CAN'T CONTROL MY MANA EITHER.
A POWERFUL BINDING SPELL, I SEE.
WHY COULDN'T HE JUST CAPTURE THE STILLE HIMSELF IF HE KNOWS A SPELL LIKE THIS...?
WELL, I SUPPOSE THIS IS USELESS IF HE CAN'T FIND ONE TO BEGIN WITH.
MY SPELL FREEZES ANY TARGET I CAN SEE.
AS LONG AS I DON'T TAKE MY EYES OFF OF YOU...
...YOU WON'T BE ABLE TO MOVE.

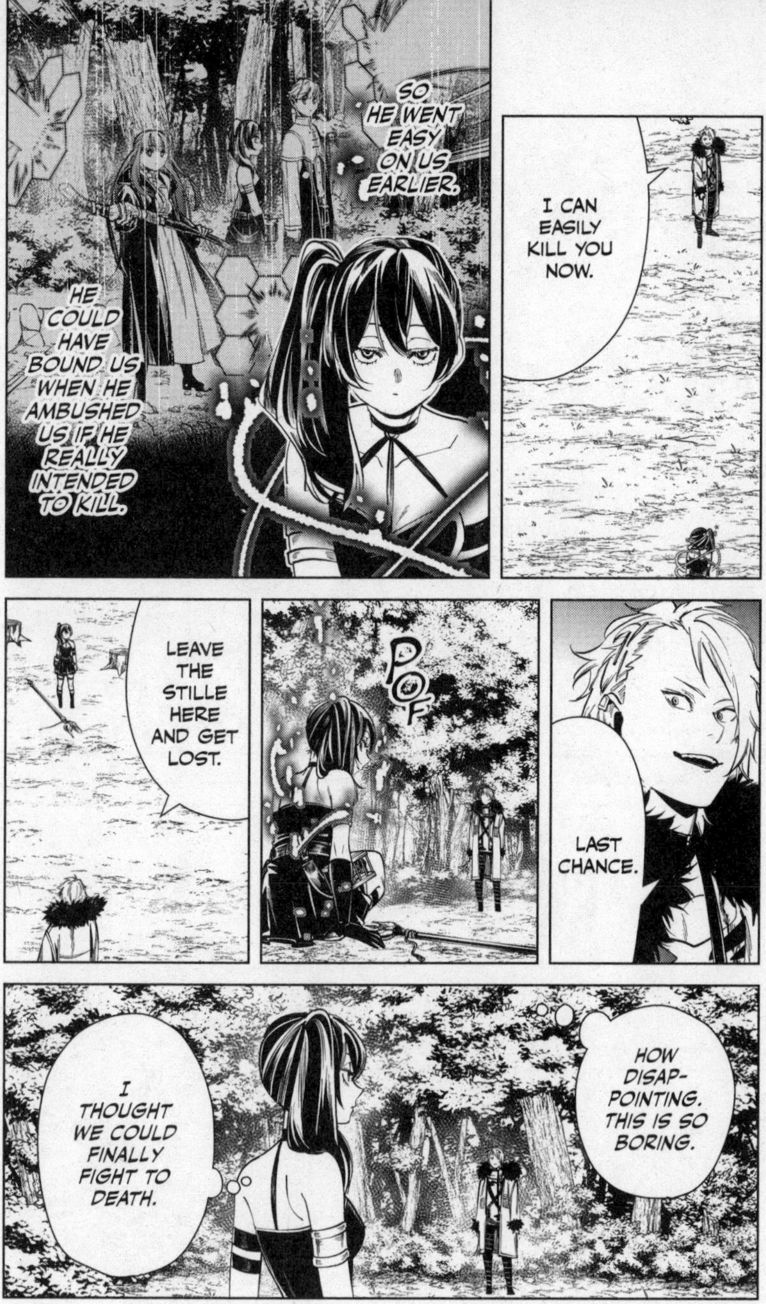
I CAN EASILY KILL YOU NOW.
SO HE WENT EASY ON US EARLIER.
HE COULD HAVE BOUND US WHEN HE AMBUSHED US IF HE REALLY INTENDED TO KILL.
LAST CHANCE.
POF
LEAVE THE STILLE HERE AND GET LOST.
HOW DISAP-POINTING. THIS IS SO BORING.
I THOUGHT WE COULD FINALLY FIGHT TO DEATH.

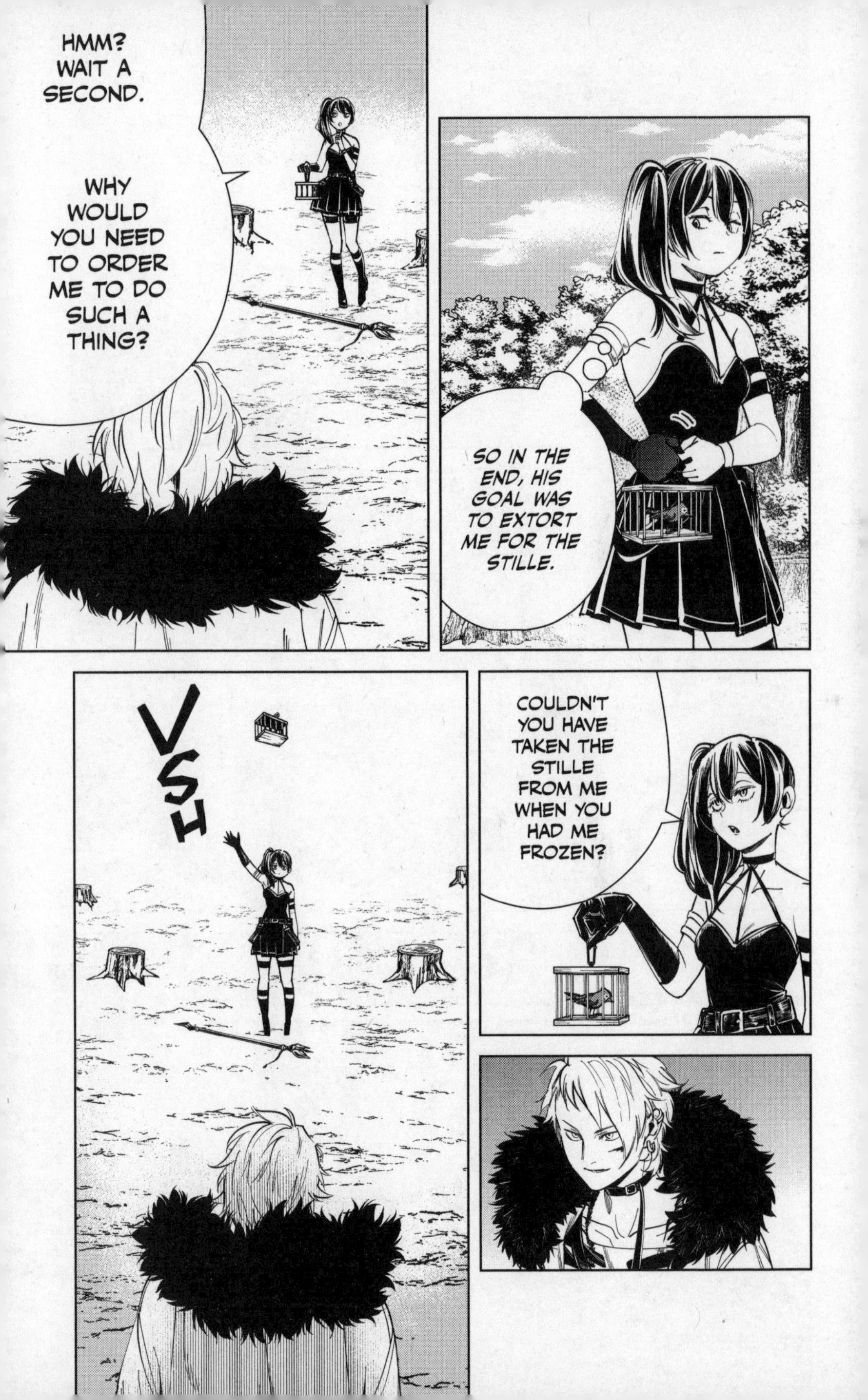
SO IN THE END, HIS GOAL WAS TO EXTORT ME FOR THE STILLE.
HMM? WAIT A SECOND.
WHY WOULD YOU NEED TO ORDER ME TO DO SUCH A THING?
COULDN'T YOU HAVE TAKEN THE STILLE FROM ME WHEN YOU HAD ME FROZEN?
VSH

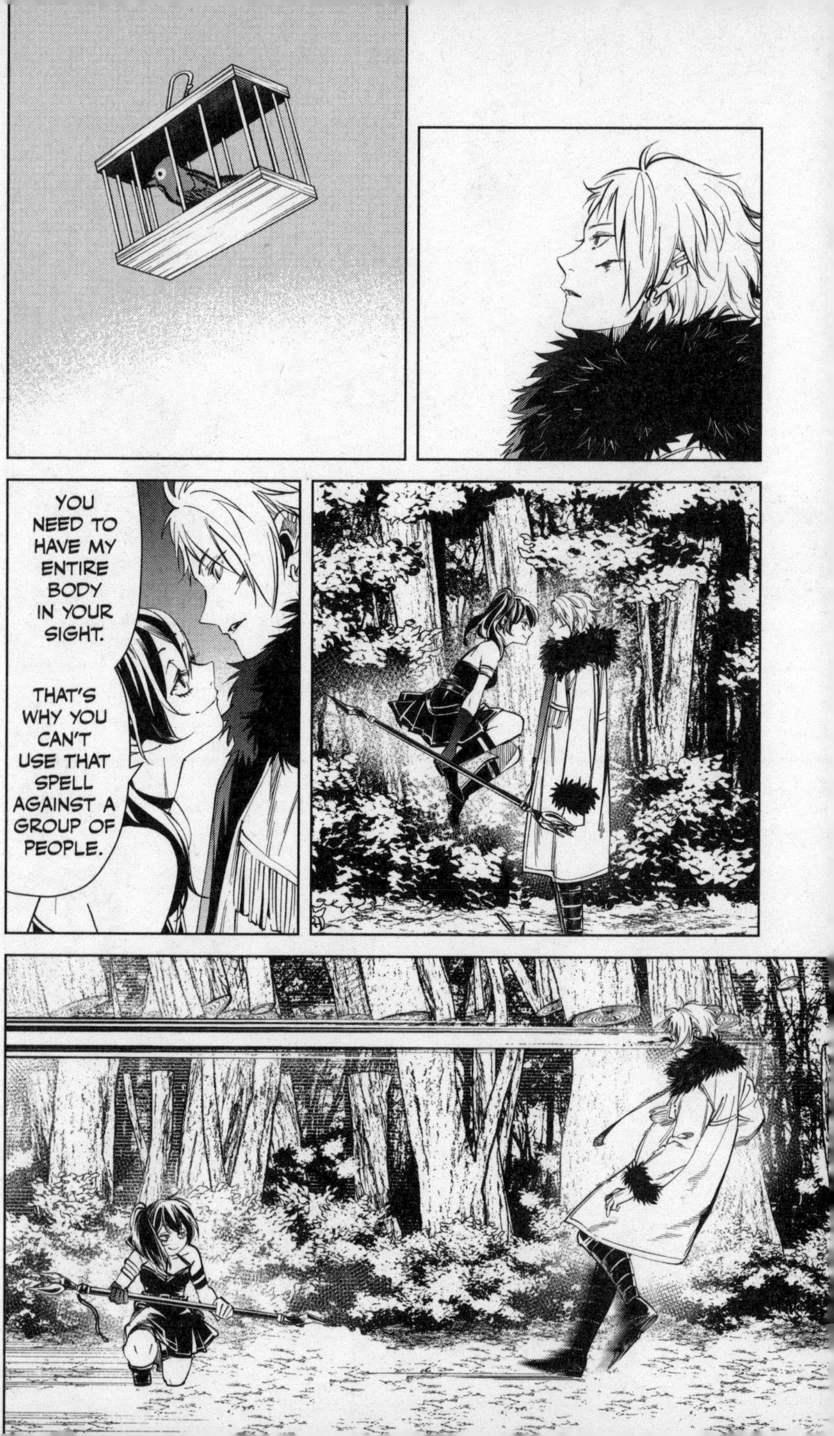
YOU NEED TO HAVE MY ENTIRE BODY IN YOUR SIGHT.
THAT'S WHY YOU CAN'T USE THAT SPELL AGAINST A GROUP OF PEOPLE.

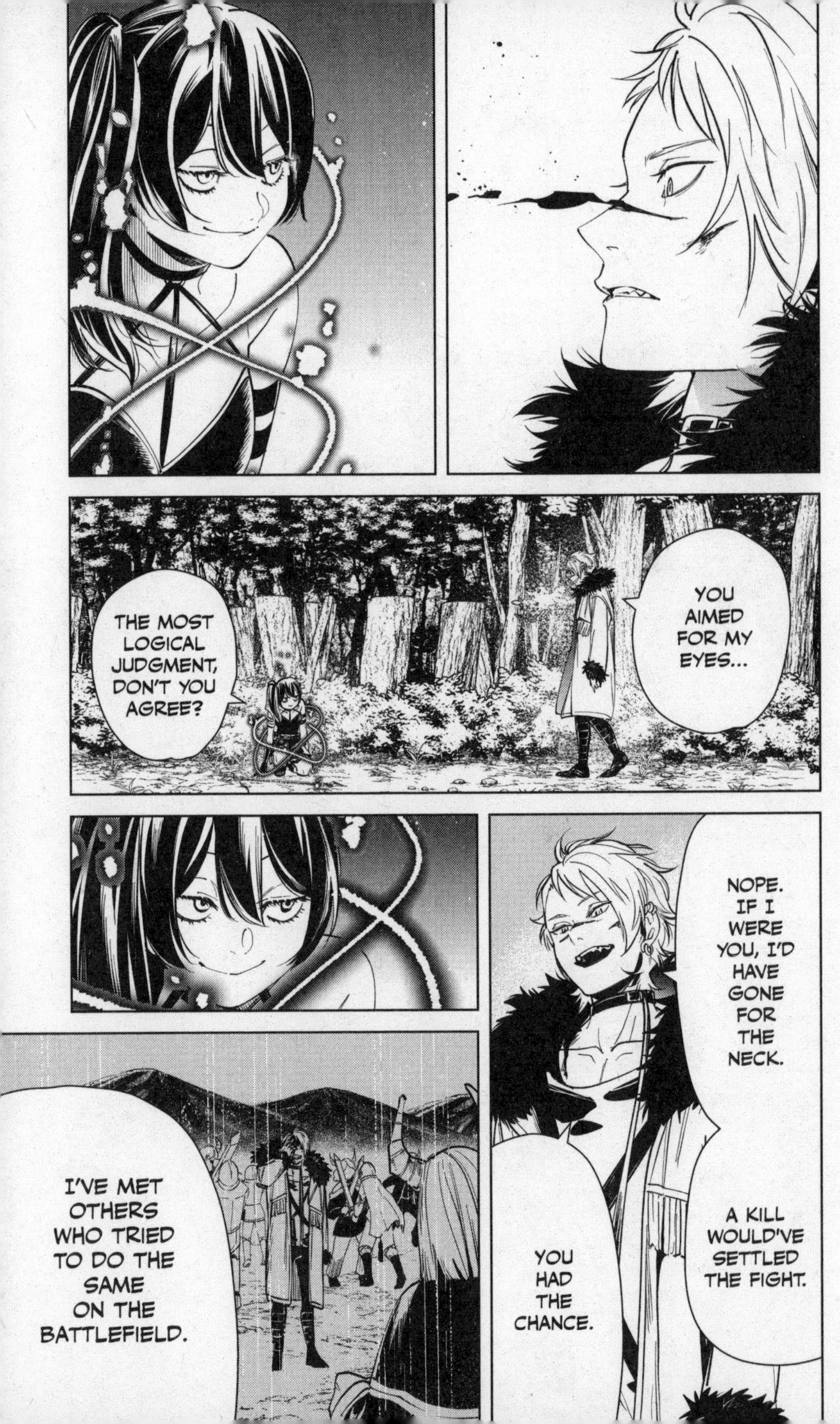
YOU AIMED FOR MY EYES...
THE MOST LOGICAL JUDGMENT, DON'T YOU AGREE?
NOPE. IF I WERE YOU, I'D HAVE GONE FOR THE NECK.
A KILL WOULD'VE SETTLED THE FIGHT.
YOU HAD THE CHANCE.
I'VE MET OTHERS WHO TRIED TO DO THE SAME ON THE BATTLEFIELD.

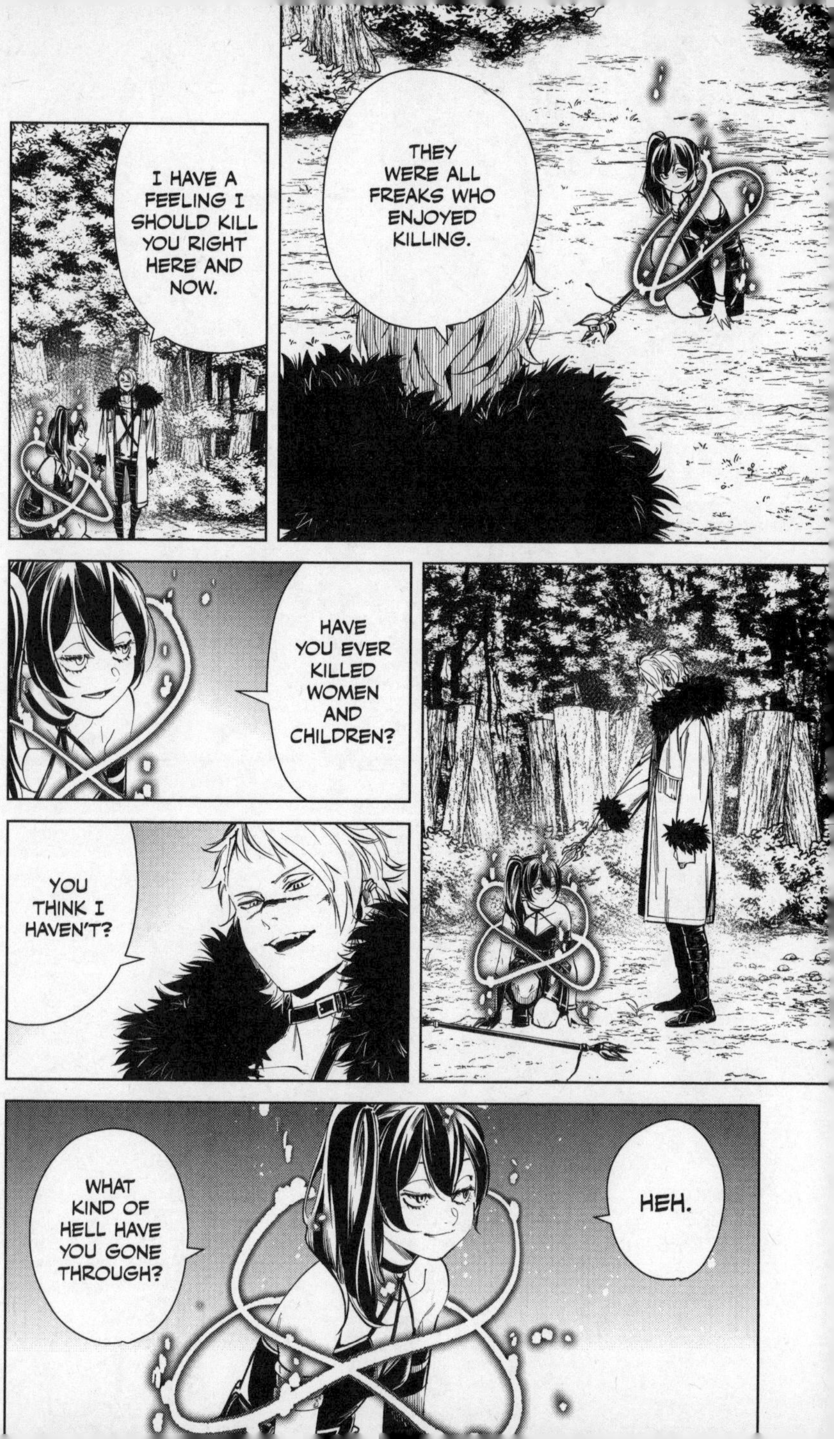
THEY WERE ALL FREAKS WHO ENJOYED KILLING.
I HAVE A FEELING I SHOULD KILL YOU RIGHT HERE AND NOW.
HAVE YOU EVER KILLED WOMEN AND CHILDREN?
YOU THINK I HAVEN'T?
HEH.
WHAT KIND OF HELL HAVE YOU GONE THROUGH?

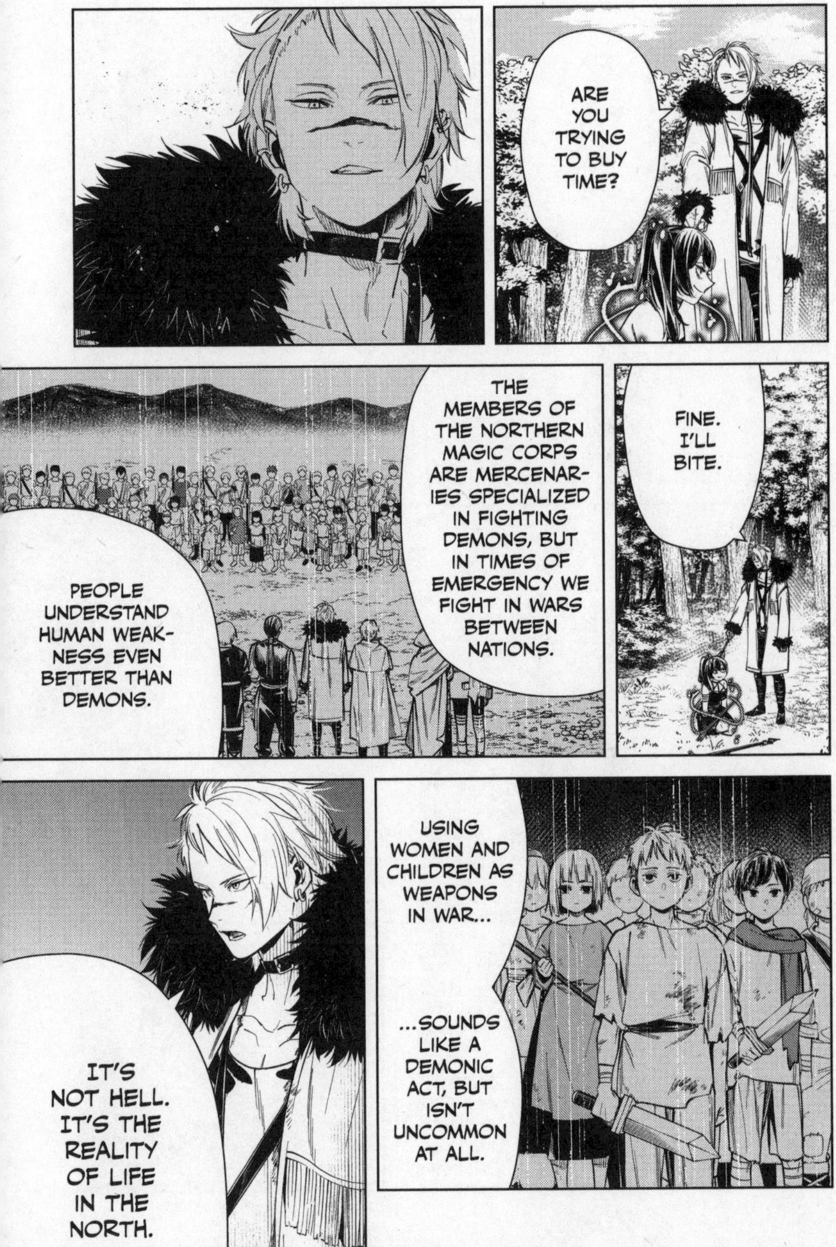
ARE YOU TRYING TO BUY TIME?
FINE. I'LL BITE.
THE MEMBERS OF THE NORTHERN MAGIC CORPS ARE MERCENARIES SPECIALIZED IN FIGHTING DEMONS, BUT IN TIMES OF EMERGENCY WE FIGHT IN WARS BETWEEN NATIONS.
PEOPLE UNDERSTAND HUMAN WEAKNESS EVEN BETTER THAN DEMONS.
USING WOMEN AND CHILDREN AS WEAPONS IN WAR...
...SOUNDS LIKE A DEMONIC ACT, BUT ISN'T UNCOMMON AT ALL.
IT'S NOT HELL. IT'S THE REALITY OF LIFE IN THE NORTH.

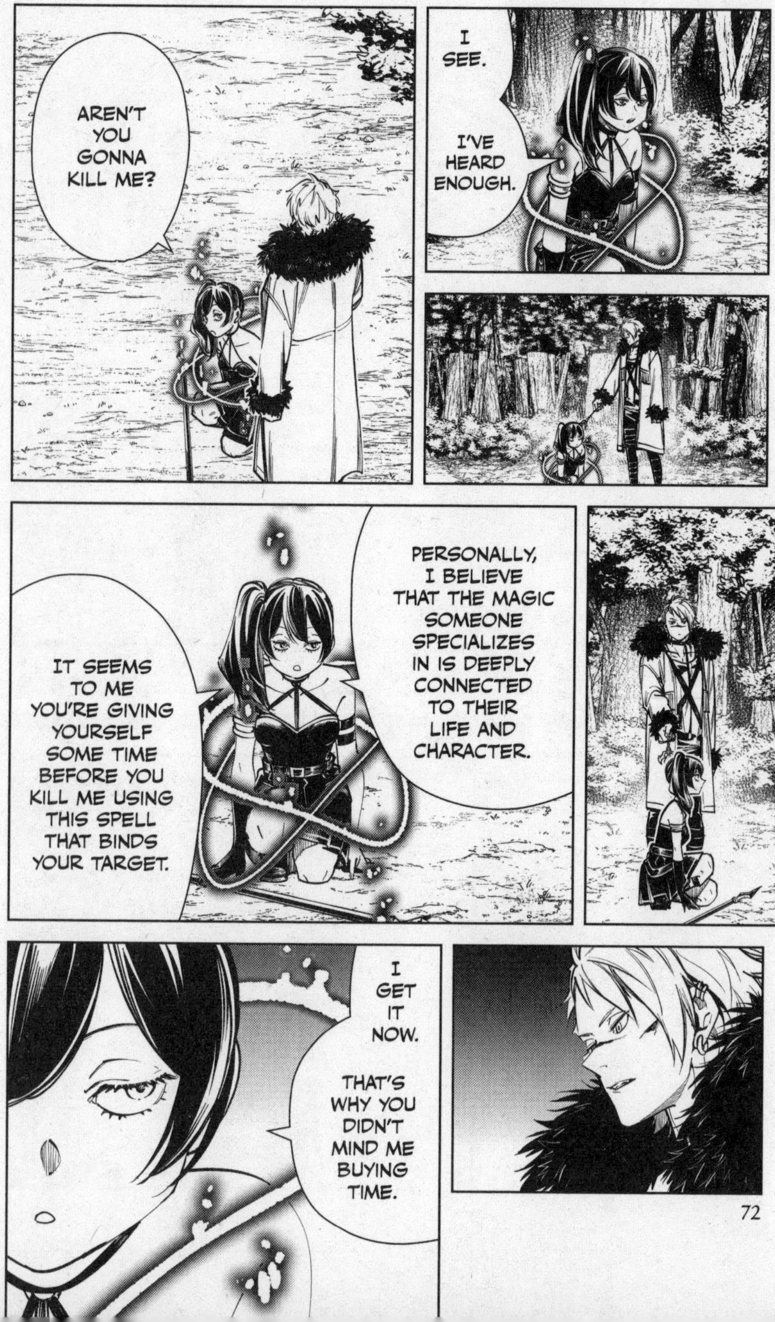
I SEE.
I'VE HEARD ENOUGH.
AREN'T YOU GONNA KILL ME?
PERSONALLY, I BELIEVE THAT THE MAGIC SOMEONE SPECIALIZES IN IS DEEPLY CONNECTED TO THEIR LIFE AND CHARACTER.
IT SEEMS TO ME YOU'RE GIVING YOURSELF SOME TIME BEFORE YOU KILL ME USING THIS SPELL THAT BINDS YOUR TARGET.
I GET IT NOW.
THAT'S WHY YOU DIDN'T MIND ME BUYING TIME.

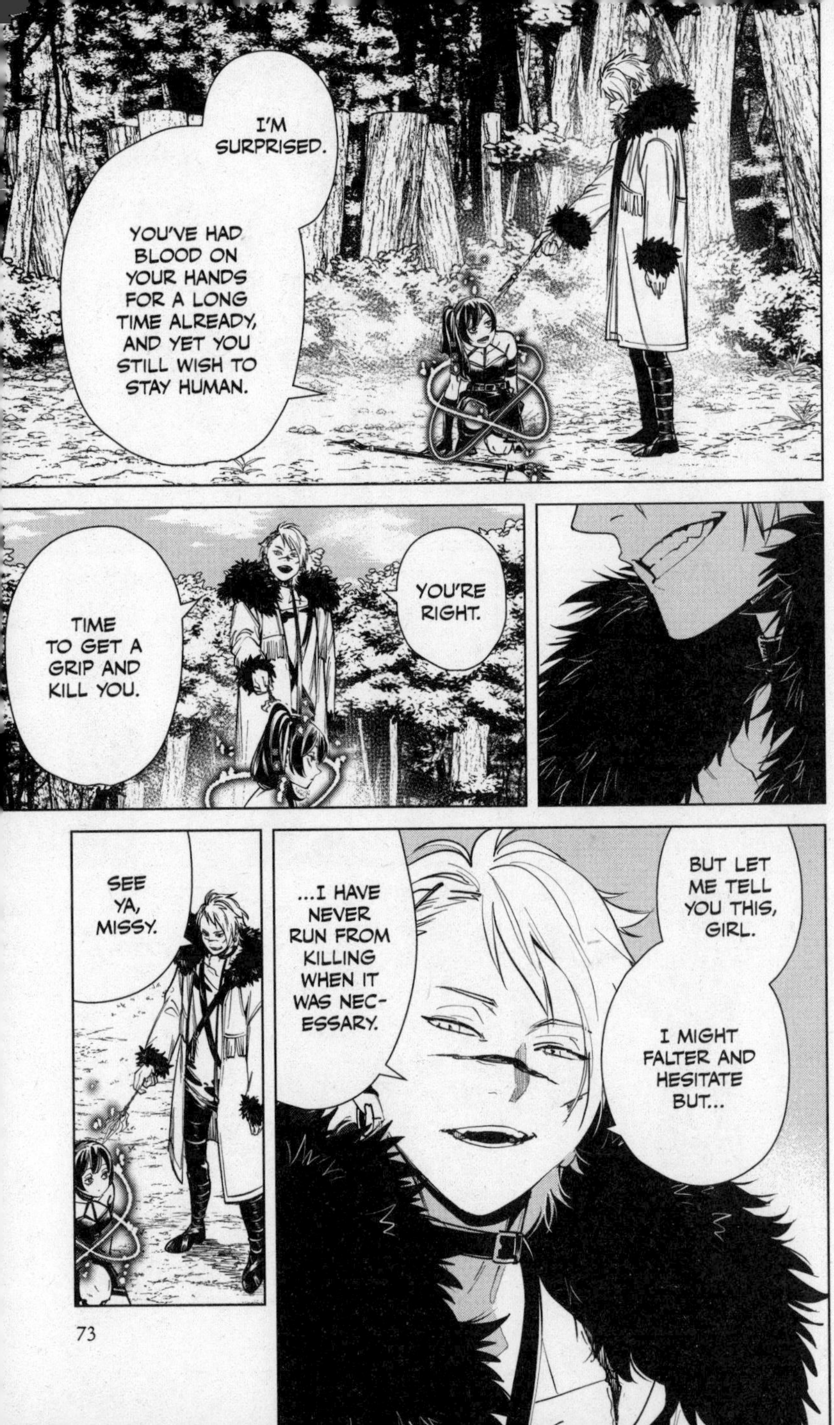
I'M SURPRISED.
YOU'VE HAD BLOOD ON YOUR HANDS FOR A LONG TIME ALREADY, AND YET YOU STILL WISH TO STAY HUMAN.
YOU'RE RIGHT.
TIME TO GET A GRIP AND KILL YOU.
BUT LET ME TELL YOU THIS, GIRL.
I MIGHT FALTER AND HESITATE BUT...
...I HAVE NEVER RUN FROM KILLING WHEN IT WAS NECESSARY.
SEE YA, MISSY.

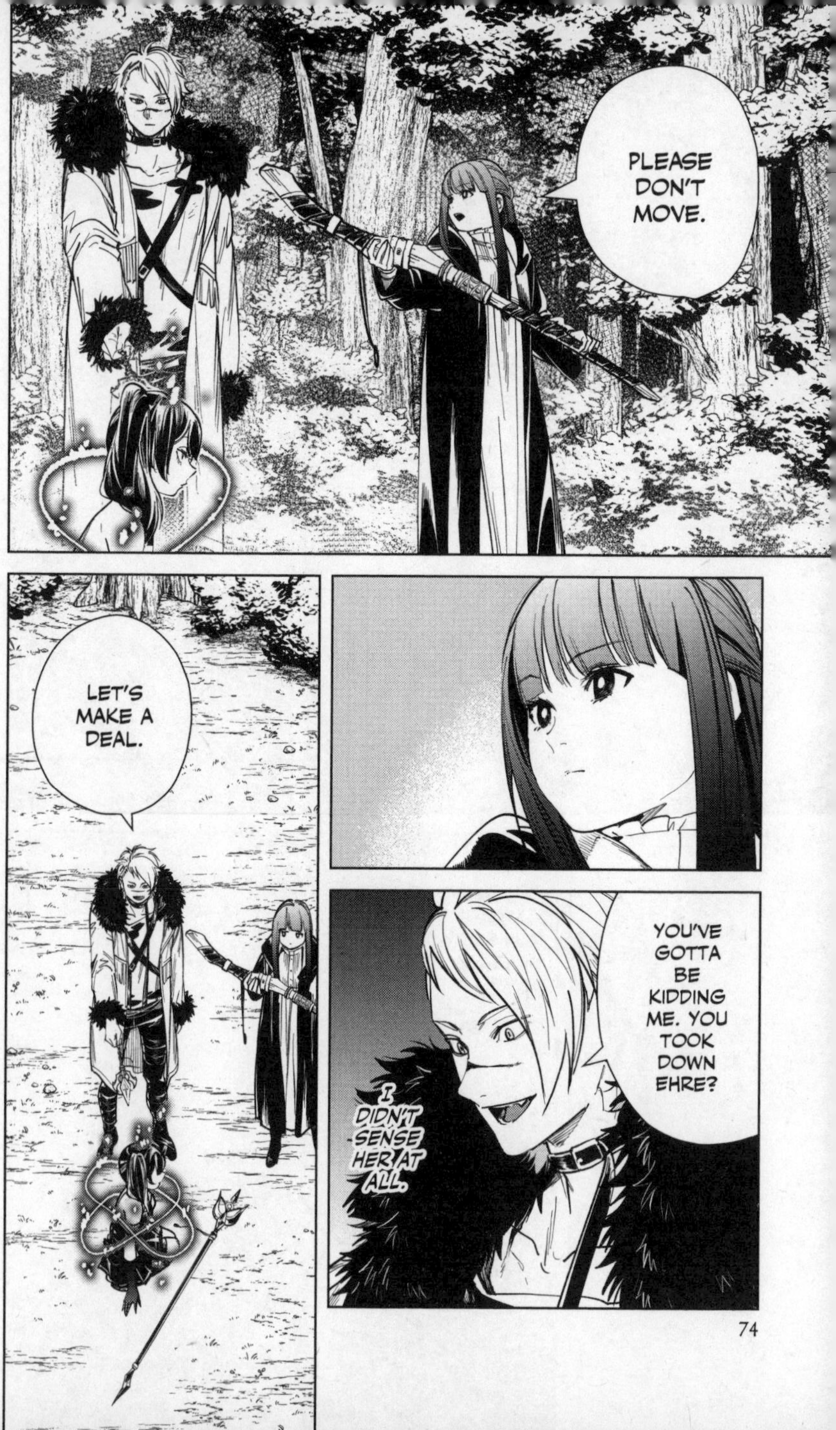
PLEASE DON'T MOVE.
YOU'VE GOTTA BE KIDDING ME. YOU TOOK DOWN EHRE?
I DIDN'T SENSE HER AT ALL.
LET'S MAKE A DEAL.

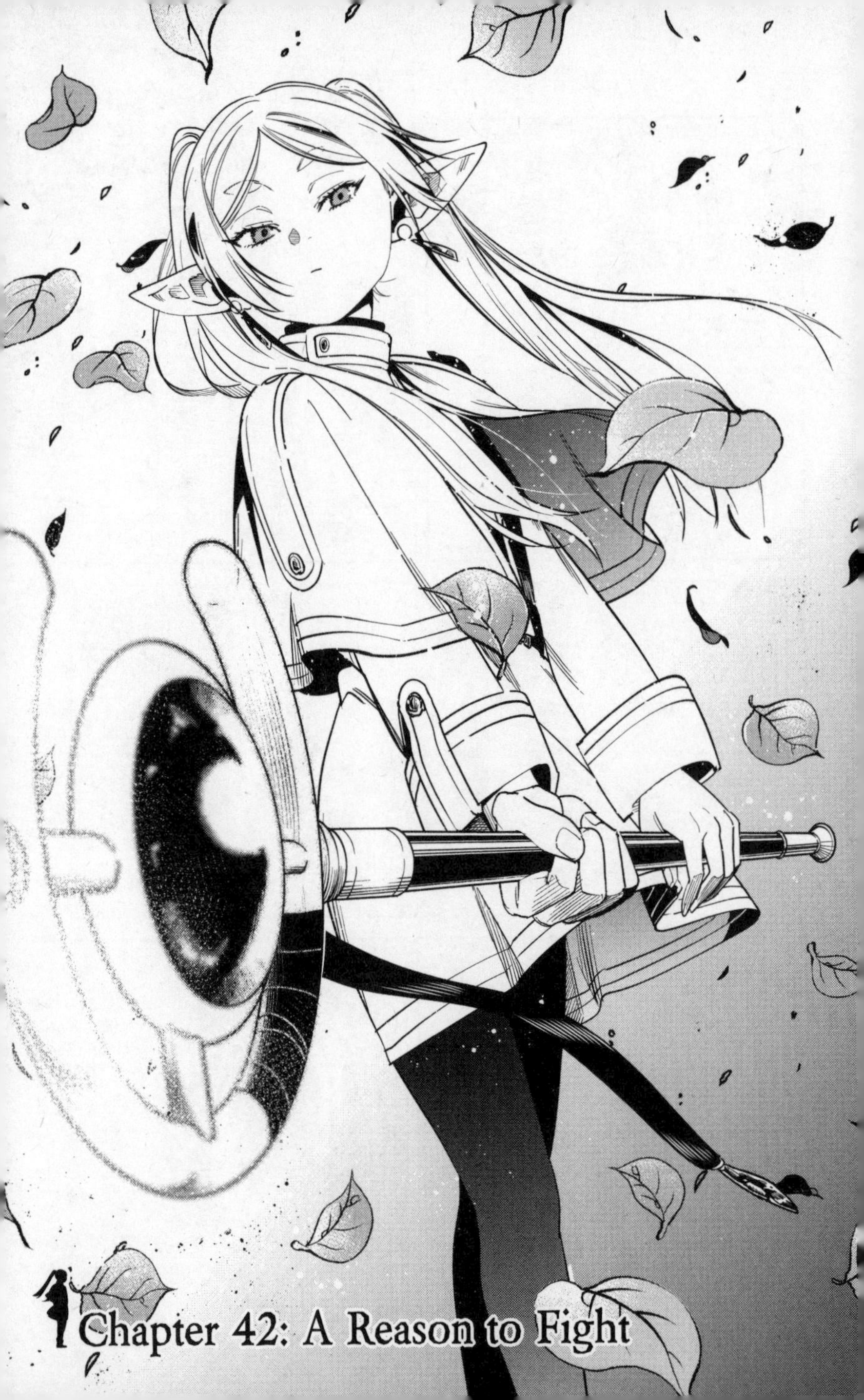

Chapter 42: A Reason to Fight

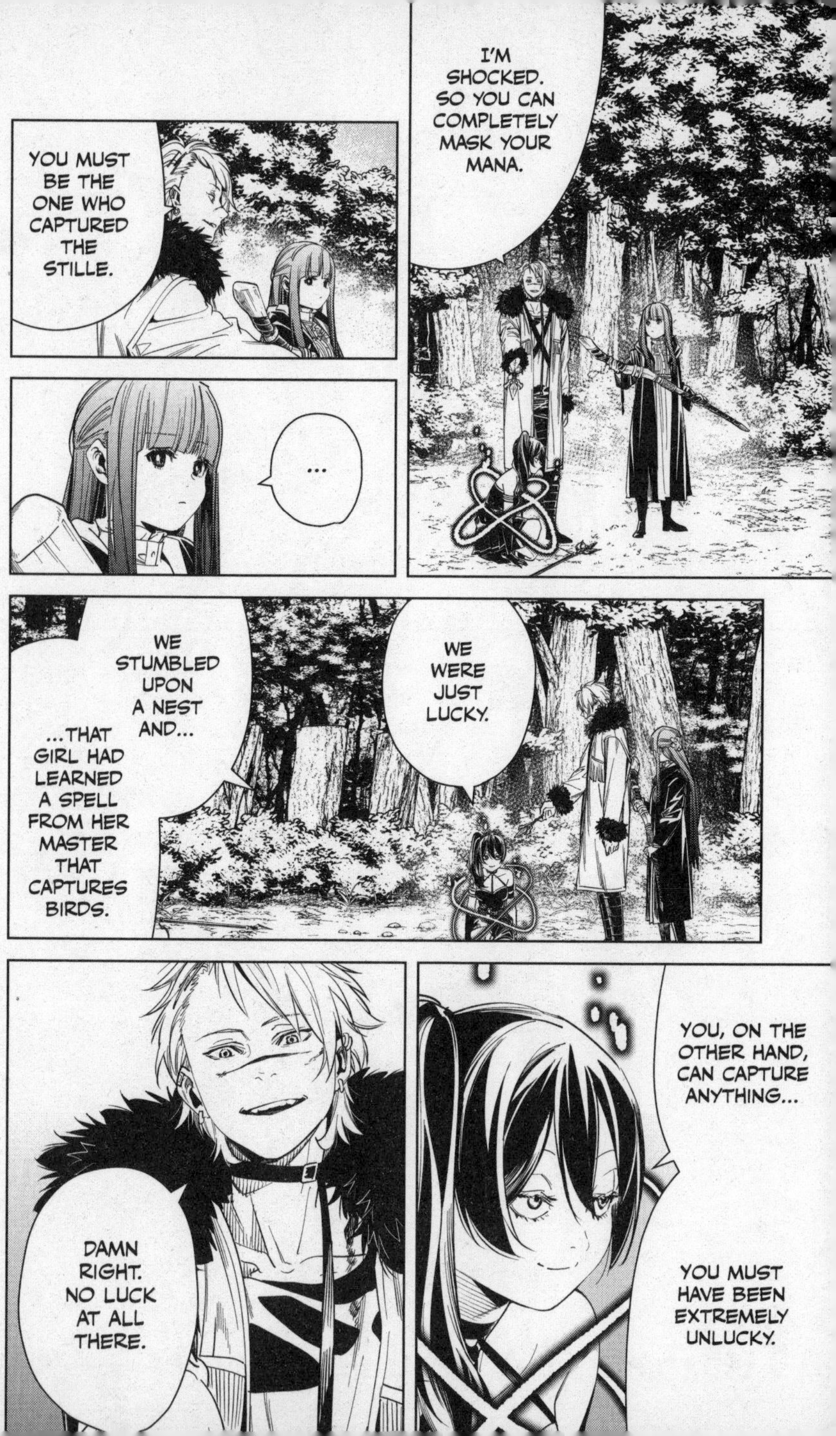
I'M SHOCKED. SO YOU CAN COMPLETELY MASK YOUR MANA.
YOU MUST BE THE ONE WHO CAPTURED THE STILLE.
...
WE WERE JUST LUCKY.
WE STUMBLED UPON A NEST AND...
...THAT GIRL HAD LEARNED A SPELL FROM HER MASTER THAT CAPTURES BIRDS.
YOU, ON THE OTHER HAND, CAN CAPTURE ANYTHING...
YOU MUST HAVE BEEN EXTREMELY UNLUCKY.
DAMN RIGHT. NO LUCK AT ALL THERE.

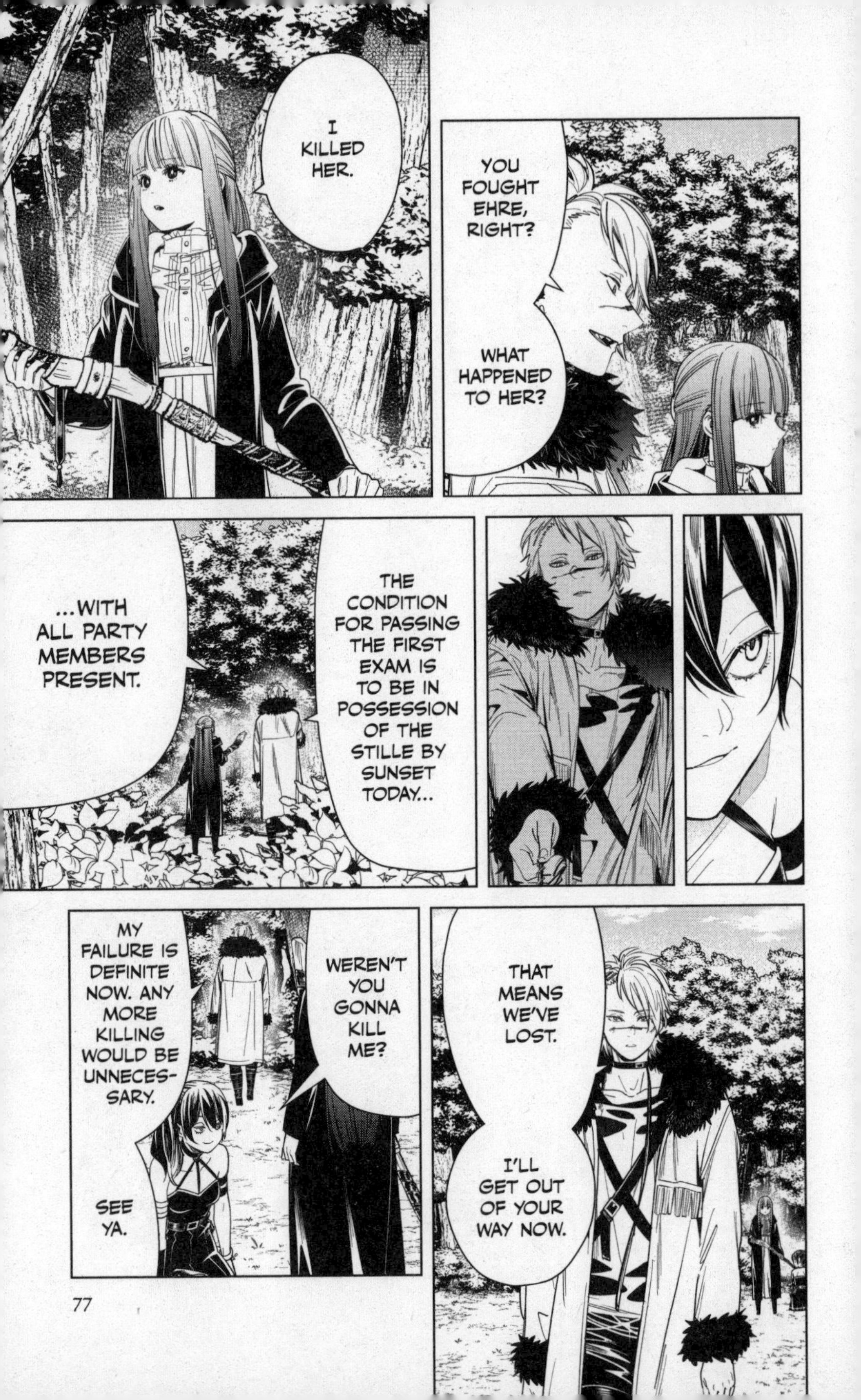
YOU FOUGHT EHRE, RIGHT?
WHAT HAPPENED TO HER?
I KILLED HER.
THE CONDITION FOR PASSING THE FIRST EXAM IS TO BE IN POSSESSION OF THE STILLE BY SUNSET TODAY...
...WITH ALL PARTY MEMBERS PRESENT.
THAT MEANS WE'VE LOST.
I'LL GET OUT OF YOUR WAY NOW.
WEREN'T YOU GONNA KILL ME?
MY FAILURE IS DEFINITE NOW. ANY MORE KILLING WOULD BE UNNECES-SARY.
SEE YA.

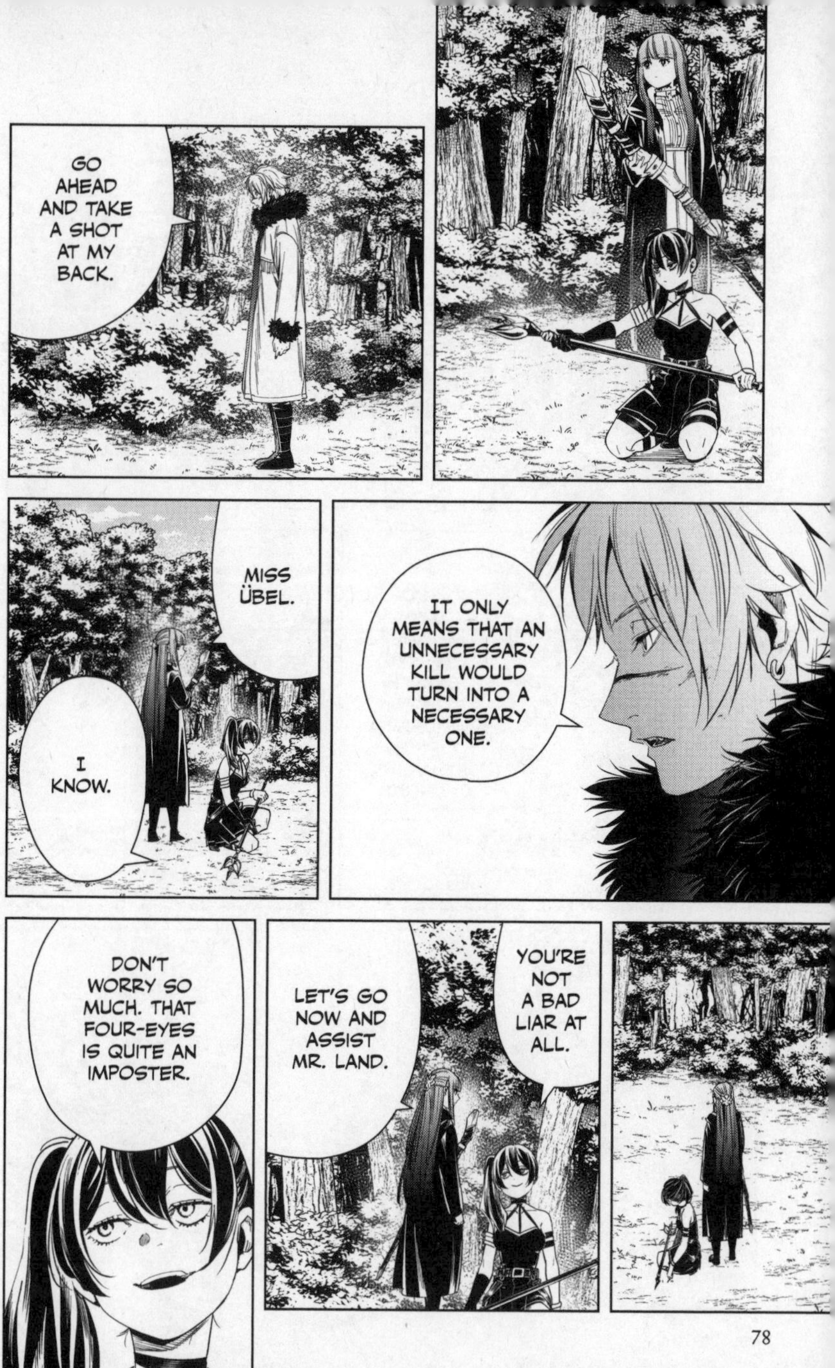
GO AHEAD AND TAKE A SHOT AT MY BACK.
IT ONLY MEANS THAT AN UNNECESSARY KILL WOULD TURN INTO A NECESSARY ONE.
MISS ÜBEL.
I KNOW.
YOU'RE NOT A BAD LIAR AT ALL.
LET'S GO NOW AND ASSIST MR. LAND.
DON'T WORRY SO MUCH. THAT FOUR-EYES IS QUITE AN IMPOSTER.

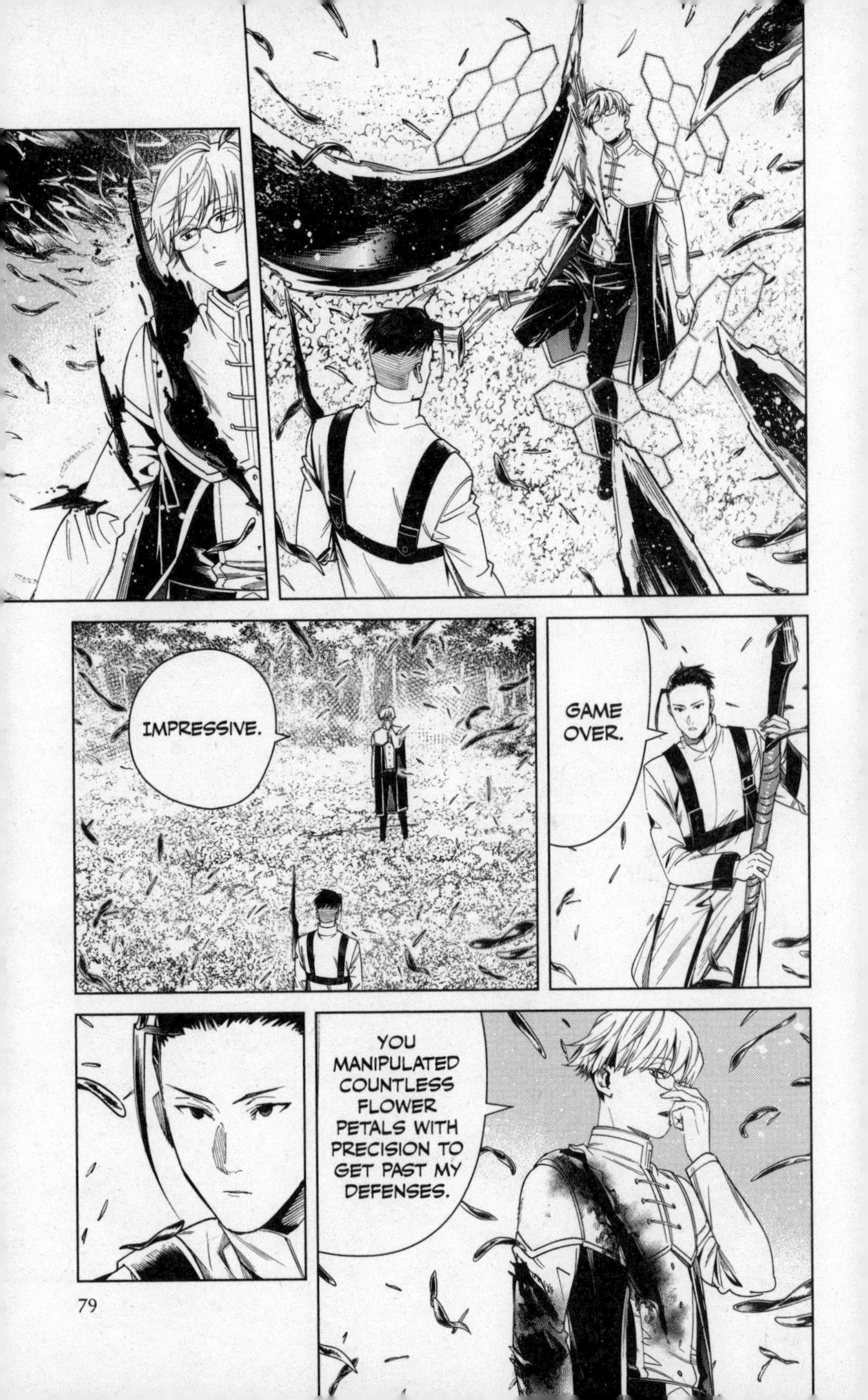
GAME OVER.
IMPRESSIVE.
YOU MANIPULATED COUNTLESS FLOWER PETALS WITH PRECISION TO GET PAST MY DEFENSES.

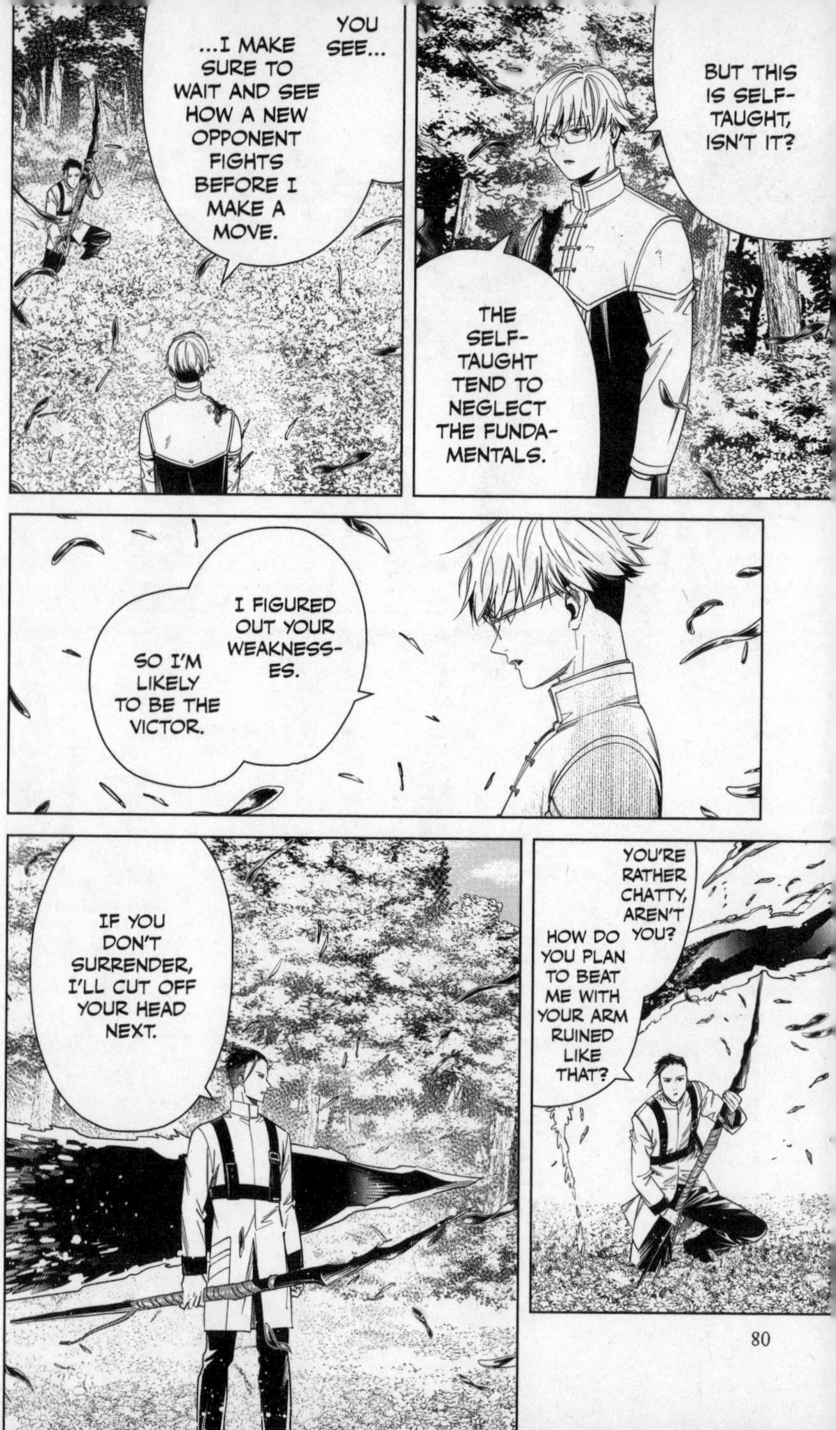
BUT THIS IS SELF-TAUGHT, ISN'T IT?
THE SELF-TAUGHT TEND TO NEGLECT THE FUNDAMENTALS.
YOU SEE...
...I MAKE SURE TO WAIT AND SEE HOW A NEW OPPONENT FIGHTS BEFORE I MAKE A MOVE.
I FIGURED OUT YOUR WEAKNESSES.
SO I'M LIKELY TO BE THE VICTOR.
YOU'RE RATHER CHATTY, AREN'T YOU?
HOW DO YOU PLAN TO BEAT ME WITH YOUR ARM RUINED LIKE THAT?
IF YOU DON'T SURRENDER, I'LL CUT OFF YOUR HEAD NEXT.

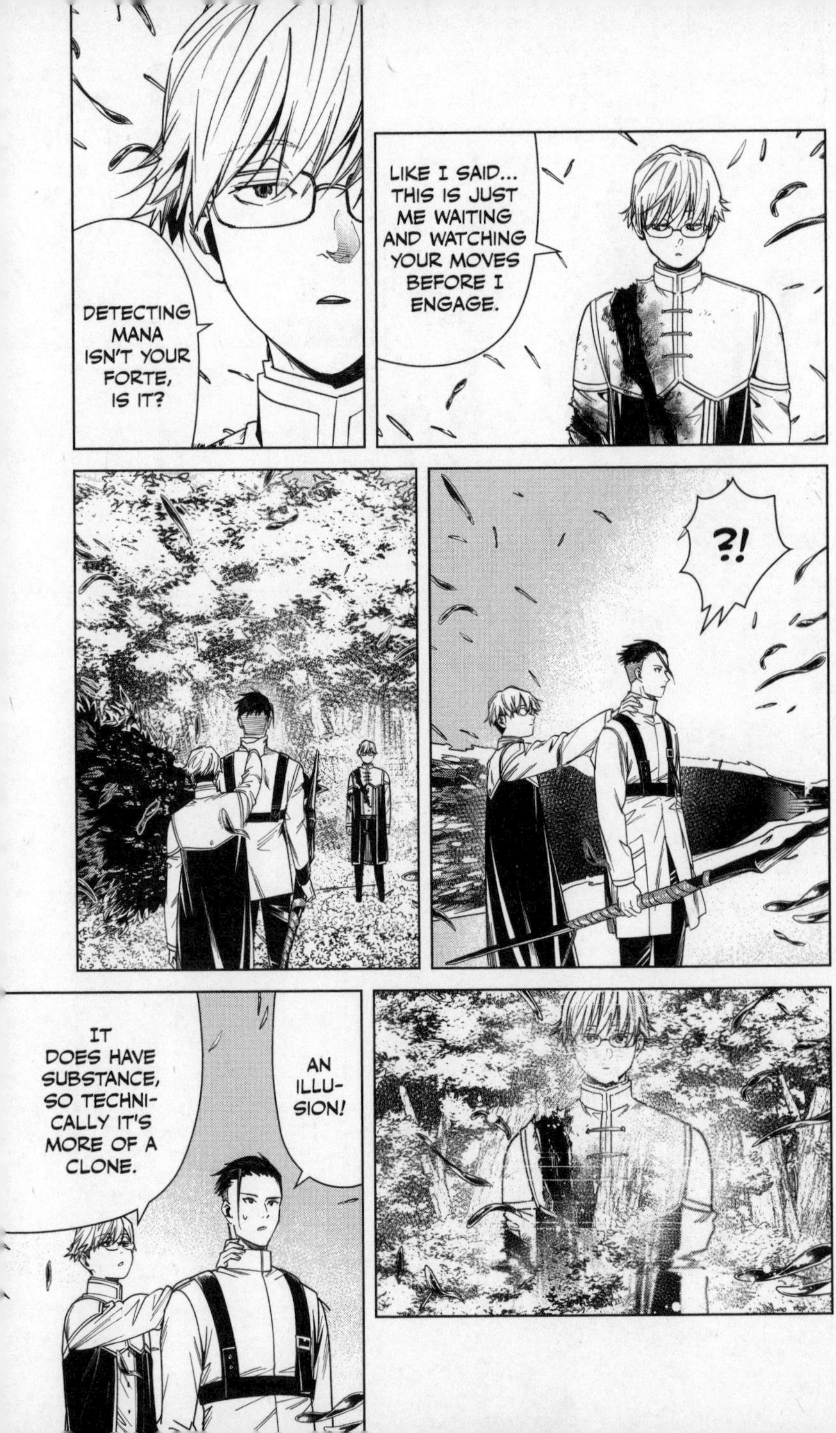
LIKE I SAID... THIS IS JUST ME WAITING AND WATCHING YOUR MOVES BEFORE I ENGAGE.
DETECTING MANA ISN'T YOUR FORTE, IS IT?
?!
AN ILLU-SION!
IT DOES HAVE SUBSTANCE, SO TECHNI-CALLY IT'S MORE OF A CLONE.

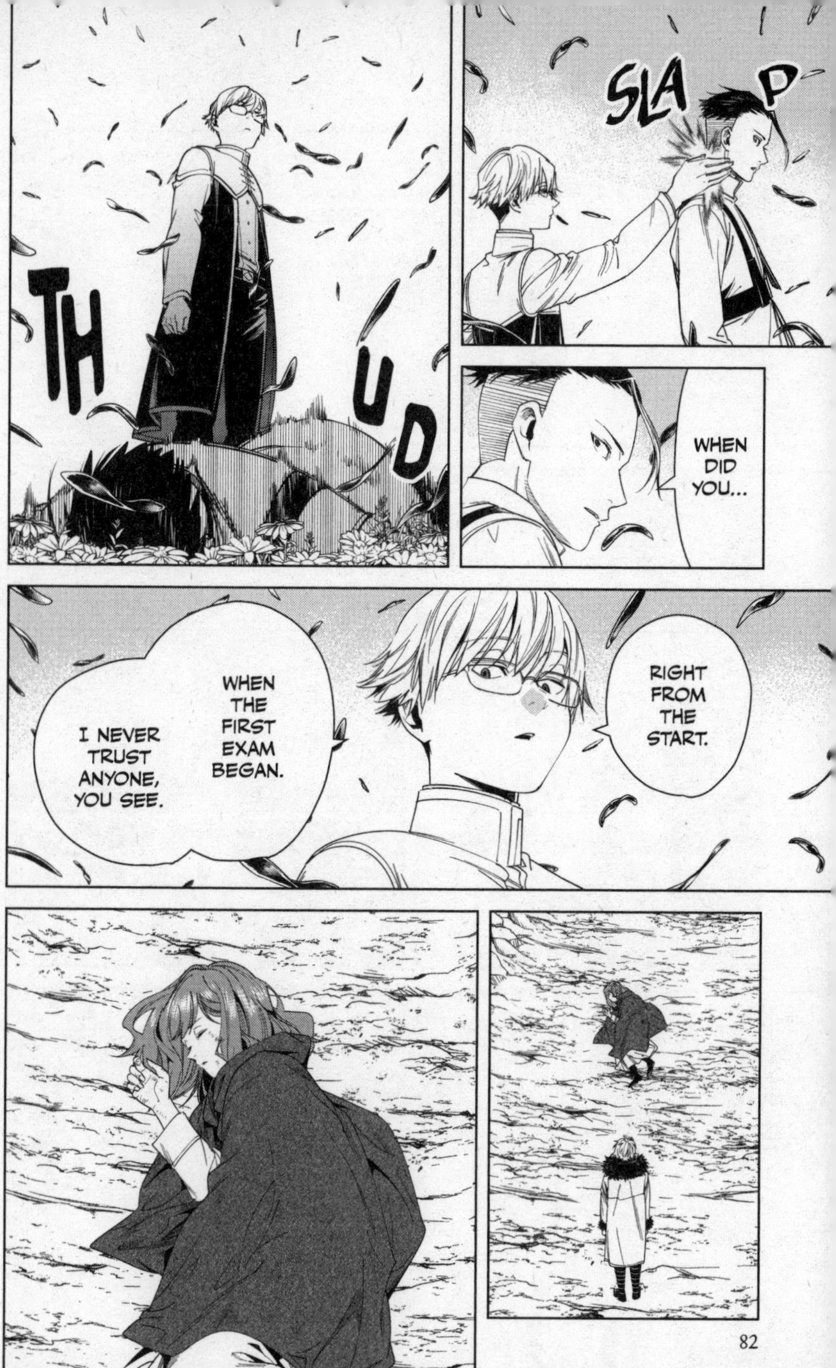
SLAP
WHEN DID YOU...
THUD
RIGHT FROM THE START.
WHEN THE FIRST EXAM BEGAN.
I NEVER TRUST ANYONE, YOU SEE.

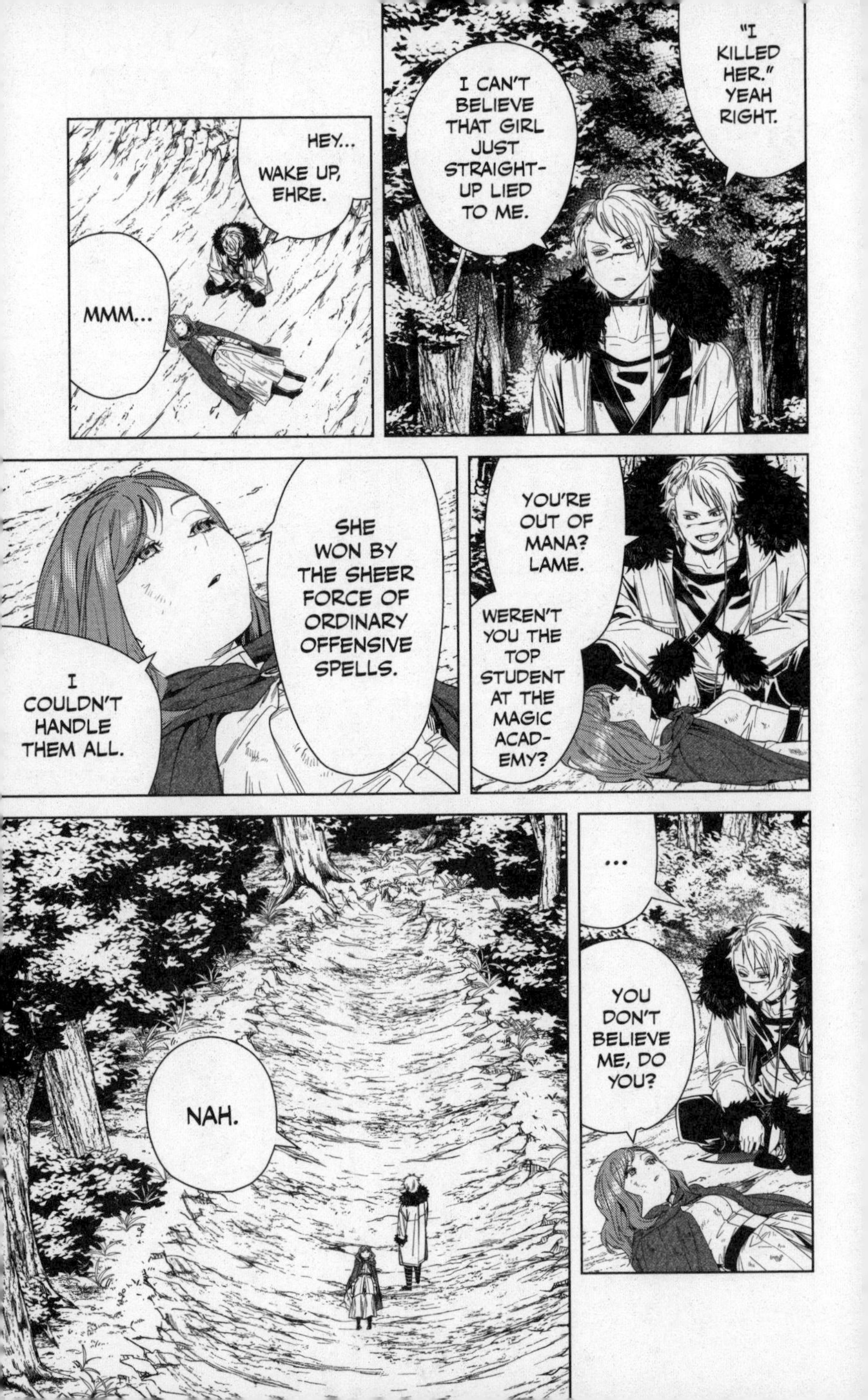
"I KILLED HER." YEAH RIGHT.
I CAN'T BELIEVE THAT GIRL JUST STRAIGHT-UP LIED TO ME.
HEY... WAKE UP, EHRE.
MMM...
YOU'RE OUT OF MANA? LAME.
WEREN'T YOU THE TOP STUDENT AT THE MAGIC ACAD-EMY?
SHE WON BY THE SHEER FORCE OF ORDINARY OFFENSIVE SPELLS.
I COULDN'T HANDLE THEM ALL.
...
YOU DON'T BELIEVE ME, DO YOU?
NAH.

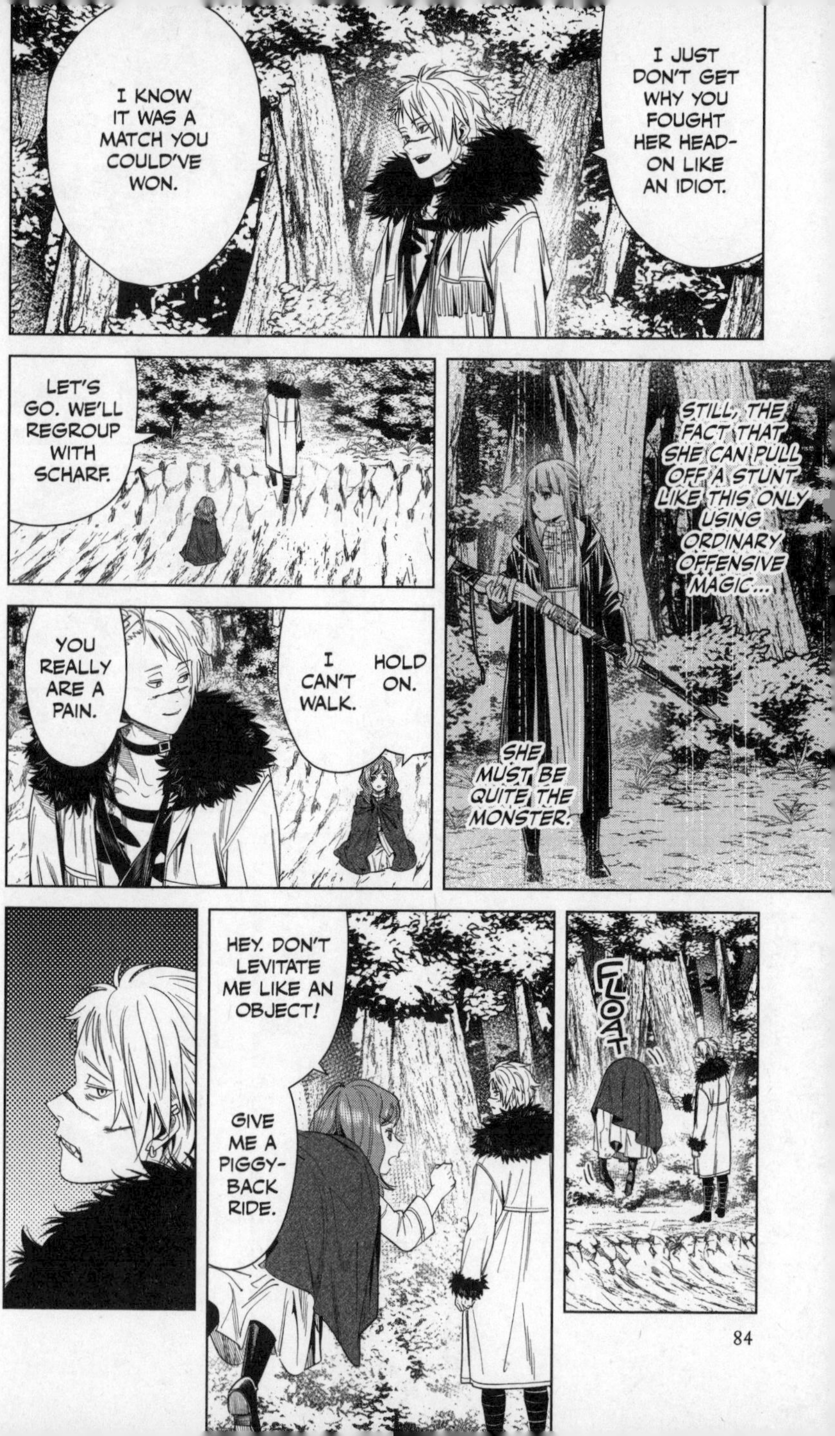
I JUST DON'T GET WHY YOU FOUGHT HER HEAD-ON LIKE AN IDIOT.
I KNOW IT WAS A MATCH YOU COULD'VE WON.
STILL, THE FACT THAT SHE CAN PULL OFF A STUNT LIKE THIS ONLY USING ORDINARY OFFENSIVE MAGIC...
SHE MUST BE QUITE THE MONSTER.
LET'S GO. WE'LL REGROUP WITH SCHARF.
HOLD ON.
I CAN'T WALK.
YOU REALLY ARE A PAIN.
FLOAT
HEY. DON'T LEVITATE ME LIKE AN OBJECT!
GIVE ME A PIGGY-BACK RIDE.

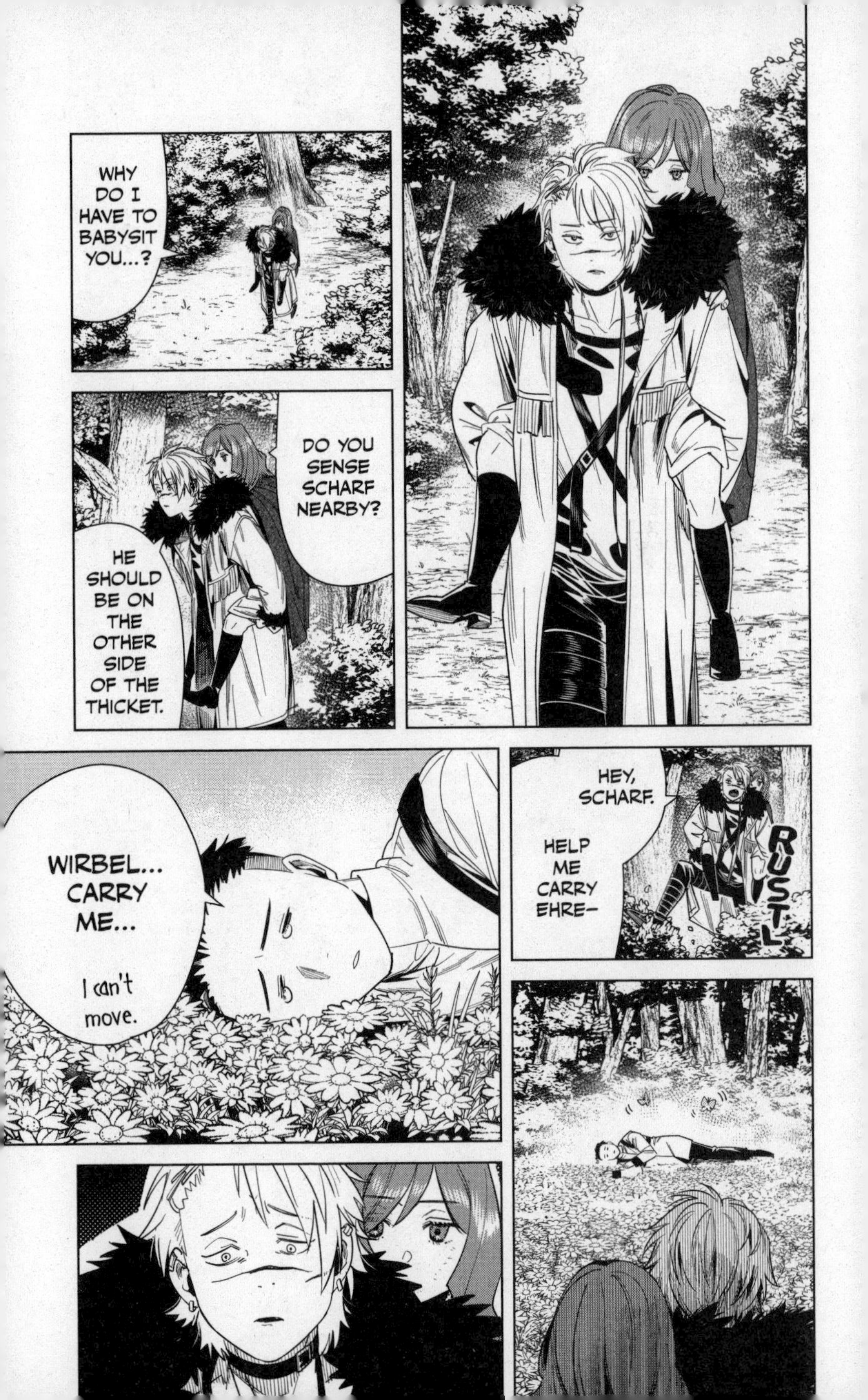
WHY DO I HAVE TO BABYSIT YOU...?
DO YOU SENSE SCHARF NEARBY?
HE SHOULD BE ON THE OTHER SIDE OF THE THICKET.
HEY, SCHARF.
HELP ME CARRY EHRE—
RUSTL
WIRBEL... CARRY ME...
I can't move.

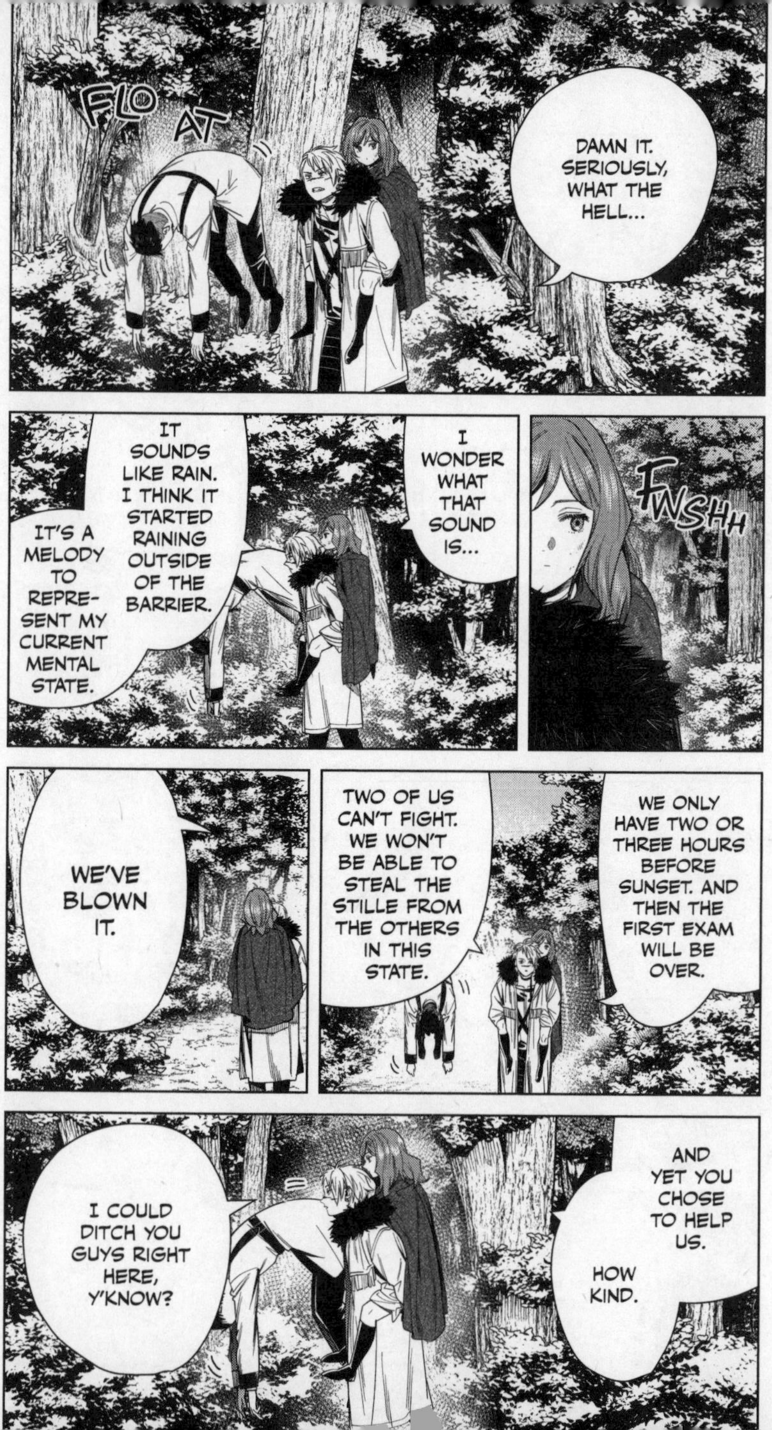
DAMN IT. SERIOUSLY, WHAT THE HELL...
FLOAT
FWSHH
I WONDER WHAT THAT SOUND IS...
IT SOUNDS LIKE RAIN. I THINK IT STARTED RAINING OUTSIDE OF THE BARRIER.
IT'S A MELODY TO REPRESENT MY CURRENT MENTAL STATE.
WE ONLY HAVE TWO OR THREE HOURS BEFORE SUNSET. AND THEN THE FIRST EXAM WILL BE OVER.
TWO OF US CAN'T FIGHT. WE WON'T BE ABLE TO STEAL THE STILLE FROM THE OTHERS IN THIS STATE.
WE'VE BLOWN IT.
AND YET YOU CHOSE TO HELP US.
HOW KIND.
I COULD DITCH YOU GUYS RIGHT HERE, Y'KNOW?

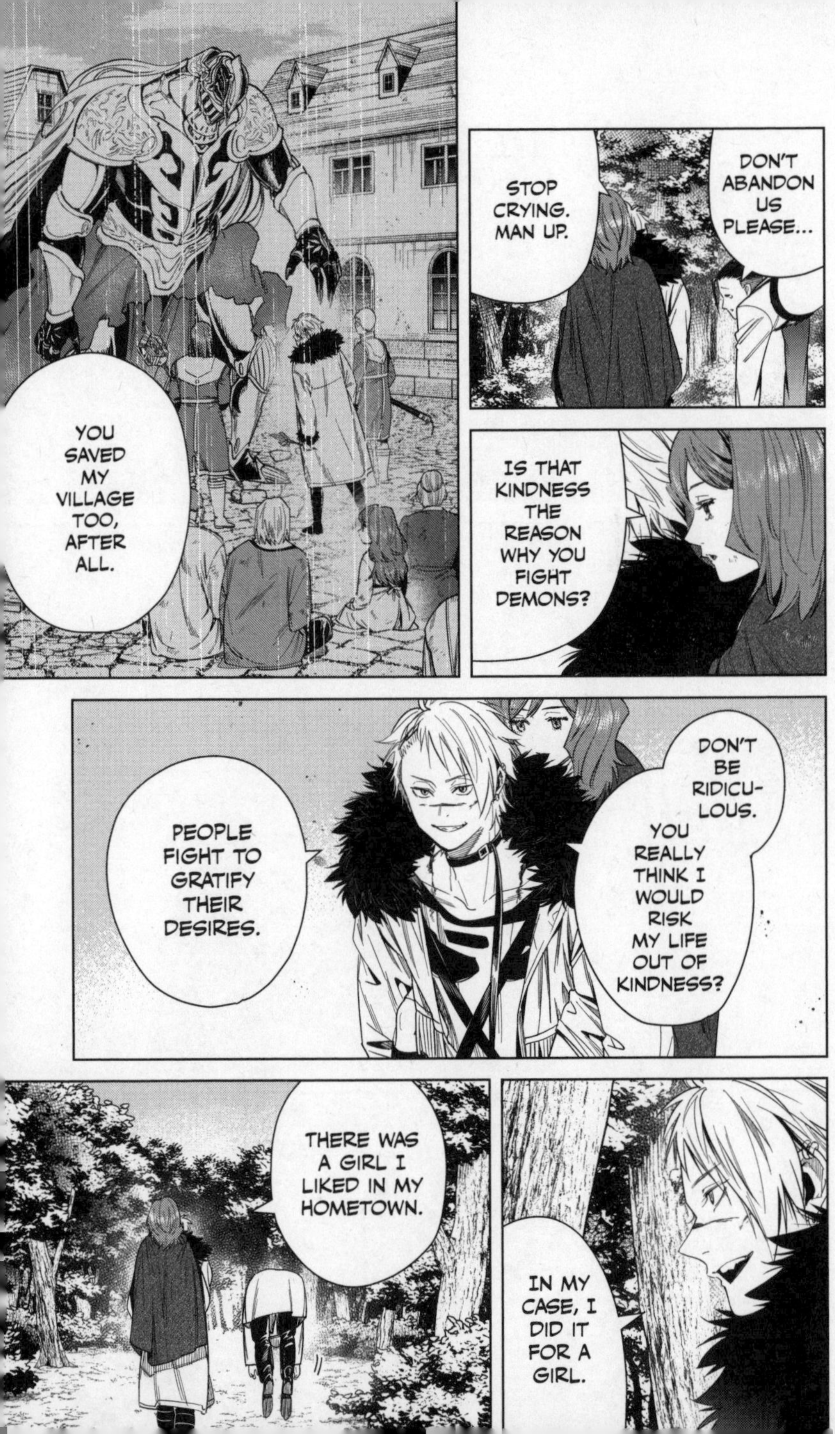
DON'T ABANDON US PLEASE...
STOP CRYING. MAN UP.
IS THAT KINDNESS THE REASON WHY YOU FIGHT DEMONS?
YOU SAVED MY VILLAGE TOO, AFTER ALL.
DON'T BE RIDICU-LOUS. YOU REALLY THINK I WOULD RISK MY LIFE OUT OF KINDNESS?
PEOPLE FIGHT TO GRATIFY THEIR DESIRES.
IN MY CASE, I DID IT FOR A GIRL.
THERE WAS A GIRL I LIKED IN MY HOMETOWN.

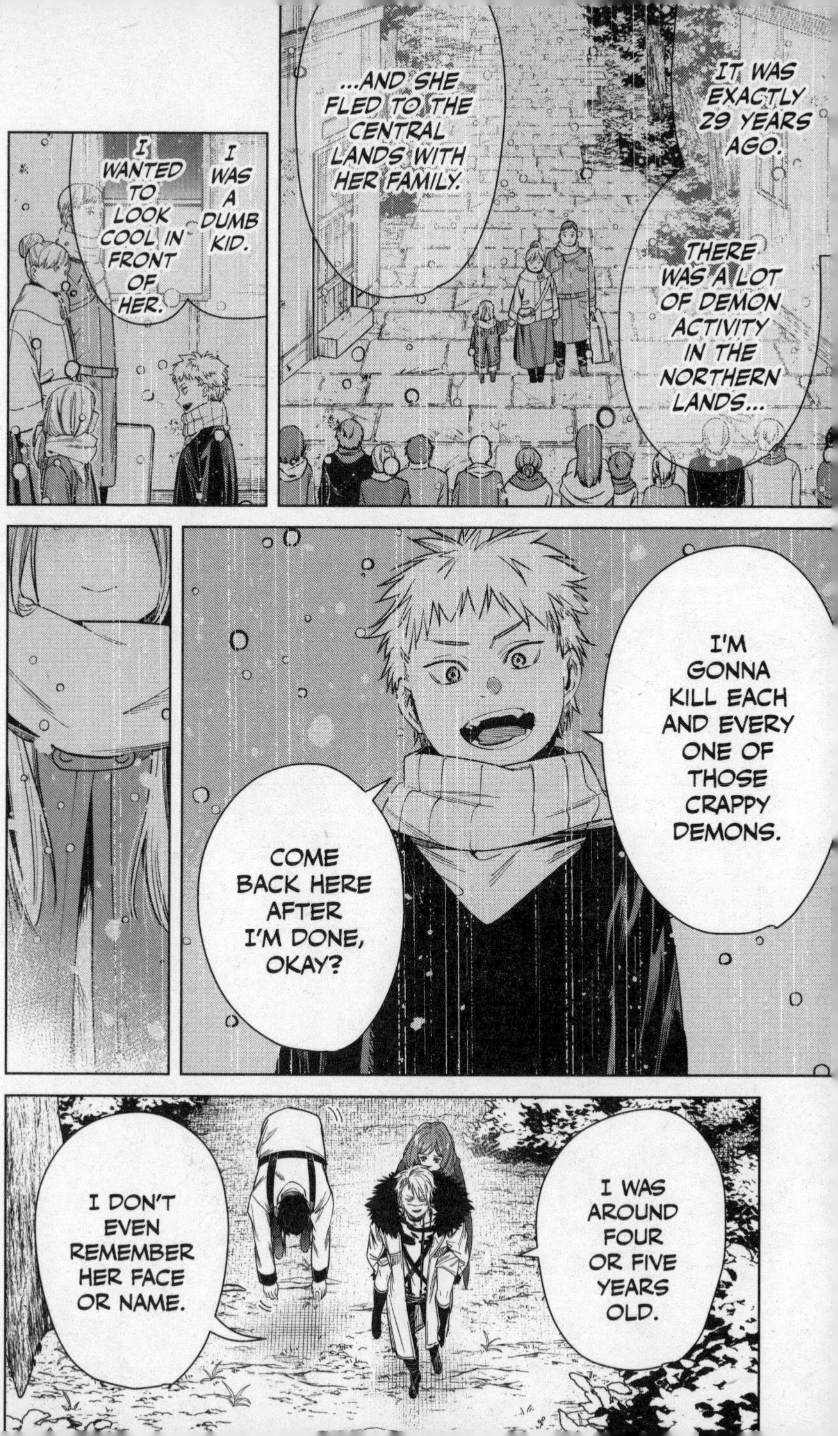
IT WAS EXACTLY 29 YEARS AGO.
THERE WAS A LOT OF DEMON ACTIVITY IN THE NORTHERN LANDS...
...AND SHE FLED TO THE CENTRAL LANDS WITH HER FAMILY.
I WAS A DUMB KID.
I WANTED TO LOOK COOL IN FRONT OF HER.
I'M GONNA KILL EACH AND EVERY ONE OF THOSE CRAPPY DEMONS.
COME BACK HERE AFTER I'M DONE, OKAY?
I WAS AROUND FOUR OR FIVE YEARS OLD.
I DON'T EVEN REMEMBER HER FACE OR NAME.

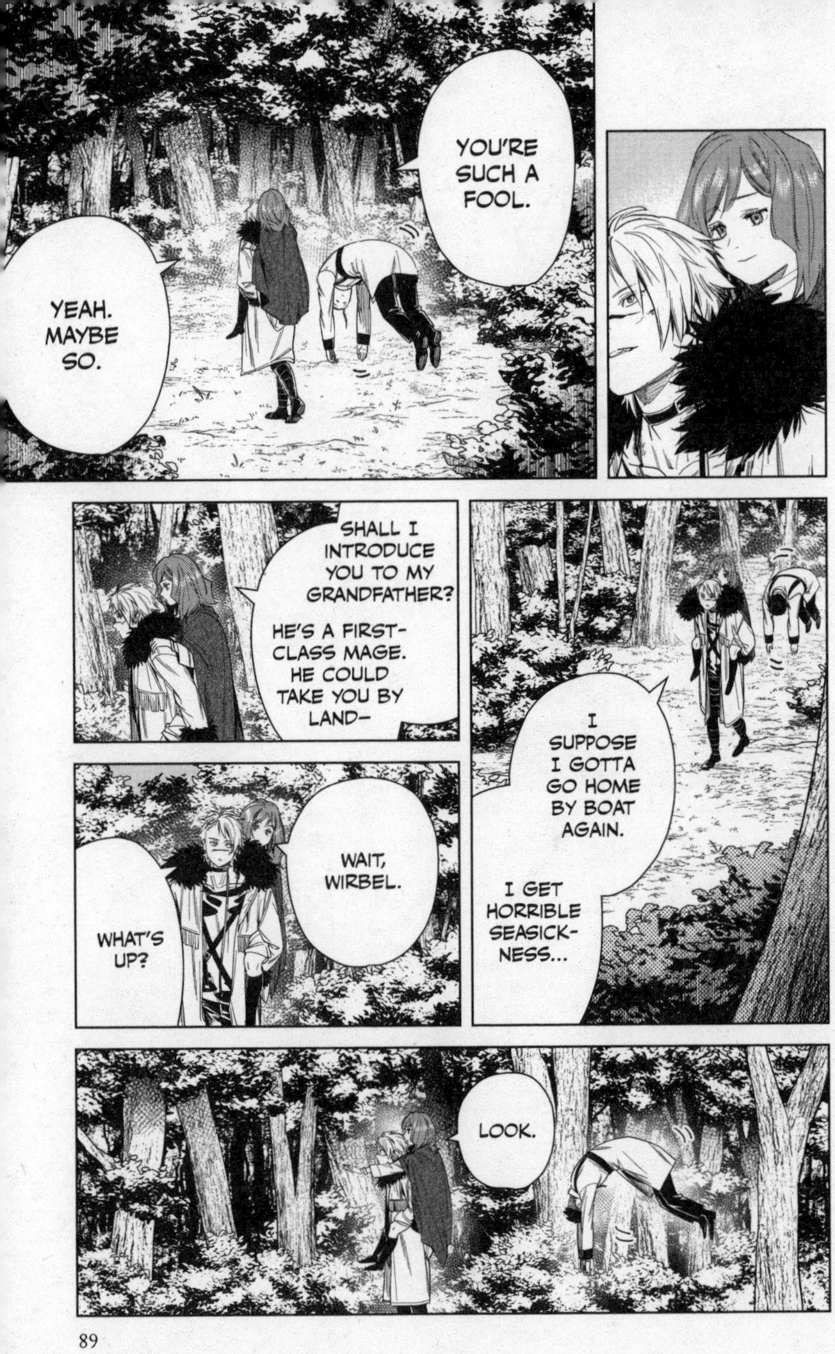
YOU'RE SUCH A FOOL.
YEAH. MAYBE SO.
I SUPPOSE I GOTTA GO HOME BY BOAT AGAIN.
I GET HORRIBLE SEASICK-NESS...
SHALL I INTRODUCE YOU TO MY GRANDFATHER?
HE'S A FIRST-CLASS MAGE. HE COULD TAKE YOU BY LAND—
WAIT, WIRBEL.
WHAT'S UP?
LOOK.

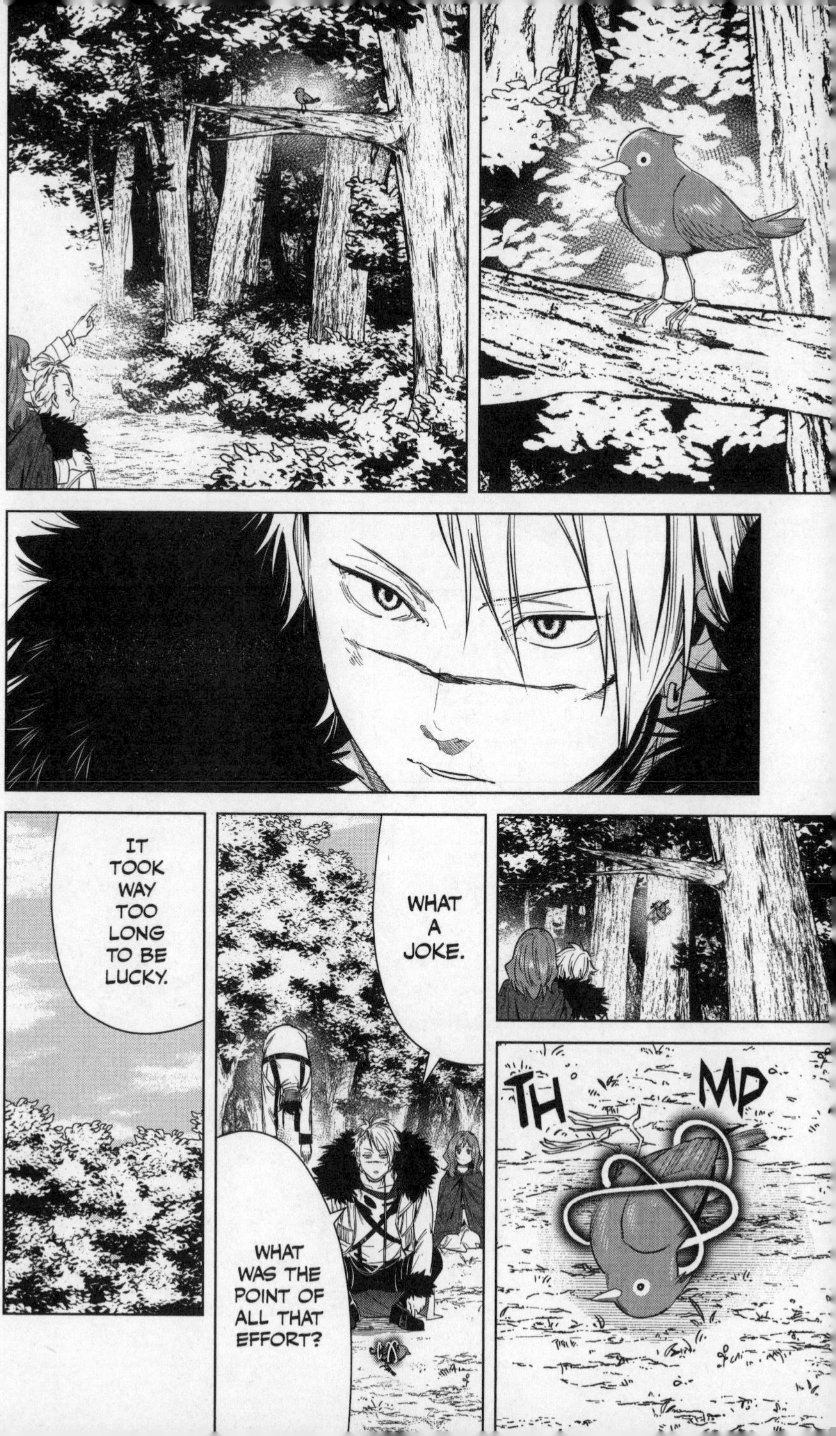
TH MP
WHAT A JOKE.
WHAT WAS THE POINT OF ALL THAT EFFORT?
IT TOOK WAY TOO LONG TO BE LUCKY.

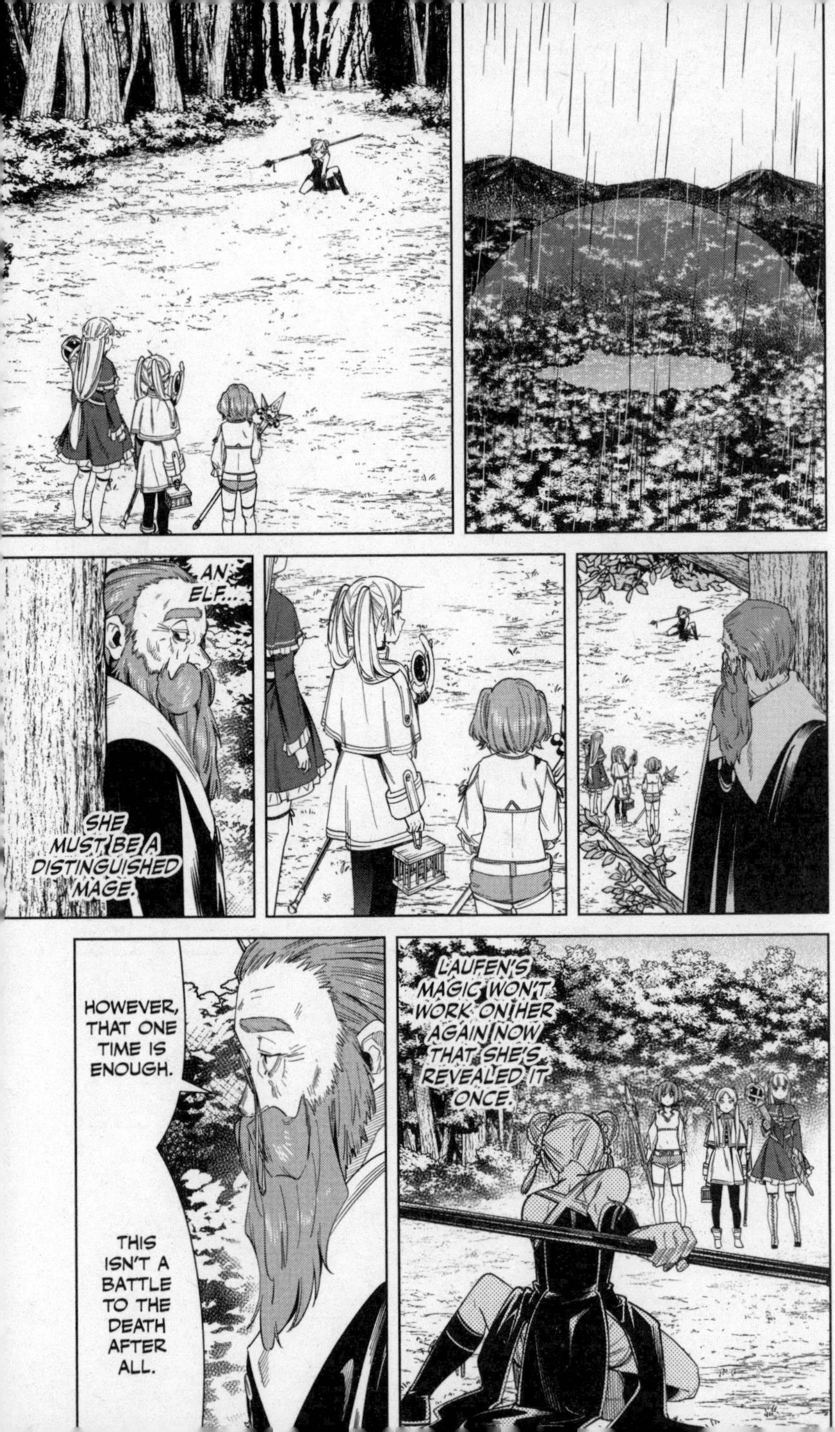
AN ELF...
SHE MUST BE A DISTINGUISHED MAGE.
LAUFEN'S MAGIC WON'T WORK ON HER AGAIN NOW THAT SHE'S REVEALED IT ONCE.
HOWEVER, THAT ONE TIME IS ENOUGH.
THIS ISN'T A BATTLE TO THE DEATH AFTER ALL.

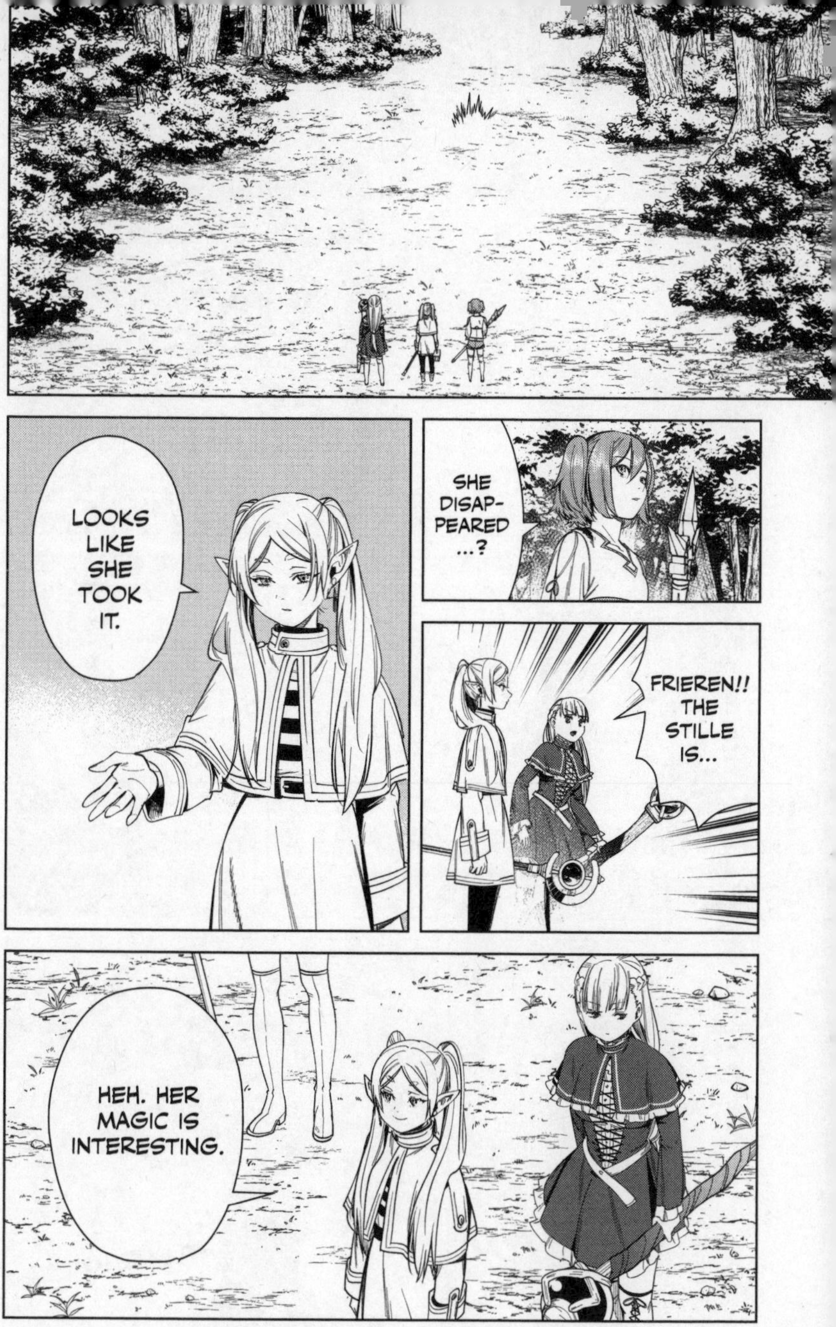
SHE DISAPPEARED...?
FRIEREN!! THE STILLE IS...
LOOKS LIKE SHE TOOK IT.
HEH. HER MAGIC IS INTERESTING.

Chapter 43: Privilege

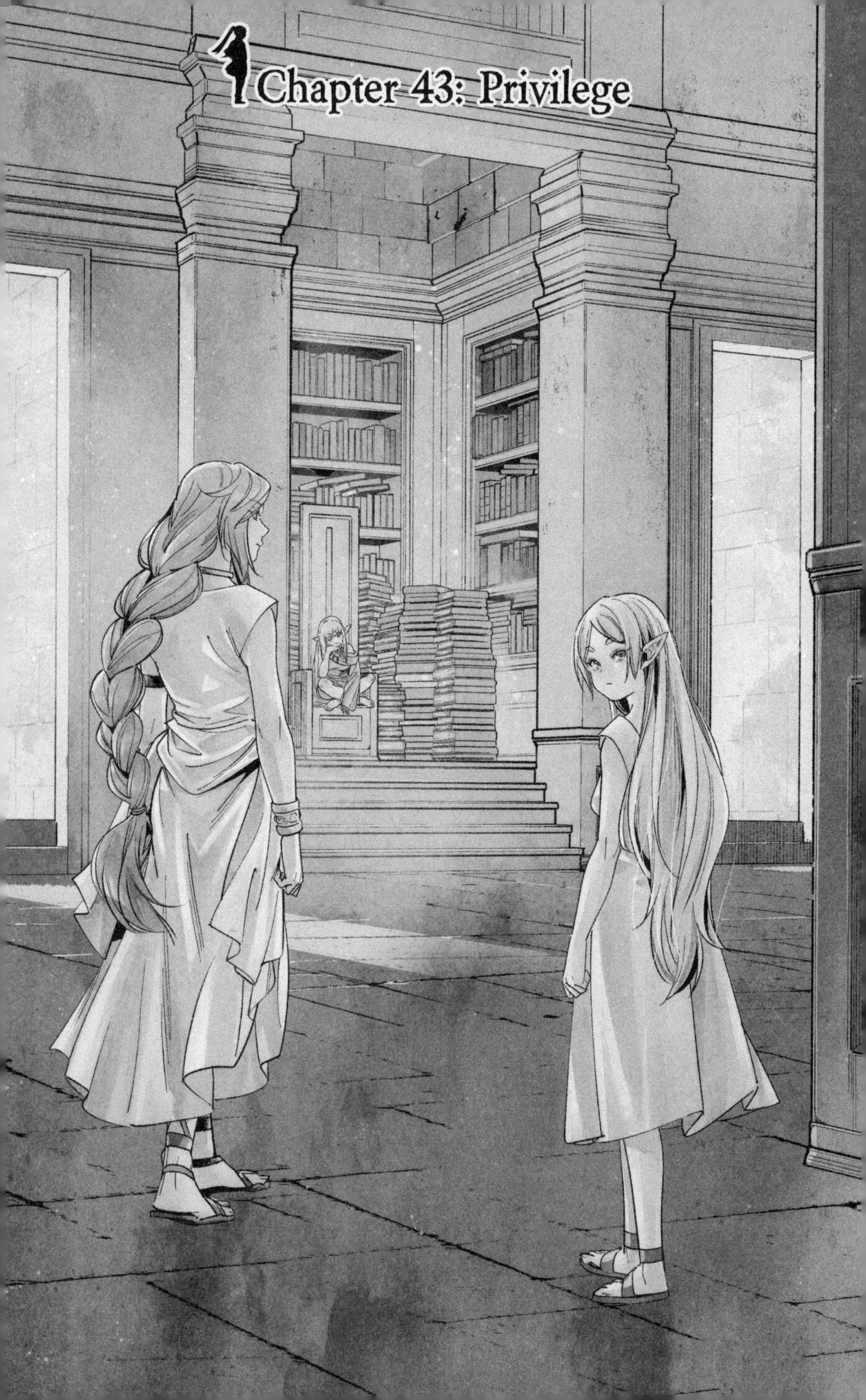

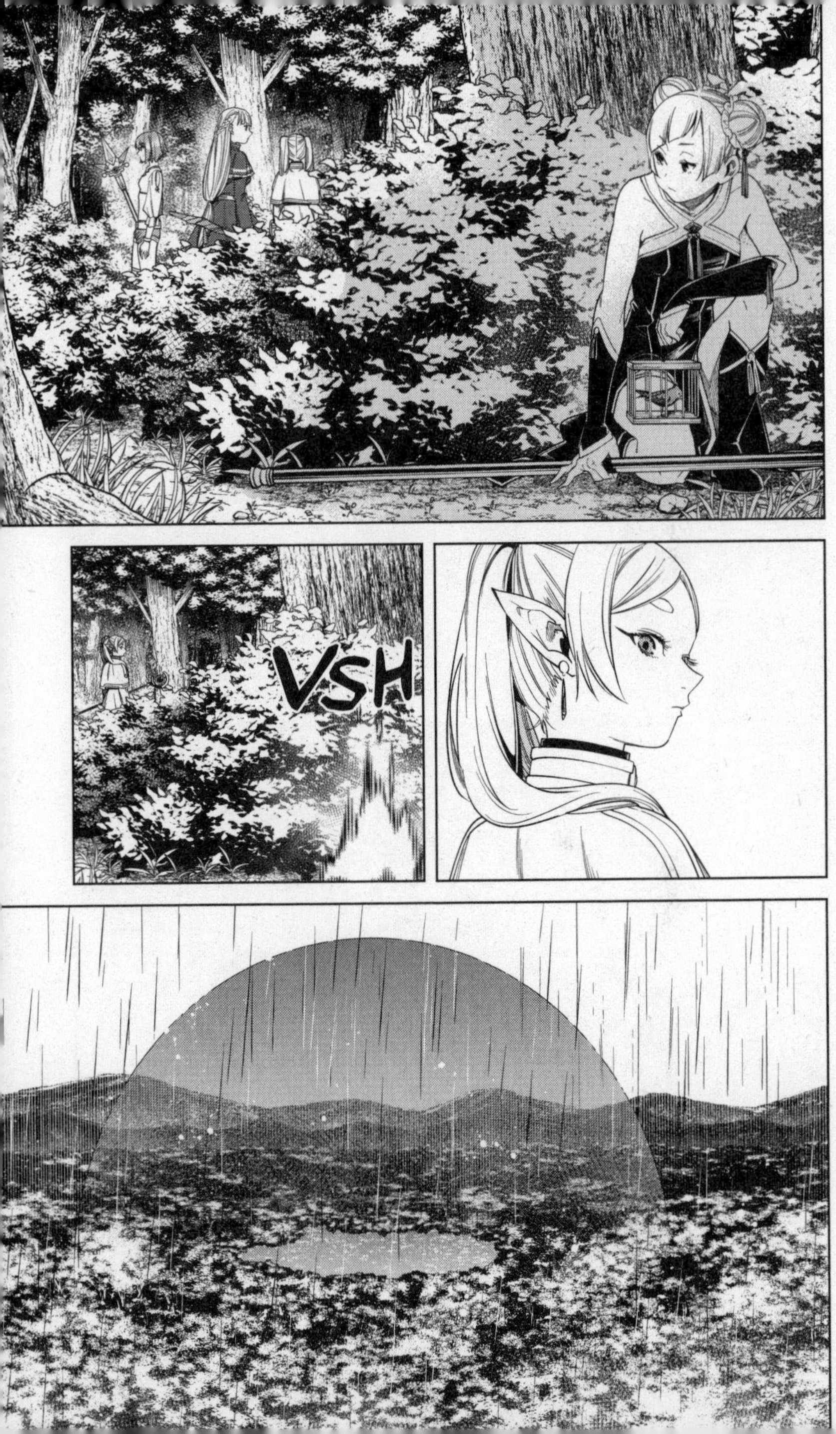
VSH

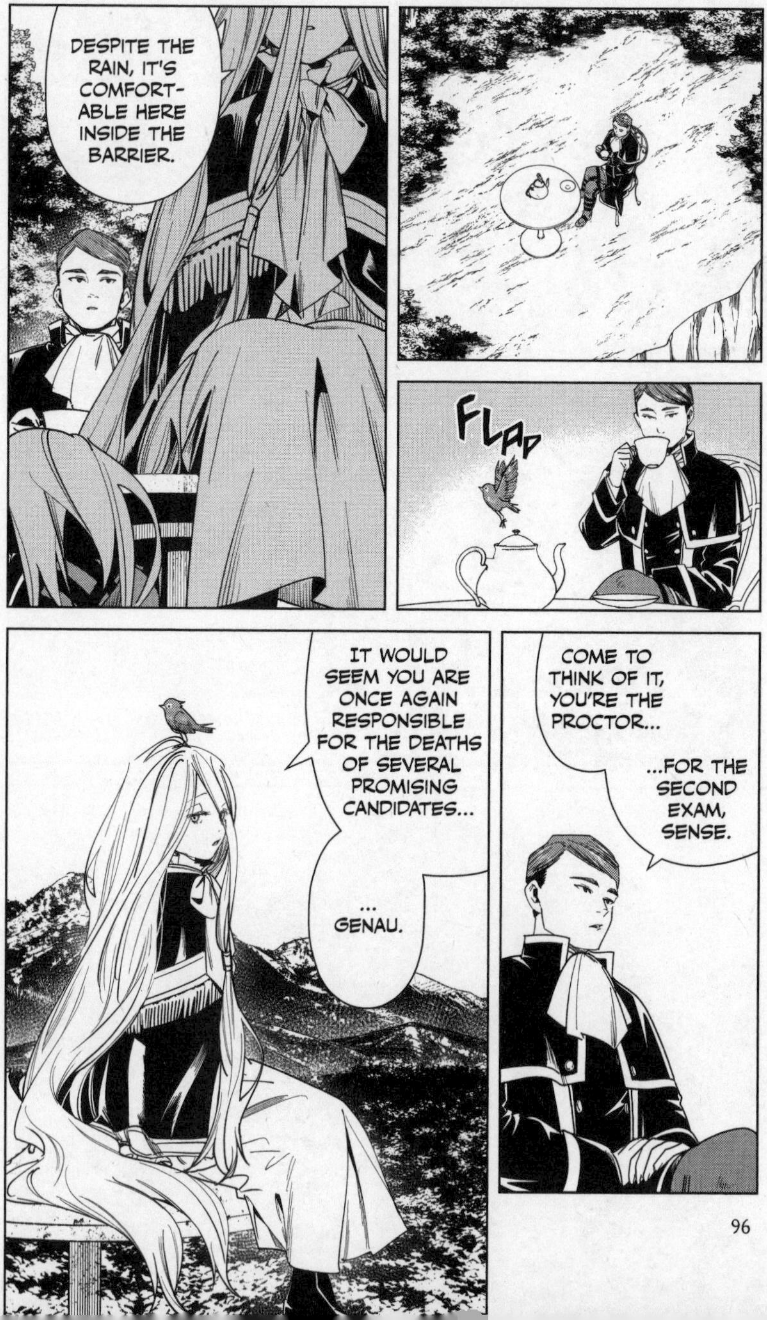
FLAP
DESPITE THE RAIN, IT'S COMFORT-ABLE HERE INSIDE THE BARRIER.
COME TO THINK OF IT, YOU'RE THE PROCTOR...
...FOR THE SECOND EXAM, SENSE.
IT WOULD SEEM YOU ARE ONCE AGAIN RESPONSIBLE FOR THE DEATHS OF SEVERAL PROMISING CANDIDATES...
... GENAU.

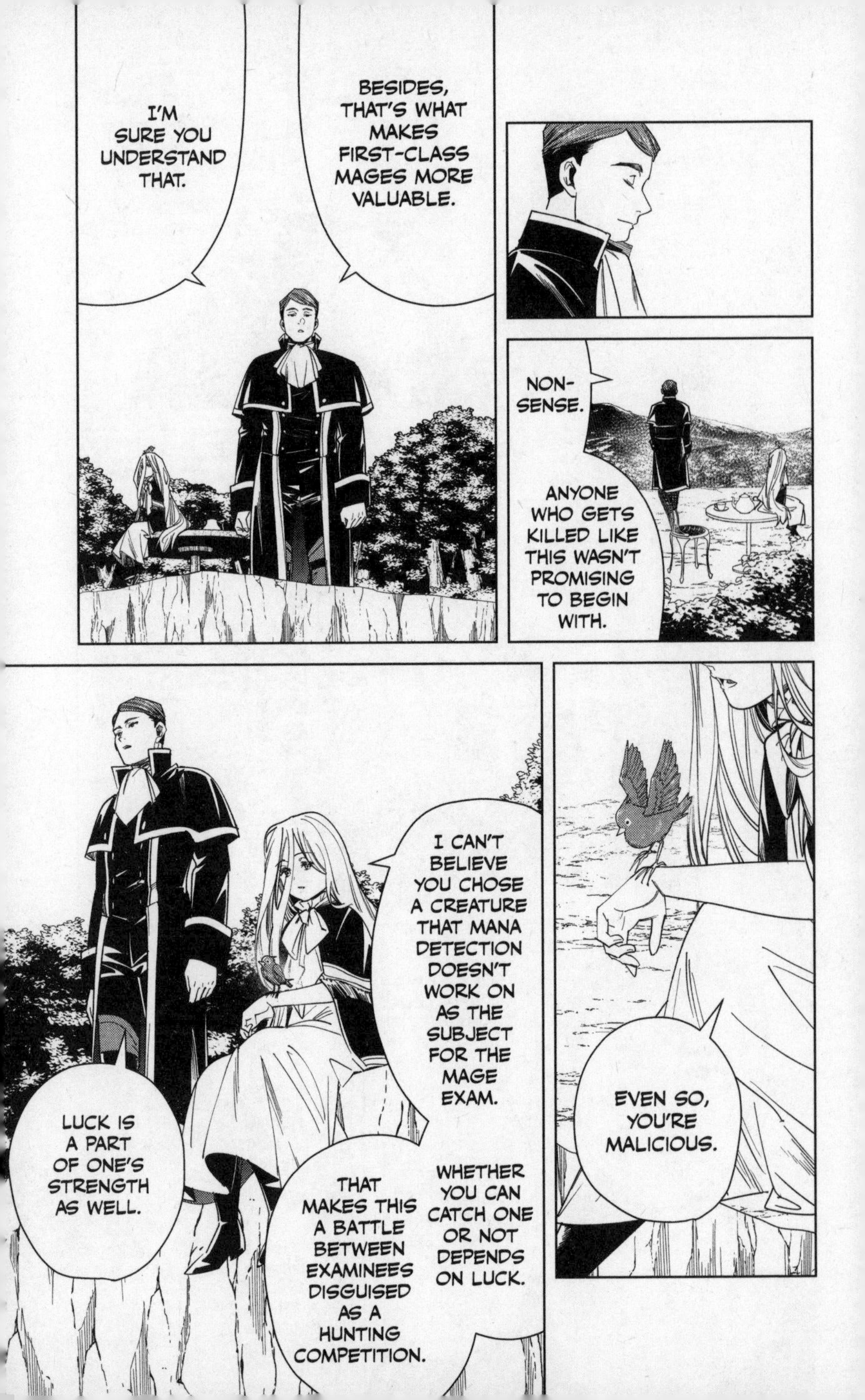
BESIDES, THAT'S WHAT MAKES FIRST-CLASS MAGES MORE VALUABLE.
I'M SURE YOU UNDERSTAND THAT.
NON-SENSE.
ANYONE WHO GETS KILLED LIKE THIS WASN'T PROMISING TO BEGIN WITH.
I CAN'T BELIEVE YOU CHOSE A CREATURE THAT MANA DETECTION DOESN'T WORK ON AS THE SUBJECT FOR THE MAGE EXAM.
WHETHER YOU CAN CATCH ONE OR NOT DEPENDS ON LUCK.
THAT MAKES THIS A BATTLE BETWEEN EXAMINEES DISGUISED AS A HUNTING COMPETITION.
LUCK IS A PART OF ONE'S STRENGTH AS WELL.
EVEN SO, YOU'RE MALICIOUS.

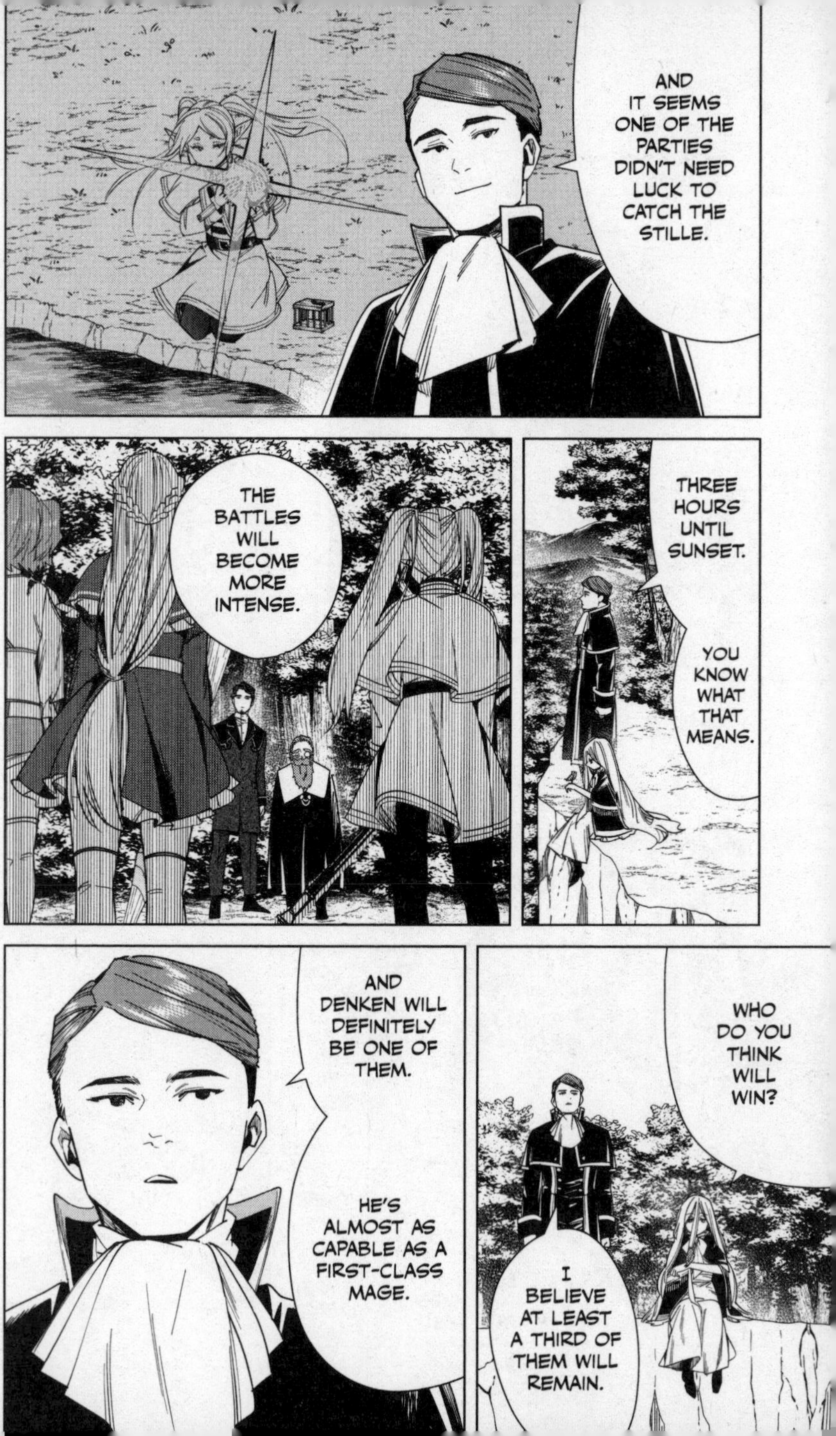
AND IT SEEMS ONE OF THE PARTIES DIDN'T NEED LUCK TO CATCH THE STILLE.
THREE HOURS UNTIL SUNSET.
YOU KNOW WHAT THAT MEANS.
THE BATTLES WILL BECOME MORE INTENSE.
WHO DO YOU THINK WILL WIN?
I BELIEVE AT LEAST A THIRD OF THEM WILL REMAIN.
AND DENKEN WILL DEFINITELY BE ONE OF THEM.
HE'S ALMOST AS CAPABLE AS A FIRST-CLASS MAGE.

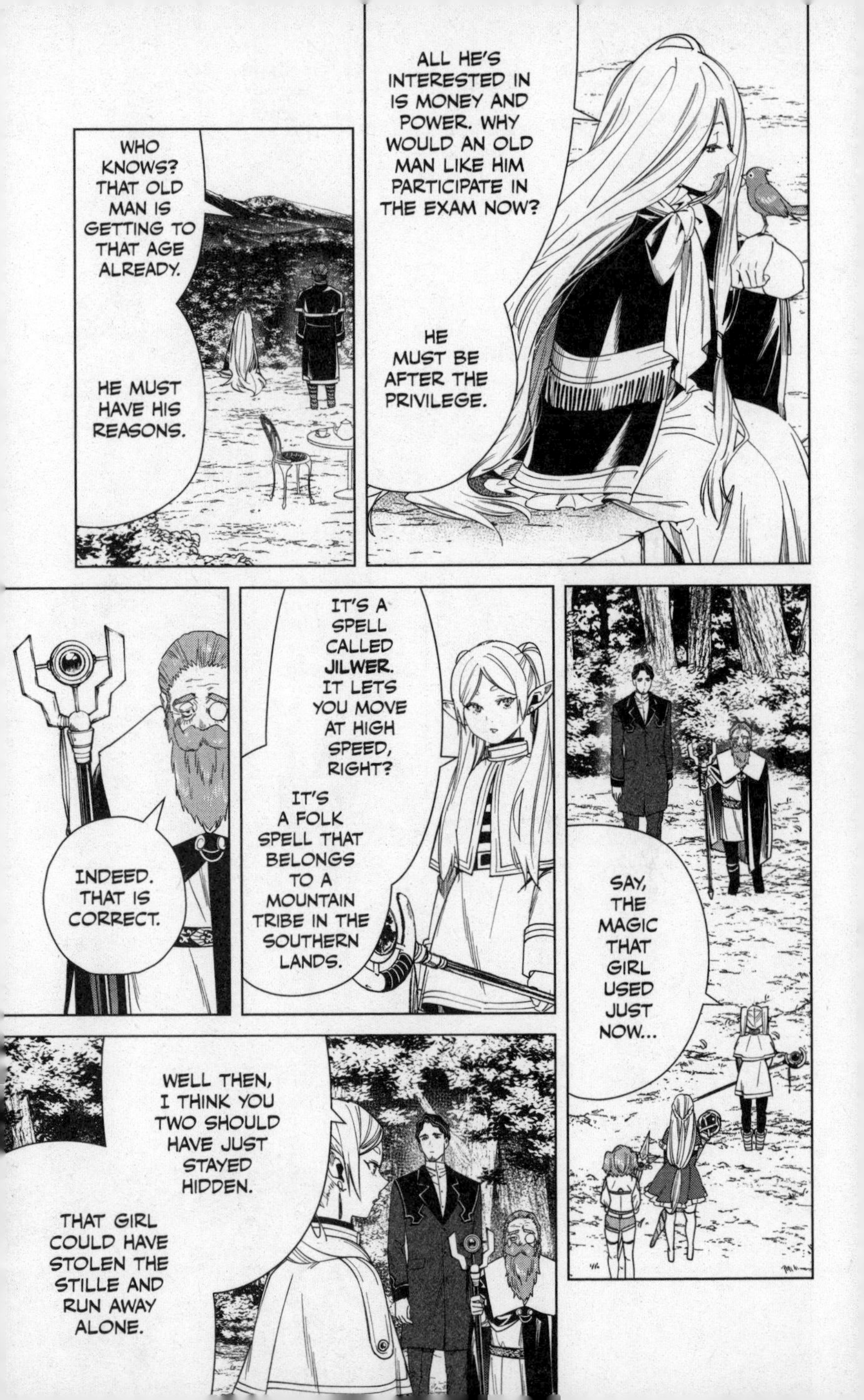
ALL HE'S INTERESTED IN IS MONEY AND POWER. WHY WOULD AN OLD MAN LIKE HIM PARTICIPATE IN THE EXAM NOW?
HE MUST BE AFTER THE PRIVILEGE.
WHO KNOWS? THAT OLD MAN IS GETTING TO THAT AGE ALREADY.
HE MUST HAVE HIS REASONS.
SAY, THE MAGIC THAT GIRL USED JUST NOW...
IT'S A SPELL CALLED **JILWER.** IT LETS YOU MOVE AT HIGH SPEED, RIGHT?
IT'S A FOLK SPELL THAT BELONGS TO A MOUNTAIN TRIBE IN THE SOUTHERN LANDS.
INDEED. THAT IS CORRECT.
WELL THEN, I THINK YOU TWO SHOULD HAVE JUST STAYED HIDDEN.
THAT GIRL COULD HAVE STOLEN THE STILLE AND RUN AWAY ALONE.

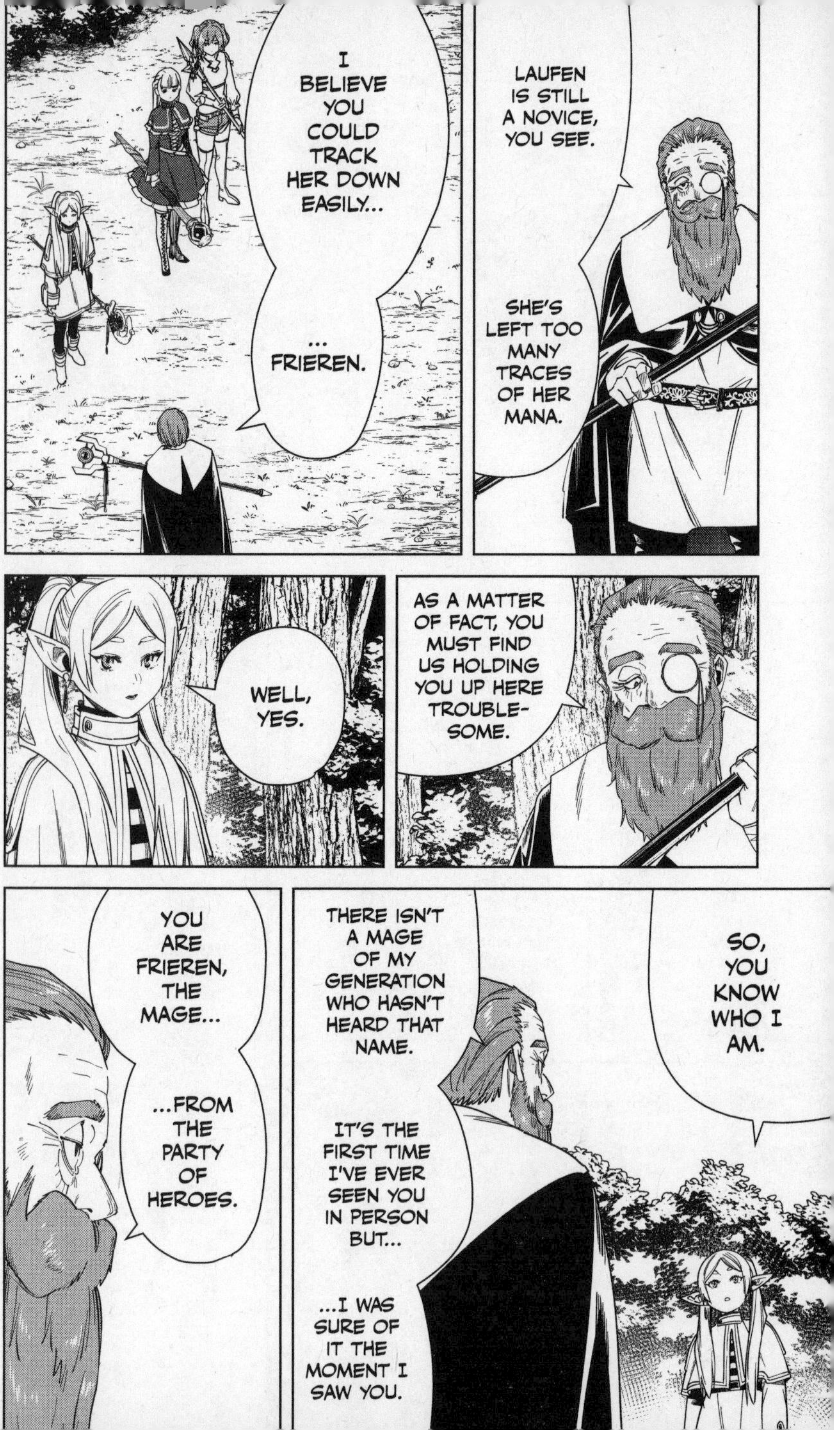
LAUFEN IS STILL A NOVICE, YOU SEE.
SHE'S LEFT TOO MANY TRACES OF HER MANA.
I BELIEVE YOU COULD TRACK HER DOWN EASILY...
... FRIEREN.
AS A MATTER OF FACT, YOU MUST FIND US HOLDING YOU UP HERE TROUBLE-SOME.
WELL, YES.
SO, YOU KNOW WHO I AM.
THERE ISN'T A MAGE OF MY GENERATION WHO HASN'T HEARD THAT NAME.
IT'S THE FIRST TIME I'VE EVER SEEN YOU IN PERSON BUT...
...I WAS SURE OF IT THE MOMENT I SAW YOU.
YOU ARE FRIEREN, THE MAGE...
...FROM THE PARTY OF HEROES.

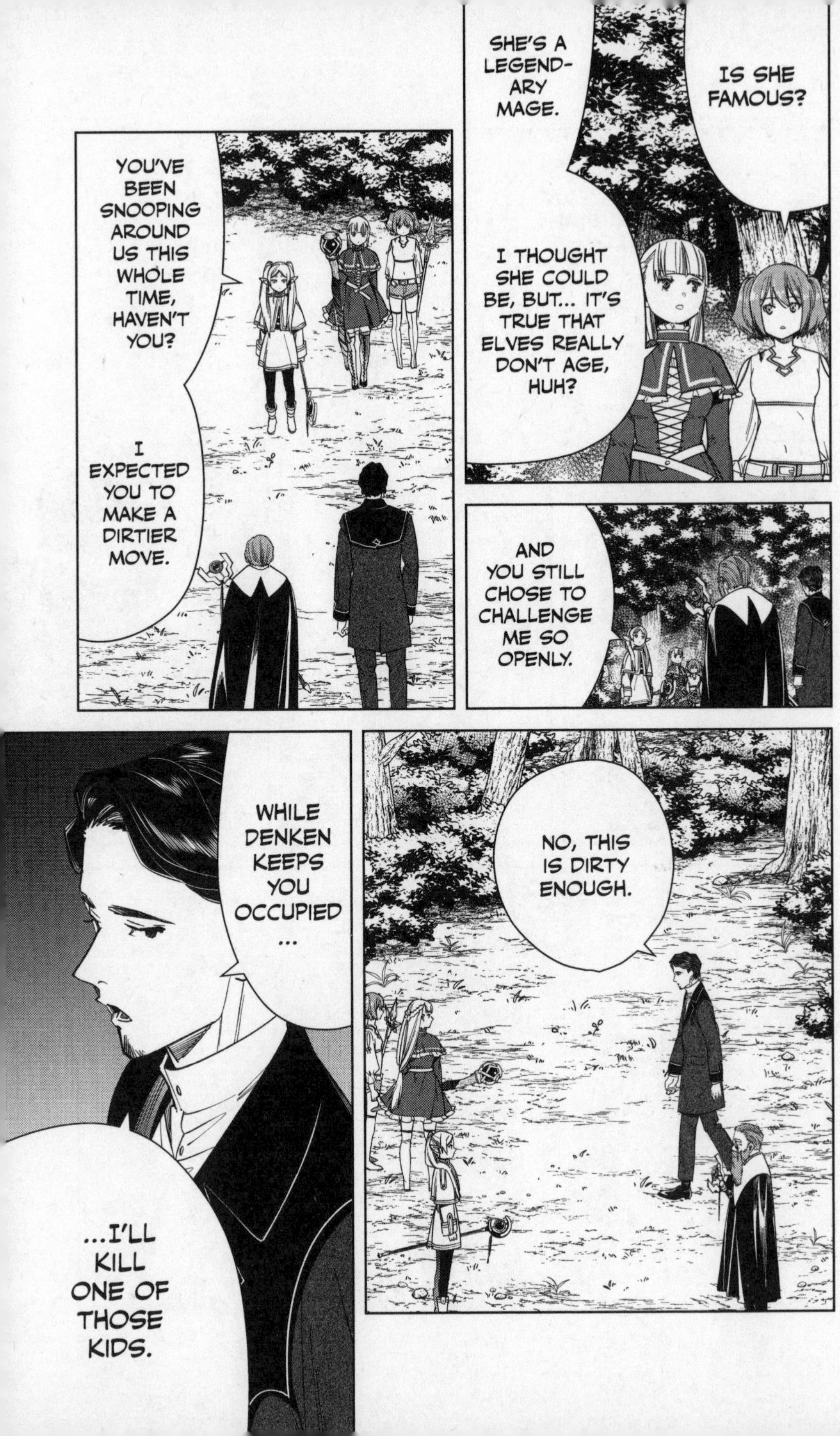
IS SHE FAMOUS?
SHE'S A LEGEND-ARY MAGE.
I THOUGHT SHE COULD BE, BUT... IT'S TRUE THAT ELVES REALLY DON'T AGE, HUH?
YOU'VE BEEN SNOOPING AROUND US THIS WHOLE TIME, HAVEN'T YOU?
I EXPECTED YOU TO MAKE A DIRTIER MOVE.
AND YOU STILL CHOSE TO CHALLENGE ME SO OPENLY.
NO, THIS IS DIRTY ENOUGH.
WHILE DENKEN KEEPS YOU OCCUPIED...
...I'LL KILL ONE OF THOSE KIDS.

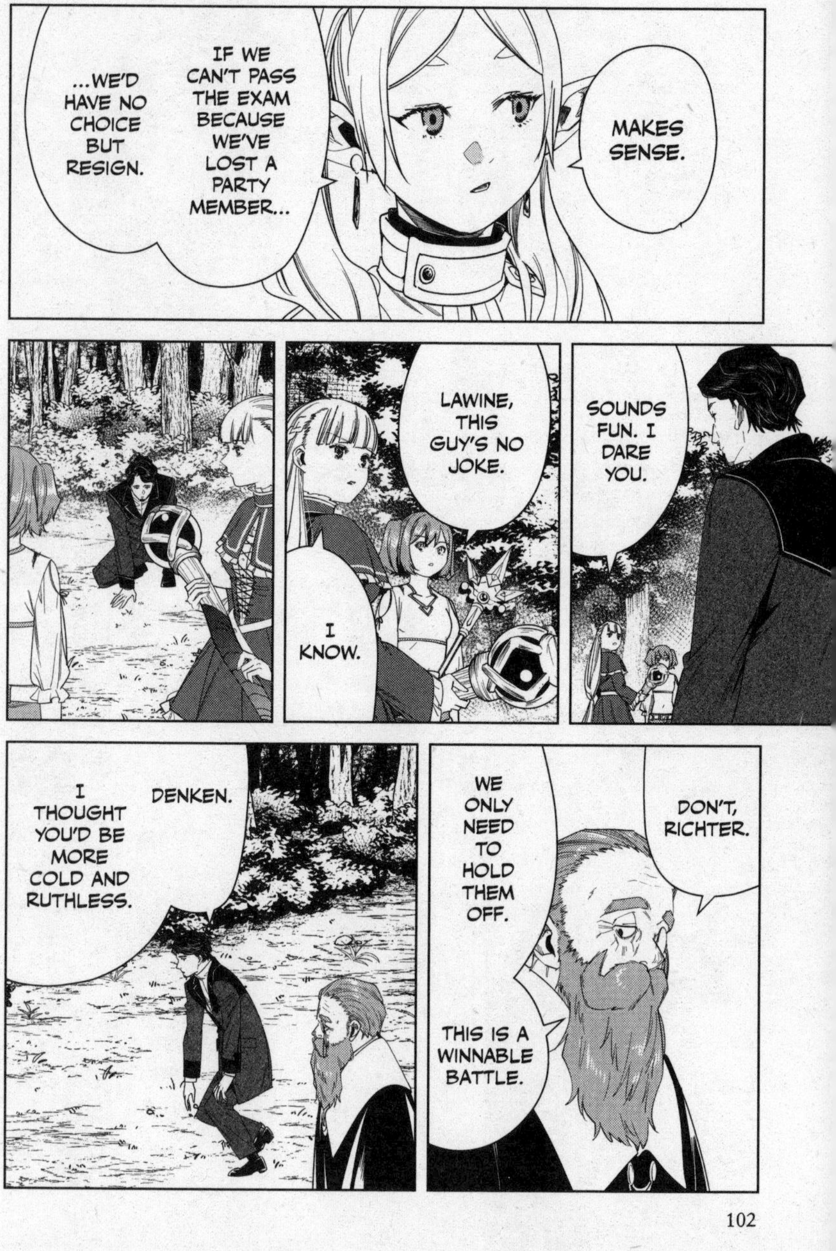
MAKES SENSE.
IF WE CAN'T PASS THE EXAM BECAUSE WE'VE LOST A PARTY MEMBER...
...WE'D HAVE NO CHOICE BUT RESIGN.
SOUNDS FUN. I DARE YOU.
LAWINE, THIS GUY'S NO JOKE.
I KNOW.
DON'T, RICHTER.
WE ONLY NEED TO HOLD THEM OFF.
THIS IS A WINNABLE BATTLE.
DENKEN.
I THOUGHT YOU'D BE MORE COLD AND RUTHLESS.

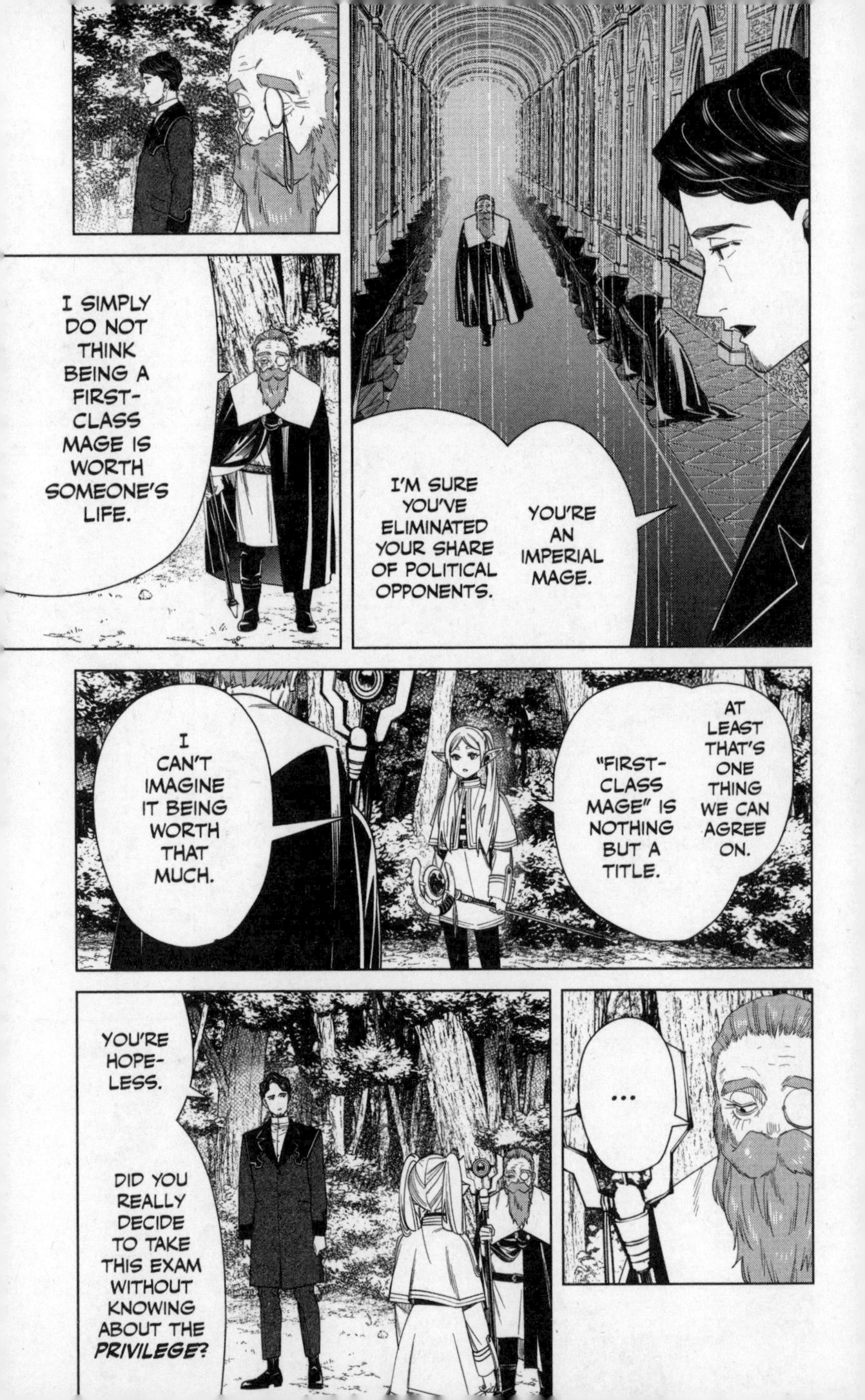
YOU'RE AN IMPERIAL MAGE.
I'M SURE YOU'VE ELIMINATED YOUR SHARE OF POLITICAL OPPONENTS.
I SIMPLY DO NOT THINK BEING A FIRST-CLASS MAGE IS WORTH SOMEONE'S LIFE.
AT LEAST THAT'S ONE THING WE CAN AGREE ON.
"FIRST-CLASS MAGE" IS NOTHING BUT A TITLE.
I CAN'T IMAGINE IT BEING WORTH THAT MUCH.
...
YOU'RE HOPE-LESS.
DID YOU REALLY DECIDE TO TAKE THIS EXAM WITHOUT KNOWING ABOUT THE *PRIVILEGE?*

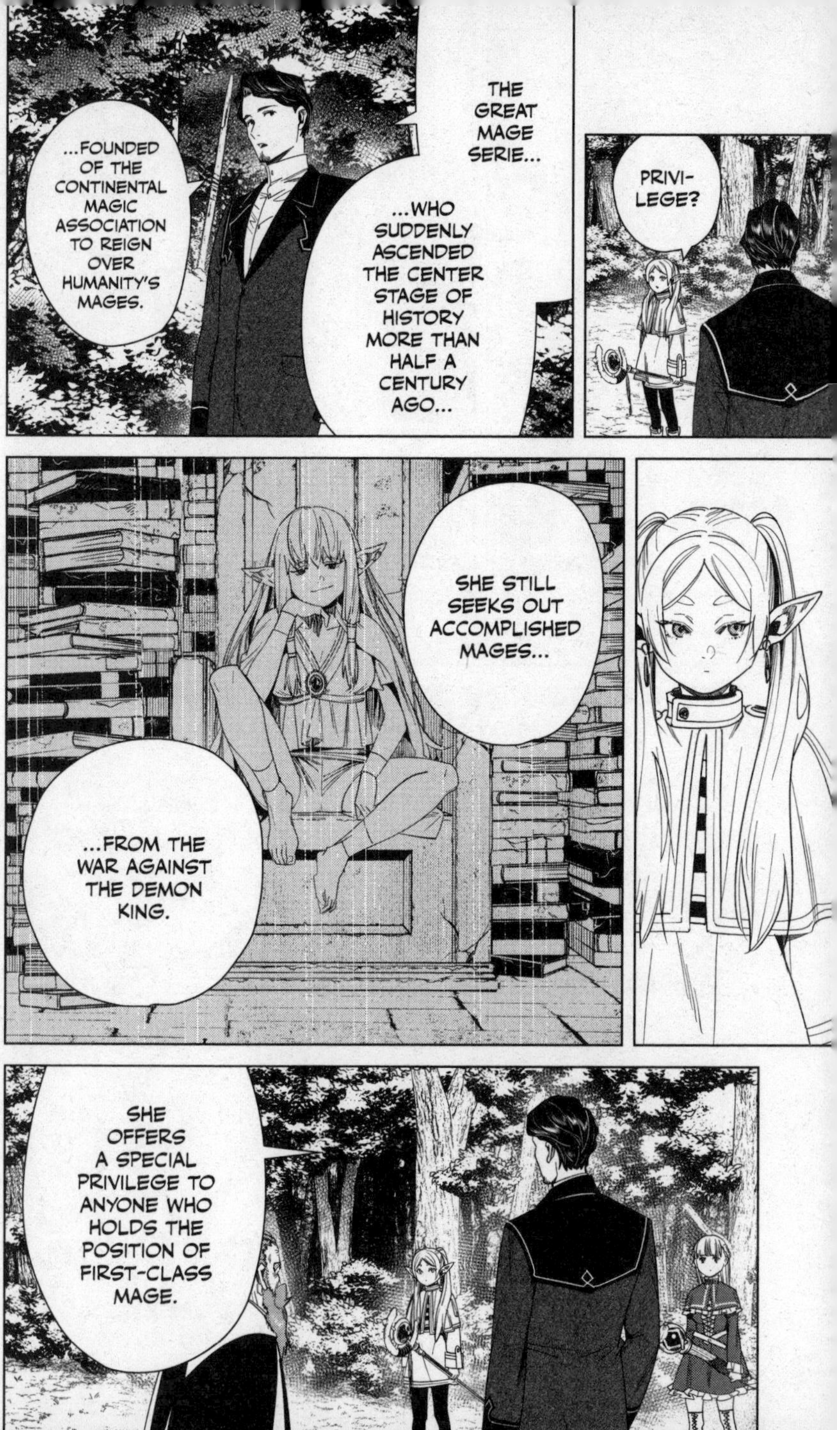
PRIVI-LEGE?
THE GREAT MAGE SERIE...
...WHO SUDDENLY ASCENDED THE CENTER STAGE OF HISTORY MORE THAN HALF A CENTURY AGO...
...FOUNDED OF THE CONTINENTAL MAGIC ASSOCIATION TO REIGN OVER HUMANITY'S MAGES.
SHE STILL SEEKS OUT ACCOMPLISHED MAGES...
...FROM THE WAR AGAINST THE DEMON KING.
SHE OFFERS A SPECIAL PRIVILEGE TO ANYONE WHO HOLDS THE POSITION OF FIRST-CLASS MAGE.

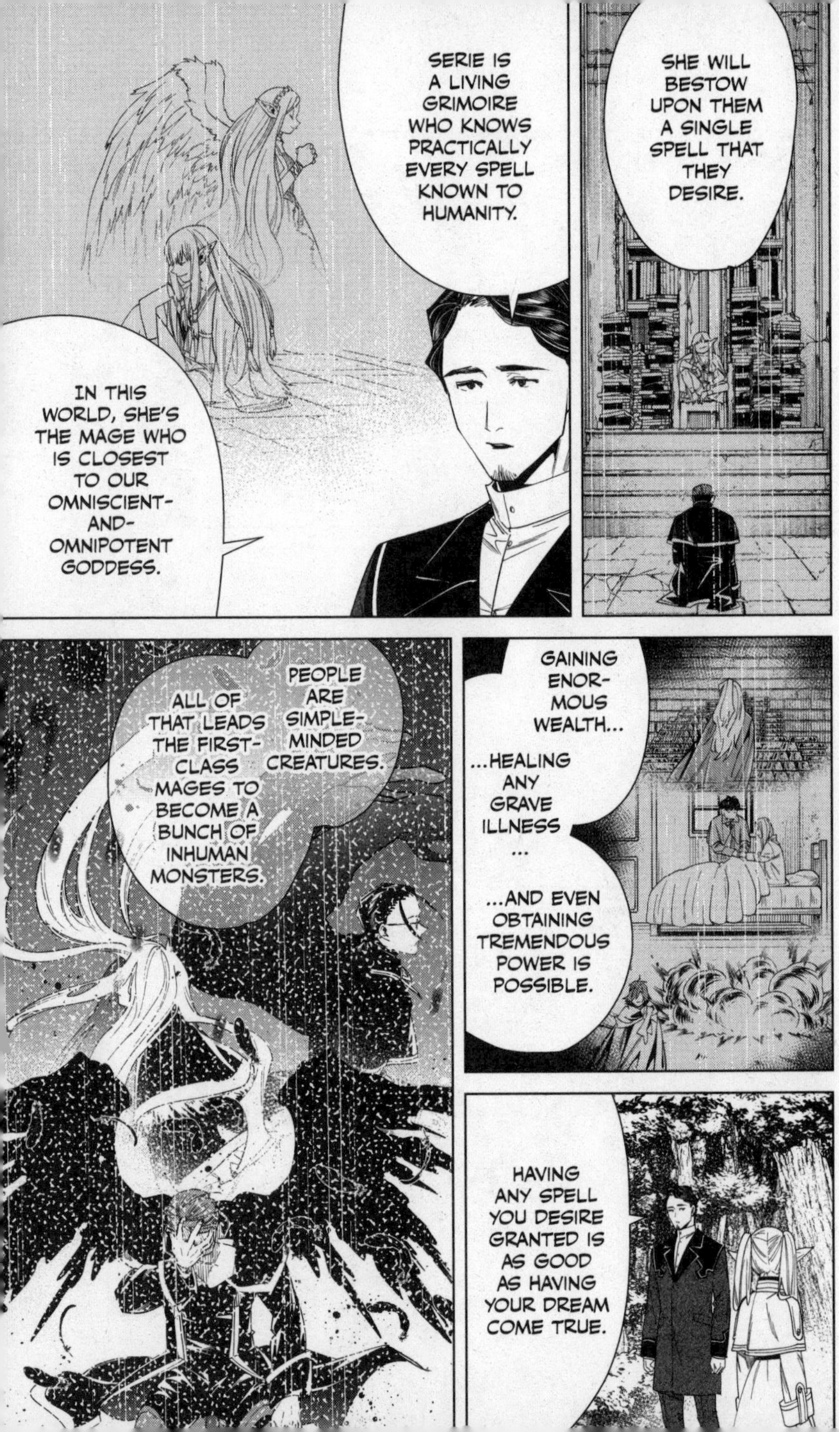
SHE WILL BESTOW UPON THEM A SINGLE SPELL THAT THEY DESIRE.
SERIE IS A LIVING GRIMOIRE WHO KNOWS PRACTICALLY EVERY SPELL KNOWN TO HUMANITY.
IN THIS WORLD, SHE'S THE MAGE WHO IS CLOSEST TO OUR OMNISCIENT-AND-OMNIPOTENT GODDESS.
GAINING ENOR-MOUS WEALTH...
...HEALING ANY GRAVE ILLNESS ...
...AND EVEN OBTAINING TREMENDOUS POWER IS POSSIBLE.
HAVING ANY SPELL YOU DESIRE GRANTED IS AS GOOD AS HAVING YOUR DREAM COME TRUE.
PEOPLE ARE SIMPLE-MINDED CREATURES.
ALL OF THAT LEADS THE FIRST-CLASS MAGES TO BECOME A BUNCH OF INHUMAN MONSTERS.

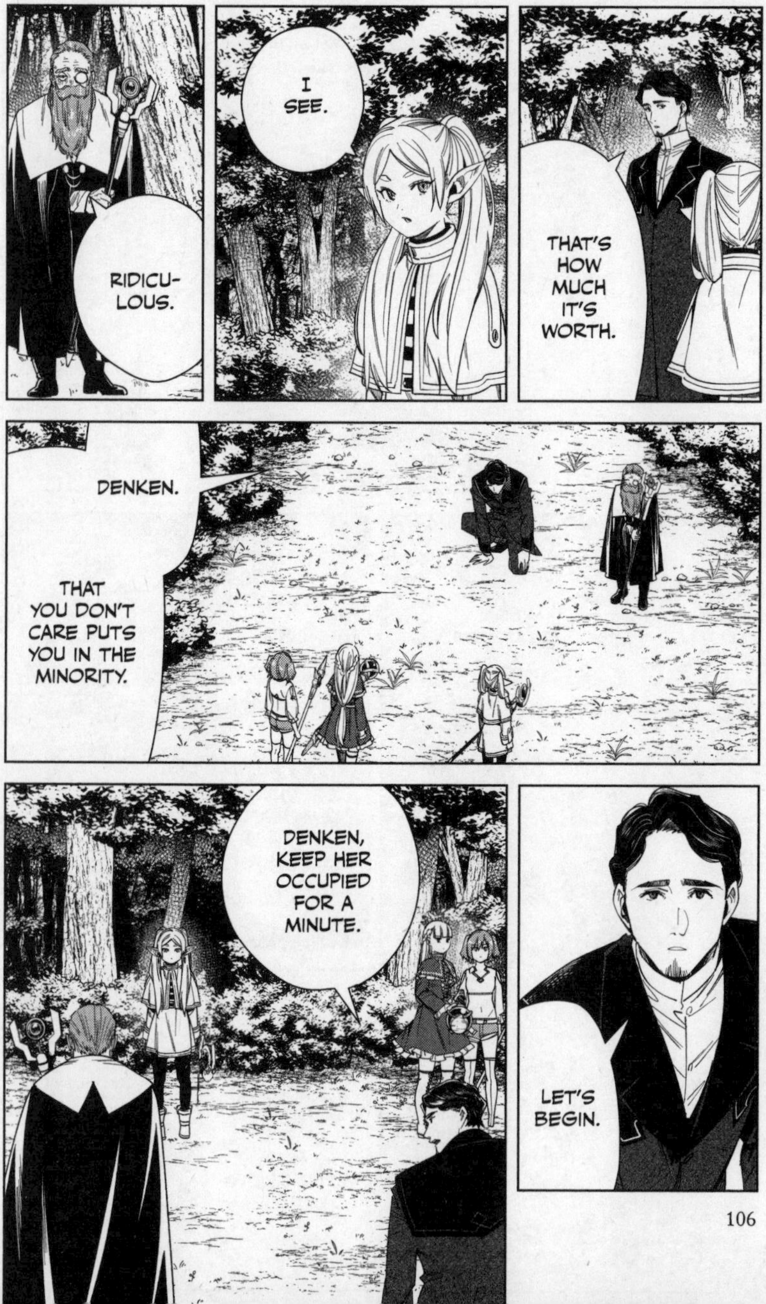
THAT'S HOW MUCH IT'S WORTH.
I SEE.
RIDICU-LOUS.
DENKEN.
THAT YOU DON'T CARE PUTS YOU IN THE MINORITY.
LET'S BEGIN.
DENKEN, KEEP HER OCCUPIED FOR A MINUTE.

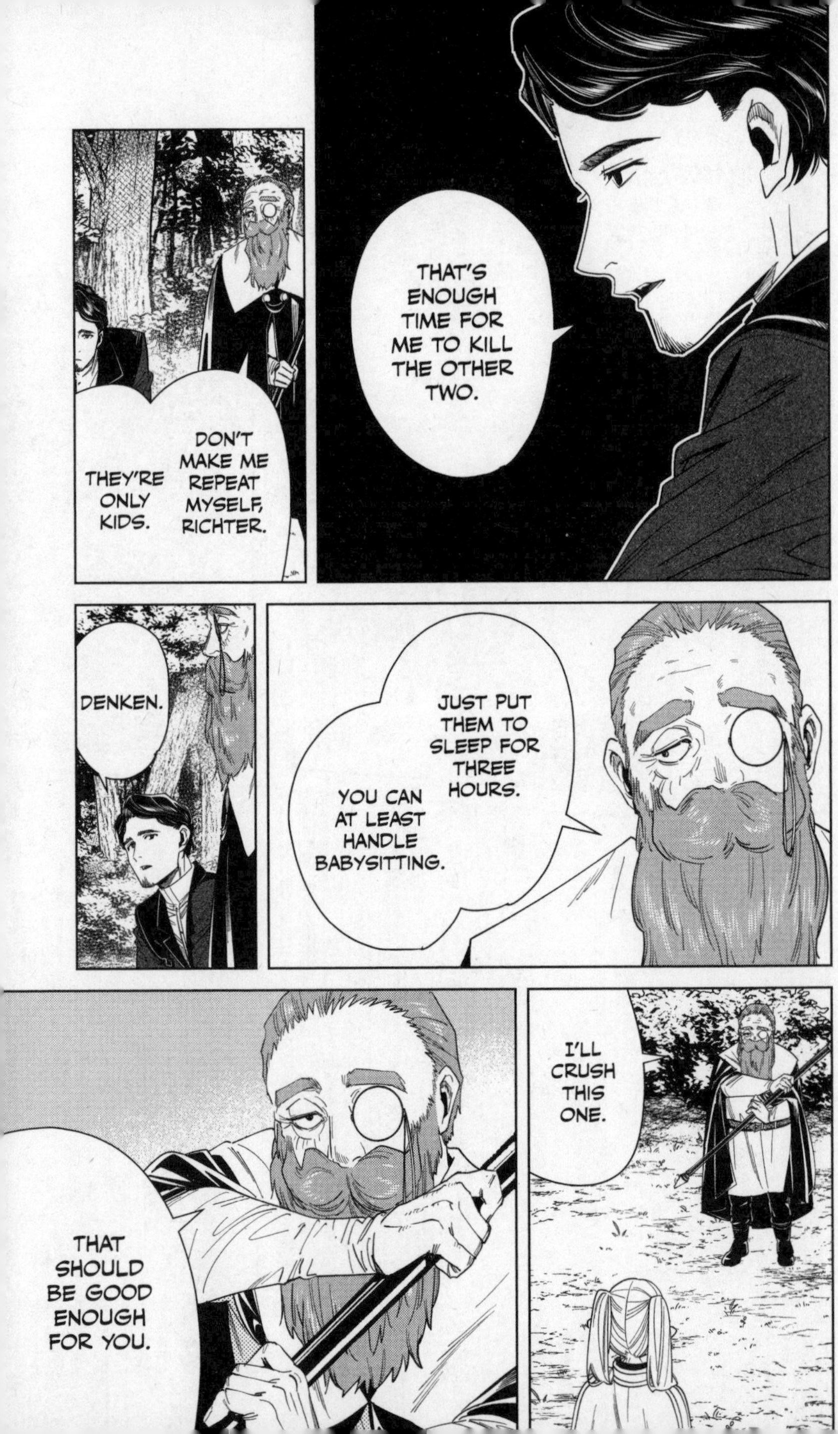
THAT'S ENOUGH TIME FOR ME TO KILL THE OTHER TWO.
DON'T MAKE ME REPEAT MYSELF, RICHTER.
THEY'RE ONLY KIDS.
JUST PUT THEM TO SLEEP FOR THREE HOURS.
YOU CAN AT LEAST HANDLE BABYSITTING.
DENKEN.
I'LL CRUSH THIS ONE.
THAT SHOULD BE GOOD ENOUGH FOR YOU.

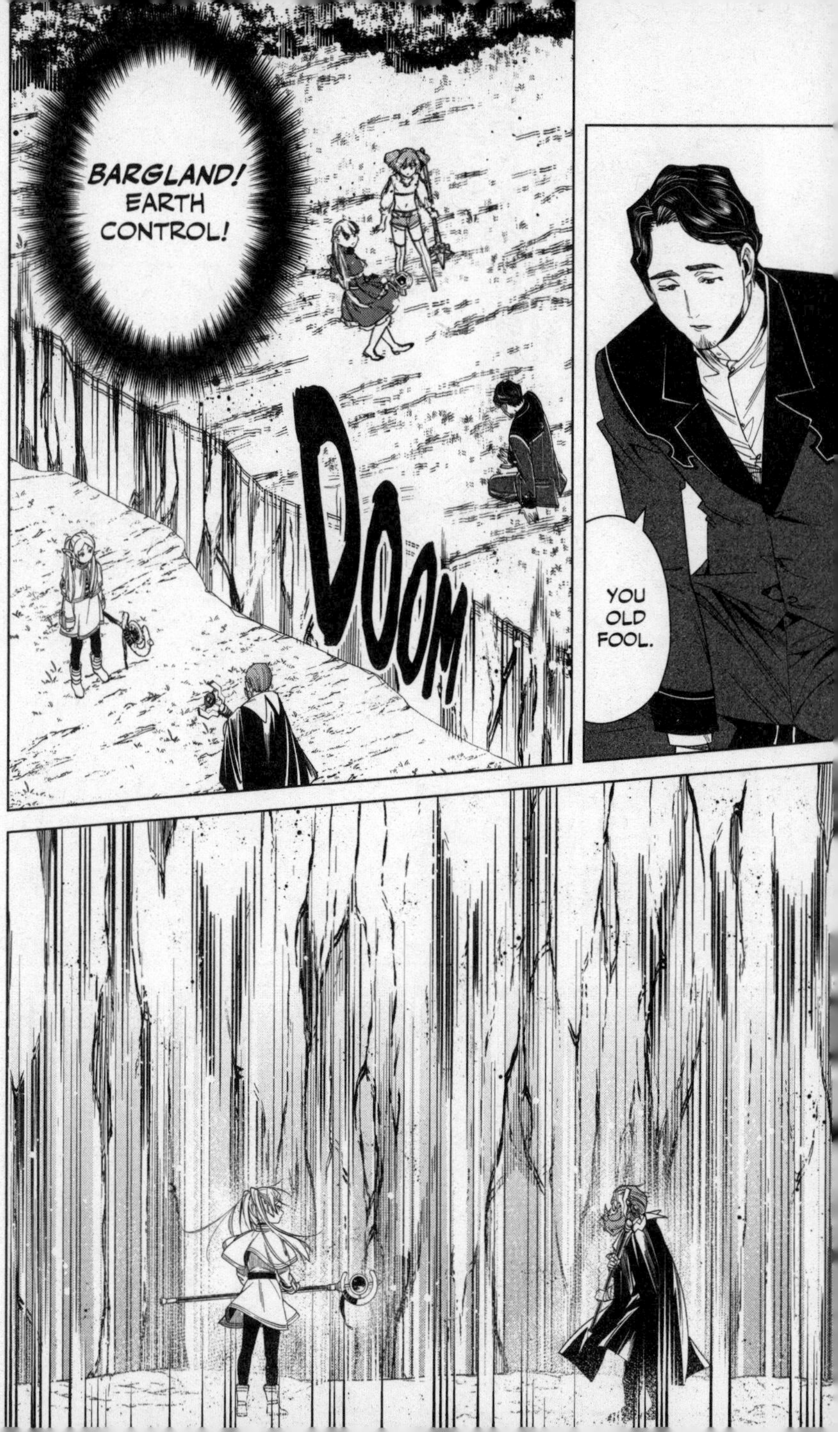
YOU OLD FOOL.
BARGLAND! EARTH CONTROL!
DOOM

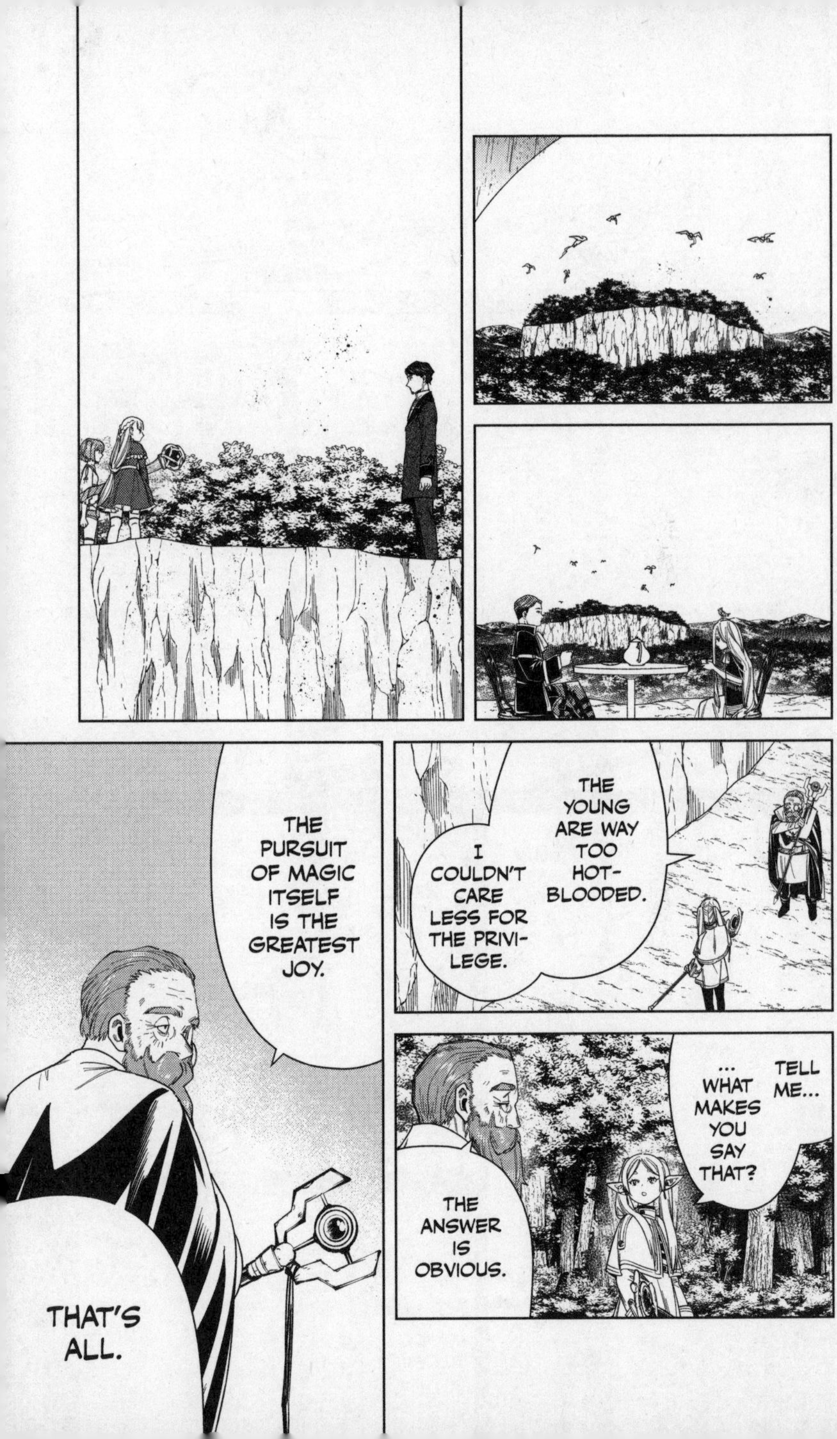
THE YOUNG ARE WAY TOO HOT-BLOODED.
I COULDN'T CARE LESS FOR THE PRIVI-LEGE.
TELL ME...
... WHAT MAKES YOU SAY THAT?
THE ANSWER IS OBVIOUS.
THE PURSUIT OF MAGIC ITSELF IS THE GREATEST JOY.
THAT'S ALL.

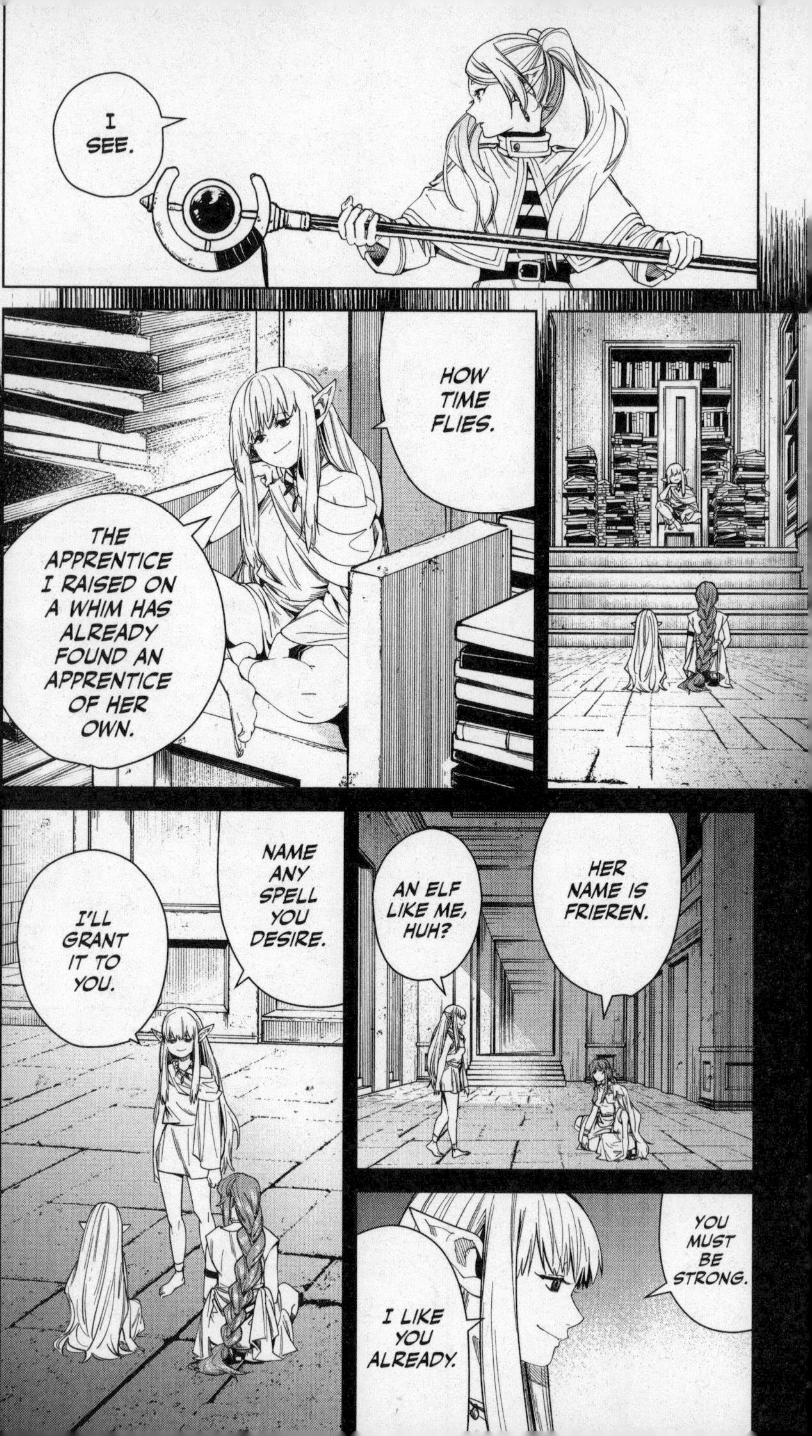
I SEE.
HOW TIME FLIES.
THE APPRENTICE I RAISED ON A WHIM HAS ALREADY FOUND AN APPRENTICE OF HER OWN.
HER NAME IS FRIEREN.
AN ELF LIKE ME, HUH?
YOU MUST BE STRONG.
I LIKE YOU ALREADY.
NAME ANY SPELL YOU DESIRE.
I'LL GRANT IT TO YOU.

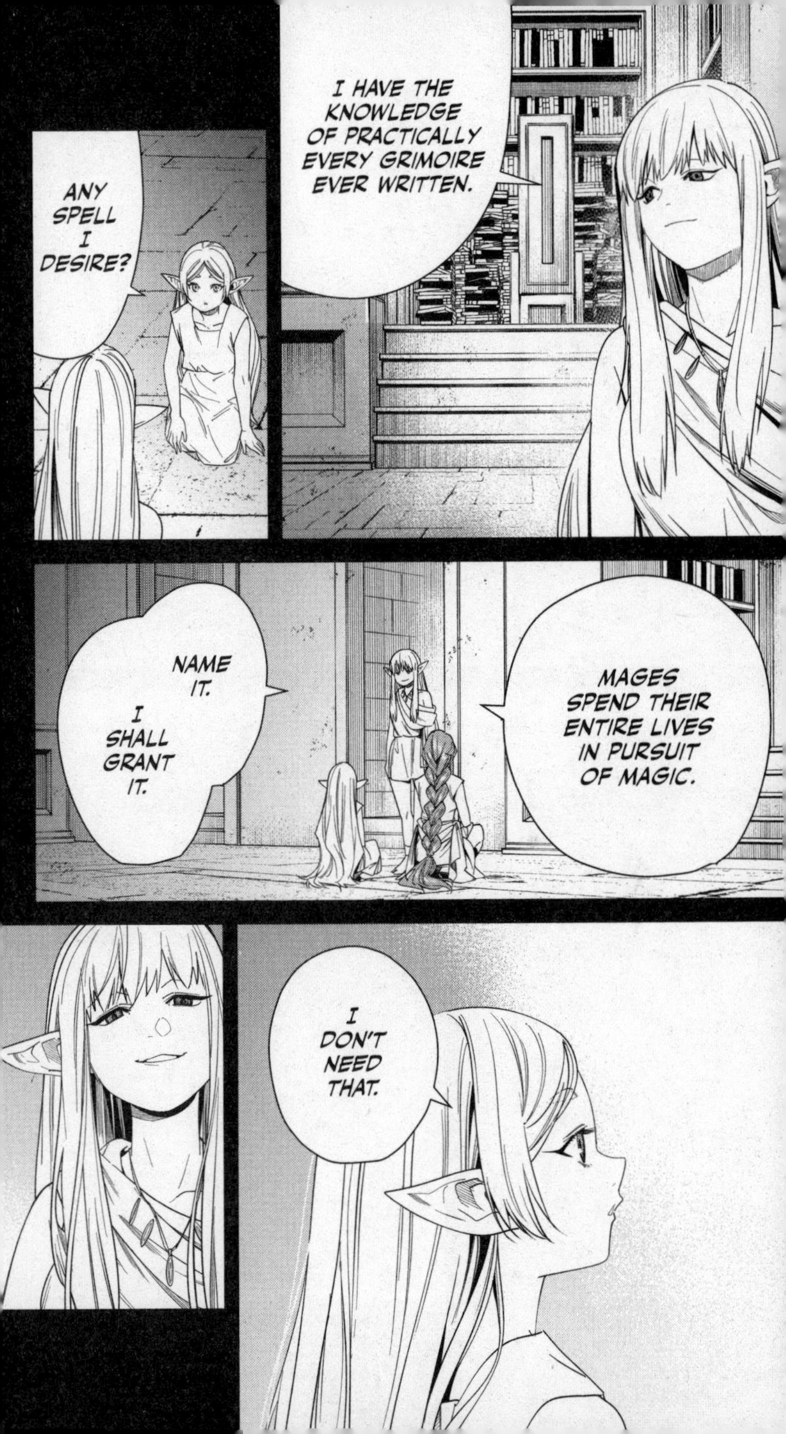
I HAVE THE KNOWLEDGE OF PRACTICALLY EVERY GRIMOIRE EVER WRITTEN.
ANY SPELL I DESIRE?
MAGES SPEND THEIR ENTIRE LIVES IN PURSUIT OF MAGIC.
NAME IT.
I SHALL GRANT IT.
I DON'T NEED THAT.

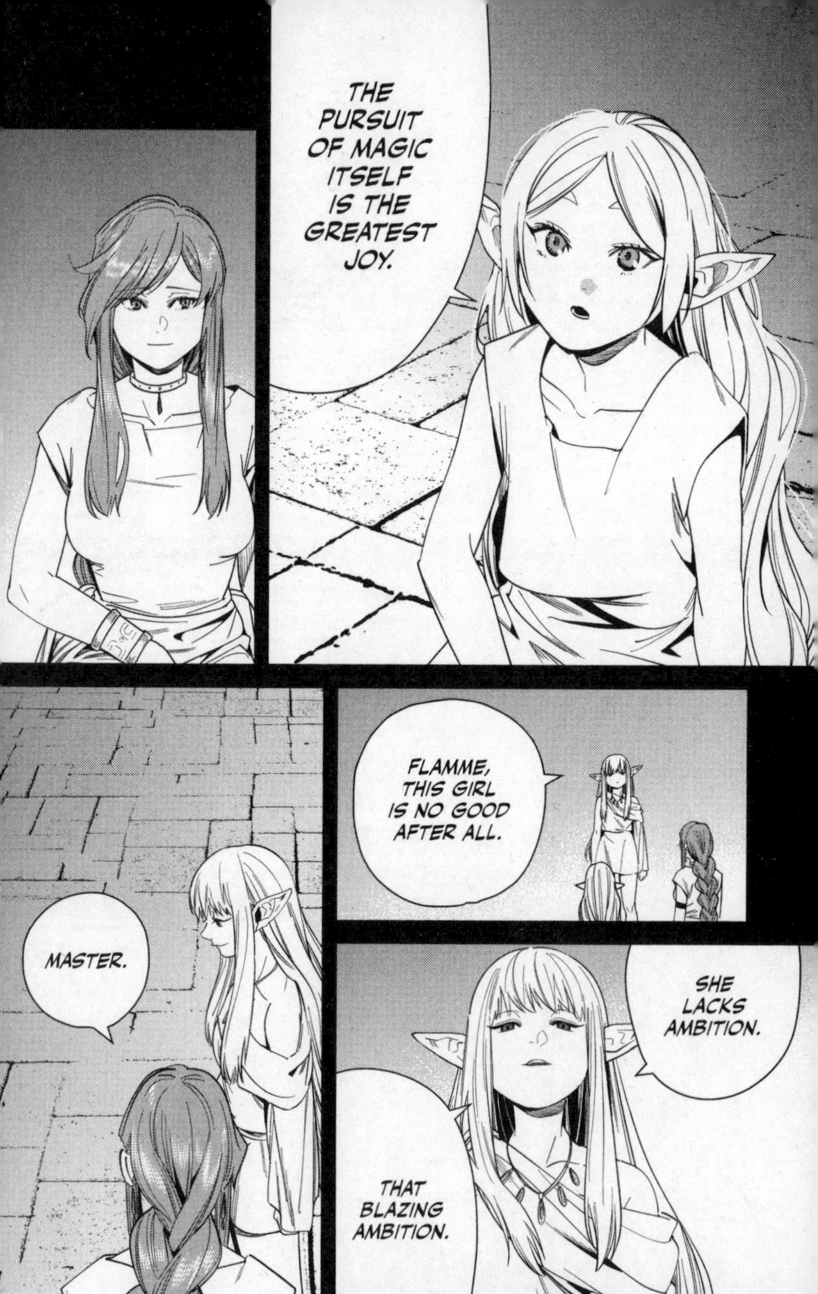
THE PURSUIT OF MAGIC ITSELF IS THE GREATEST JOY.
FLAMME, THIS GIRL IS NO GOOD AFTER ALL.
SHE LACKS AMBITION.
THAT BLAZING AMBITION.
MASTER.

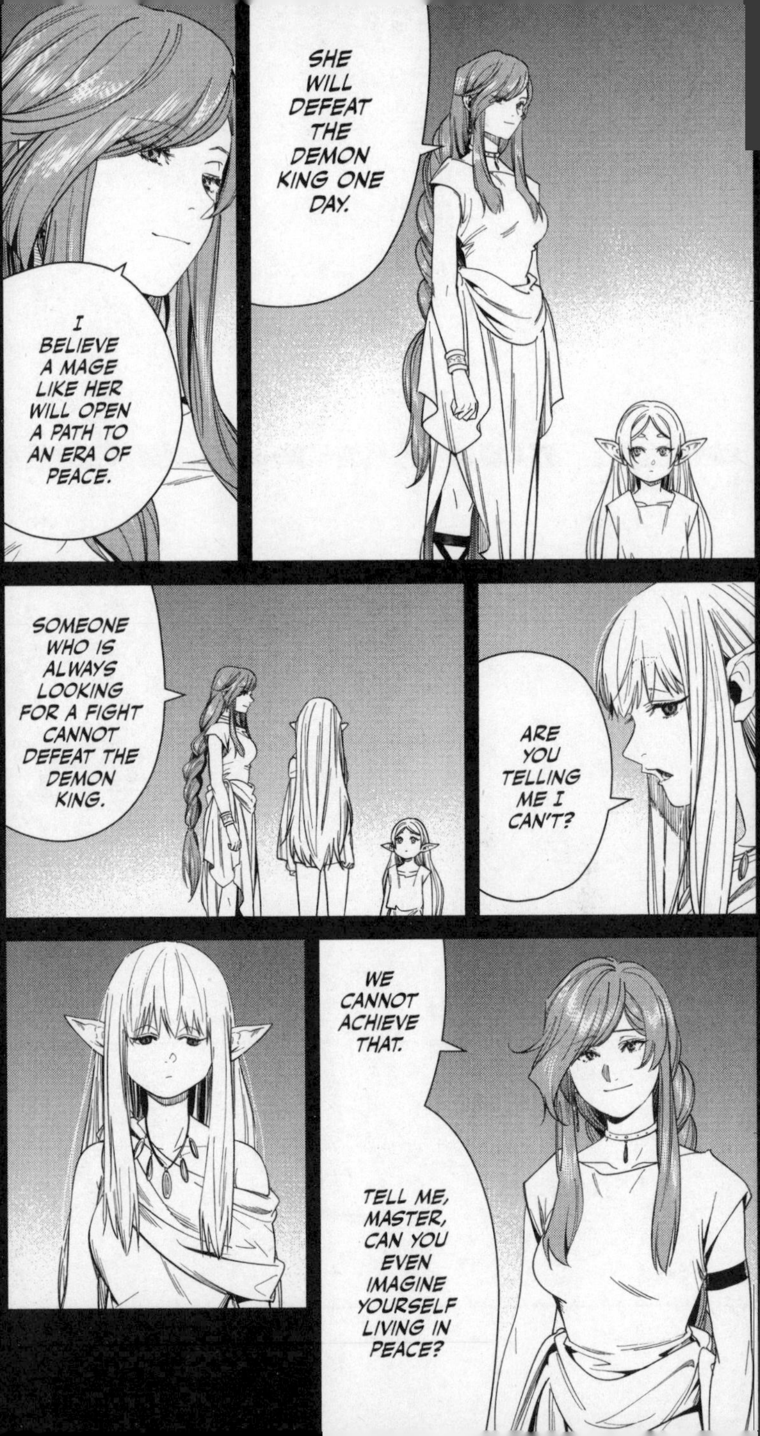
I BELIEVE A MAGE LIKE HER WILL OPEN A PATH TO AN ERA OF PEACE.
SHE WILL DEFEAT THE DEMON KING ONE DAY.
SOMEONE WHO IS ALWAYS LOOKING FOR A FIGHT CANNOT DEFEAT THE DEMON KING.
ARE YOU TELLING ME I CAN'T?
WE CANNOT ACHIEVE THAT.
TELL ME, MASTER, CAN YOU EVEN IMAGINE YOURSELF LIVING IN PEACE?

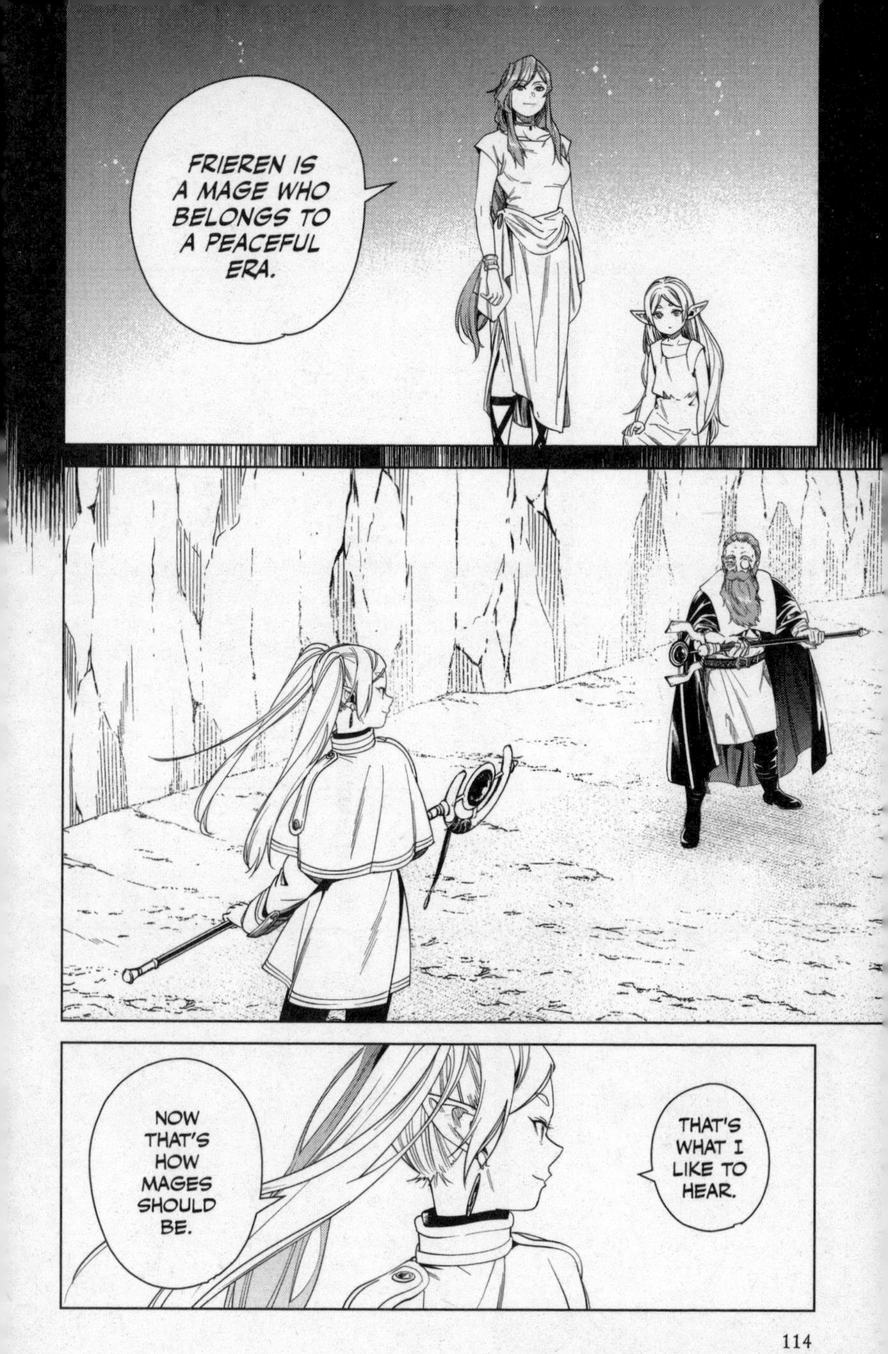
FRIEREN IS A MAGE WHO BELONGS TO A PEACEFUL ERA.
THAT'S WHAT I LIKE TO HEAR.
NOW THAT'S HOW MAGES SHOULD BE.

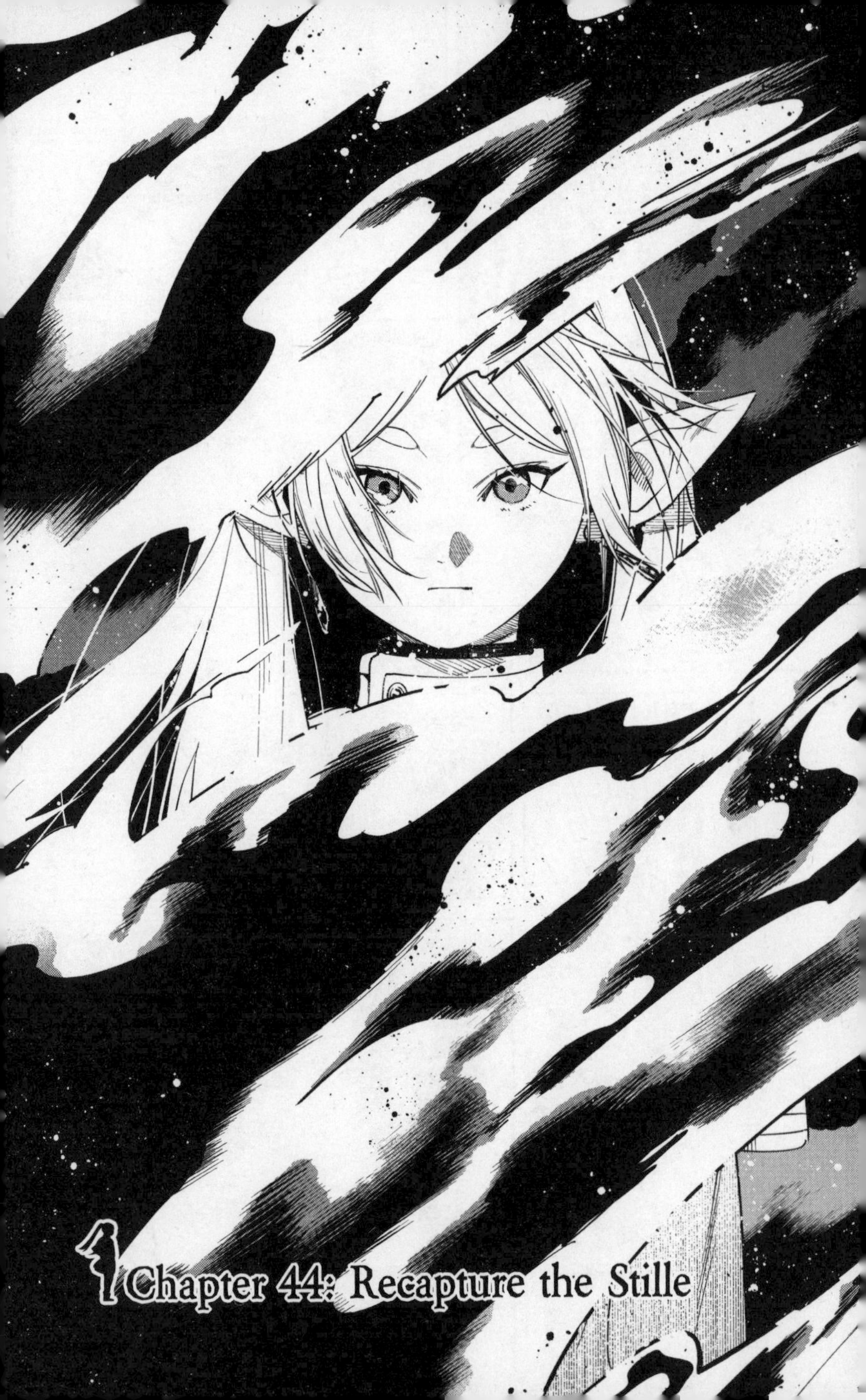
Chapter 44: Recapture the Stille

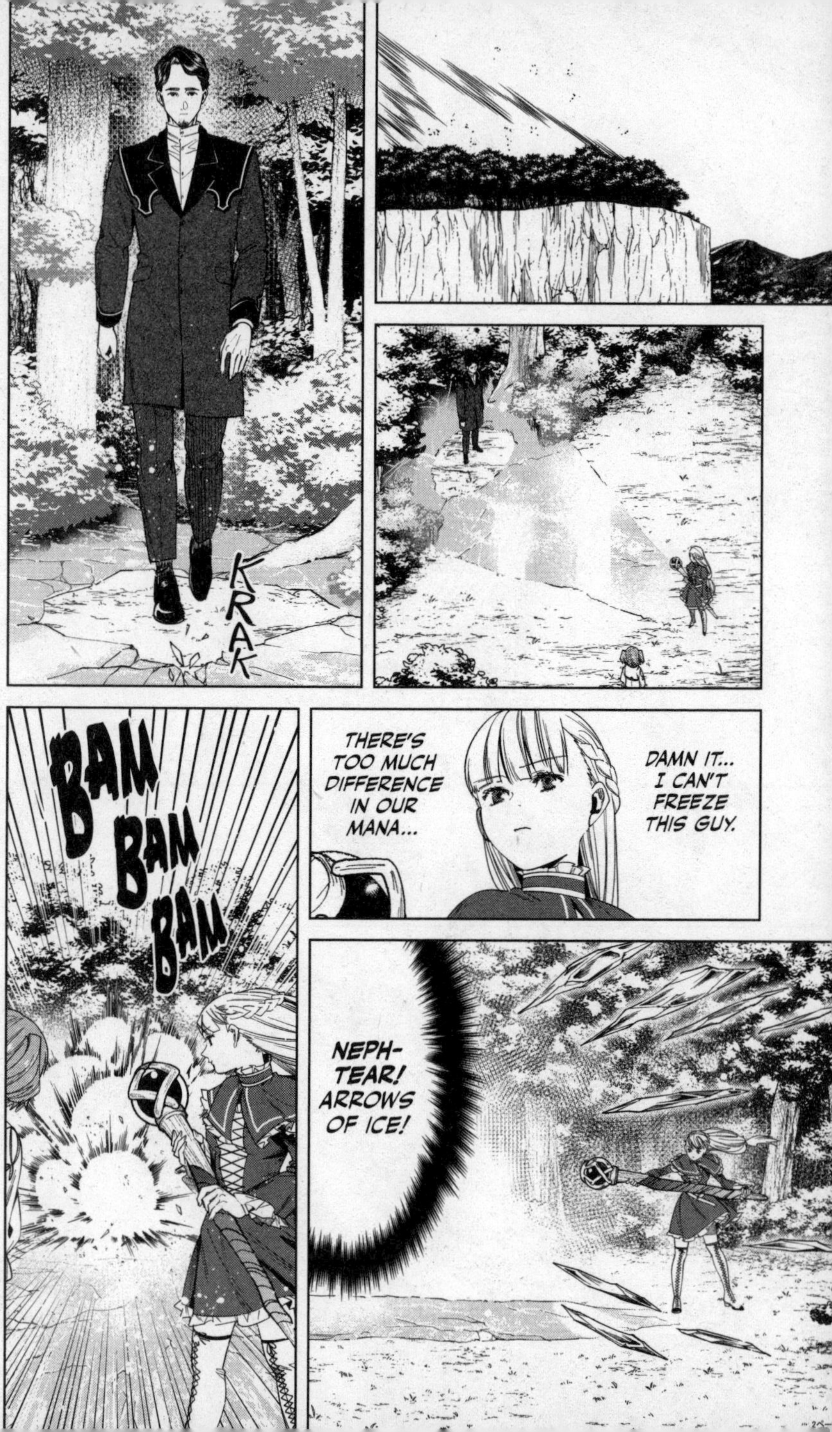
KRAK
DAMN IT... I CAN'T FREEZE THIS GUY.
THERE'S TOO MUCH DIFFERENCE IN OUR MANA...
NEPH-TEAR! ARROWS OF ICE!
BAM BAM BAM

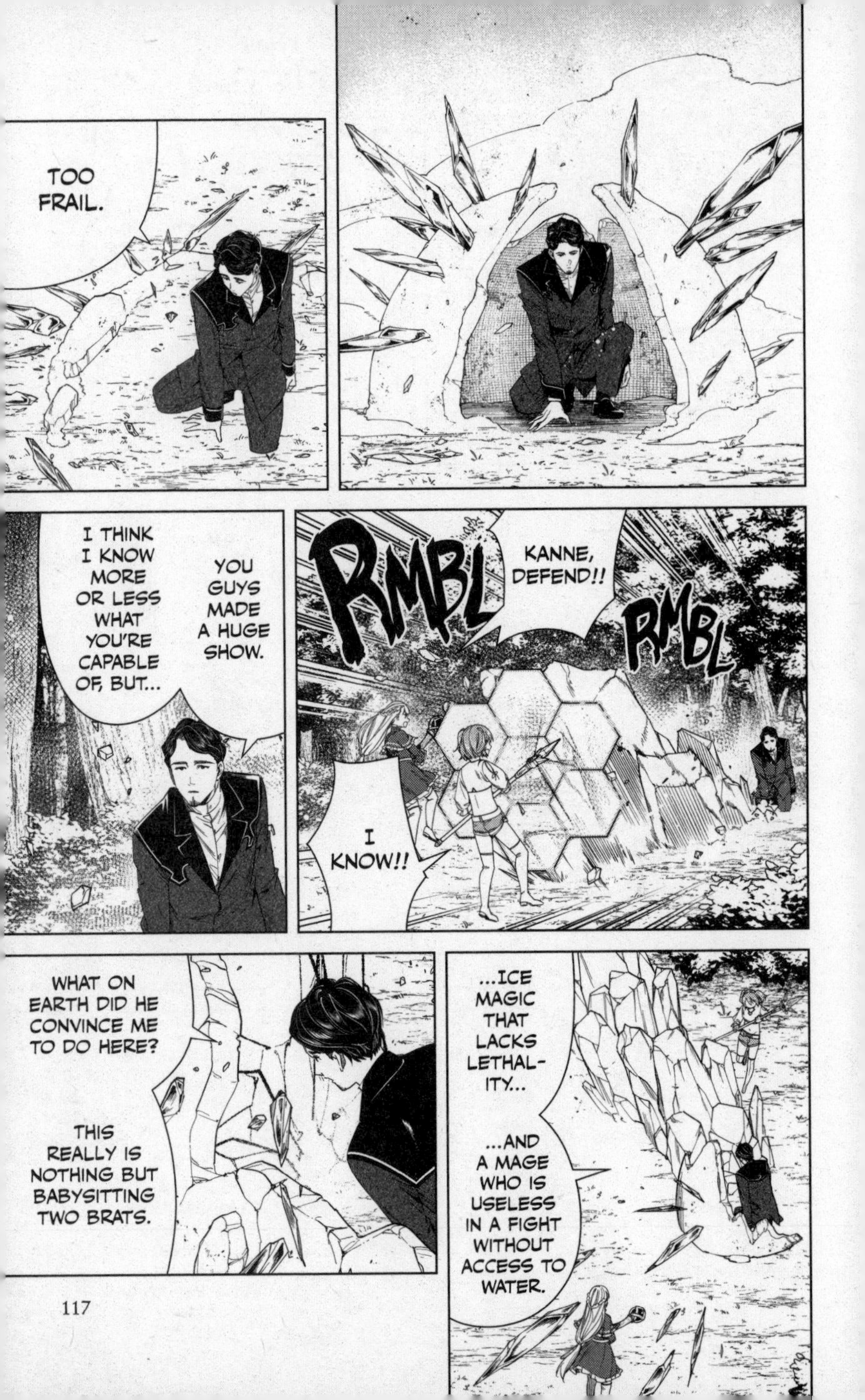
TOO FRAIL.
KANNE, DEFEND!!
RMBL
RMBL
I KNOW!!
YOU GUYS MADE A HUGE SHOW.
I THINK I KNOW MORE OR LESS WHAT YOU'RE CAPABLE OF, BUT...
...ICE MAGIC THAT LACKS LETHAL-ITY...
...AND A MAGE WHO IS USELESS IN A FIGHT WITHOUT ACCESS TO WATER.
WHAT ON EARTH DID HE CONVINCE ME TO DO HERE?
THIS REALLY IS NOTHING BUT BABYSITTING TWO BRATS.

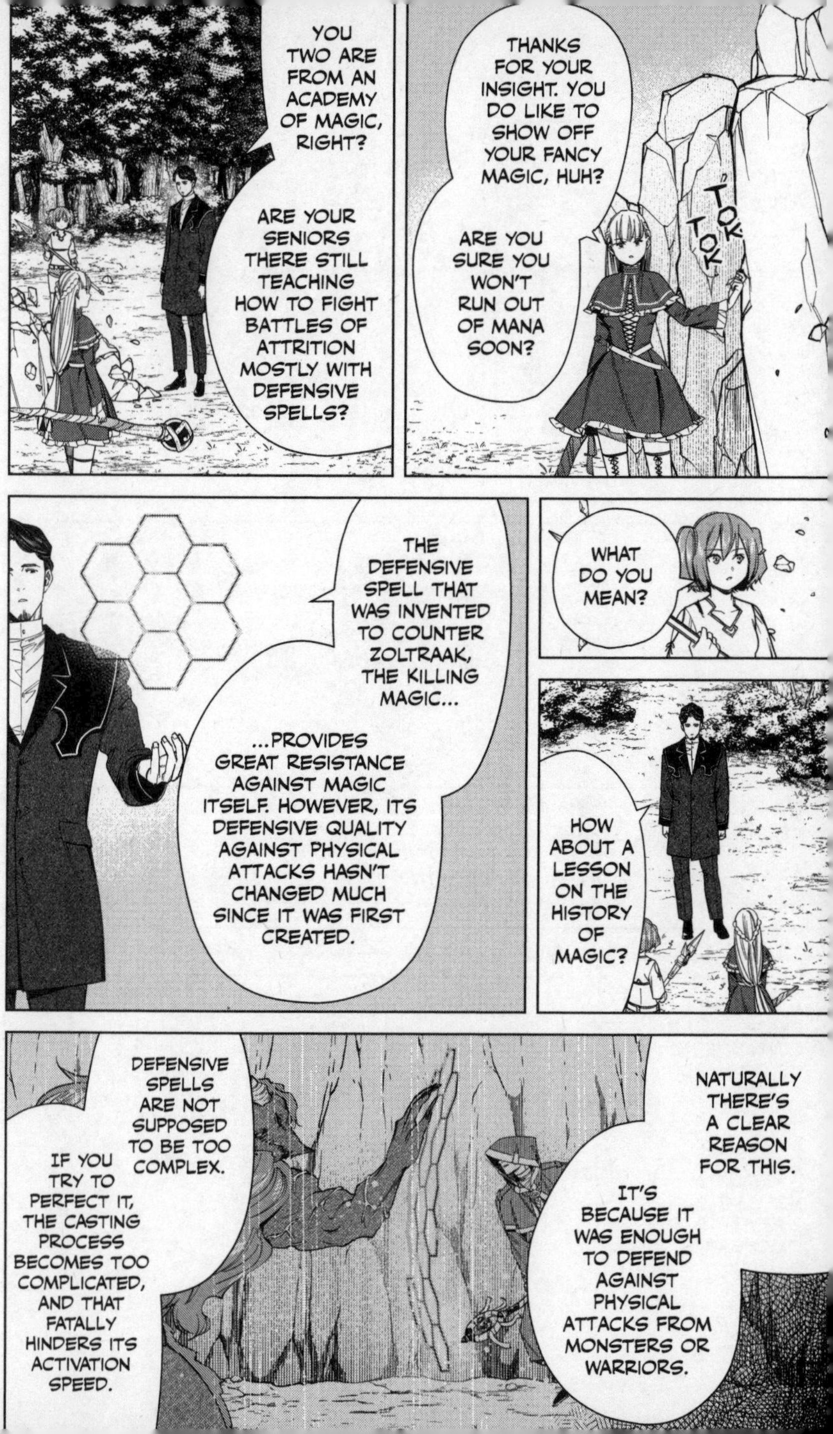
THANKS FOR YOUR INSIGHT. YOU DO LIKE TO SHOW OFF YOUR FANCY MAGIC, HUH?
ARE YOU SURE YOU WON'T RUN OUT OF MANA SOON?
TOK TOK
YOU TWO ARE FROM AN ACADEMY OF MAGIC, RIGHT?
ARE YOUR SENIORS THERE STILL TEACHING HOW TO FIGHT BATTLES OF ATTRITION MOSTLY WITH DEFENSIVE SPELLS?
WHAT DO YOU MEAN?
HOW ABOUT A LESSON ON THE HISTORY OF MAGIC?
THE DEFENSIVE SPELL THAT WAS INVENTED TO COUNTER ZOLTRAAK, THE KILLING MAGIC...
...PROVIDES GREAT RESISTANCE AGAINST MAGIC ITSELF. HOWEVER, ITS DEFENSIVE QUALITY AGAINST PHYSICAL ATTACKS HASN'T CHANGED MUCH SINCE IT WAS FIRST CREATED.
NATURALLY THERE'S A CLEAR REASON FOR THIS.
IT'S BECAUSE IT WAS ENOUGH TO DEFEND AGAINST PHYSICAL ATTACKS FROM MONSTERS OR WARRIORS.
DEFENSIVE SPELLS ARE NOT SUPPOSED TO BE TOO COMPLEX.
IF YOU TRY TO PERFECT IT, THE CASTING PROCESS BECOMES TOO COMPLICATED, AND THAT FATALLY HINDERS ITS ACTIVATION SPEED.

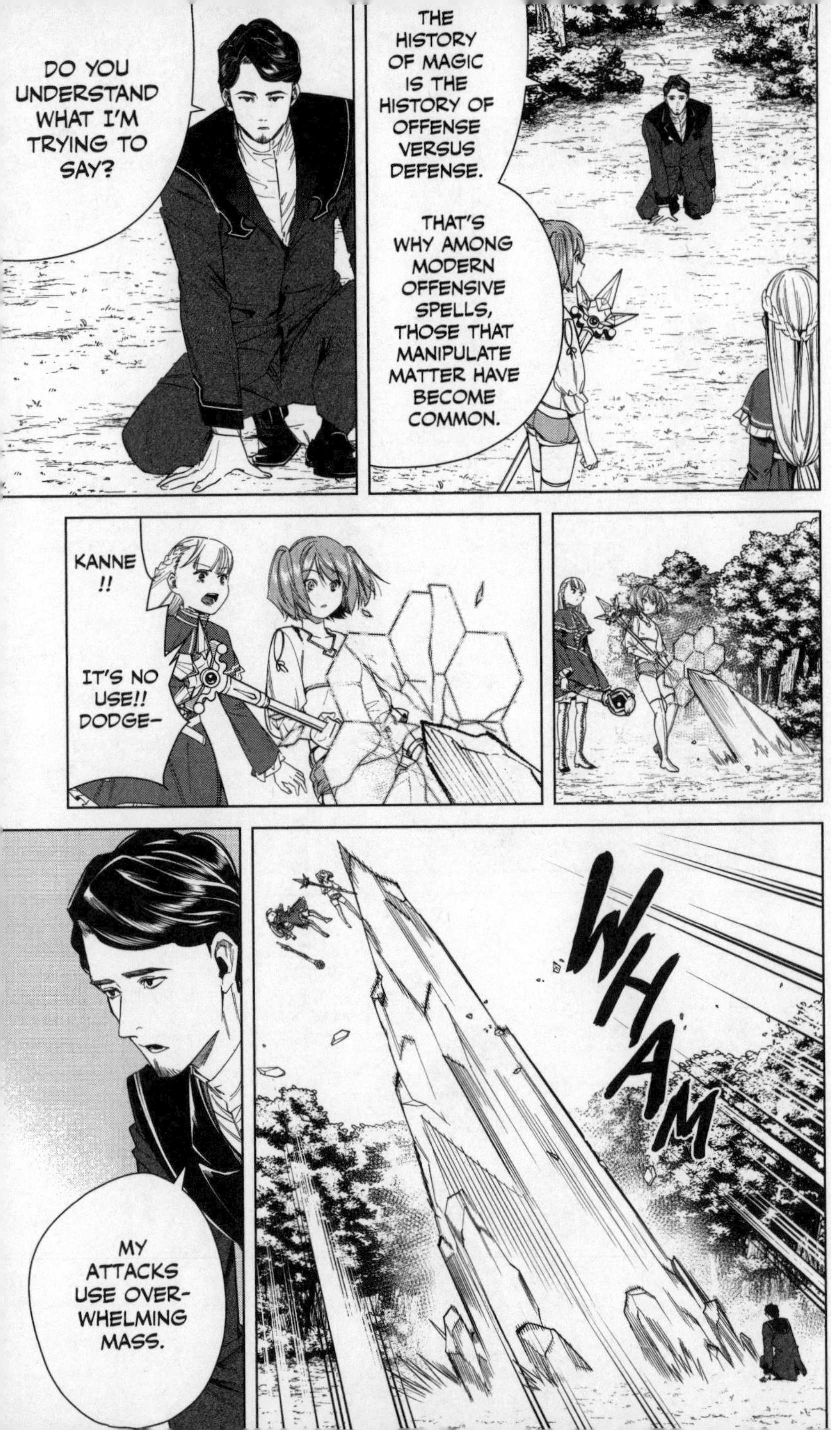
THE HISTORY OF MAGIC IS THE HISTORY OF OFFENSE VERSUS DEFENSE.
THAT'S WHY AMONG MODERN OFFENSIVE SPELLS, THOSE THAT MANIPULATE MATTER HAVE BECOME COMMON.
DO YOU UNDERSTAND WHAT I'M TRYING TO SAY?
KANNE !!
IT'S NO USE!! DODGE-
WHAM
MY ATTACKS USE OVER-WHELMING MASS.

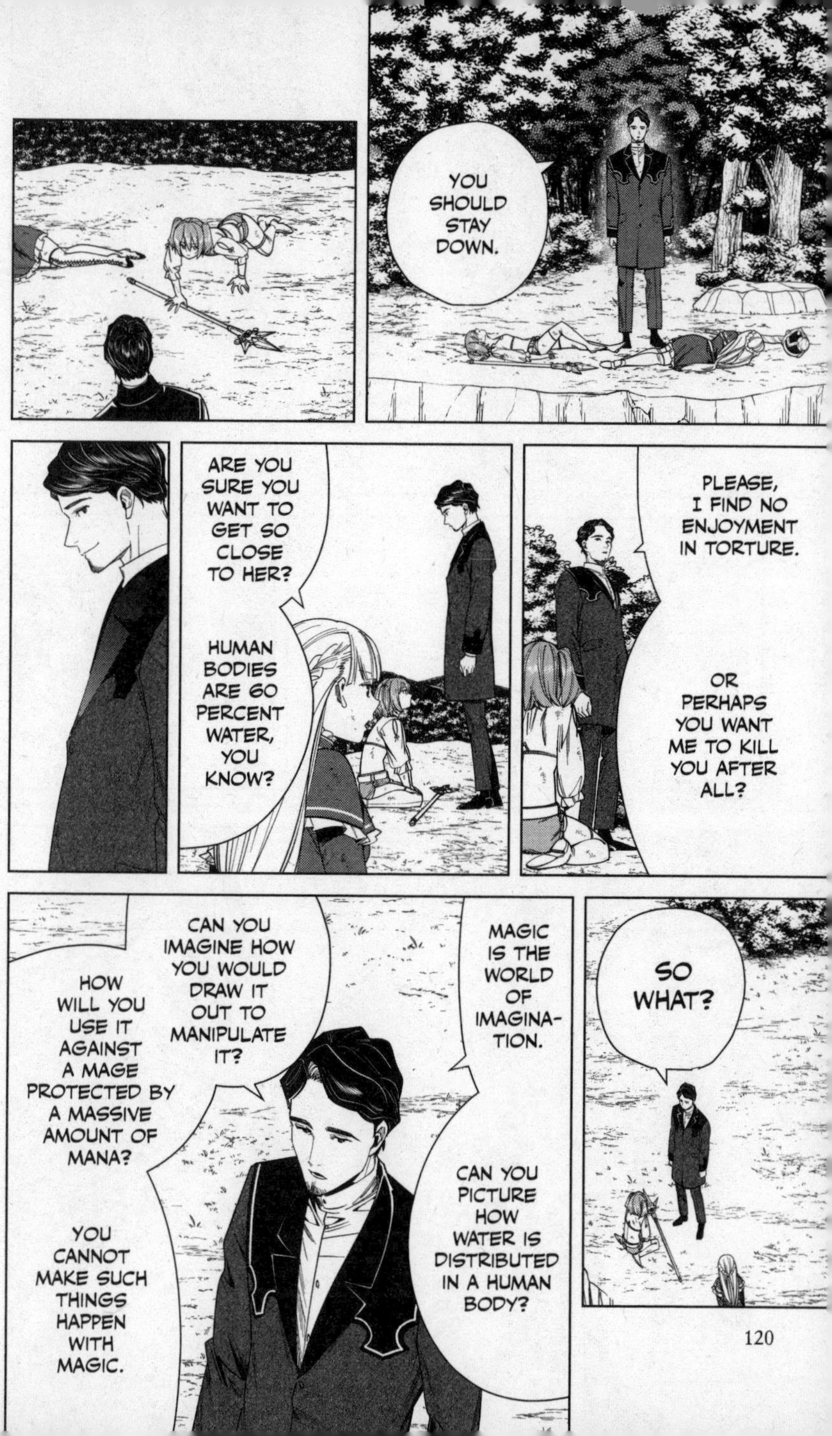
YOU SHOULD STAY DOWN.
PLEASE, I FIND NO ENJOYMENT IN TORTURE.
OR PERHAPS YOU WANT ME TO KILL YOU AFTER ALL?
ARE YOU SURE YOU WANT TO GET SO CLOSE TO HER?
HUMAN BODIES ARE 60 PERCENT WATER, YOU KNOW?
SO WHAT?
MAGIC IS THE WORLD OF IMAGINA-TION.
CAN YOU PICTURE HOW WATER IS DISTRIBUTED IN A HUMAN BODY?
CAN YOU IMAGINE HOW YOU WOULD DRAW IT OUT TO MANIPULATE IT?
HOW WILL YOU USE IT AGAINST A MAGE PROTECTED BY A MASSIVE AMOUNT OF MANA?
YOU CANNOT MAKE SUCH THINGS HAPPEN WITH MAGIC.

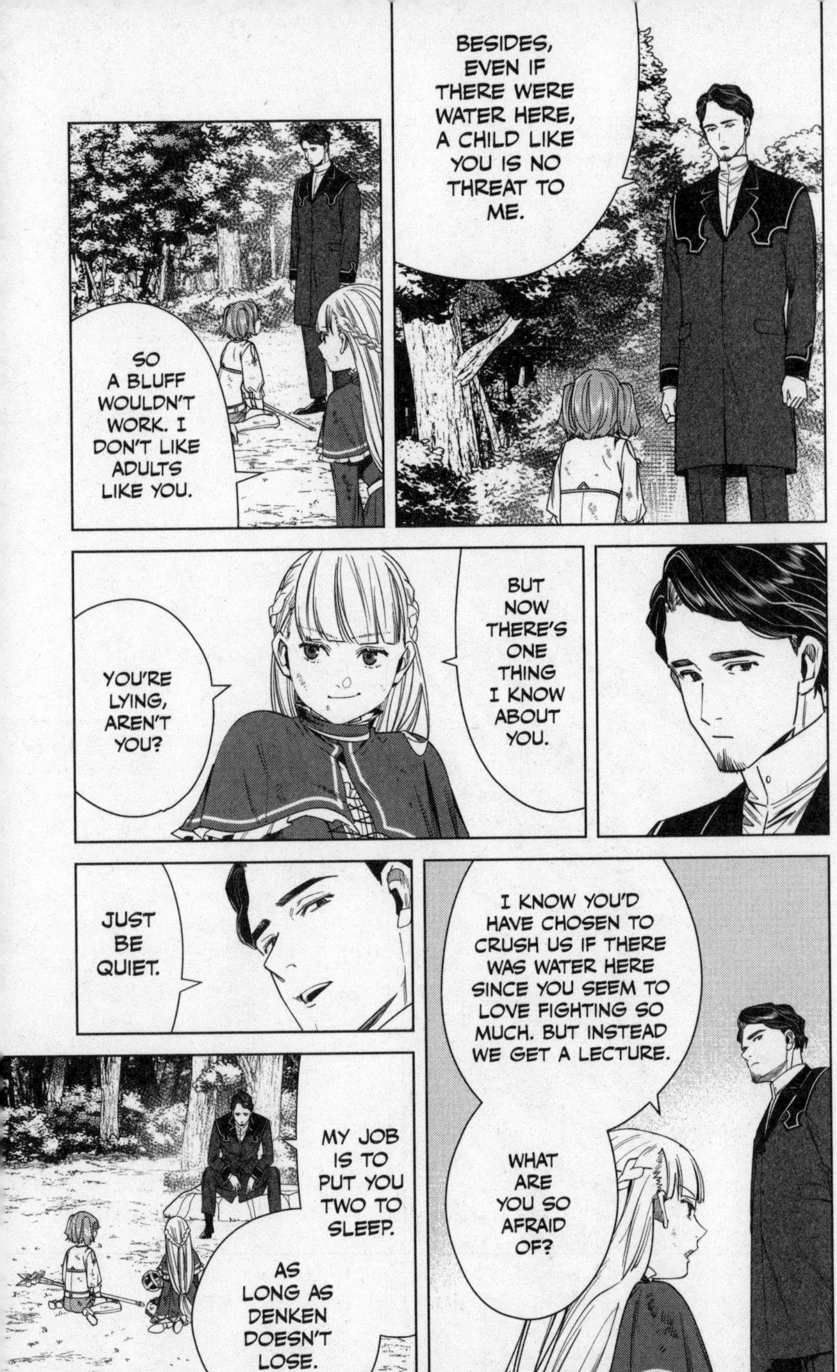
BESIDES, EVEN IF THERE WERE WATER HERE, A CHILD LIKE YOU IS NO THREAT TO ME.
SO A BLUFF WOULDN'T WORK. I DON'T LIKE ADULTS LIKE YOU.
BUT NOW THERE'S ONE THING I KNOW ABOUT YOU.
YOU'RE LYING, AREN'T YOU?
I KNOW YOU'D HAVE CHOSEN TO CRUSH US IF THERE WAS WATER HERE SINCE YOU SEEM TO LOVE FIGHTING SO MUCH. BUT INSTEAD WE GET A LECTURE.
WHAT ARE YOU SO AFRAID OF?
JUST BE QUIET.
MY JOB IS TO PUT YOU TWO TO SLEEP.
AS LONG AS DENKEN DOESN'T LOSE.

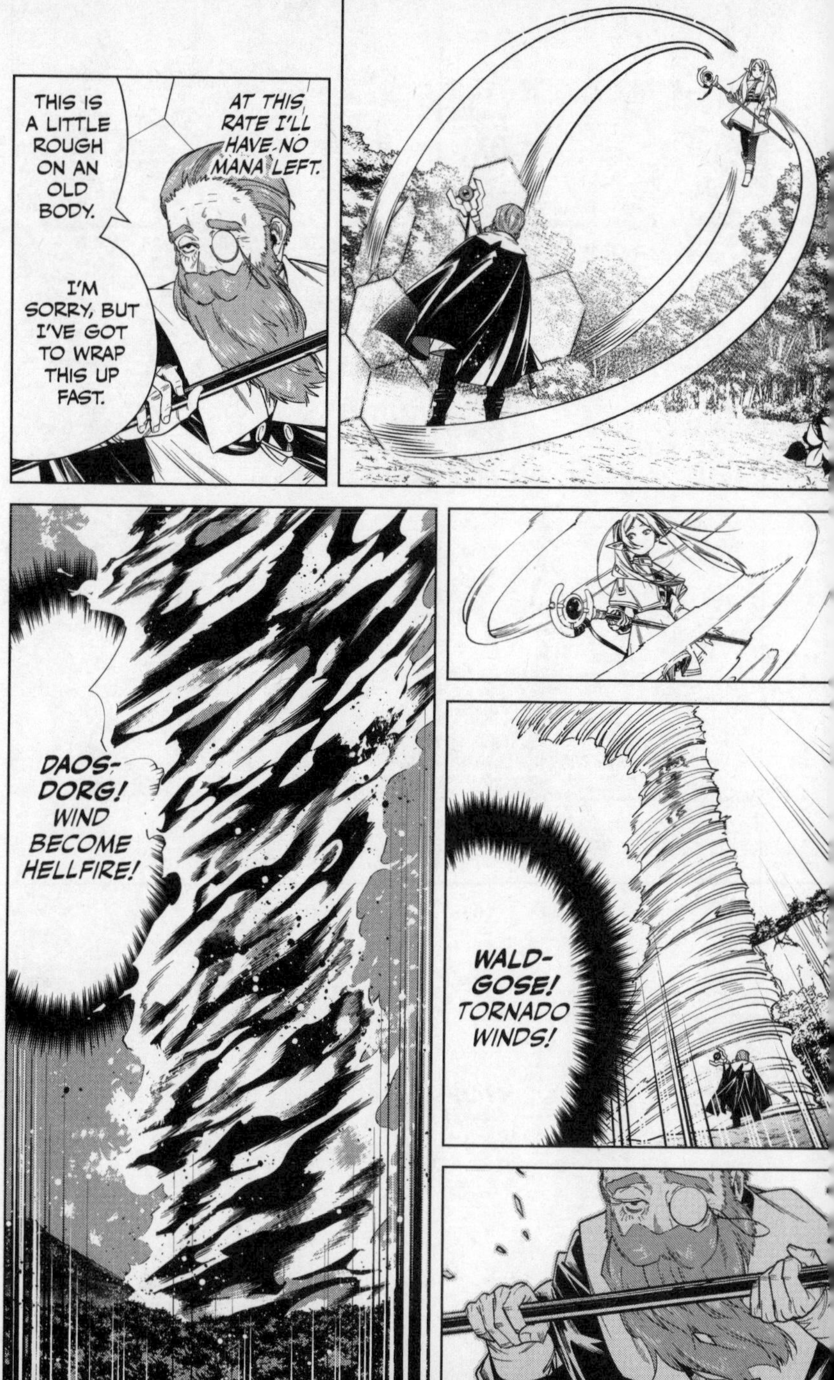
AT THIS RATE I'LL HAVE NO MANA LEFT.
THIS IS A LITTLE ROUGH ON AN OLD BODY.
I'M SORRY, BUT I'VE GOT TO WRAP THIS UP FAST.
WALD-GOSE! TORNADO WINDS!
DAOS-DORG! WIND BECOME HELLFIRE!

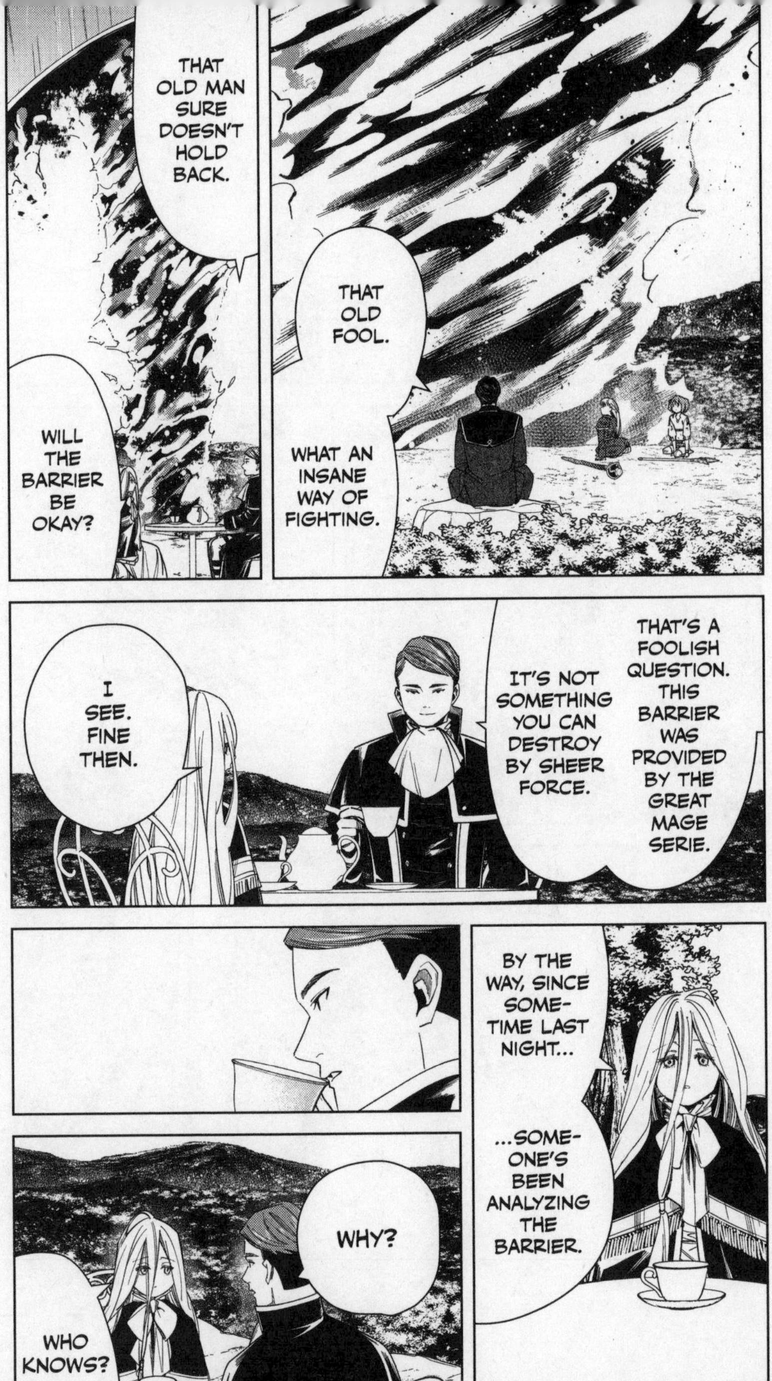
THAT OLD FOOL.
WHAT AN INSANE WAY OF FIGHTING.
THAT OLD MAN SURE DOESN'T HOLD BACK.
WILL THE BARRIER BE OKAY?
THAT'S A FOOLISH QUESTION. THIS BARRIER WAS PROVIDED BY THE GREAT MAGE SERIE.
IT'S NOT SOMETHING YOU CAN DESTROY BY SHEER FORCE.
I SEE. FINE THEN.
BY THE WAY, SINCE SOME-TIME LAST NIGHT...
...SOME-ONE'S BEEN ANALYZING THE BARRIER.
WHY?
WHO KNOWS?

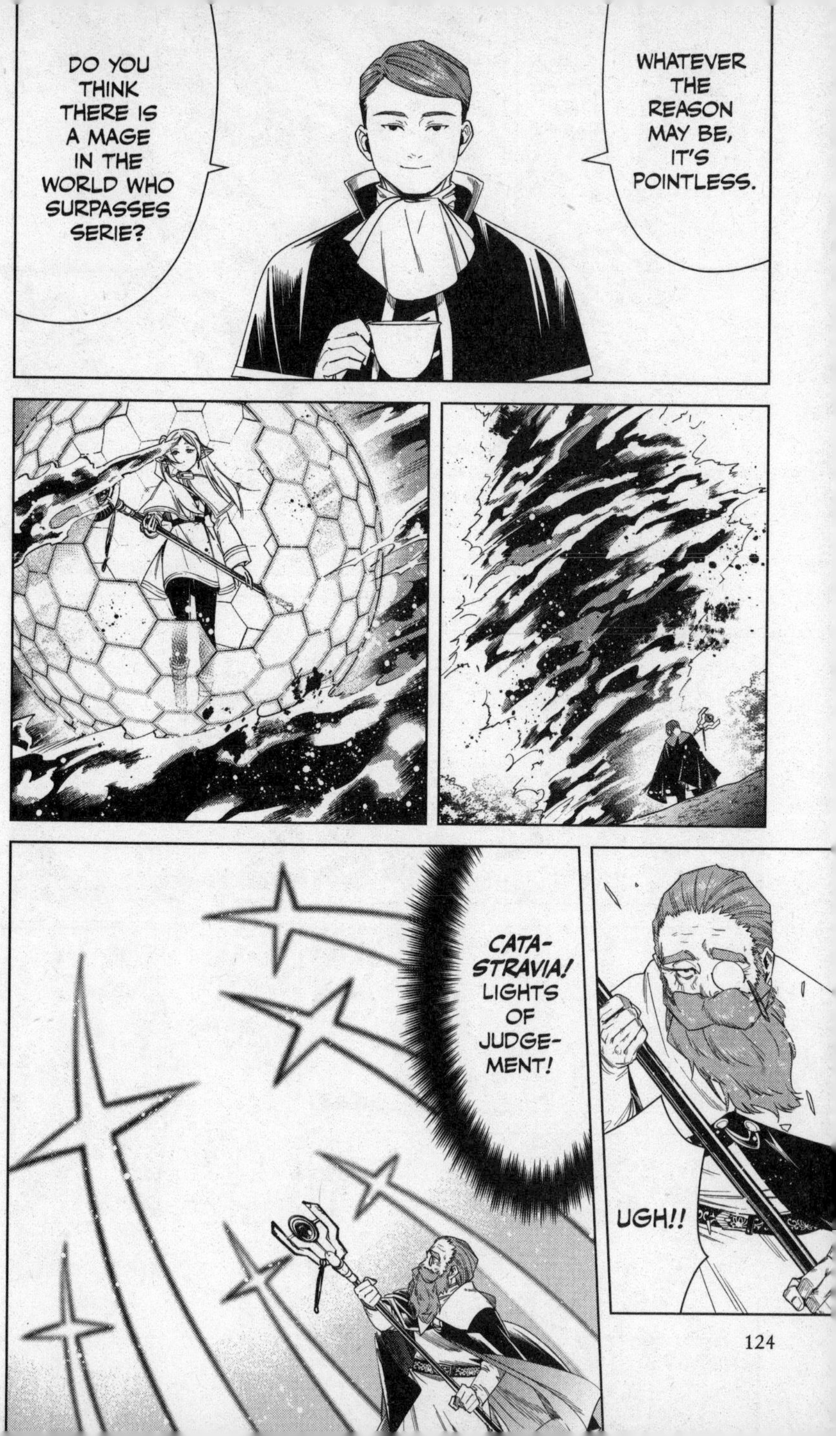
WHATEVER THE REASON MAY BE, IT'S POINTLESS.
DO YOU THINK THERE IS A MAGE IN THE WORLD WHO SURPASSES SERIE?
UGH!!
CATA-STRAVIA! LIGHTS OF JUDGE-MENT!

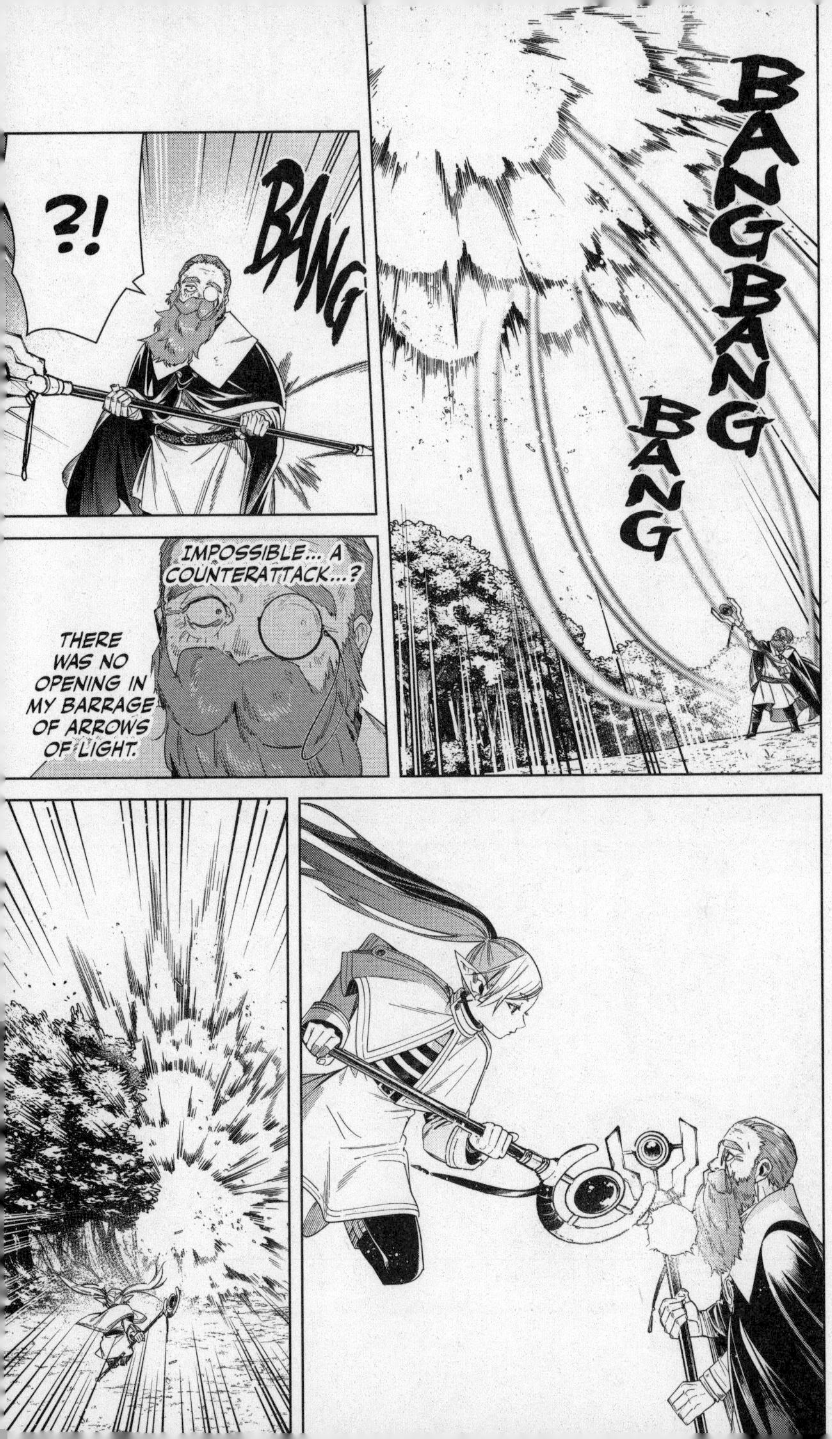
BANG
BANG
BANG
?!
BANG
IMPOSSIBLE... A COUNTERATTACK...?
THERE WAS NO OPENING IN MY BARRAGE OF ARROWS OF LIGHT.

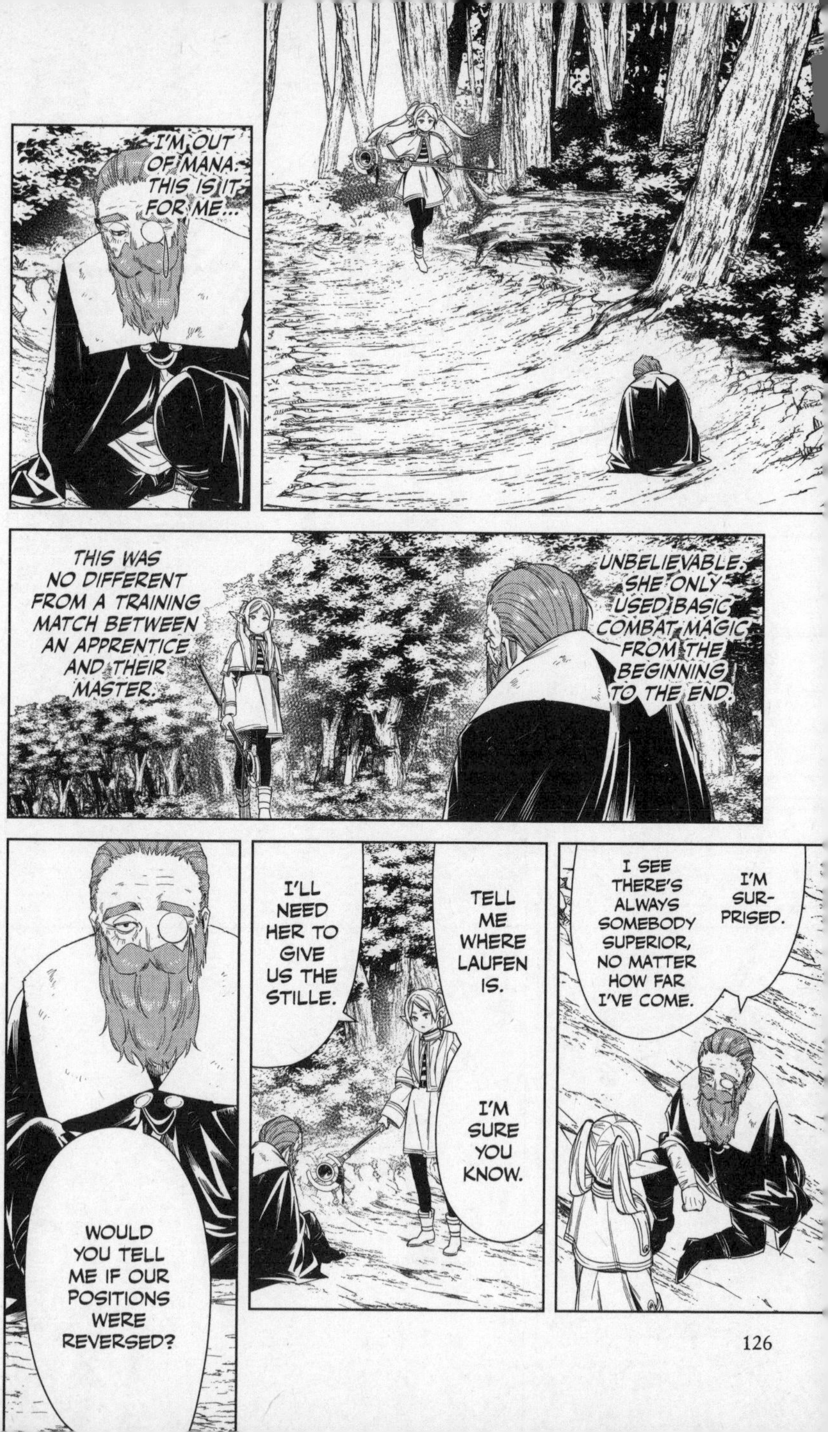
I'M OUT OF MANA. THIS IS IT FOR ME...
UNBELIEVABLE. SHE ONLY USED BASIC COMBAT MAGIC FROM THE BEGINNING TO THE END.
THIS WAS NO DIFFERENT FROM A TRAINING MATCH BETWEEN AN APPRENTICE AND THEIR MASTER.
I'M SUR-PRISED.
I SEE THERE'S ALWAYS SOMEBODY SUPERIOR, NO MATTER HOW FAR I'VE COME.
TELL ME WHERE LAUFEN IS.
I'M SURE YOU KNOW.
I'LL NEED HER TO GIVE US THE STILLE.
WOULD YOU TELL ME IF OUR POSITIONS WERE REVERSED?

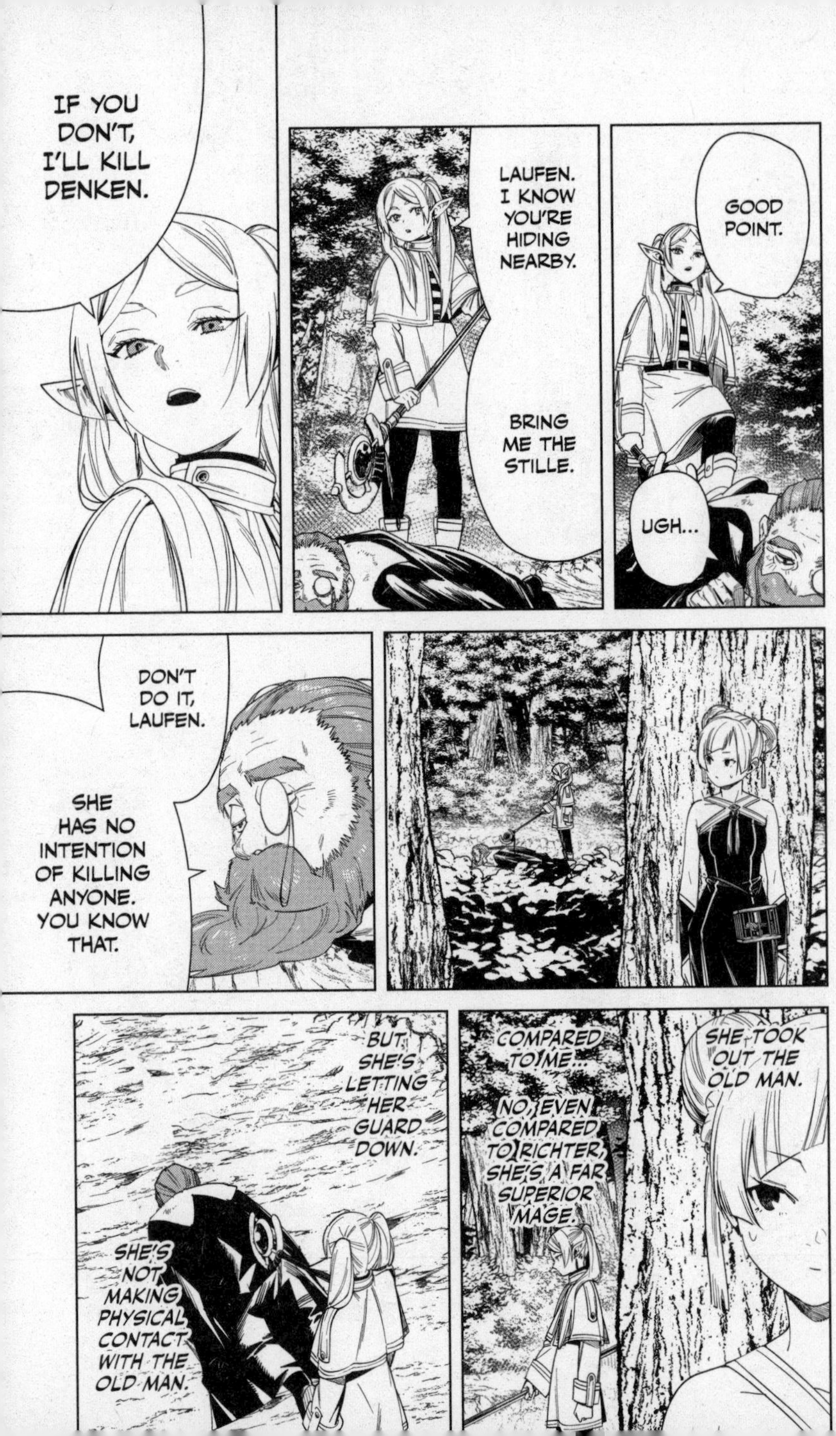
GOOD POINT.
UGH...
LAUFEN. I KNOW YOU'RE HIDING NEARBY.
BRING ME THE STILLE.
IF YOU DON'T, I'LL KILL DENKEN.
DON'T DO IT, LAUFEN.
SHE HAS NO INTENTION OF KILLING ANYONE. YOU KNOW THAT.
SHE TOOK OUT THE OLD MAN.
COMPARED TO ME...
NO, EVEN COMPARED TO RICHTER, SHE'S A FAR SUPERIOR MAGE.
BUT SHE'S LETTING HER GUARD DOWN.
SHE'S NOT MAKING PHYSICAL CONTACT WITH THE OLD MAN.

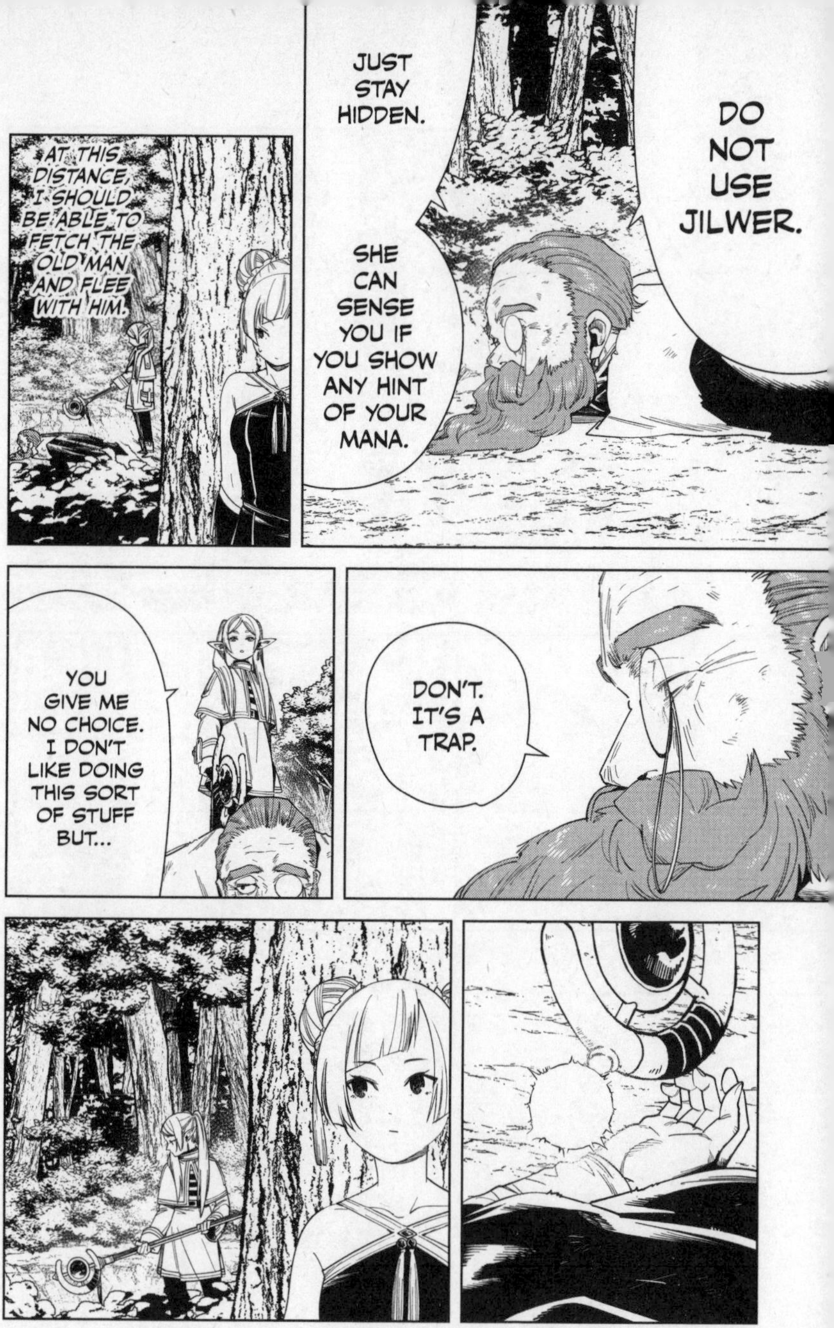
DO NOT USE JILWER.
JUST STAY HIDDEN.
SHE CAN SENSE YOU IF YOU SHOW ANY HINT OF YOUR MANA.
AT THIS DISTANCE, I SHOULD BE ABLE TO FETCH THE OLD MAN AND FLEE WITH HIM.
DON'T. IT'S A TRAP.
YOU GIVE ME NO CHOICE. I DON'T LIKE DOING THIS SORT OF STUFF BUT...

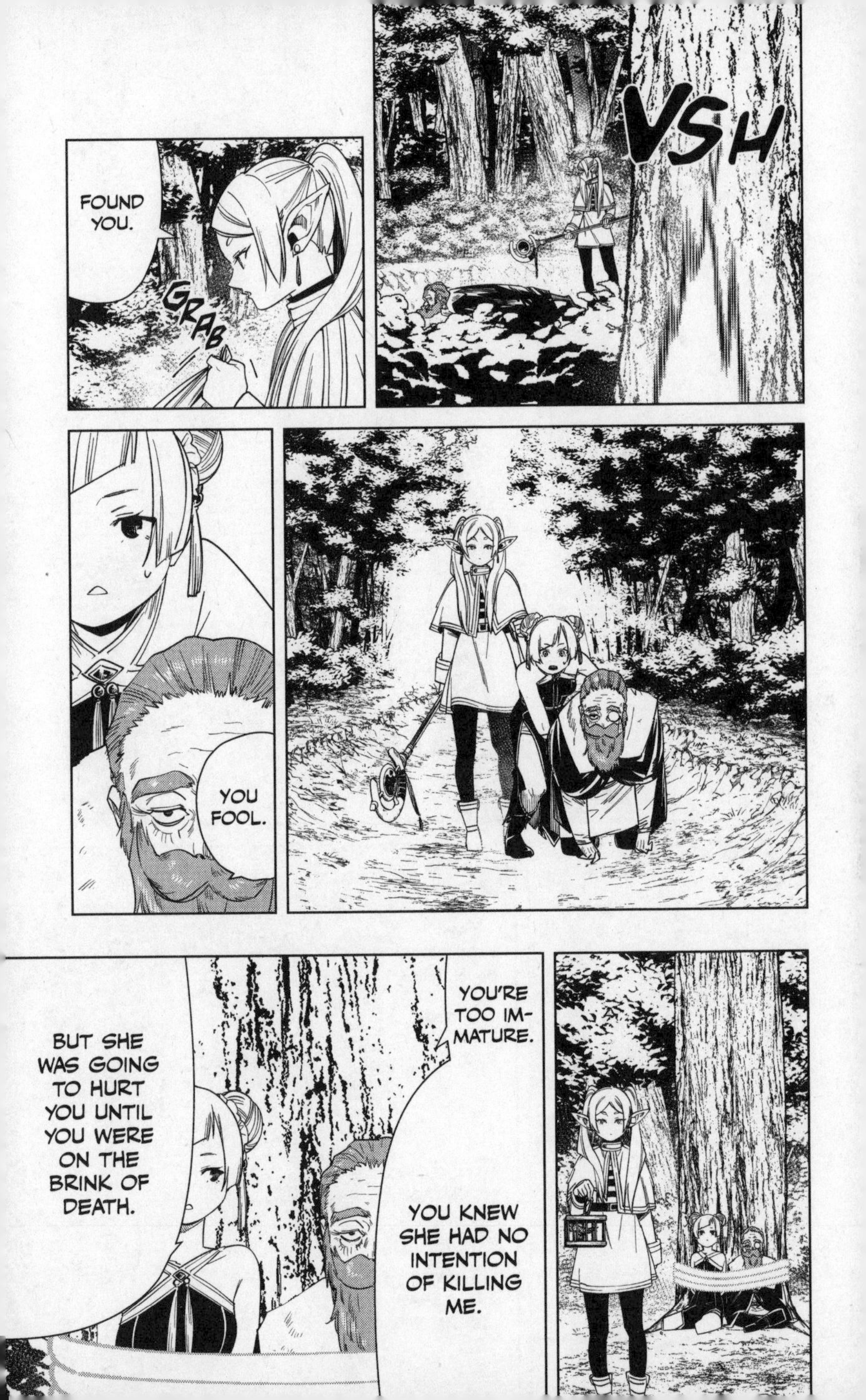
VSH
FOUND YOU.
GRAB
YOU FOOL.
YOU'RE TOO IM-MATURE.
YOU KNEW SHE HAD NO INTENTION OF KILLING ME.
BUT SHE WAS GOING TO HURT YOU UNTIL YOU WERE ON THE BRINK OF DEATH.

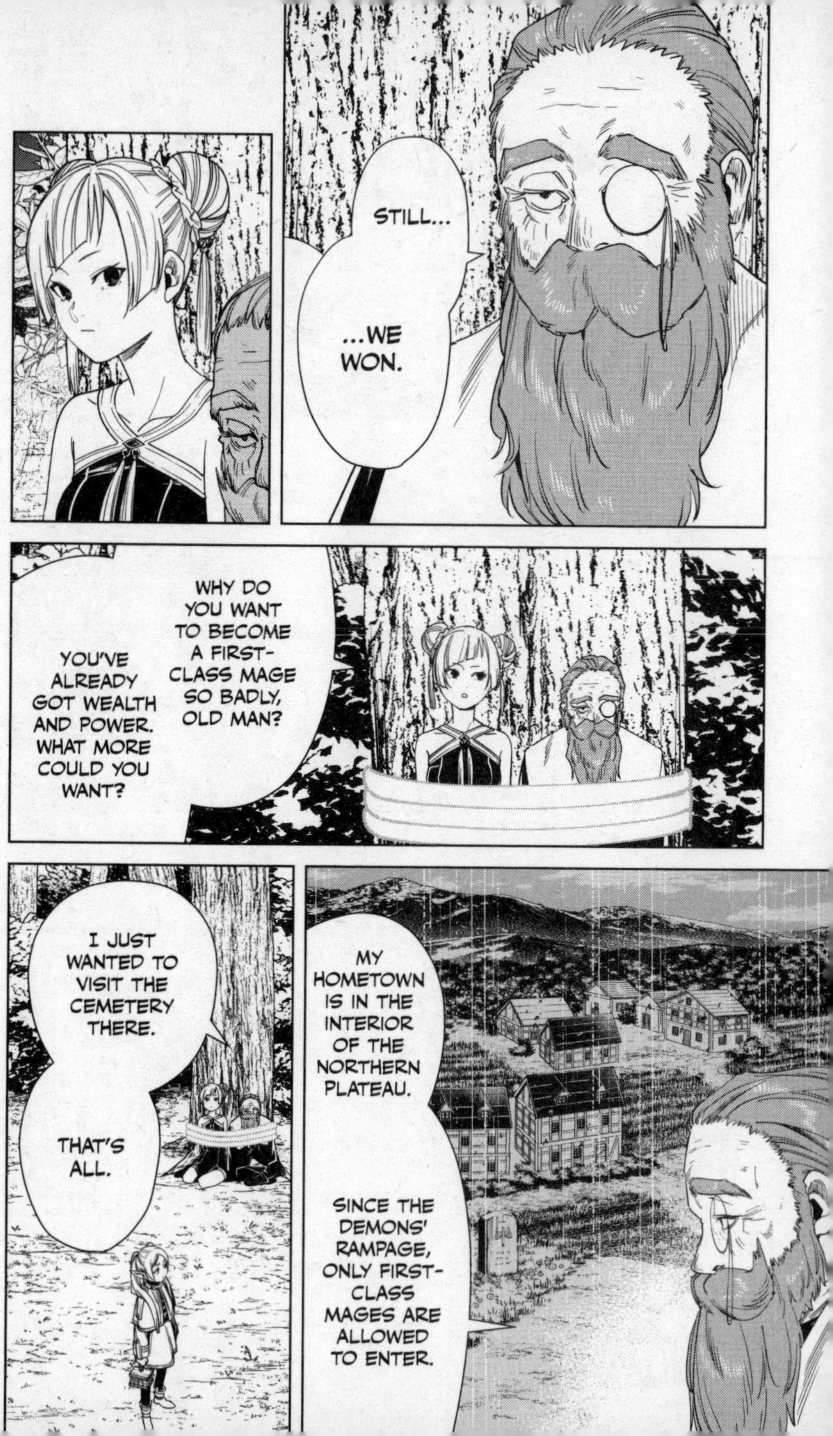
STILL...
...WE WON.
WHY DO YOU WANT TO BECOME A FIRST-CLASS MAGE SO BADLY, OLD MAN?
YOU'VE ALREADY GOT WEALTH AND POWER. WHAT MORE COULD YOU WANT?
MY HOMETOWN IS IN THE INTERIOR OF THE NORTHERN PLATEAU.
SINCE THE DEMONS' RAMPAGE, ONLY FIRST-CLASS MAGES ARE ALLOWED TO ENTER.
I JUST WANTED TO VISIT THE CEMETERY THERE.
THAT'S ALL.

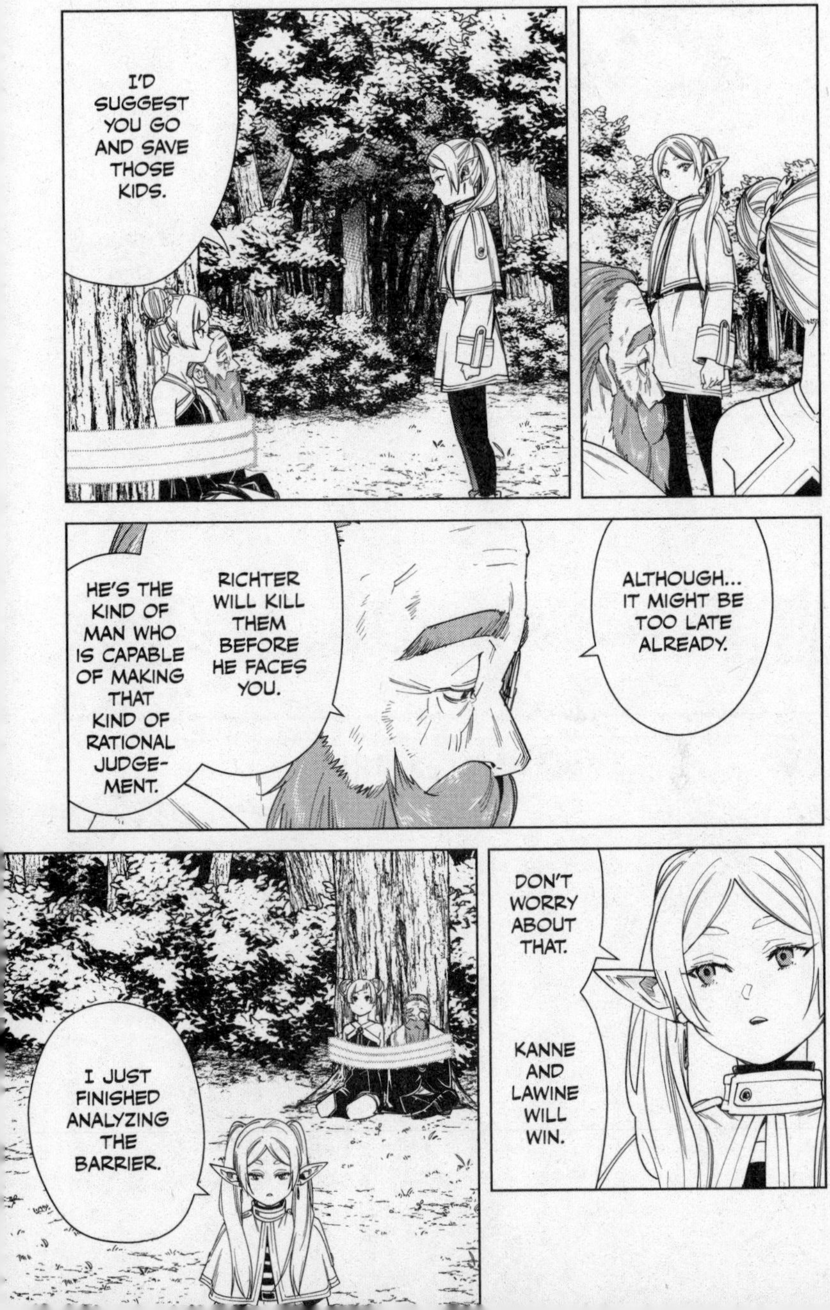
I'D SUGGEST YOU GO AND SAVE THOSE KIDS.
ALTHOUGH... IT MIGHT BE TOO LATE ALREADY.
RICHTER WILL KILL THEM BEFORE HE FACES YOU.
HE'S THE KIND OF MAN WHO IS CAPABLE OF MAKING THAT KIND OF RATIONAL JUDGE-MENT.
DON'T WORRY ABOUT THAT.
KANNE AND LAWINE WILL WIN.
I JUST FINISHED ANALYZING THE BARRIER.

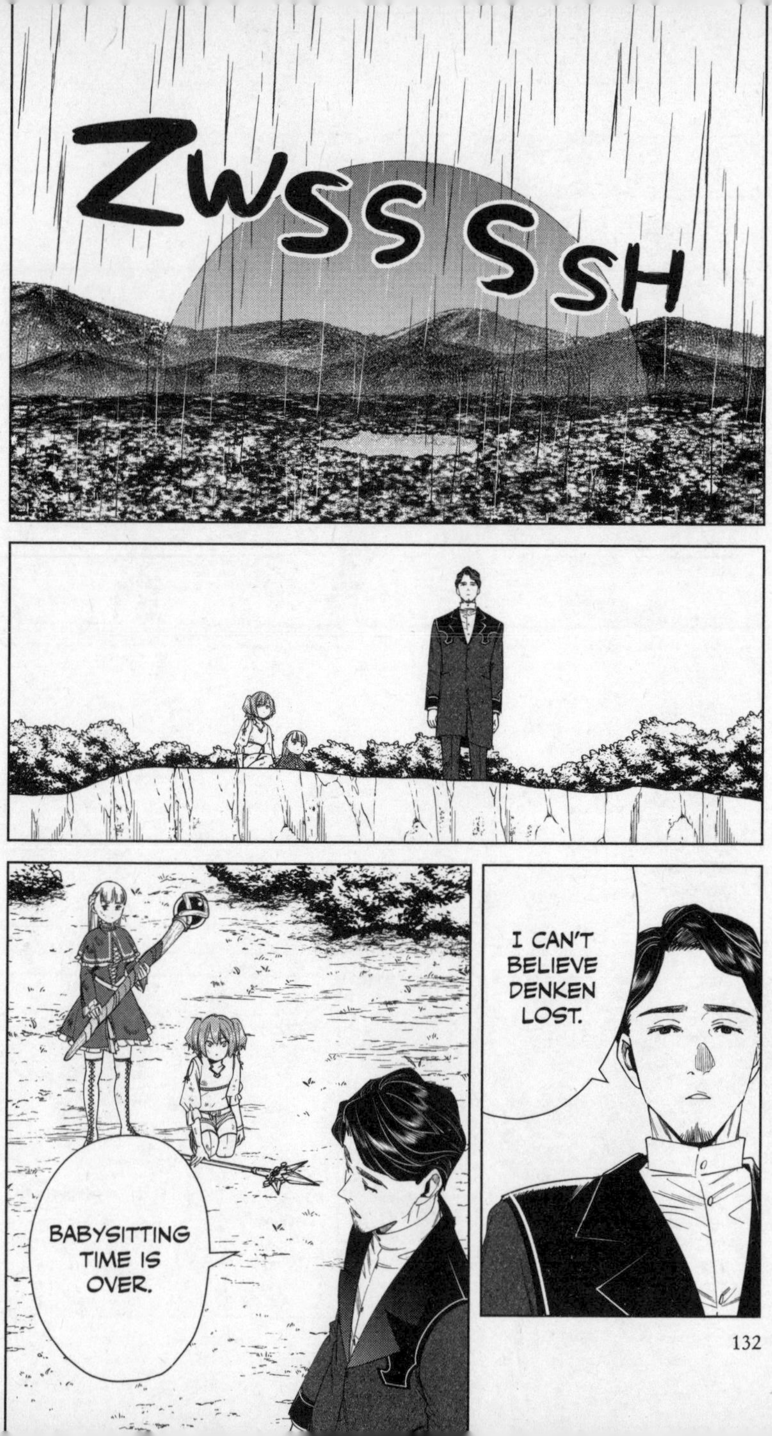
ZWSSSSH
I CAN'T BELIEVE DENKEN LOST.
BABYSITTING TIME IS OVER.

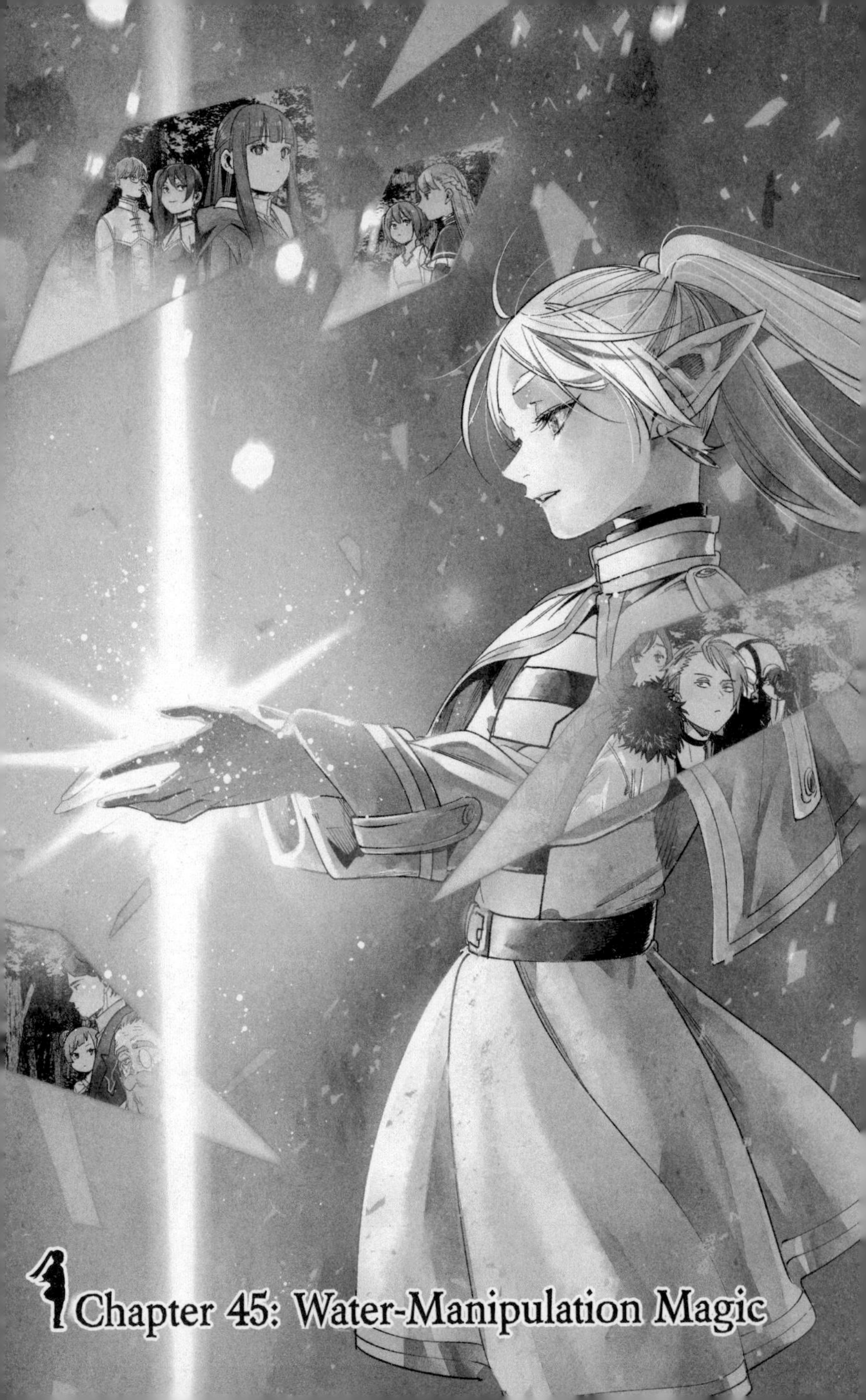

Chapter 45: Water-Manipulation Magic

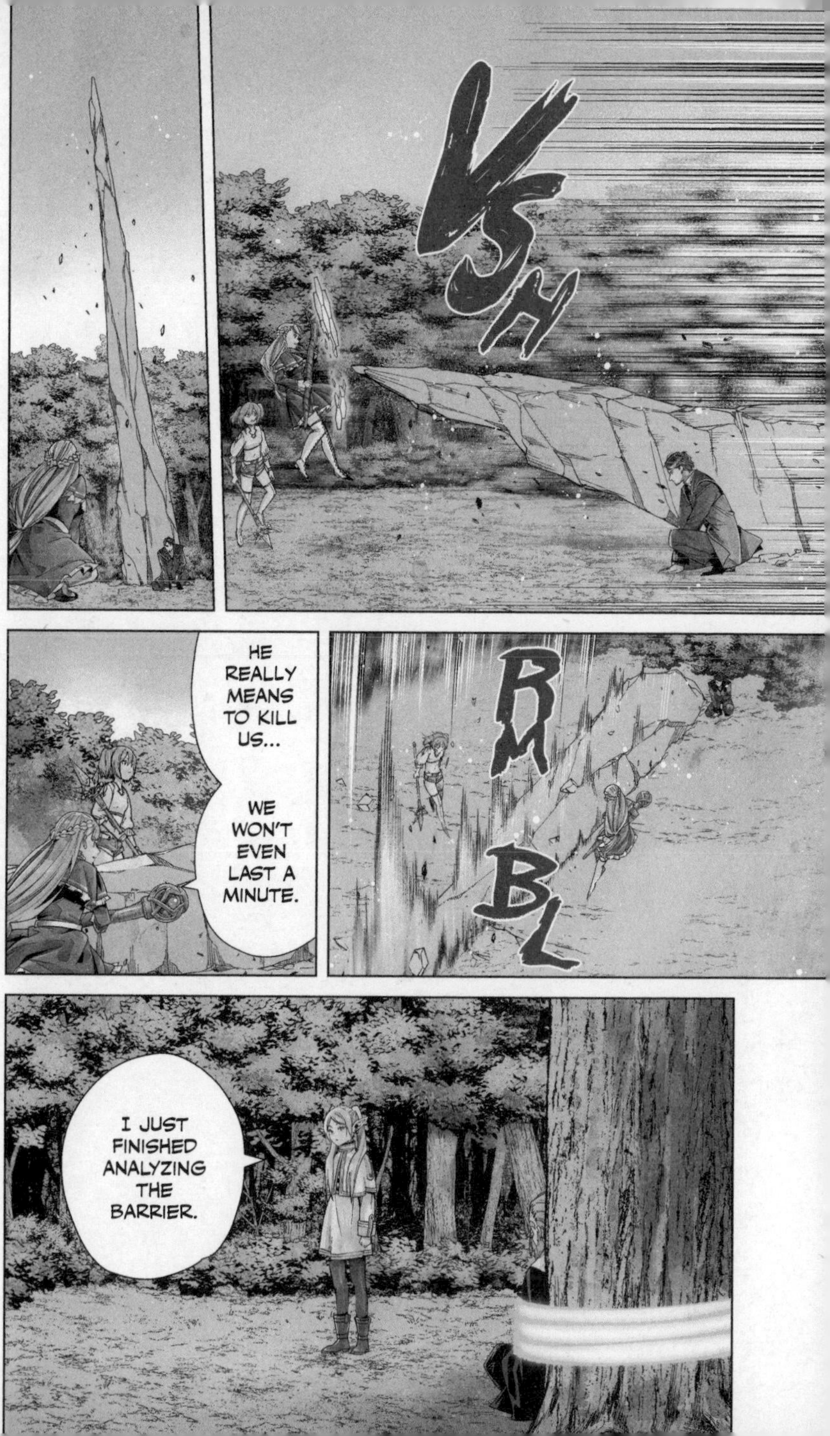
VSH
RMBL
HE REALLY MEANS TO KILL US... WE WON'T EVEN LAST A MINUTE.
I JUST FINISHED ANALYZING THE BARRIER.

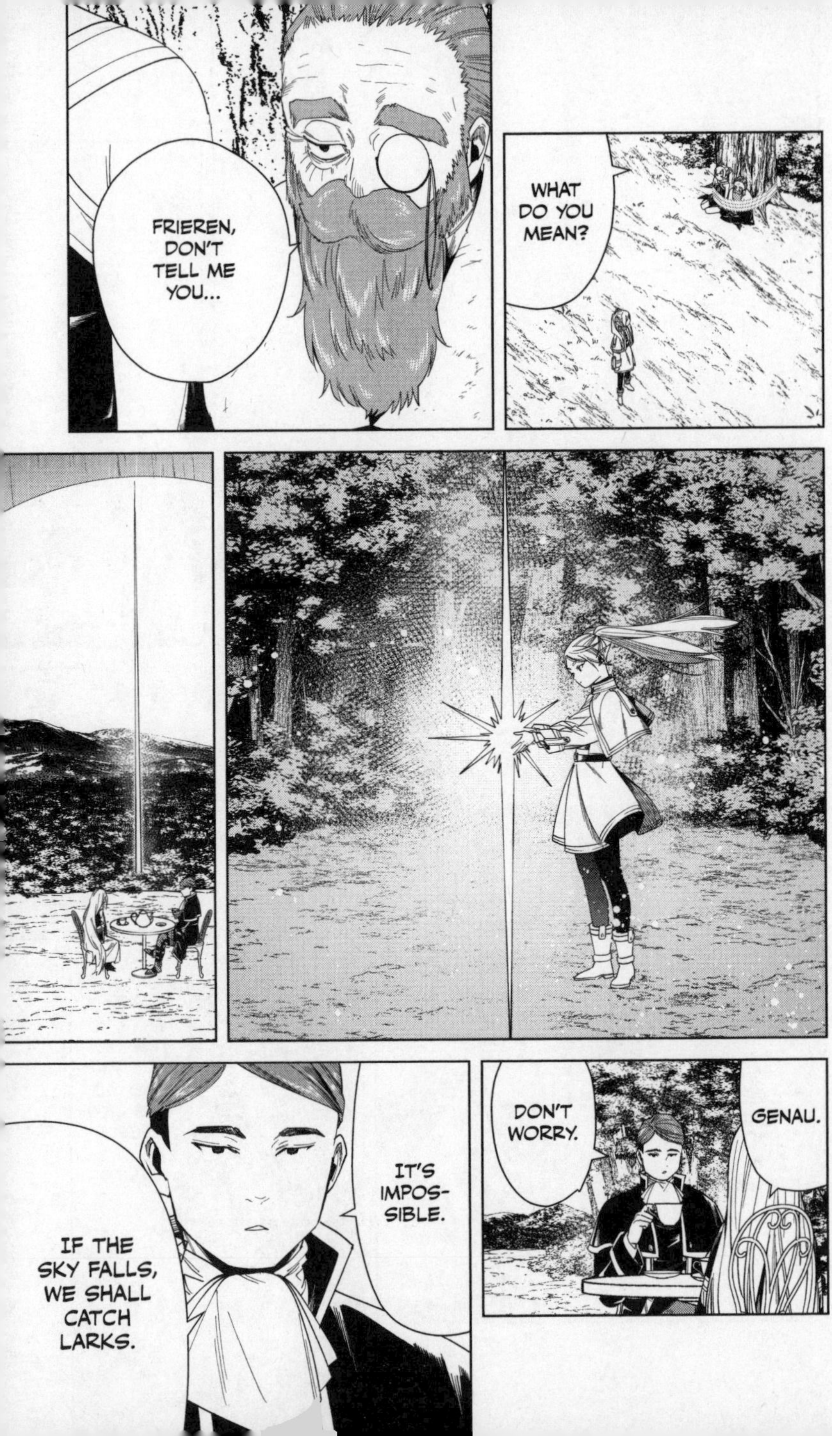
WHAT DO YOU MEAN?
FRIEREN, DON'T TELL ME YOU...
GENAU.
DON'T WORRY.
IT'S IMPOS-SIBLE.
IF THE SKY FALLS, WE SHALL CATCH LARKS.

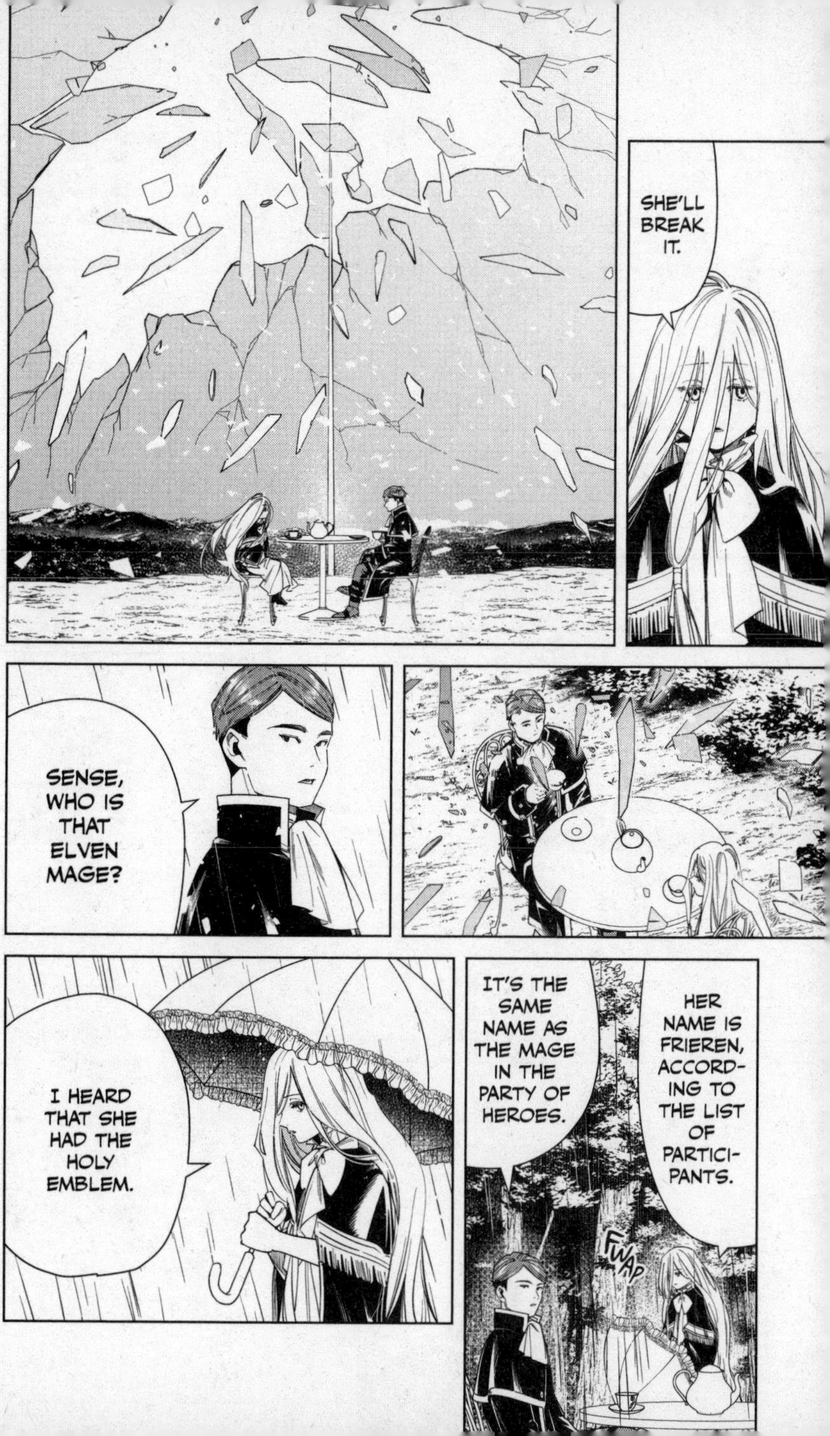
SHE'LL BREAK IT.
SENSE, WHO IS THAT ELVEN MAGE?
HER NAME IS FRIEREN, ACCORDING TO THE LIST OF PARTICIPANTS.
IT'S THE SAME NAME AS THE MAGE IN THE PARTY OF HEROES.
FWAP
I HEARD THAT SHE HAD THE HOLY EMBLEM.

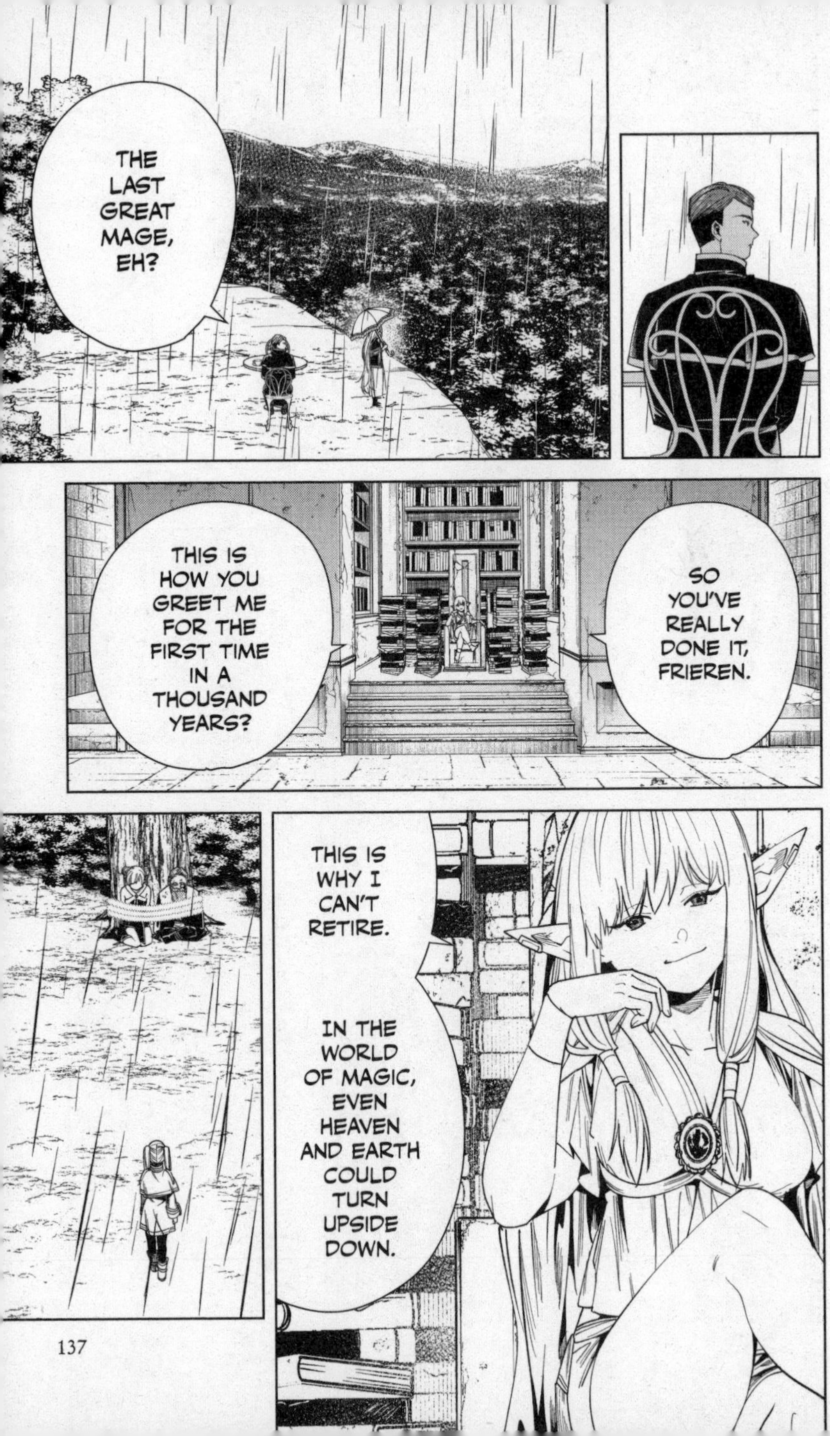
THE LAST GREAT MAGE, EH?
SO YOU'VE REALLY DONE IT, FRIEREN.
THIS IS HOW YOU GREET ME FOR THE FIRST TIME IN A THOUSAND YEARS?
THIS IS WHY I CAN'T RETIRE.
IN THE WORLD OF MAGIC, EVEN HEAVEN AND EARTH COULD TURN UPSIDE DOWN.

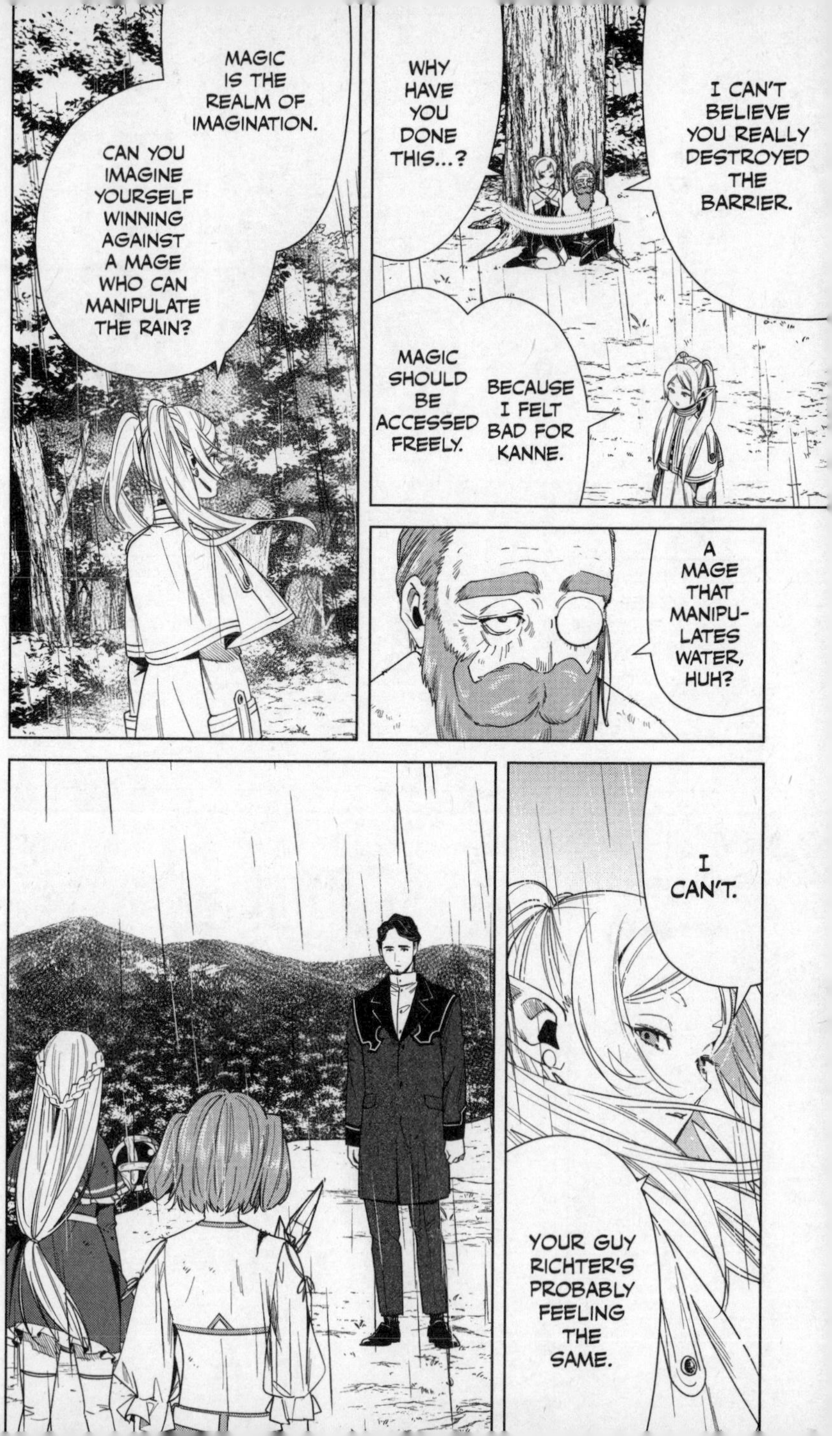
I CAN'T BELIEVE YOU REALLY DESTROYED THE BARRIER.
WHY HAVE YOU DONE THIS...?
BECAUSE I FELT BAD FOR KANNE.
MAGIC SHOULD BE ACCESSED FREELY.
A MAGE THAT MANIPU-LATES WATER, HUH?
MAGIC IS THE REALM OF IMAGINATION.
CAN YOU IMAGINE YOURSELF WINNING AGAINST A MAGE WHO CAN MANIPULATE THE RAIN?
I CAN'T.
YOUR GUY RICHTER'S PROBABLY FEELING THE SAME.

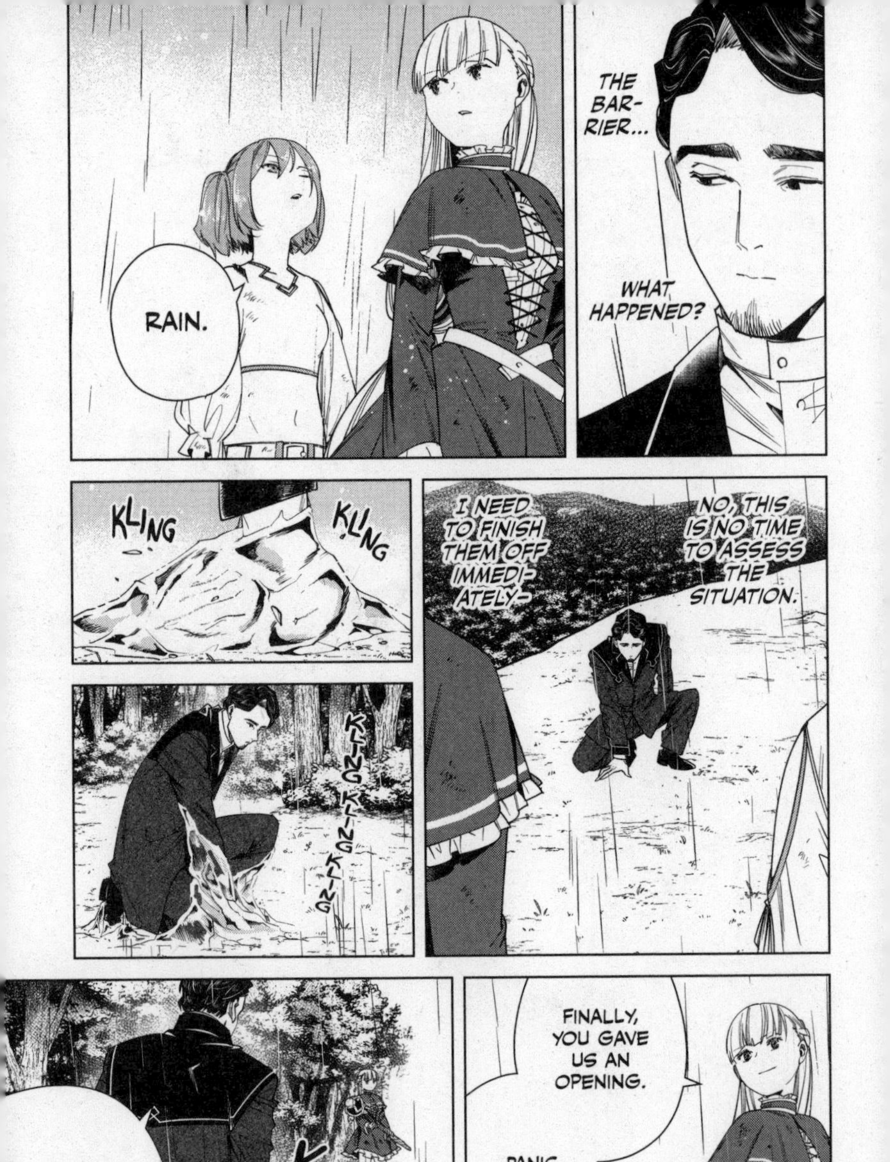
THE BARRIER...
WHAT HAPPENED?
RAIN.
NO, THIS IS NO TIME TO ASSESS THE SITUATION.
I NEED TO FINISH THEM OFF IMMEDIATELY-
KLING
KLING
KLING KLING KLING
FINALLY, YOU GAVE US AN OPENING.
PANIC MADE YOUR MANA UNSTABLE.
KLING
BUYING TIME LIKE THIS WON'T...

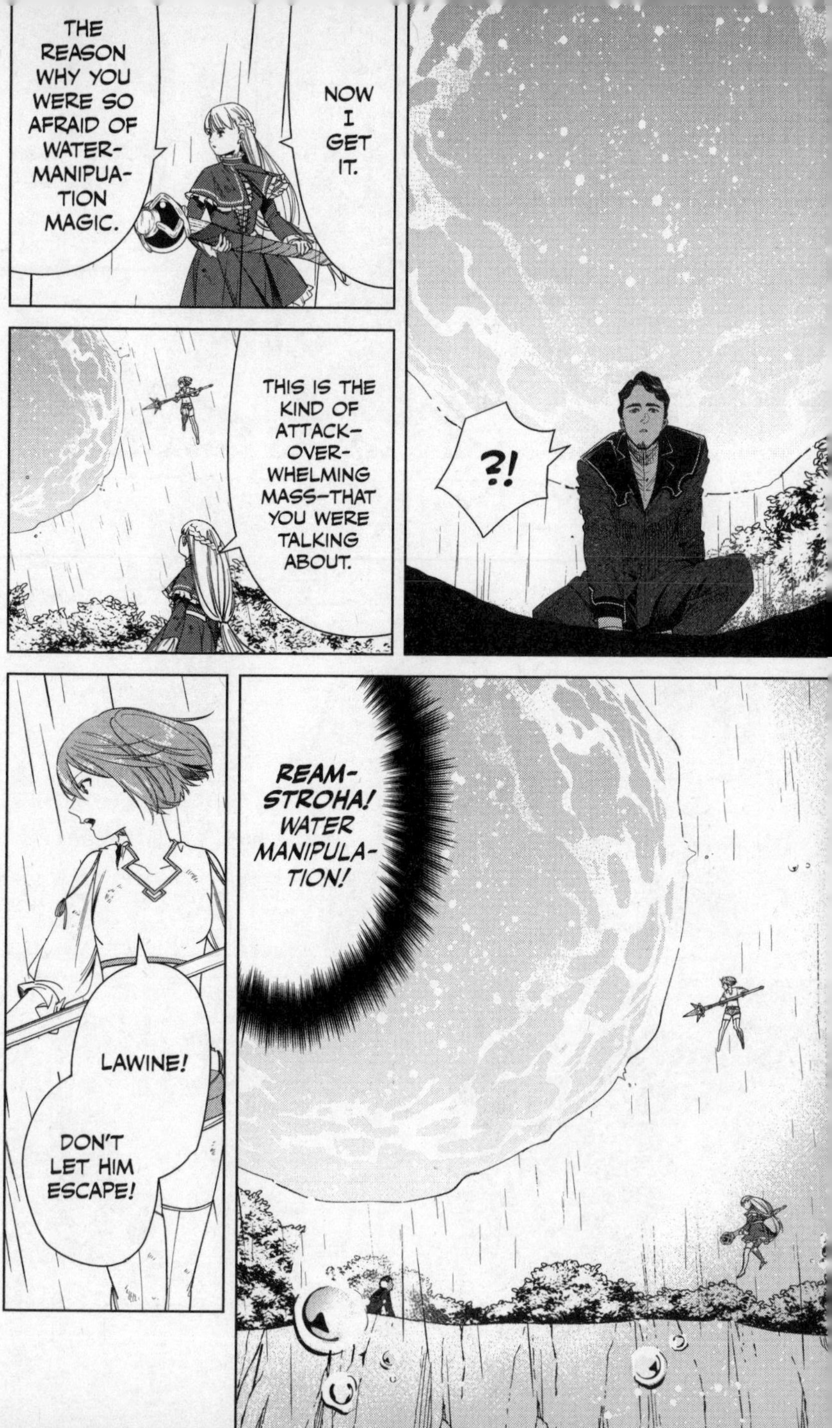
?!
NOW I GET IT.
THE REASON WHY YOU WERE SO AFRAID OF WATER-MANIPUATION MAGIC.
THIS IS THE KIND OF ATTACK—OVERWHELMING MASS—THAT YOU WERE TALKING ABOUT.
REAM-STROHA! WATER MANIPULATION!
LAWINE!
DON'T LET HIM ESCAPE!

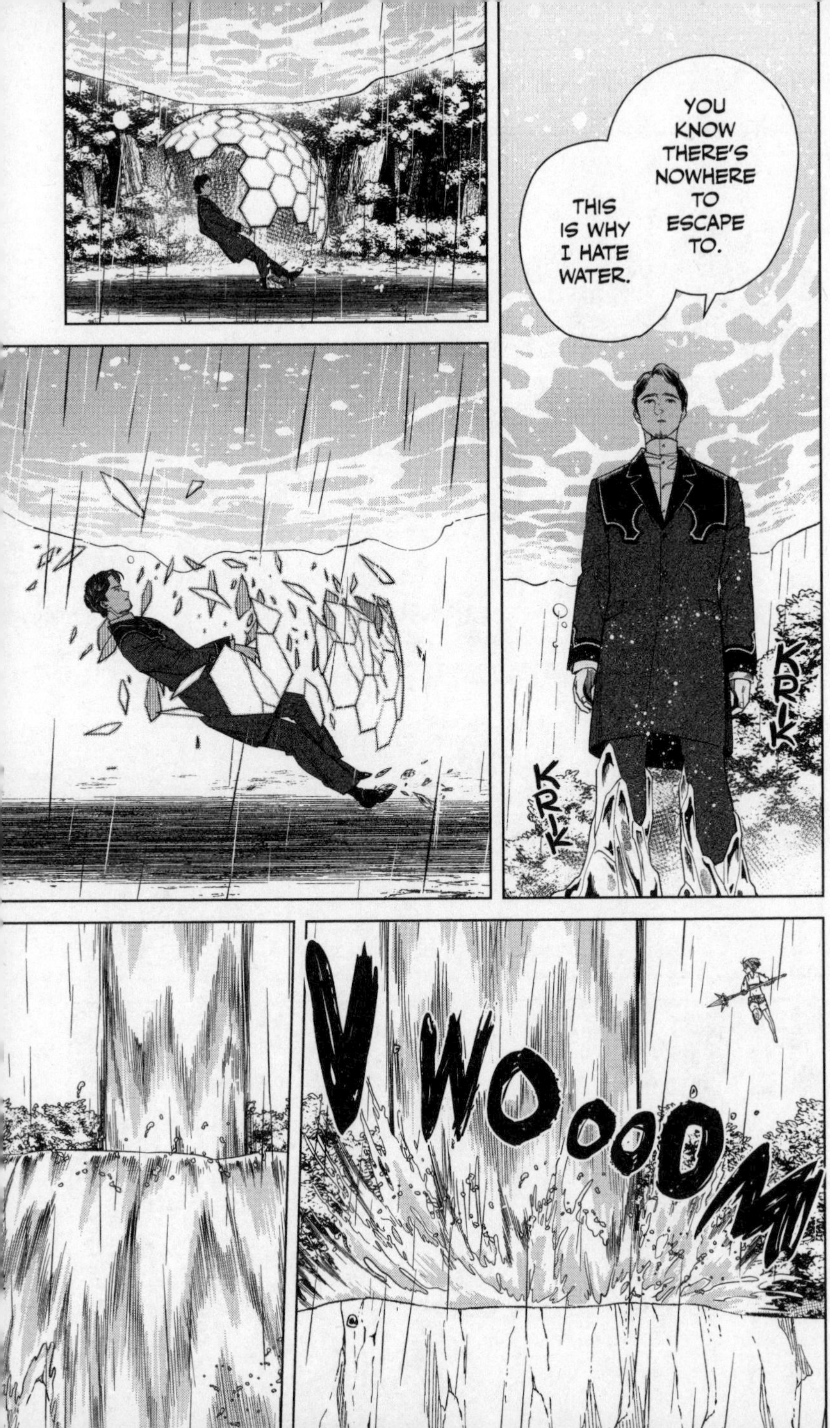
YOU KNOW THERE'S NOWHERE TO ESCAPE TO.
THIS IS WHY I HATE WATER.
KRIK KRIK
KRIK KRIK
VWOOOOM

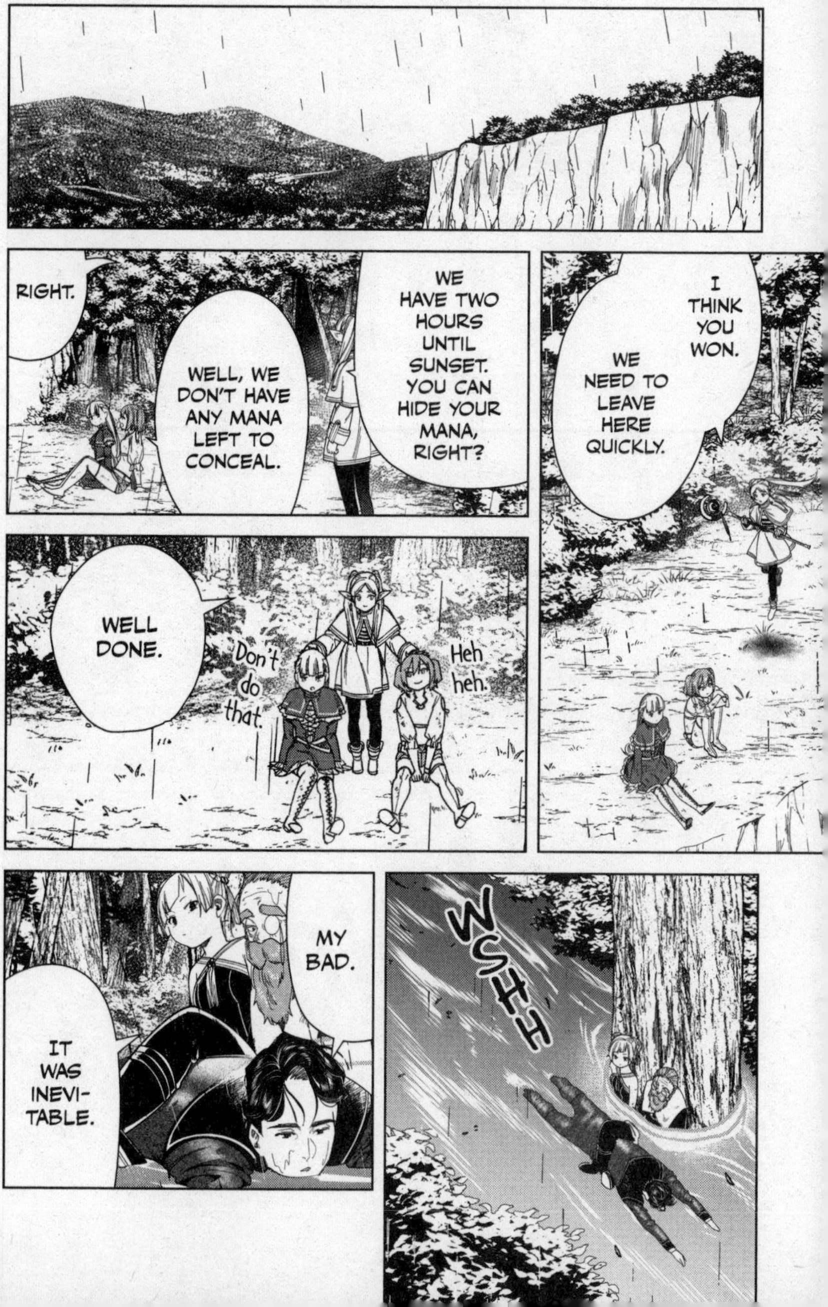

I THINK YOU WON.
WE NEED TO LEAVE HERE QUICKLY.
WE HAVE TWO HOURS UNTIL SUNSET. YOU CAN HIDE YOUR MANA, RIGHT?
WELL, WE DON'T HAVE ANY MANA LEFT TO CONCEAL.
RIGHT.
WELL DONE.
Heh heh.
Don't do that.
WSHH
MY BAD.
IT WAS INEVI-TABLE.

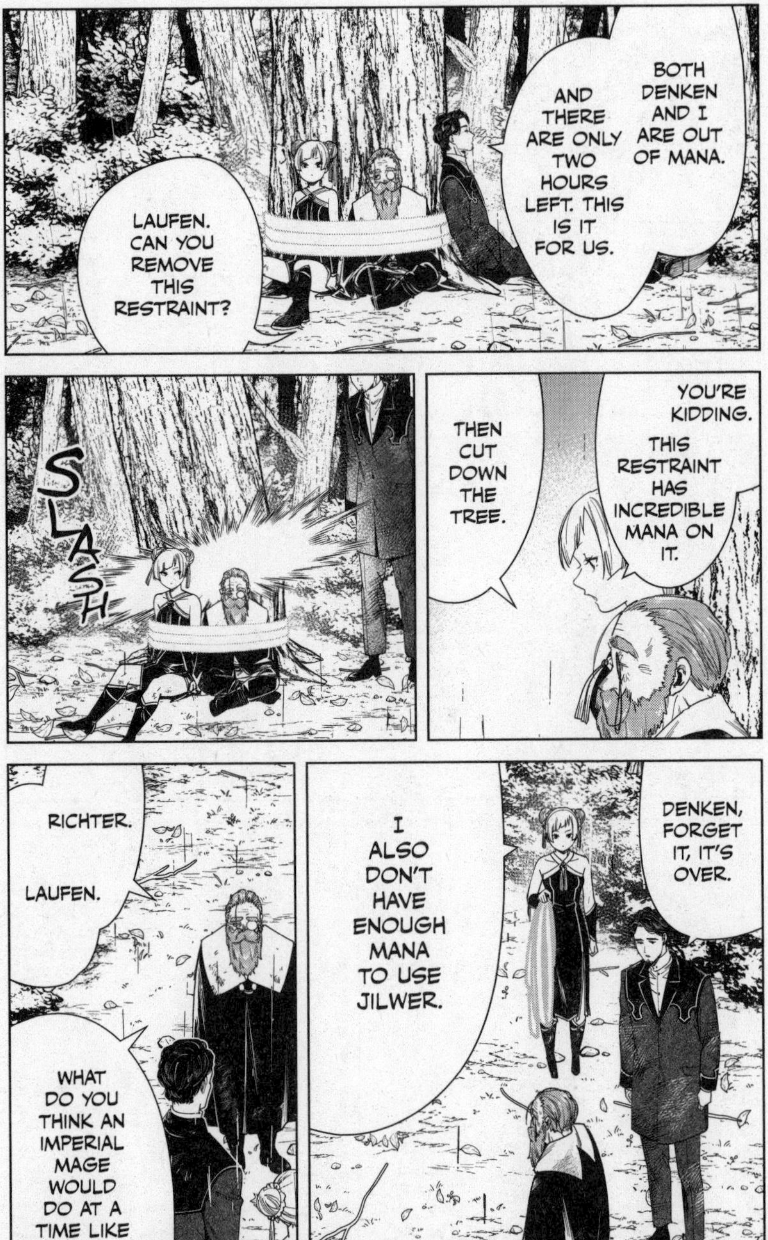
BOTH DENKEN AND I ARE OUT OF MANA.
AND THERE ARE ONLY TWO HOURS LEFT. THIS IS IT FOR US.
LAUFEN. CAN YOU REMOVE THIS RESTRAINT?
YOU'RE KIDDING.
THIS RESTRAINT HAS INCREDIBLE MANA ON IT.
THEN CUT DOWN THE TREE.
SLASH
DENKEN, FORGET IT, IT'S OVER.
I ALSO DON'T HAVE ENOUGH MANA TO USE JILWER.
RICHTER.
LAUFEN.
WHAT DO YOU THINK AN IMPERIAL MAGE WOULD DO AT A TIME LIKE THIS?

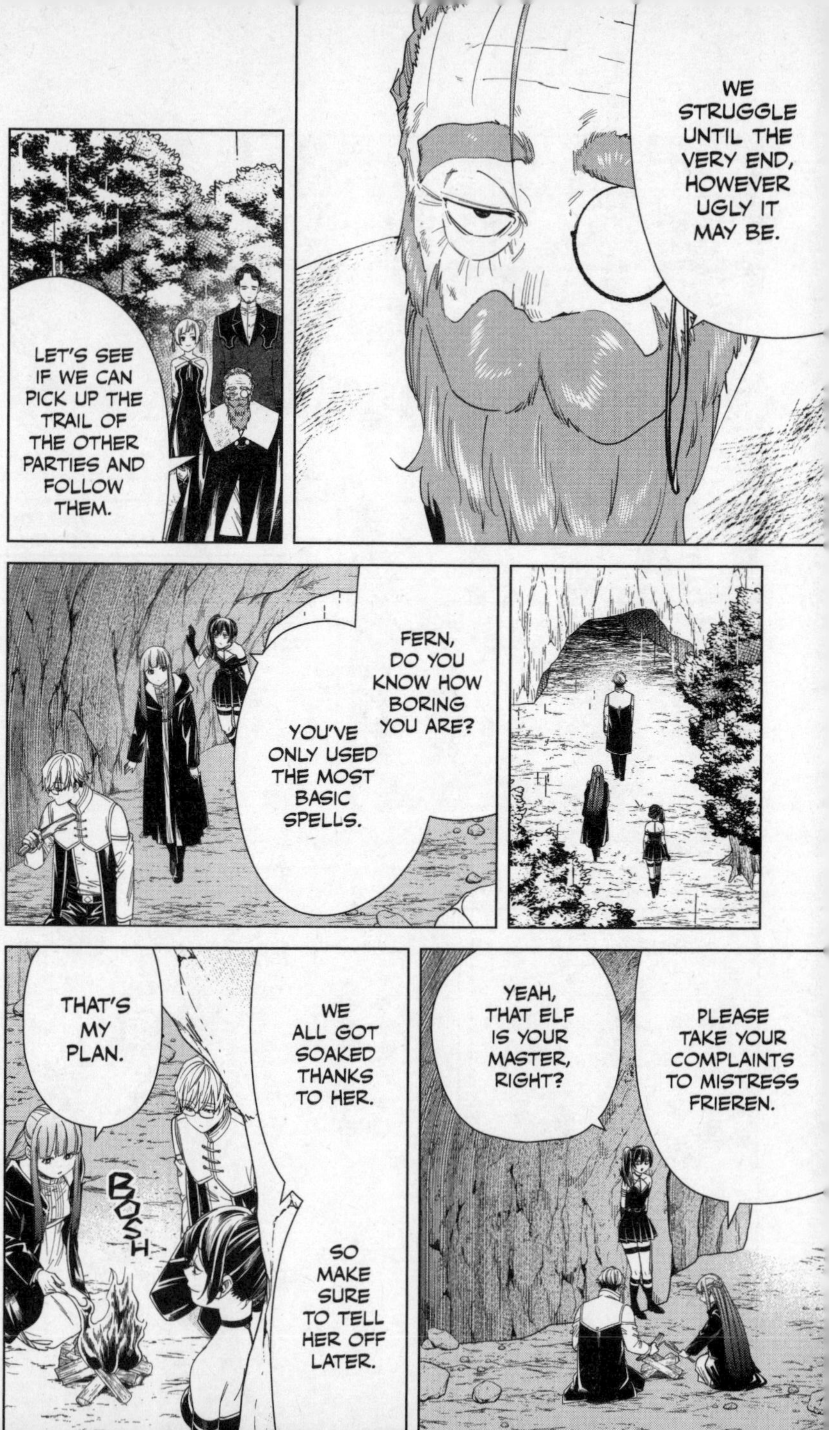
WE STRUGGLE UNTIL THE VERY END, HOWEVER UGLY IT MAY BE.
LET'S SEE IF WE CAN PICK UP THE TRAIL OF THE OTHER PARTIES AND FOLLOW THEM.
FERN, DO YOU KNOW HOW BORING YOU ARE?
YOU'VE ONLY USED THE MOST BASIC SPELLS.
PLEASE TAKE YOUR COMPLAINTS TO MISTRESS FRIEREN.
YEAH, THAT ELF IS YOUR MASTER, RIGHT?
WE ALL GOT SOAKED THANKS TO HER.
SO MAKE SURE TO TELL HER OFF LATER.
THAT'S MY PLAN.
BOSH

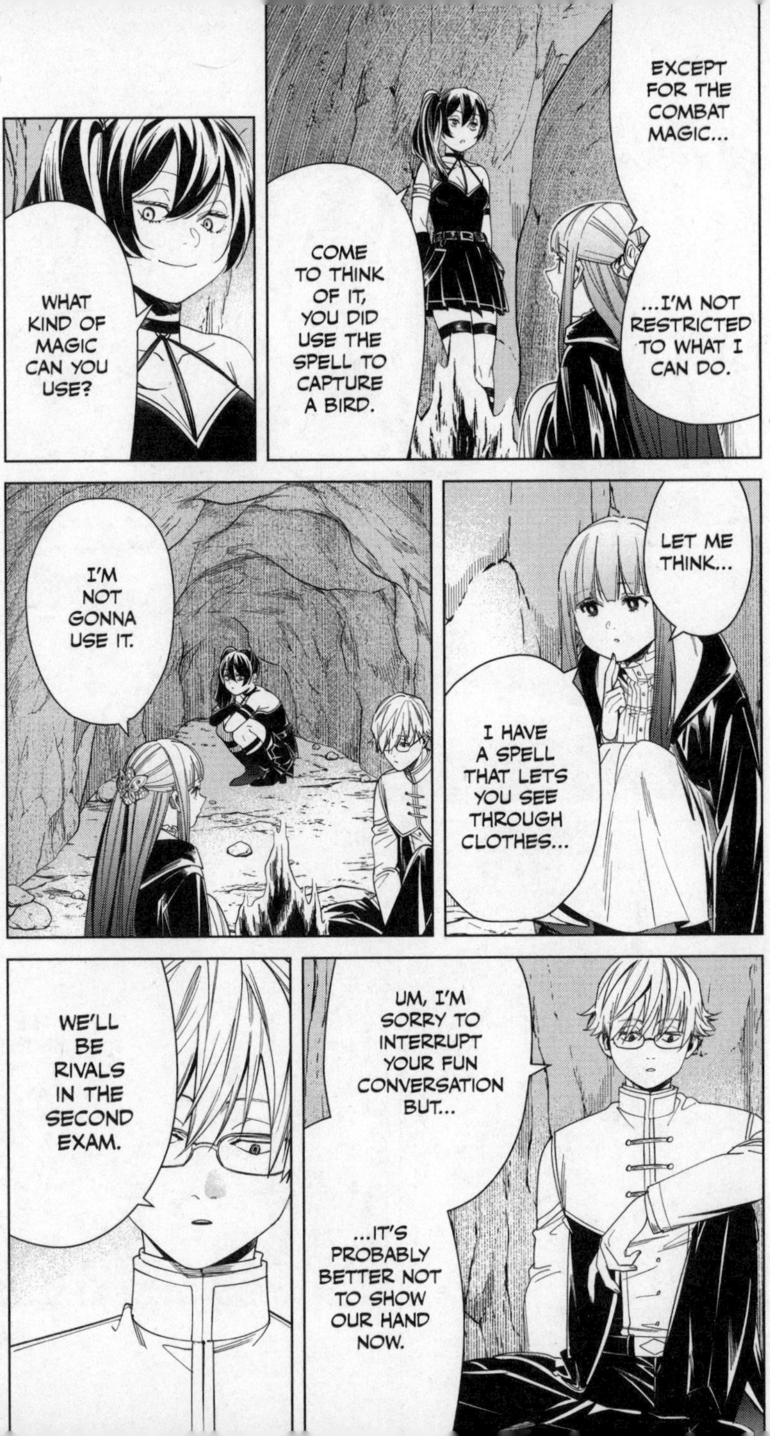
EXCEPT FOR THE COMBAT MAGIC...
...I'M NOT RESTRICTED TO WHAT I CAN DO.
COME TO THINK OF IT, YOU DID USE THE SPELL TO CAPTURE A BIRD.
WHAT KIND OF MAGIC CAN YOU USE?
LET ME THINK...
I HAVE A SPELL THAT LETS YOU SEE THROUGH CLOTHES...
I'M NOT GONNA USE IT.
UM, I'M SORRY TO INTERRUPT YOUR FUN CONVERSATION BUT...
...IT'S PROBABLY BETTER NOT TO SHOW OUR HAND NOW.
WE'LL BE RIVALS IN THE SECOND EXAM.

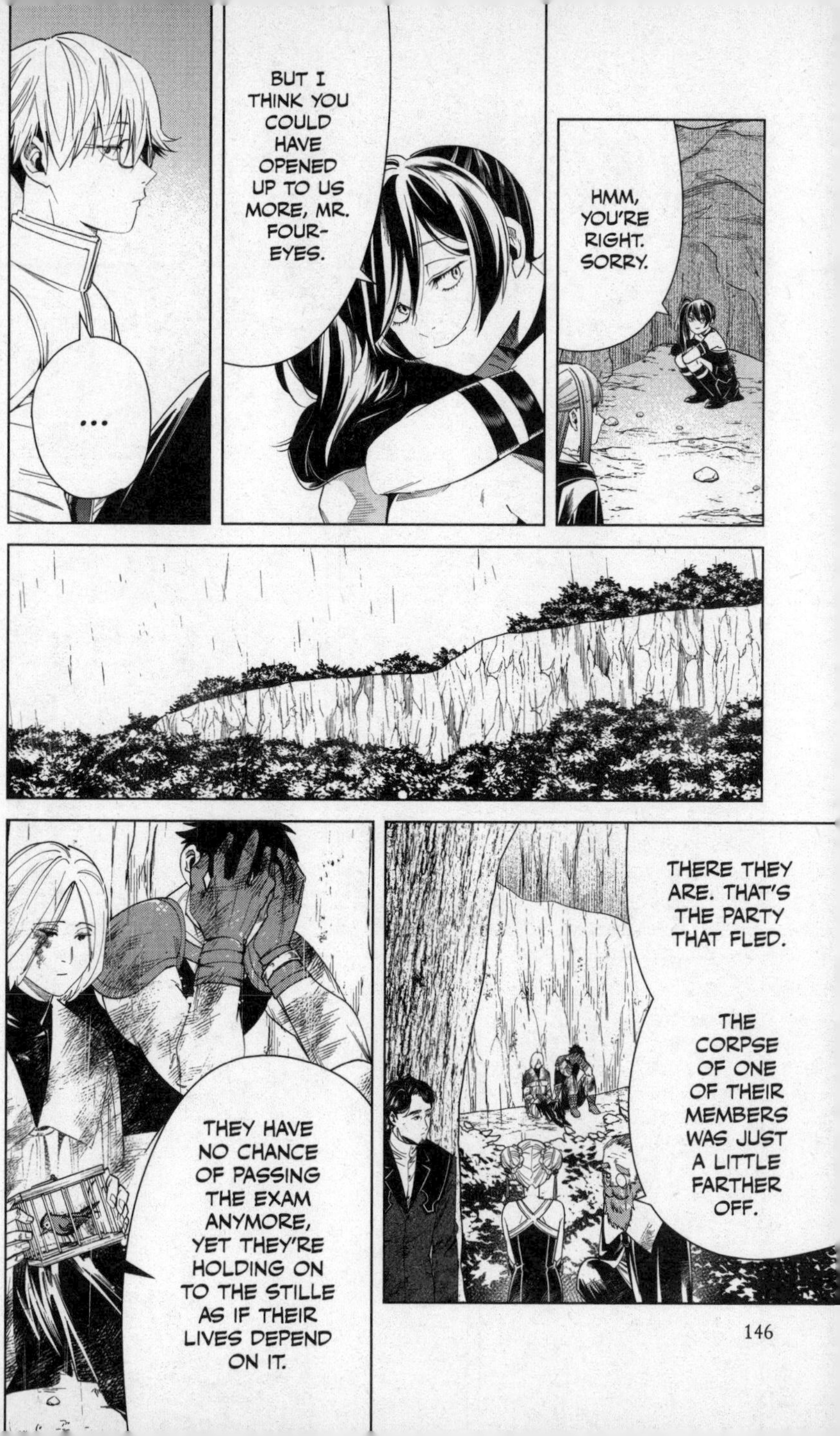
HMM, YOU'RE RIGHT. SORRY.
BUT I THINK YOU COULD HAVE OPENED UP TO US MORE, MR. FOUR-EYES.
...
THERE THEY ARE. THAT'S THE PARTY THAT FLED.
THE CORPSE OF ONE OF THEIR MEMBERS WAS JUST A LITTLE FARTHER OFF.
THEY HAVE NO CHANCE OF PASSING THE EXAM ANYMORE, YET THEY'RE HOLDING ON TO THE STILLE AS IF THEIR LIVES DEPEND ON IT.

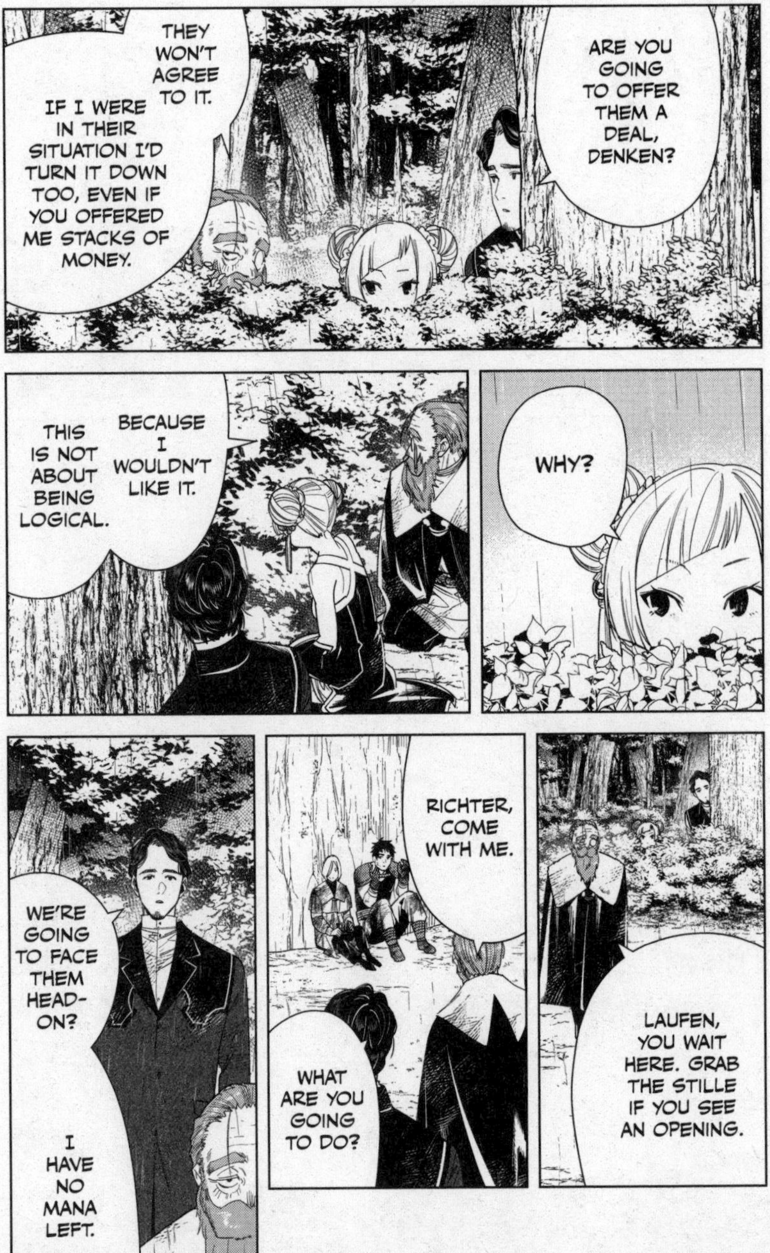
ARE YOU GOING TO OFFER THEM A DEAL, DENKEN?
THEY WON'T AGREE TO IT.
IF I WERE IN THEIR SITUATION I'D TURN IT DOWN TOO, EVEN IF YOU OFFERED ME STACKS OF MONEY.
WHY?
BECAUSE I WOULDN'T LIKE IT.
THIS IS NOT ABOUT BEING LOGICAL.
LAUFEN, YOU WAIT HERE. GRAB THE STILLE IF YOU SEE AN OPENING.
RICHTER, COME WITH ME.
WHAT ARE YOU GOING TO DO?
WE'RE GOING TO FACE THEM HEAD-ON?
I HAVE NO MANA LEFT.

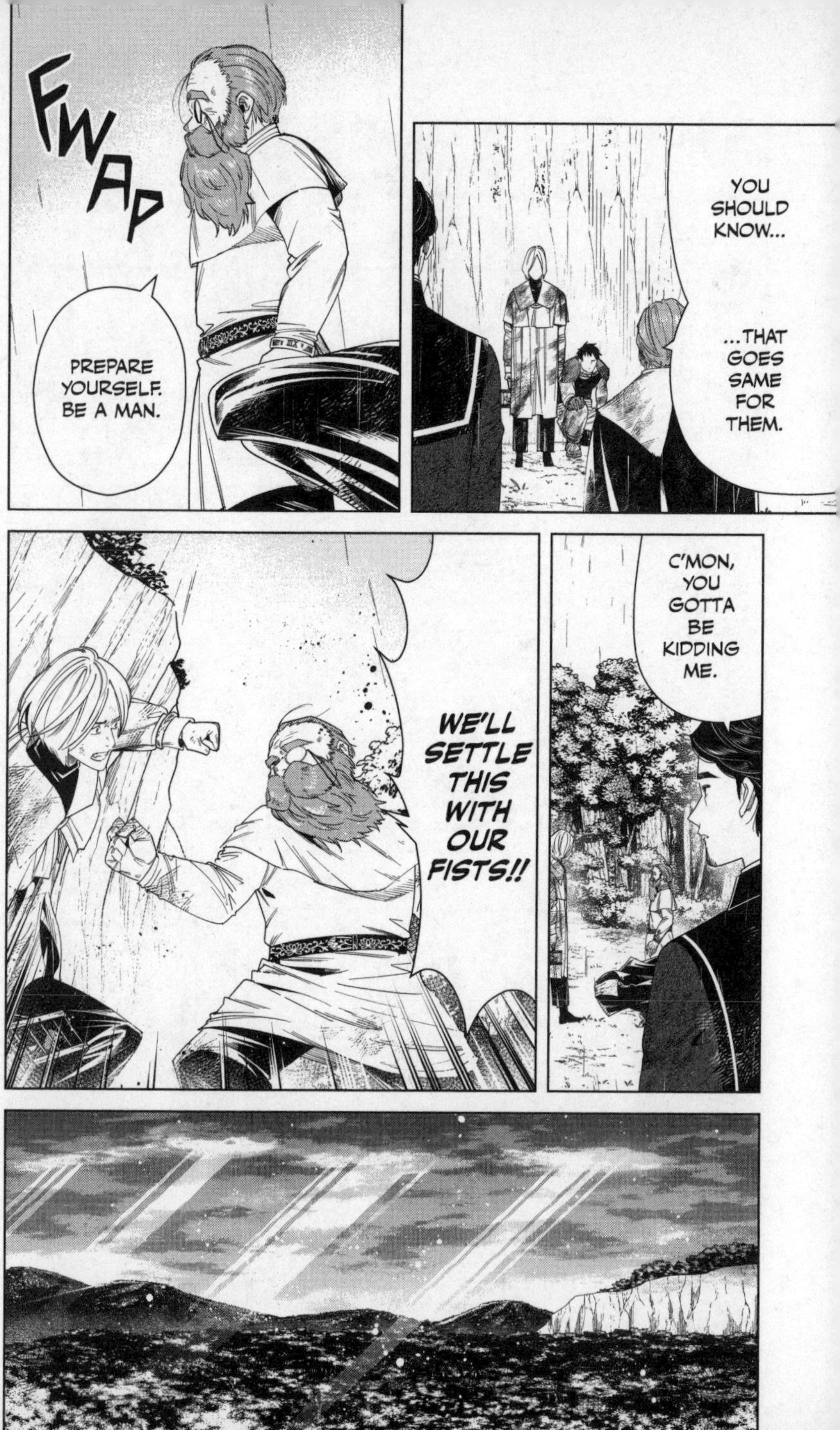
YOU SHOULD KNOW...
...THAT GOES SAME FOR THEM.
FWAP
PREPARE YOURSELF. BE A MAN.
C'MON, YOU GOTTA BE KIDDING ME.
WE'LL SETTLE THIS WITH OUR FISTS!!

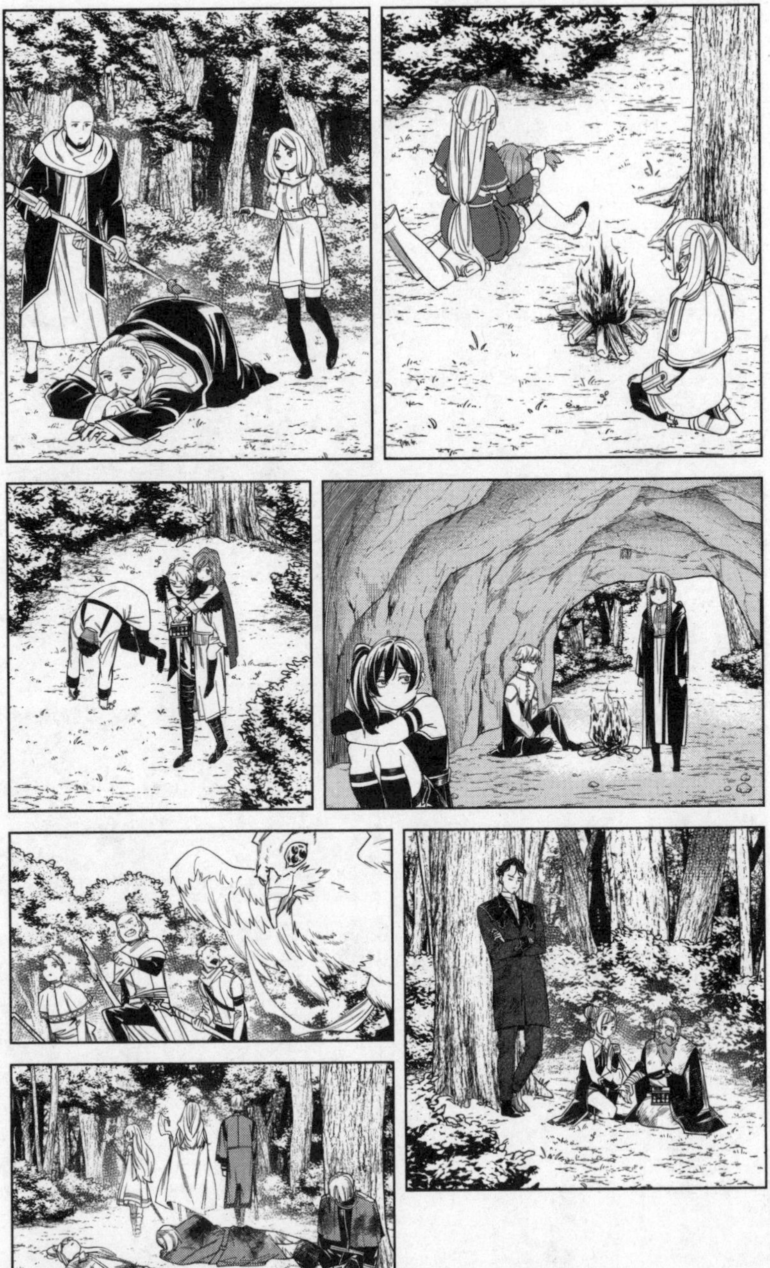

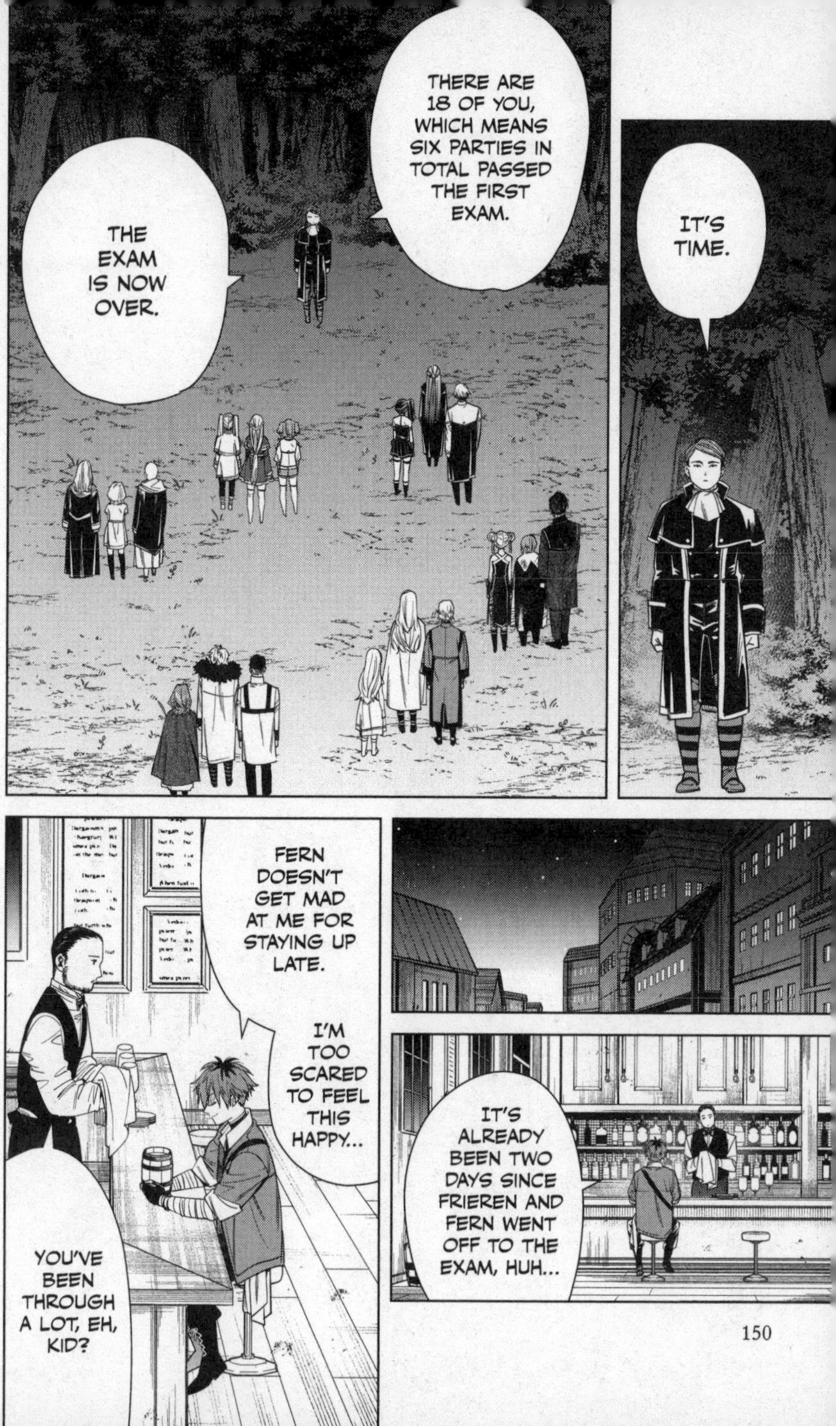
IT'S TIME.
THERE ARE 18 OF YOU, WHICH MEANS SIX PARTIES IN TOTAL PASSED THE FIRST EXAM.
THE EXAM IS NOW OVER.
IT'S ALREADY BEEN TWO DAYS SINCE FRIEREN AND FERN WENT OFF TO THE EXAM, HUH...
FERN DOESN'T GET MAD AT ME FOR STAYING UP LATE.
I'M TOO SCARED TO FEEL THIS HAPPY...
YOU'VE BEEN THROUGH A LOT, EH, KID?

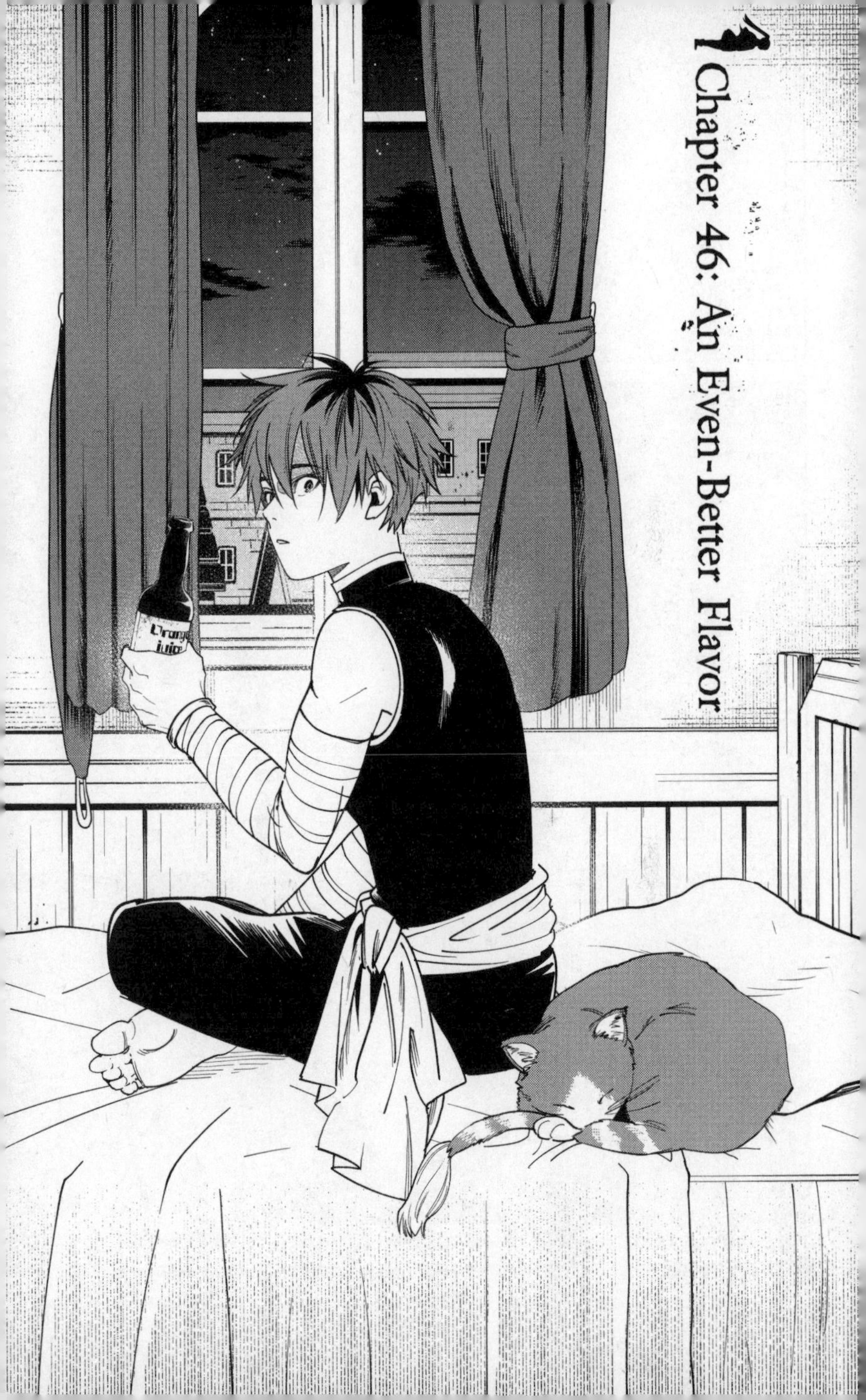
Chapter 46: An Even-Better Flavor
Orange juice

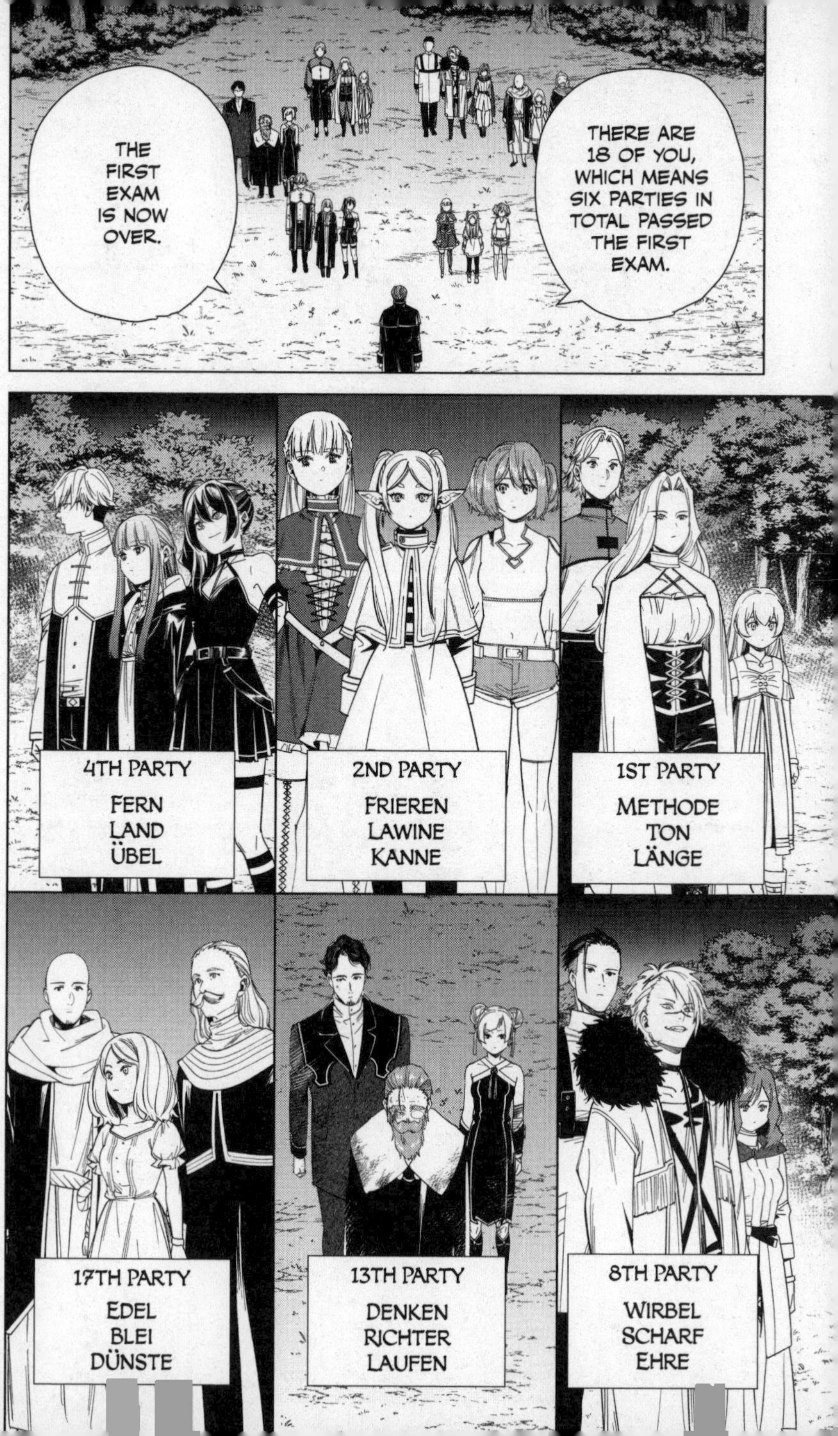
THERE ARE 18 OF YOU, WHICH MEANS SIX PARTIES IN TOTAL PASSED THE FIRST EXAM.
THE FIRST EXAM IS NOW OVER.
1ST PARTY
METHODE
TON
LÄNGE
2ND PARTY
FRIEREN
LAWINE
KANNE
4TH PARTY
FERN
LAND
ÜBEL
8TH PARTY
WIRBEL
SCHARF
EHRE
13TH PARTY
DENKEN
RICHTER
LAUFEN
17TH PARTY
EDEL
BLEI
DÜNSTE

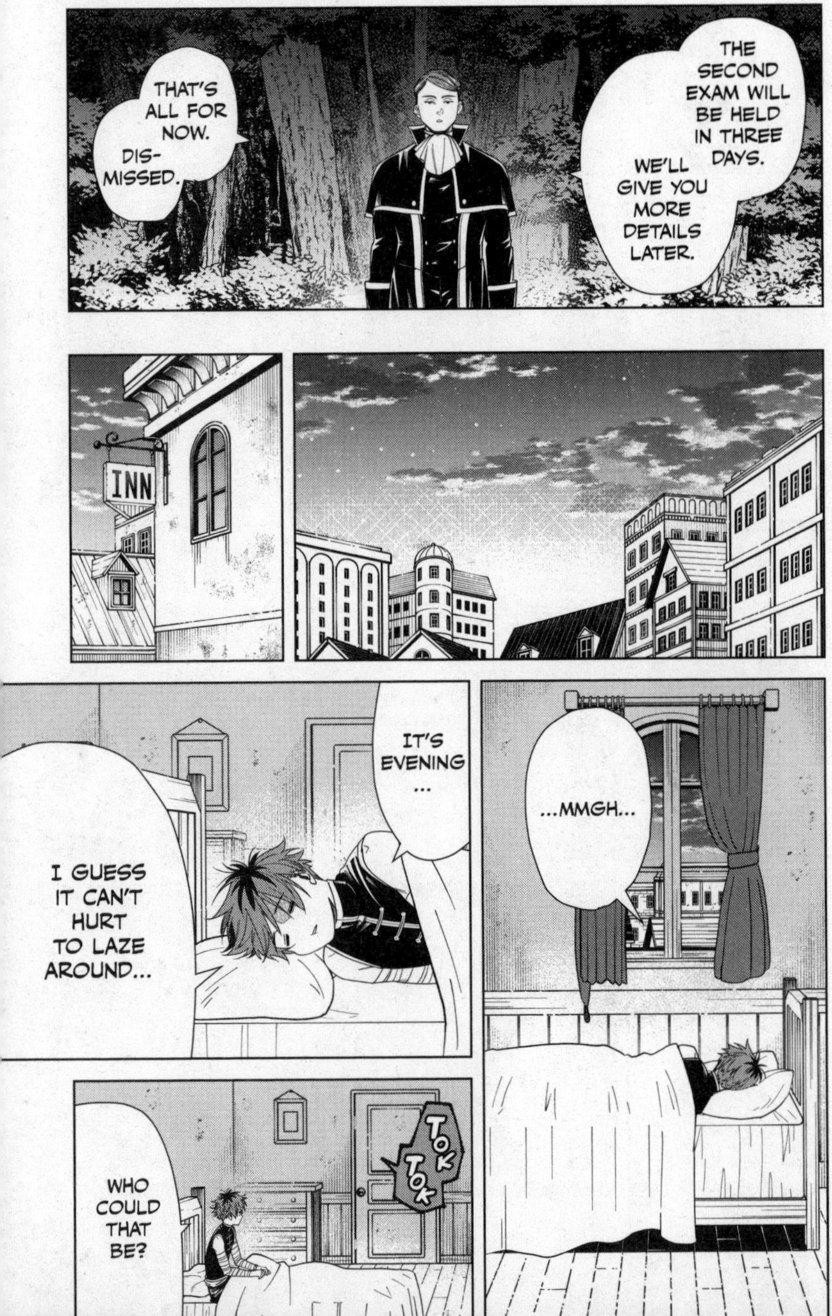
THE SECOND EXAM WILL BE HELD IN THREE DAYS.
WE'LL GIVE YOU MORE DETAILS LATER.
THAT'S ALL FOR NOW.
DIS-MISSED.
INN
...MMGH...
IT'S EVENING...
I GUESS IT CAN'T HURT TO LAZE AROUND...
TOK TOK
WHO COULD THAT BE?

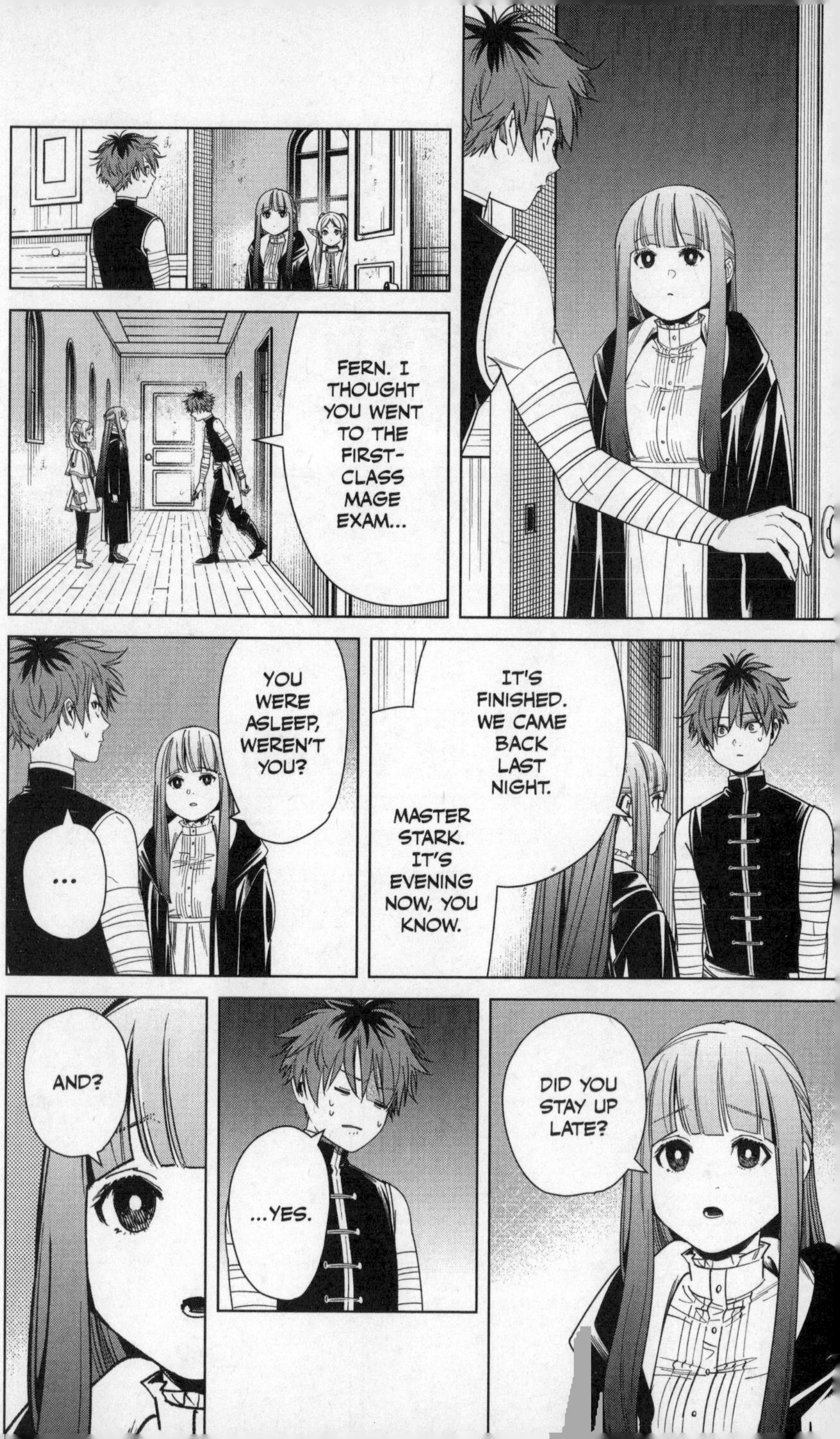
FERN. I THOUGHT YOU WENT TO THE FIRST-CLASS MAGE EXAM...
IT'S FINISHED. WE CAME BACK LAST NIGHT.
MASTER STARK. IT'S EVENING NOW, YOU KNOW.
YOU WERE ASLEEP, WEREN'T YOU?
...
DID YOU STAY UP LATE?
...YES.
AND?

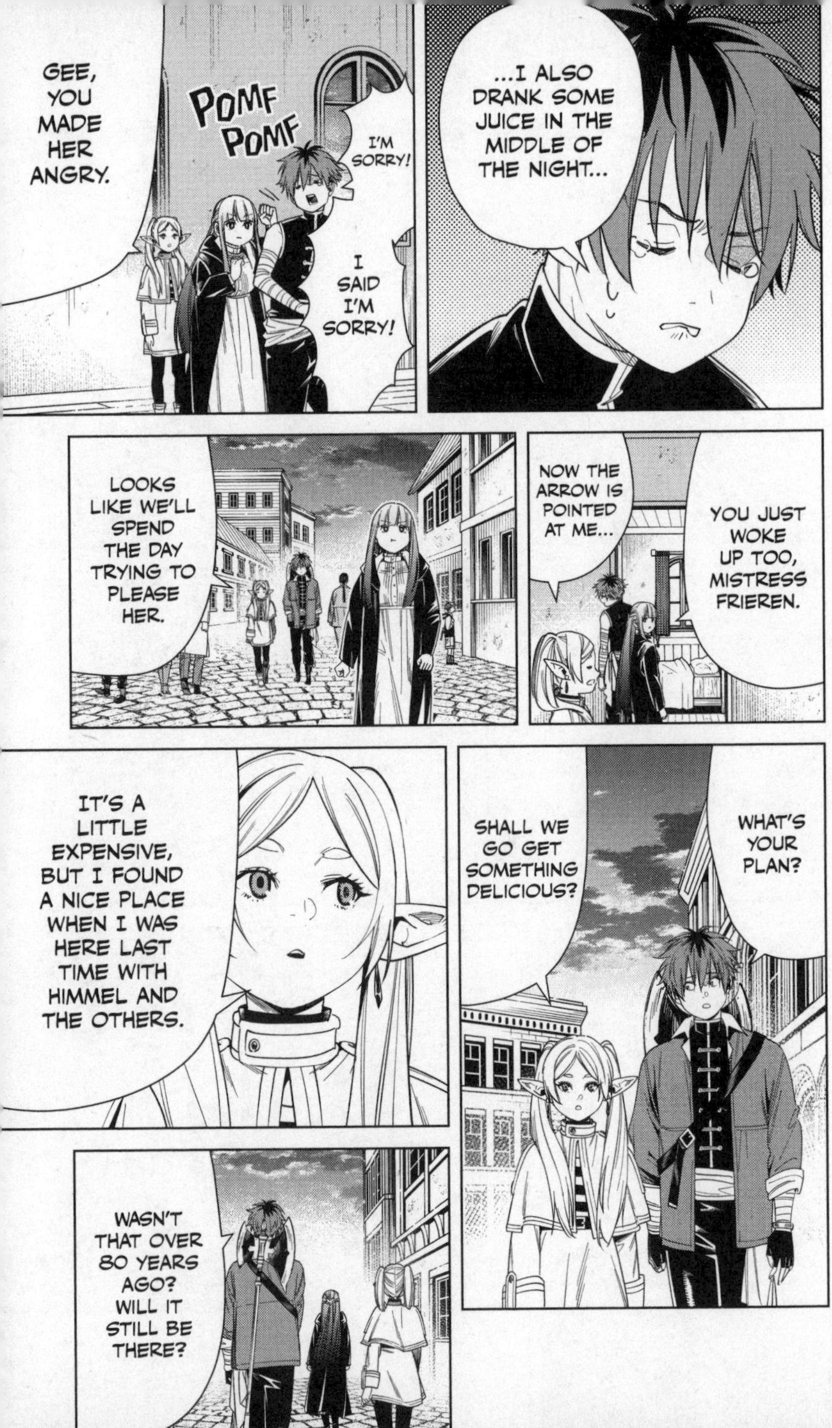
...I ALSO DRANK SOME JUICE IN THE MIDDLE OF THE NIGHT...
I'M SORRY!
POMF POMF
I SAID I'M SORRY!
GEE, YOU MADE HER ANGRY.
YOU JUST WOKE UP TOO, MISTRESS FRIEREN.
NOW THE ARROW IS POINTED AT ME...
LOOKS LIKE WE'LL SPEND THE DAY TRYING TO PLEASE HER.
WHAT'S YOUR PLAN?
SHALL WE GO GET SOMETHING DELICIOUS?
IT'S A LITTLE EXPENSIVE, BUT I FOUND A NICE PLACE WHEN I WAS HERE LAST TIME WITH HIMMEL AND THE OTHERS.
WASN'T THAT OVER 80 YEARS AGO? WILL IT STILL BE THERE?

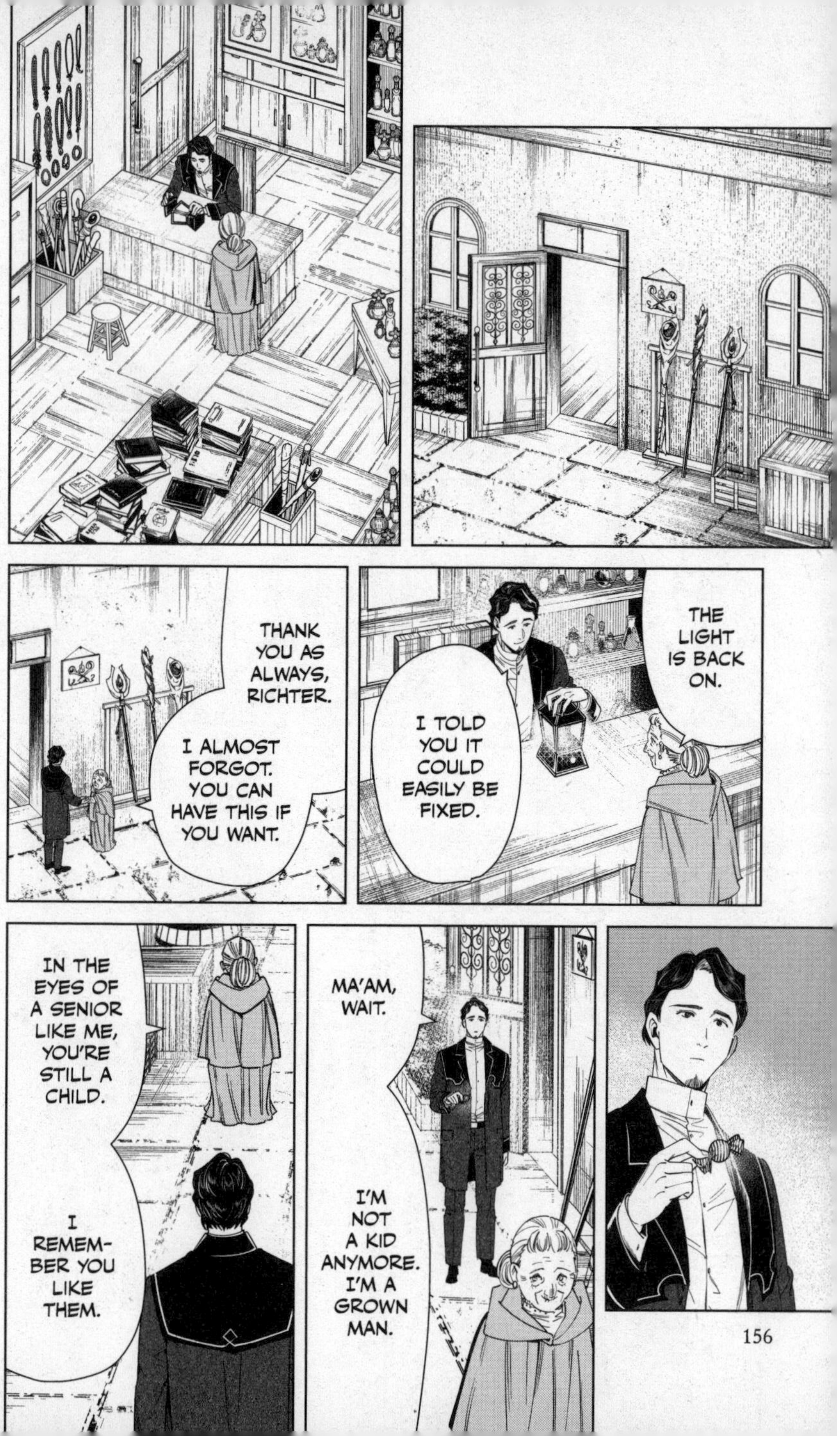
THE LIGHT IS BACK ON.
I TOLD YOU IT COULD EASILY BE FIXED.
THANK YOU AS ALWAYS, RICHTER.
I ALMOST FORGOT. YOU CAN HAVE THIS IF YOU WANT.
MA'AM, WAIT.
I'M NOT A KID ANYMORE. I'M A GROWN MAN.
IN THE EYES OF A SENIOR LIKE ME, YOU'RE STILL A CHILD.
I REMEMBER YOU LIKE THEM.

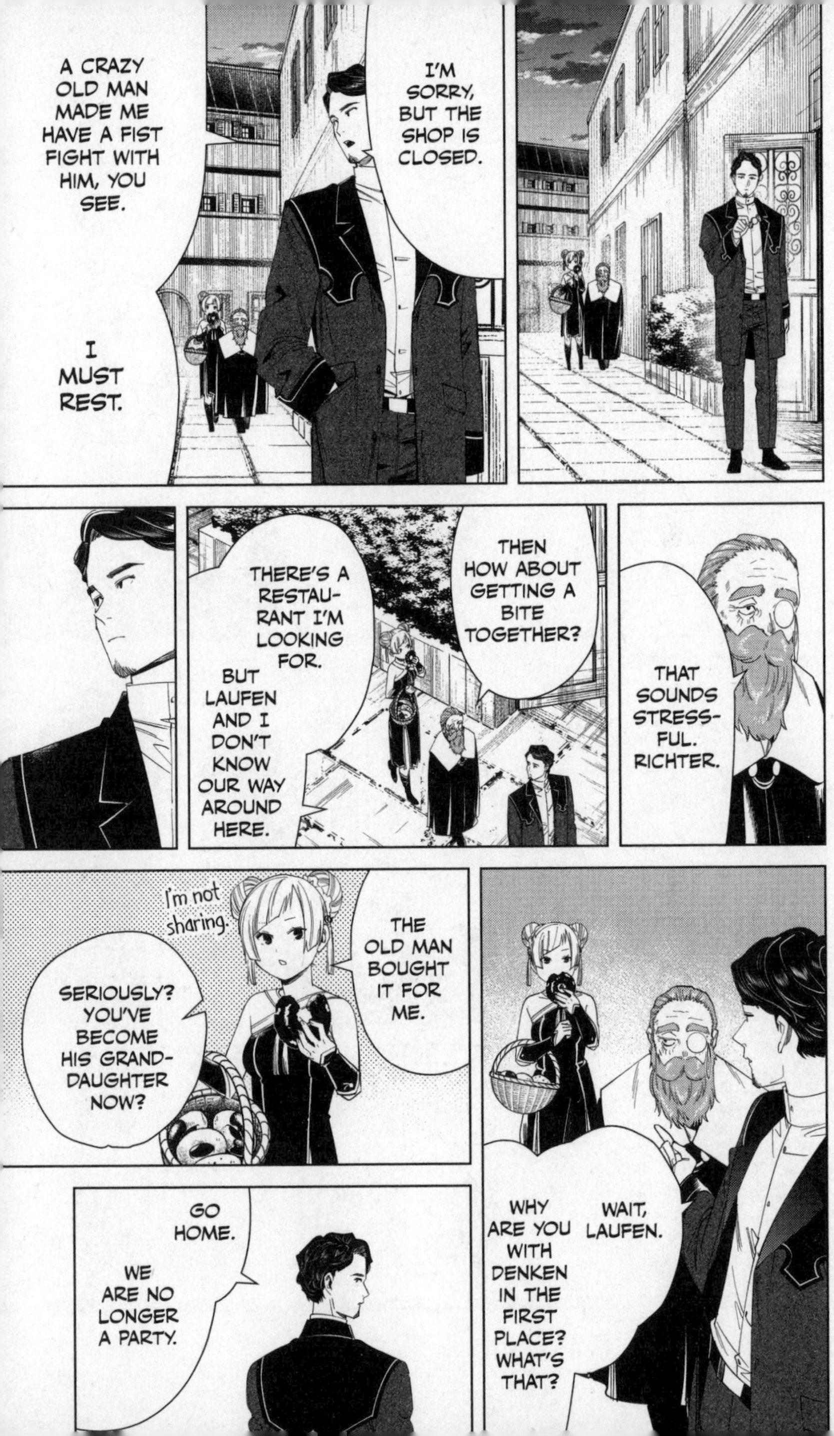
I'M SORRY, BUT THE SHOP IS CLOSED.
A CRAZY OLD MAN MADE ME HAVE A FIST FIGHT WITH HIM, YOU SEE.
I MUST REST.
THAT SOUNDS STRESSFUL. RICHTER.
THEN HOW ABOUT GETTING A BITE TOGETHER?
THERE'S A RESTAURANT I'M LOOKING FOR.
BUT LAUFEN AND I DON'T KNOW OUR WAY AROUND HERE.
WAIT, LAUFEN.
WHY ARE YOU WITH DENKEN IN THE FIRST PLACE? WHAT'S THAT?
THE OLD MAN BOUGHT IT FOR ME.
I'm not sharing.
SERIOUSLY? YOU'VE BECOME HIS GRANDDAUGHTER NOW?
GO HOME.
WE ARE NO LONGER A PARTY.

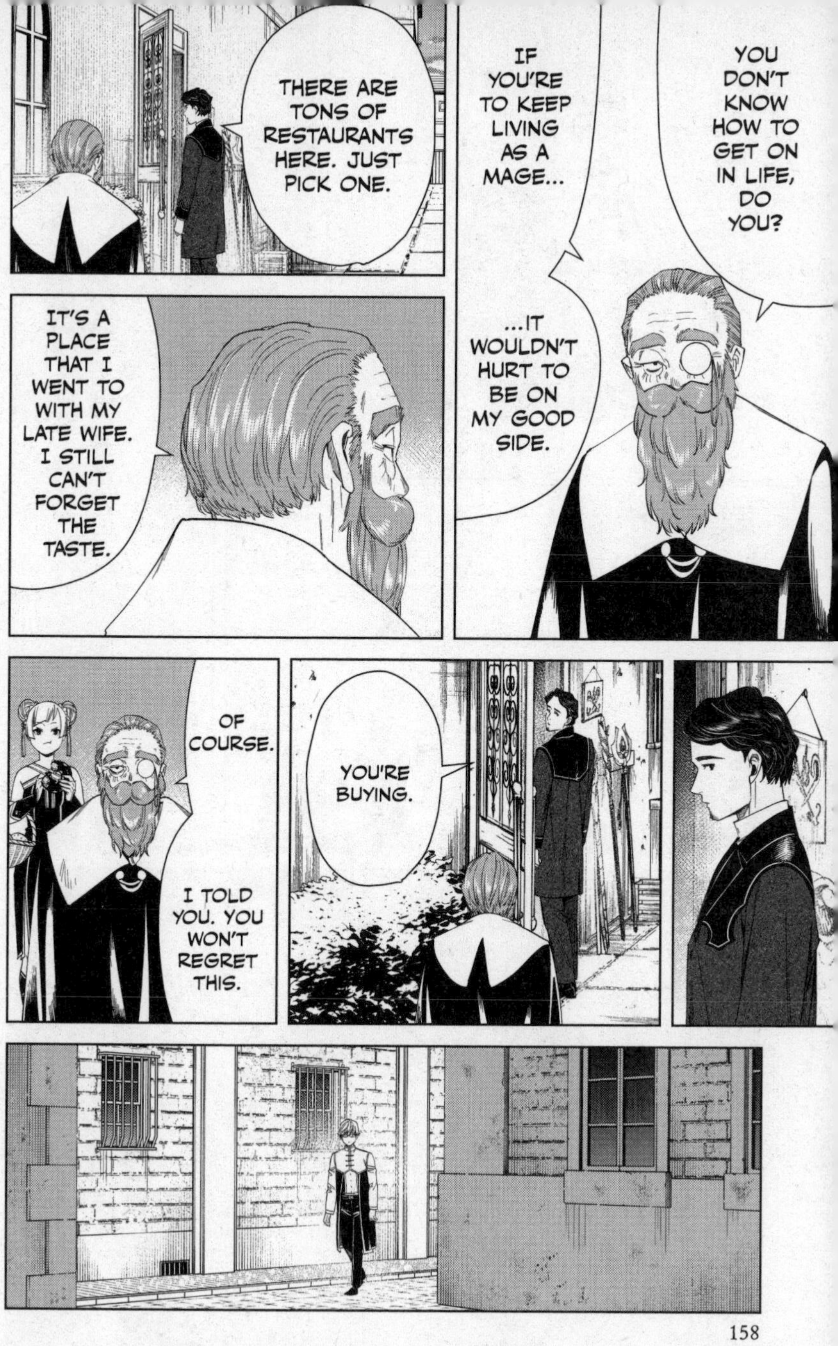
YOU DON'T KNOW HOW TO GET ON IN LIFE, DO YOU?
IF YOU'RE TO KEEP LIVING AS A MAGE...
...IT WOULDN'T HURT TO BE ON MY GOOD SIDE.
THERE ARE TONS OF RESTAURANTS HERE. JUST PICK ONE.
IT'S A PLACE THAT I WENT TO WITH MY LATE WIFE. I STILL CAN'T FORGET THE TASTE.
YOU'RE BUYING.
OF COURSE.
I TOLD YOU. YOU WON'T REGRET THIS.

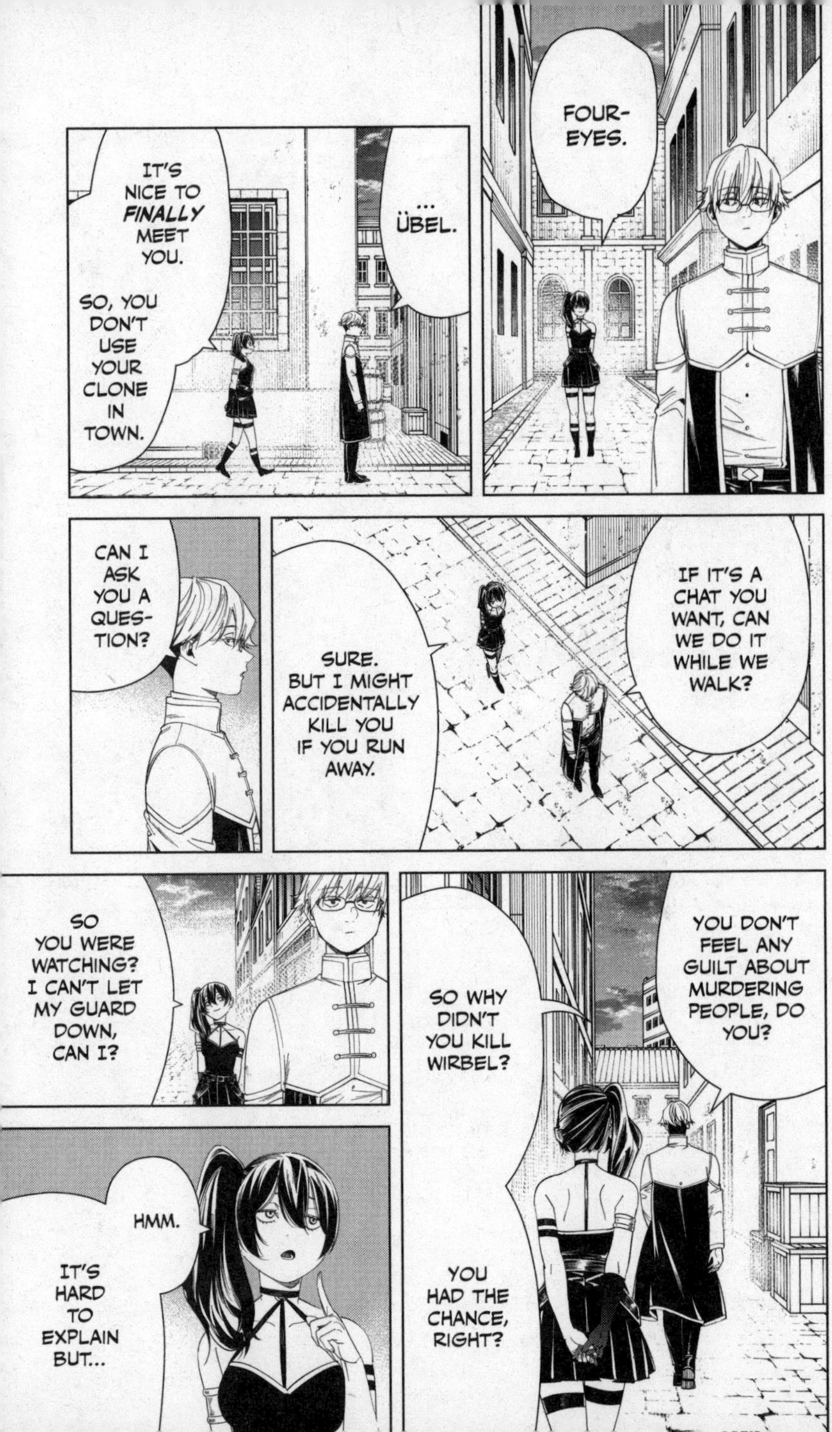
FOUR-EYES.
... ÜBEL.
IT'S NICE TO *FINALLY* MEET YOU.
SO, YOU DON'T USE YOUR CLONE IN TOWN.
IF IT'S A CHAT YOU WANT, CAN WE DO IT WHILE WE WALK?
SURE. BUT I MIGHT ACCIDENTALLY KILL YOU IF YOU RUN AWAY.
CAN I ASK YOU A QUESTION?
YOU DON'T FEEL ANY GUILT ABOUT MURDERING PEOPLE, DO YOU?
SO WHY DIDN'T YOU KILL WIRBEL?
YOU HAD THE CHANCE, RIGHT?
SO YOU WERE WATCHING? I CAN'T LET MY GUARD DOWN, CAN I?
HMM.
IT'S HARD TO EXPLAIN BUT...

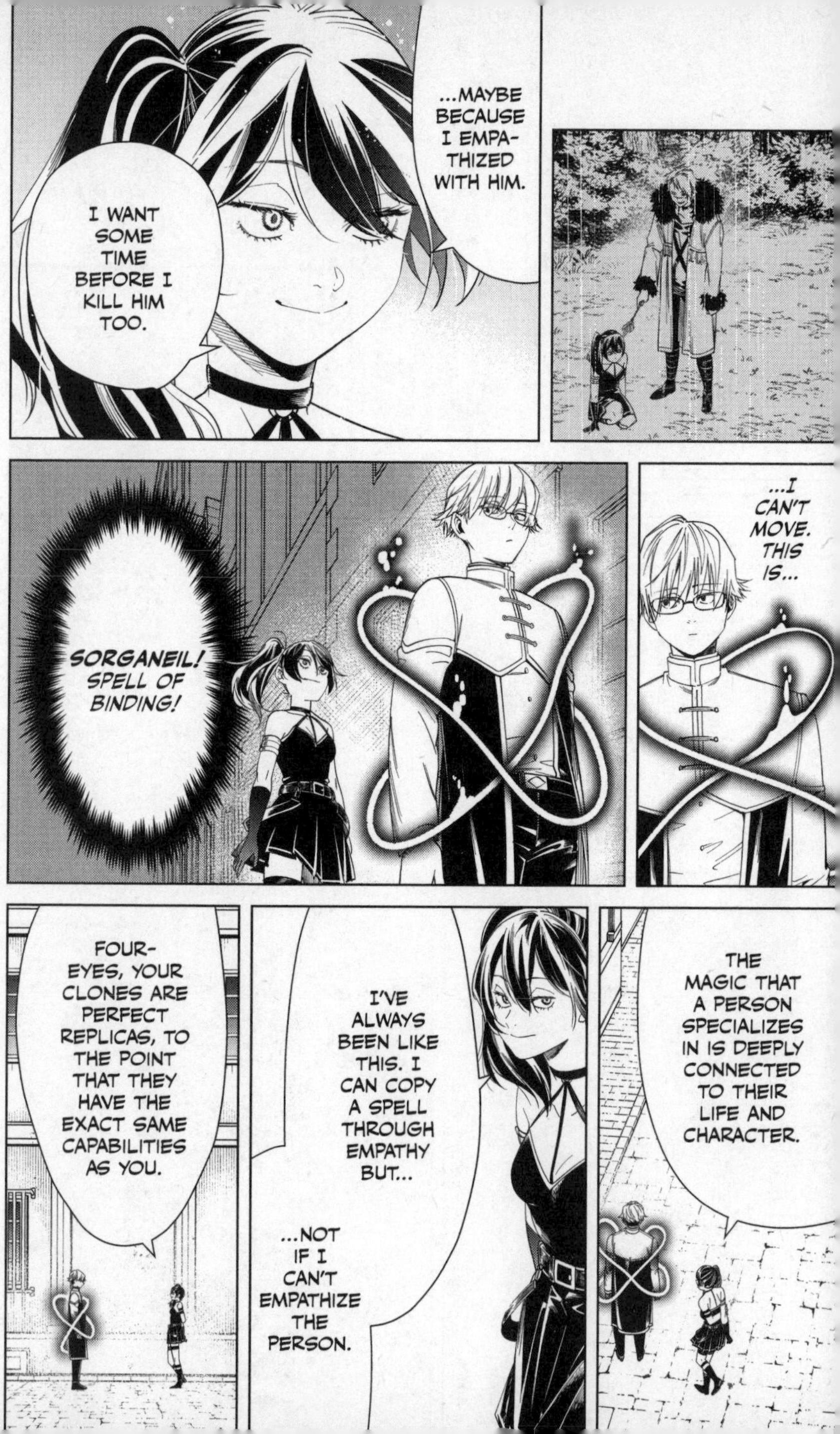
...MAYBE BECAUSE I EMPATHIZED WITH HIM.
I WANT SOME TIME BEFORE I KILL HIM TOO.
...I CAN'T MOVE. THIS IS...
SORGANEIL! SPELL OF BINDING!
THE MAGIC THAT A PERSON SPECIALIZES IN IS DEEPLY CONNECTED TO THEIR LIFE AND CHARACTER.
I'VE ALWAYS BEEN LIKE THIS. I CAN COPY A SPELL THROUGH EMPATHY BUT...
...NOT IF I CAN'T EMPATHIZE THE PERSON.
FOUR-EYES, YOUR CLONES ARE PERFECT REPLICAS, TO THE POINT THAT THEY HAVE THE EXACT SAME CAPABILITIES AS YOU.

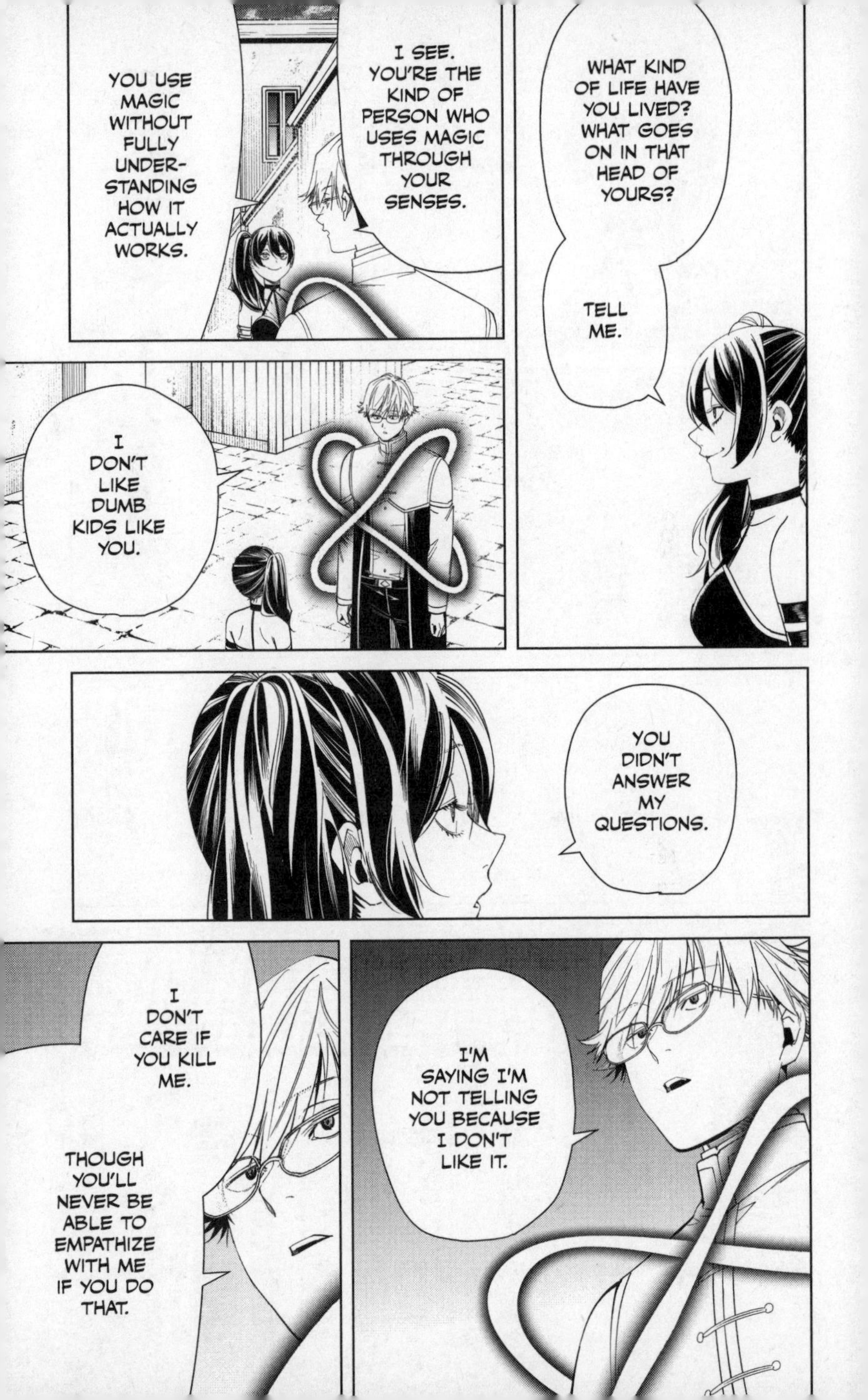
WHAT KIND OF LIFE HAVE YOU LIVED? WHAT GOES ON IN THAT HEAD OF YOURS?
TELL ME.
I SEE. YOU'RE THE KIND OF PERSON WHO USES MAGIC THROUGH YOUR SENSES.
YOU USE MAGIC WITHOUT FULLY UNDER-STANDING HOW IT ACTUALLY WORKS.
I DON'T LIKE DUMB KIDS LIKE YOU.
YOU DIDN'T ANSWER MY QUESTIONS.
I'M SAYING I'M NOT TELLING YOU BECAUSE I DON'T LIKE IT.
I DON'T CARE IF YOU KILL ME.
THOUGH YOU'LL NEVER BE ABLE TO EMPATHIZE WITH ME IF YOU DO THAT.

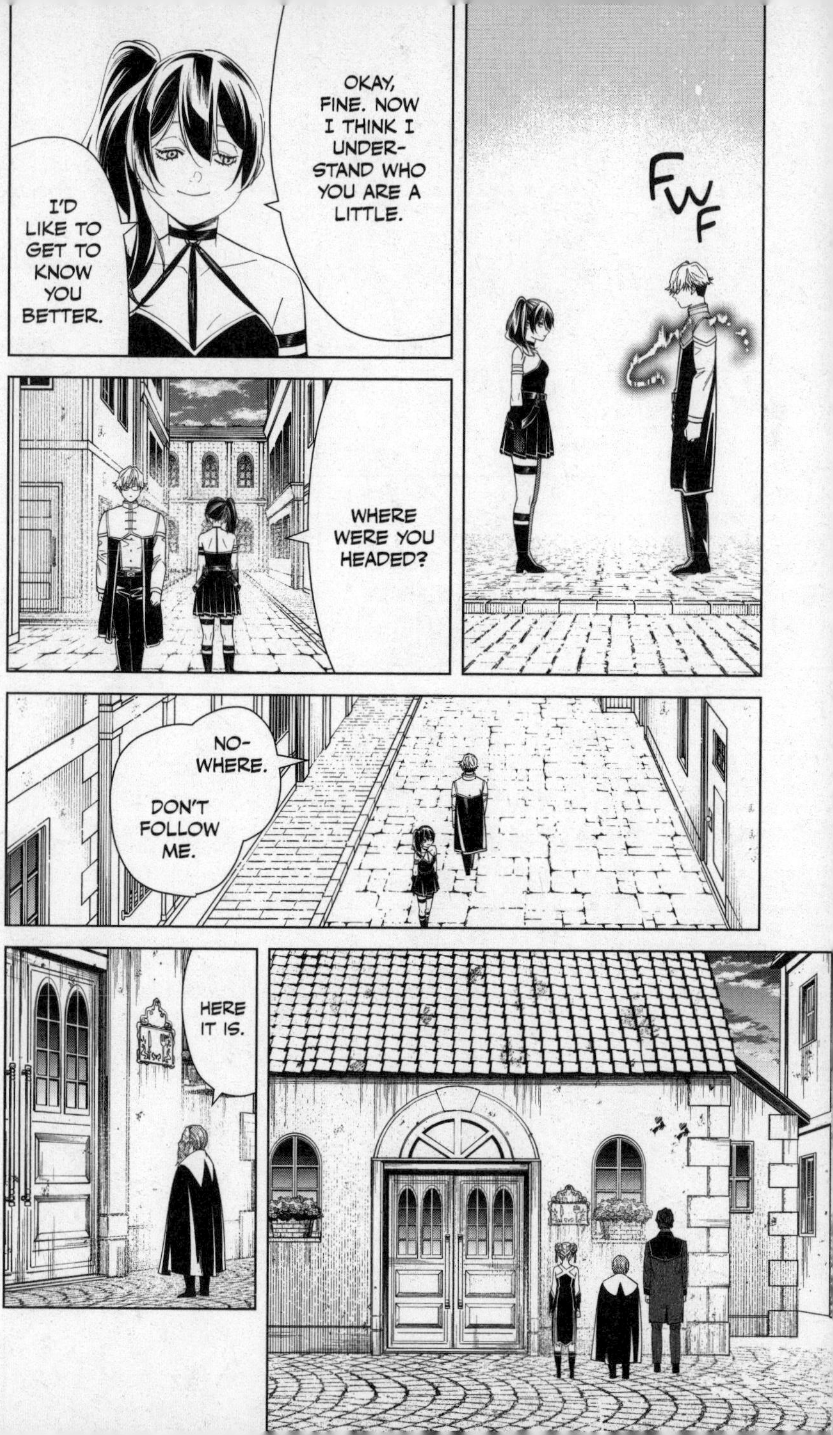
FWF
OKAY, FINE. NOW I THINK I UNDER-STAND WHO YOU ARE A LITTLE.
I'D LIKE TO GET TO KNOW YOU BETTER.
WHERE WERE YOU HEADED?
NO-WHERE.
DON'T FOLLOW ME.
HERE IT IS.

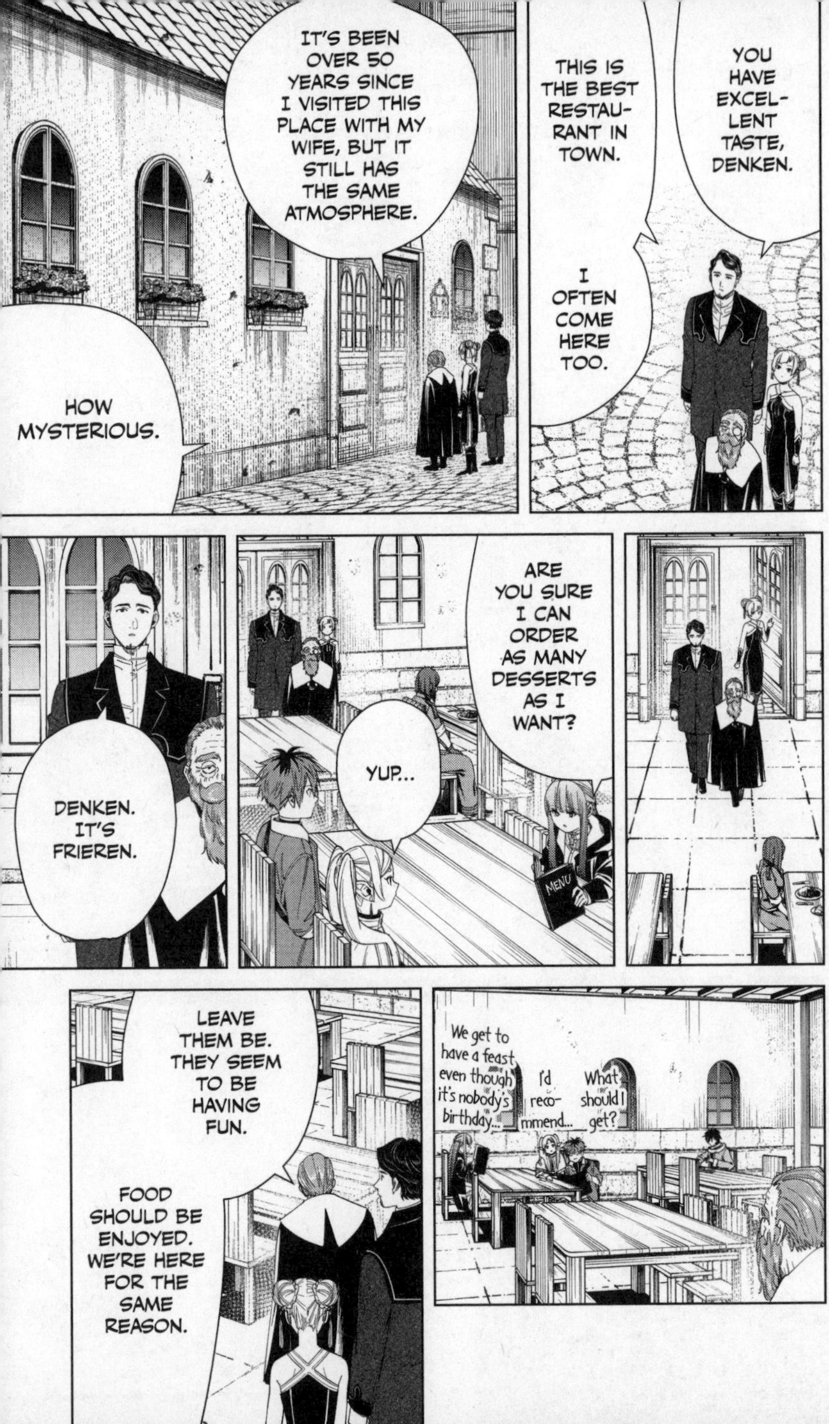
YOU HAVE EXCEL-LENT TASTE, DENKEN.
THIS IS THE BEST RESTAU-RANT IN TOWN.
I OFTEN COME HERE TOO.
IT'S BEEN OVER 50 YEARS SINCE I VISITED THIS PLACE WITH MY WIFE, BUT IT STILL HAS THE SAME ATMOSPHERE.
HOW MYSTERIOUS.
ARE YOU SURE I CAN ORDER AS MANY DESSERTS AS I WANT?
YUP...
MENU
DENKEN. IT'S FRIEREN.
What should I get?
I'd reco-mmend...
We get to have a feast even though it's nobody's birthday...
LEAVE THEM BE. THEY SEEM TO BE HAVING FUN.
FOOD SHOULD BE ENJOYED. WE'RE HERE FOR THE SAME REASON.

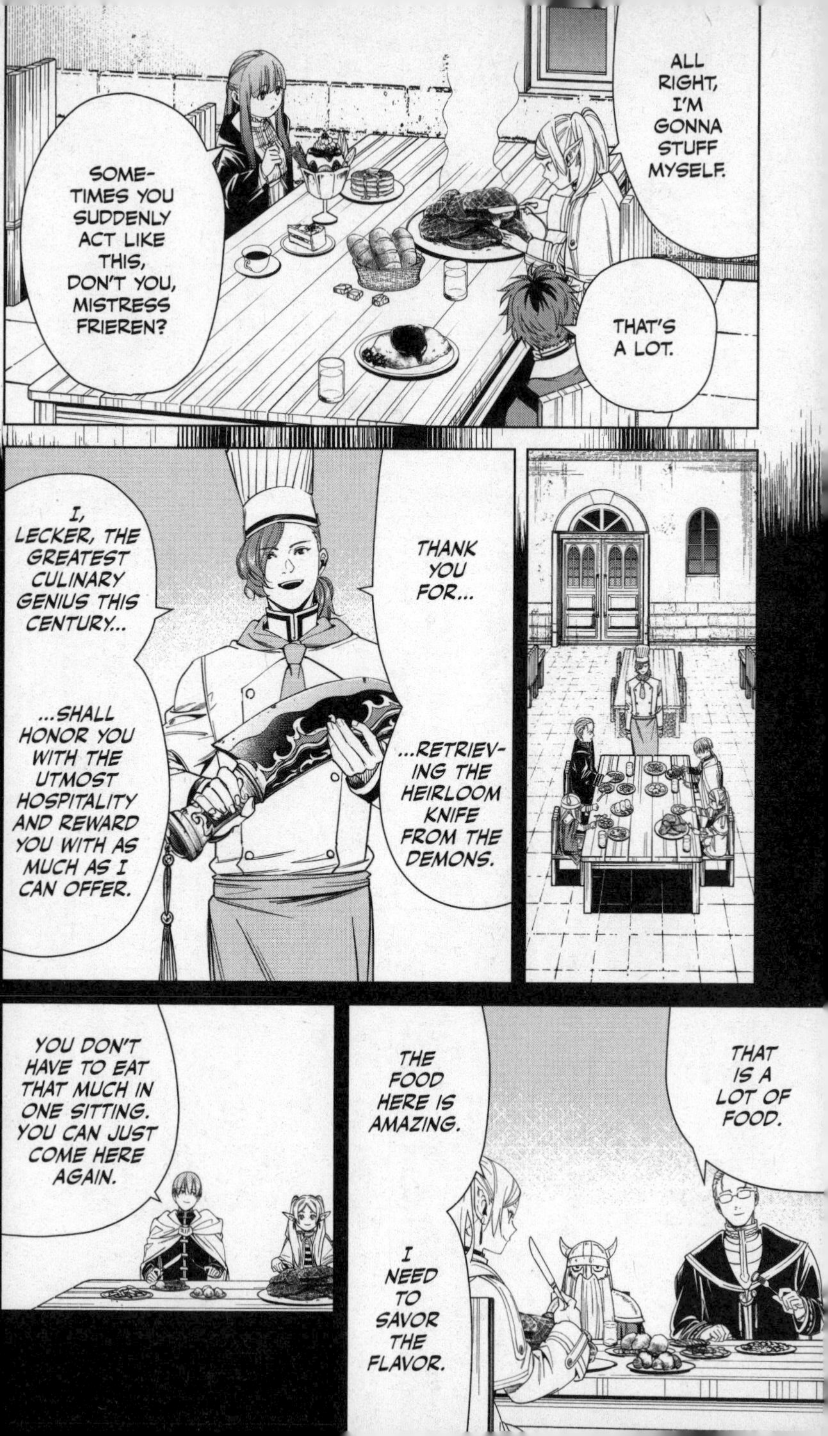
ALL RIGHT, I'M GONNA STUFF MYSELF.
THAT'S A LOT.
SOME-TIMES YOU SUDDENLY ACT LIKE THIS, DON'T YOU, MISTRESS FRIEREN?
THANK YOU FOR...
...RETRIEV-ING THE HEIRLOOM KNIFE FROM THE DEMONS.
I, LECKER, THE GREATEST CULINARY GENIUS THIS CENTURY...
...SHALL HONOR YOU WITH THE UTMOST HOSPITALITY AND REWARD YOU WITH AS MUCH AS I CAN OFFER.
THAT IS A LOT OF FOOD.
THE FOOD HERE IS AMAZING.
I NEED TO SAVOR THE FLAVOR.
YOU DON'T HAVE TO EAT THAT MUCH IN ONE SITTING. YOU CAN JUST COME HERE AGAIN.

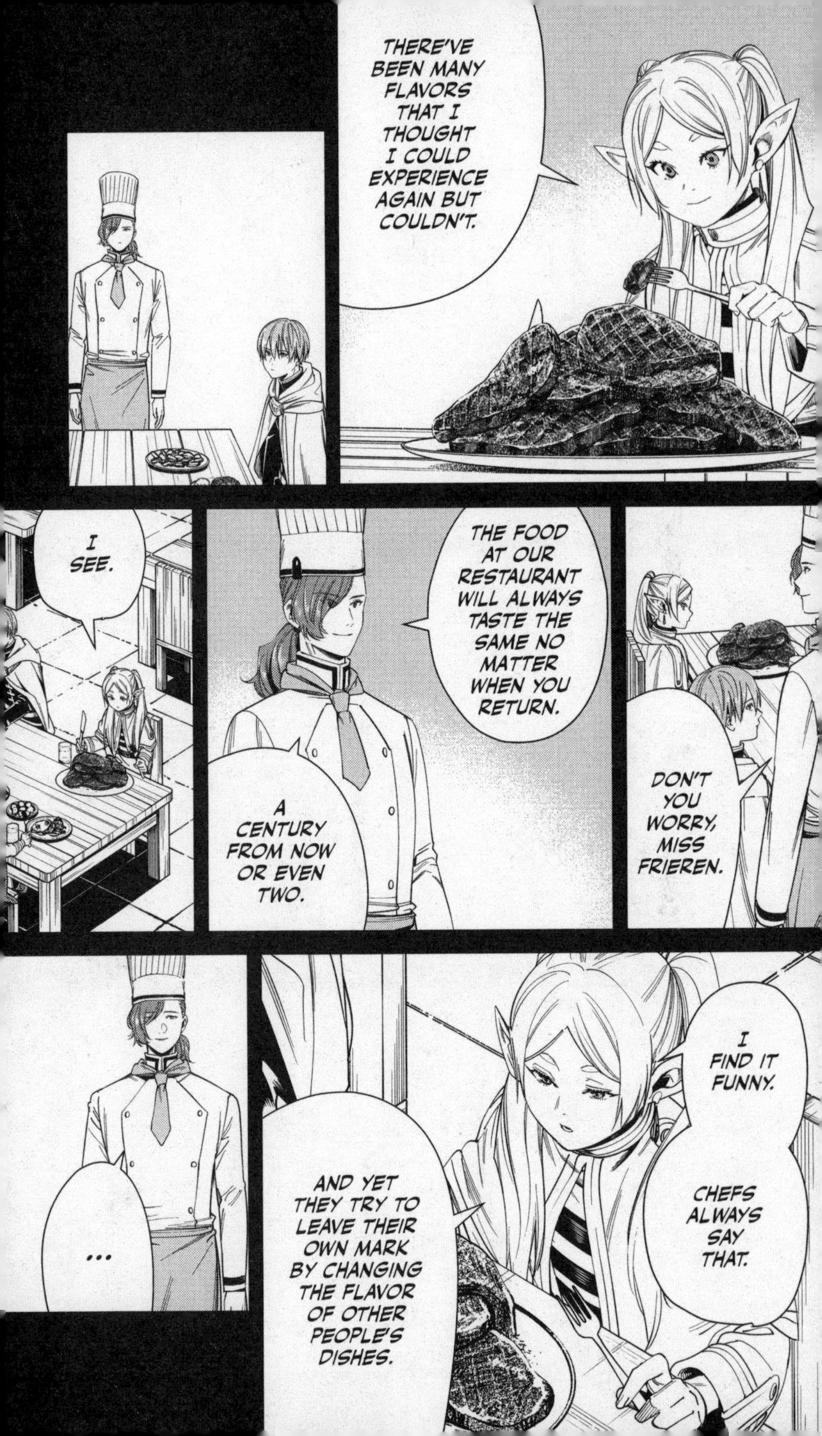
THERE'VE BEEN MANY FLAVORS THAT I THOUGHT I COULD EXPERIENCE AGAIN BUT COULDN'T.
DON'T YOU WORRY, MISS FRIEREN.
THE FOOD AT OUR RESTAURANT WILL ALWAYS TASTE THE SAME NO MATTER WHEN YOU RETURN.
A CENTURY FROM NOW OR EVEN TWO.
I SEE.
I FIND IT FUNNY.
CHEFS ALWAYS SAY THAT.
AND YET THEY TRY TO LEAVE THEIR OWN MARK BY CHANGING THE FLAVOR OF OTHER PEOPLE'S DISHES.
...

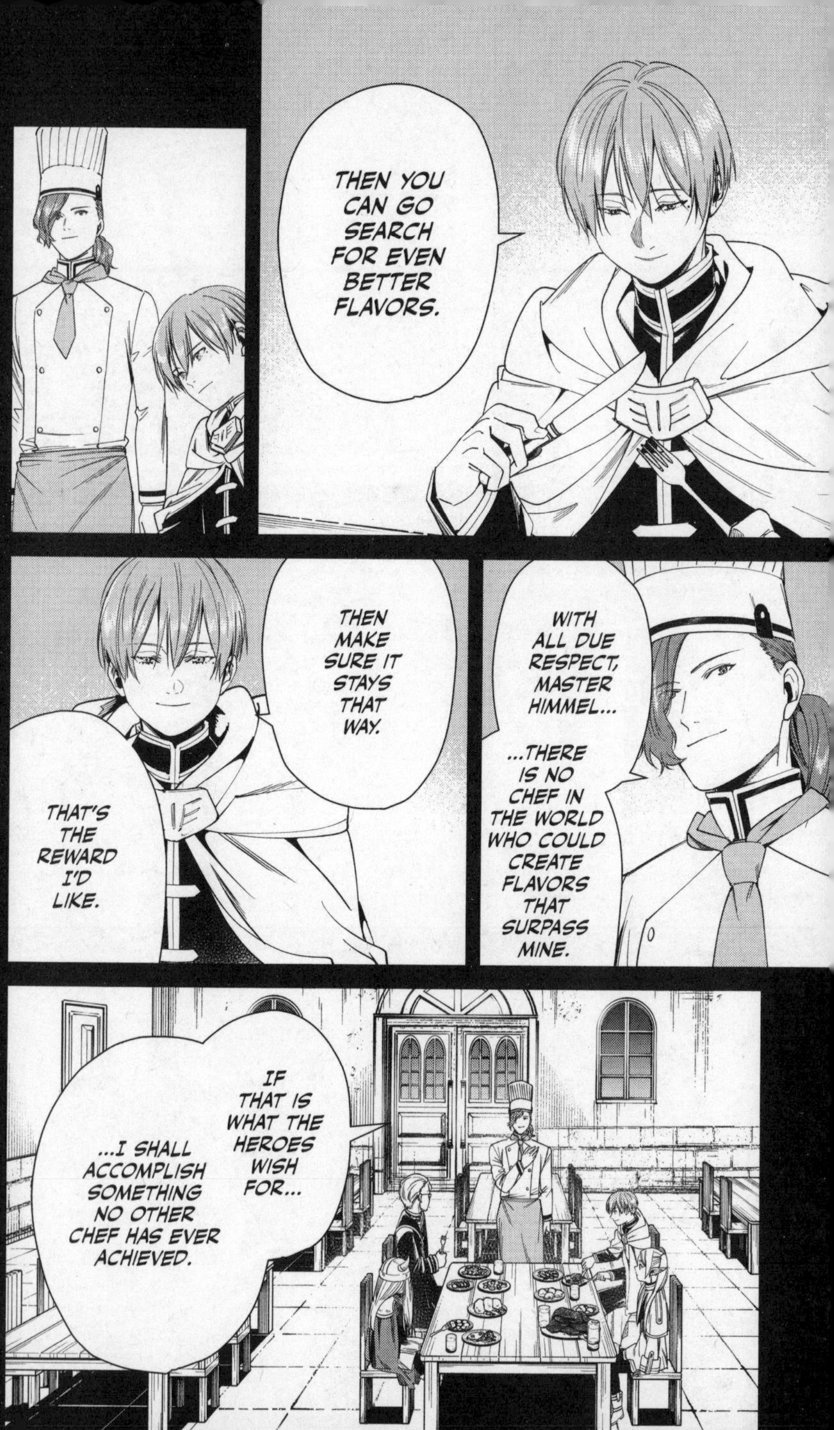
THEN YOU CAN GO SEARCH FOR EVEN BETTER FLAVORS.
WITH ALL DUE RESPECT, MASTER HIMMEL...
...THERE IS NO CHEF IN THE WORLD WHO COULD CREATE FLAVORS THAT SURPASS MINE.
THEN MAKE SURE IT STAYS THAT WAY.
THAT'S THE REWARD I'D LIKE.
IF THAT IS WHAT THE HEROES WISH FOR...
...I SHALL ACCOMPLISH SOMETHING NO OTHER CHEF HAS EVER ACHIEVED.

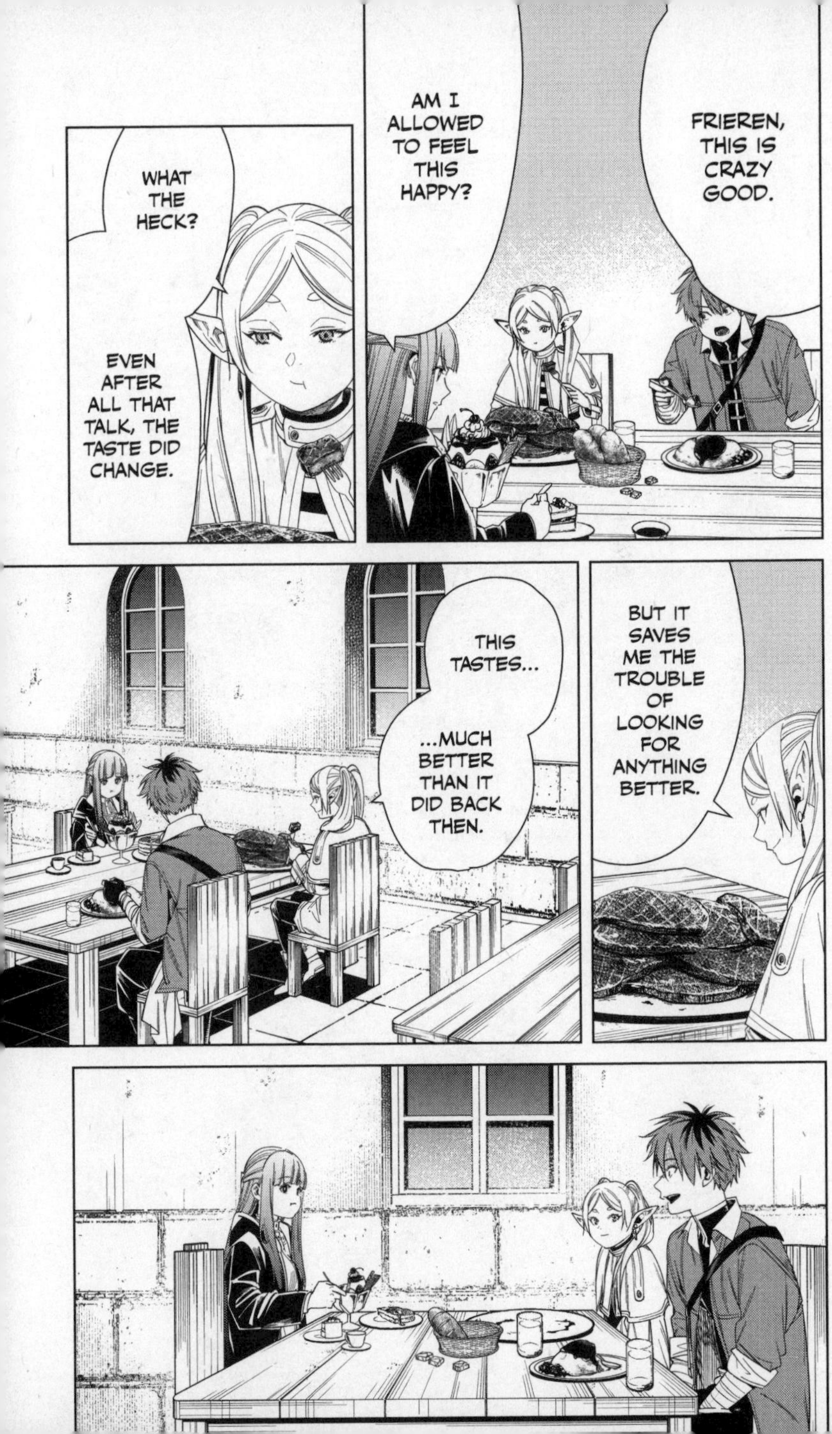
FRIEREN, THIS IS CRAZY GOOD.
AM I ALLOWED TO FEEL THIS HAPPY?
WHAT THE HECK?
EVEN AFTER ALL THAT TALK, THE TASTE DID CHANGE.
BUT IT SAVES ME THE TROUBLE OF LOOKING FOR ANYTHING BETTER.
THIS TASTES...
...MUCH BETTER THAN IT DID BACK THEN.

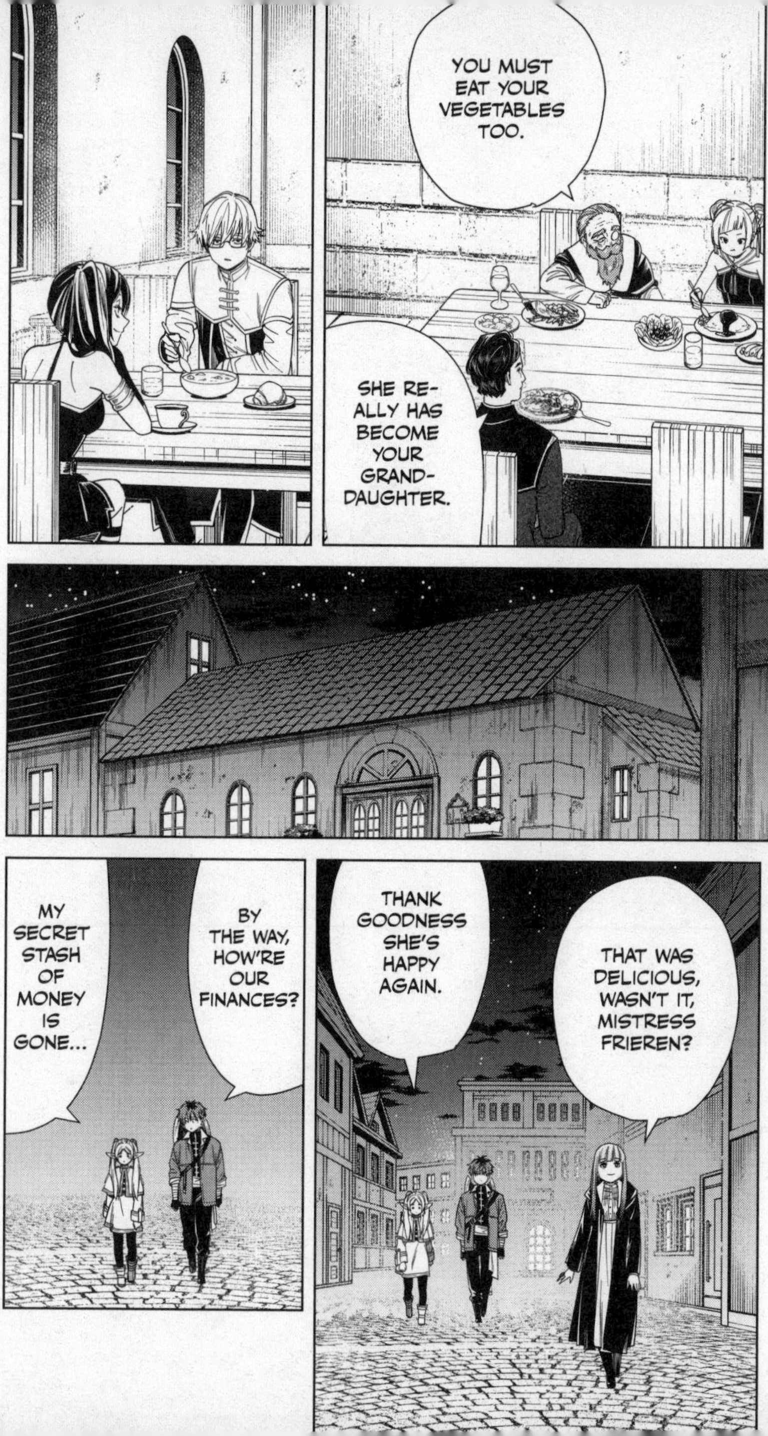
YOU MUST EAT YOUR VEGETABLES TOO.
SHE REALLY HAS BECOME YOUR GRANDDAUGHTER.
THAT WAS DELICIOUS, WASN'T IT, MISTRESS FRIEREN?
THANK GOODNESS SHE'S HAPPY AGAIN.
BY THE WAY, HOW'RE OUR FINANCES?
MY SECRET STASH OF MONEY IS GONE...

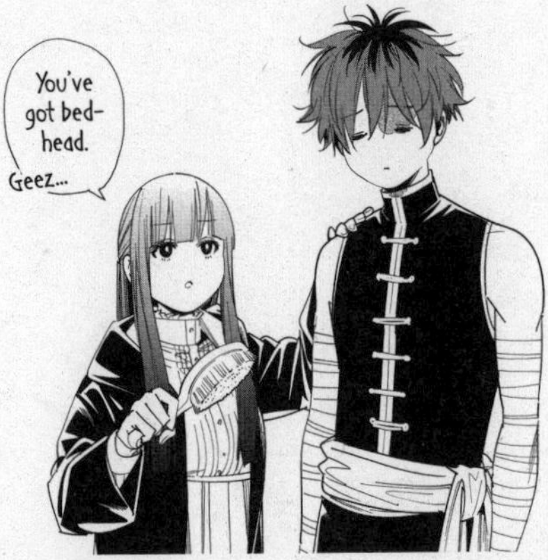
You've got bed-head.
Geez...

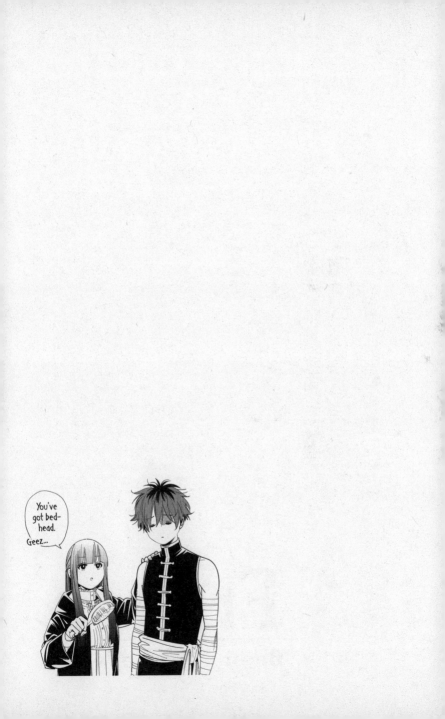

Frieren

Beyond Journey's End

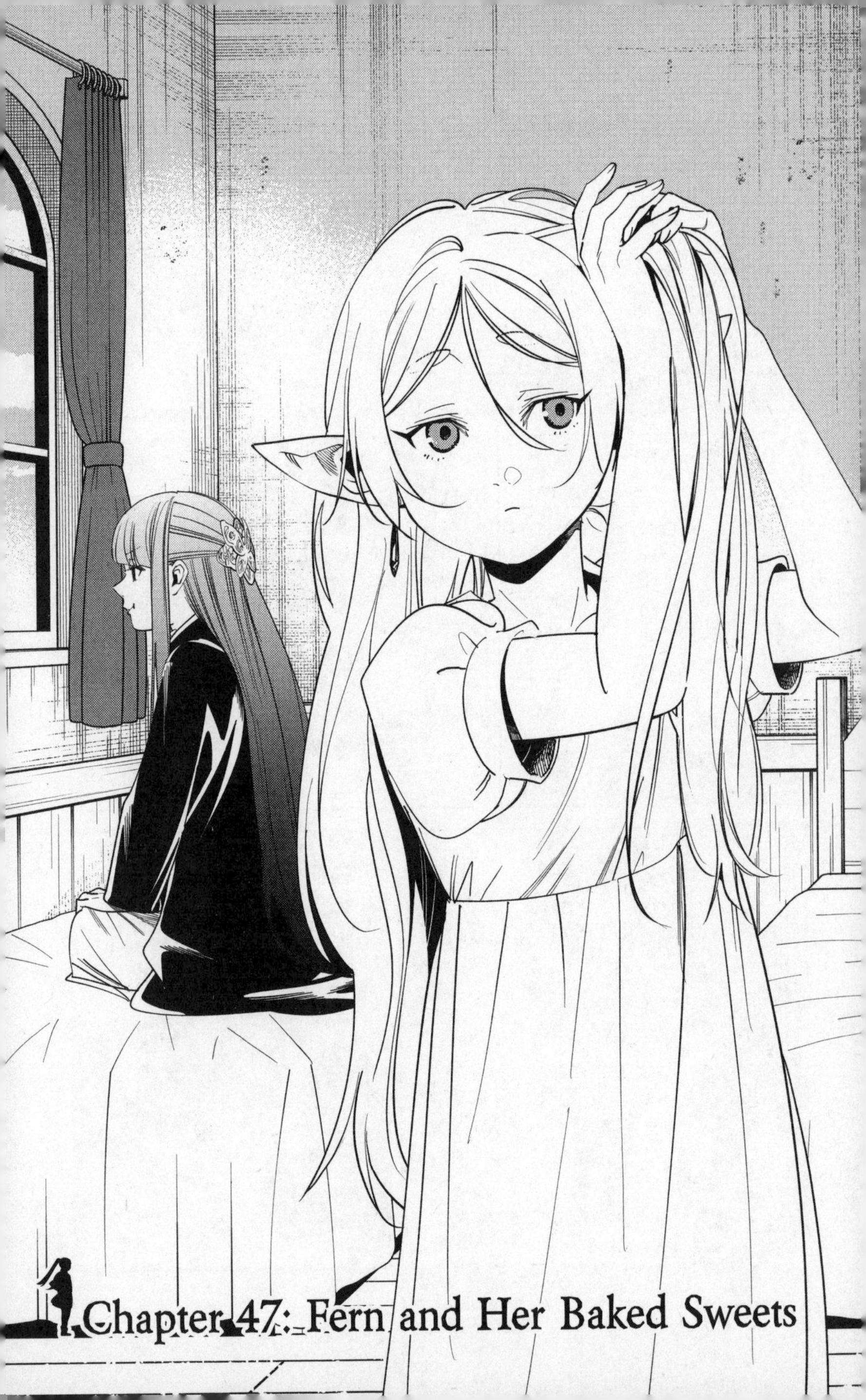

Chapter 47: Fern and Her Baked Sweets

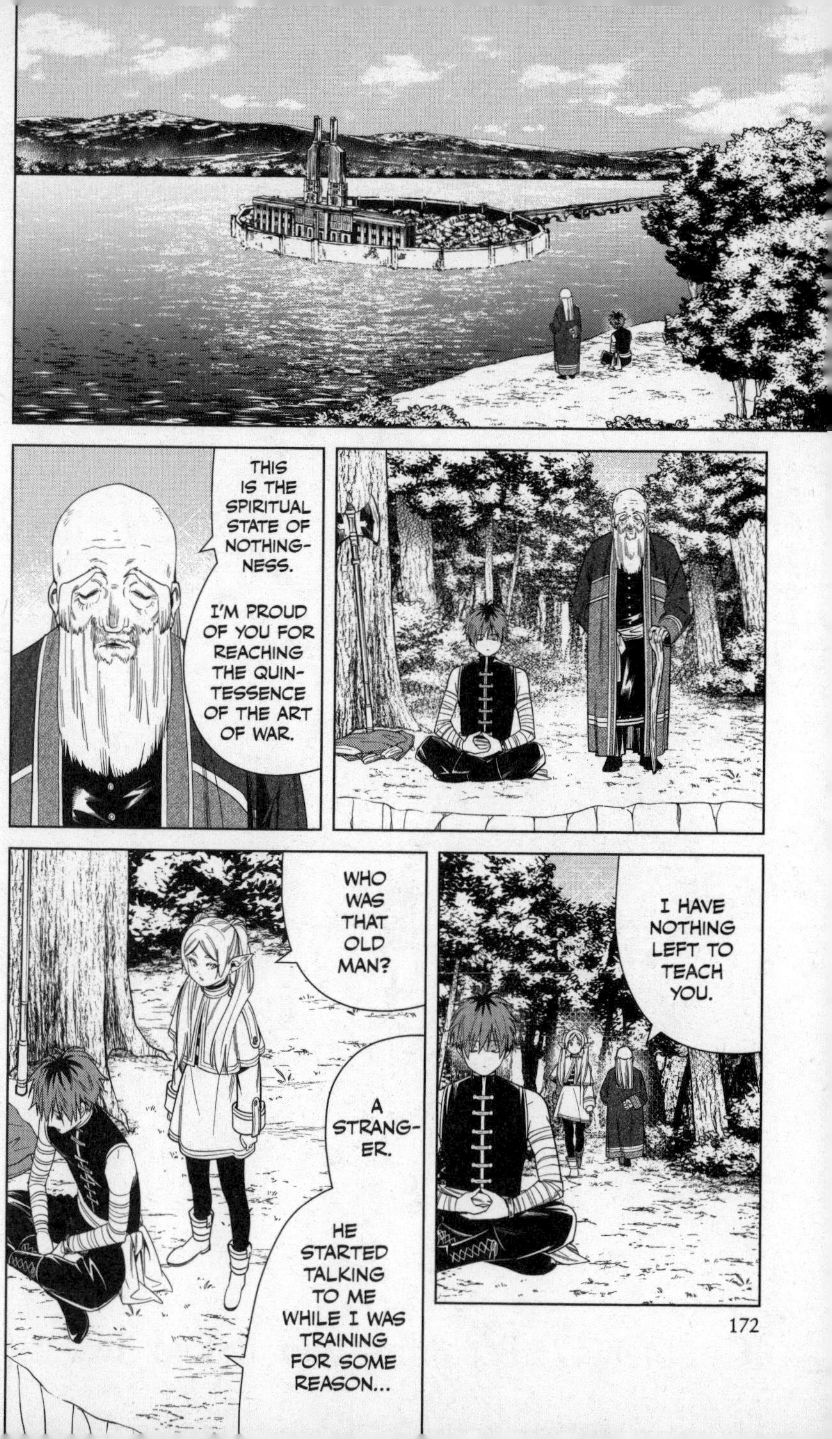
THIS IS THE SPIRITUAL STATE OF NOTHING-NESS.
I'M PROUD OF YOU FOR REACHING THE QUIN-TESSENCE OF THE ART OF WAR.
I HAVE NOTHING LEFT TO TEACH YOU.
WHO WAS THAT OLD MAN?
A STRANG-ER.
HE STARTED TALKING TO ME WHILE I WAS TRAINING FOR SOME REASON...

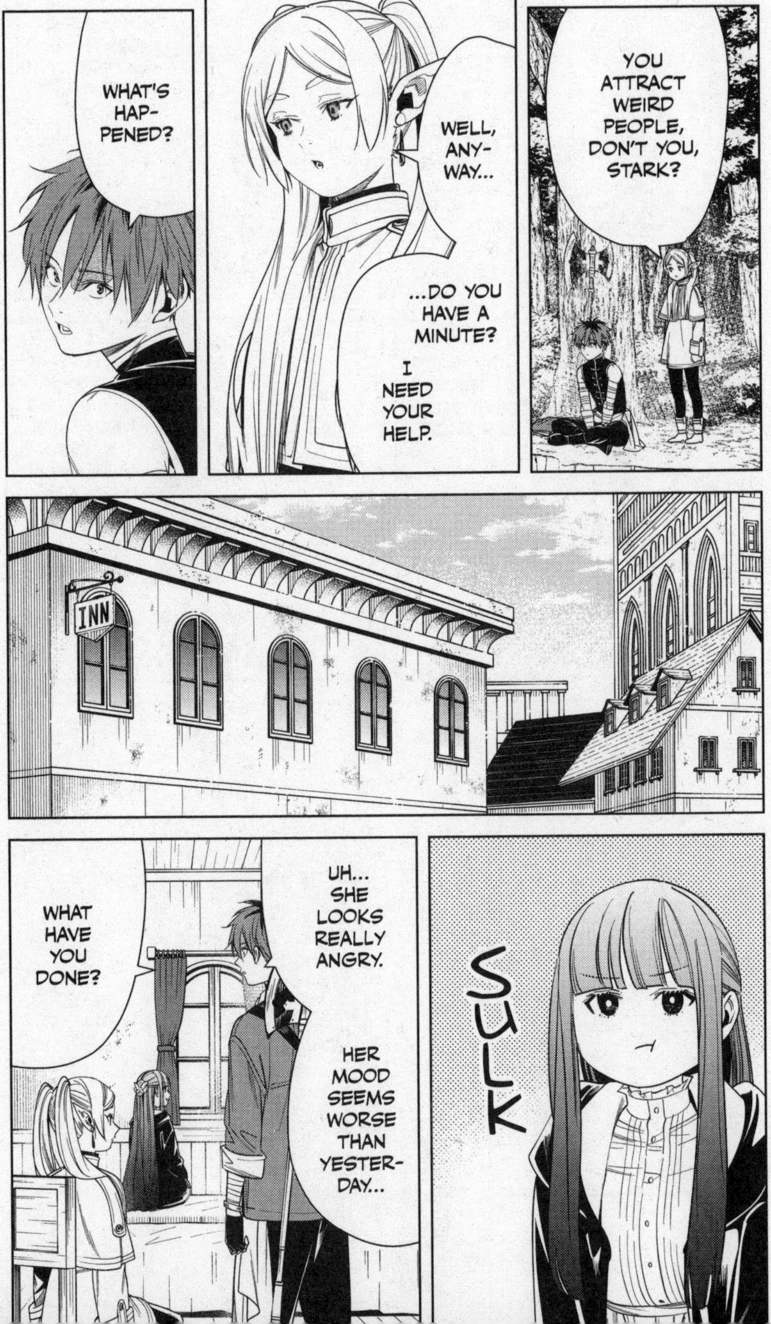
YOU ATTRACT WEIRD PEOPLE, DON'T YOU, STARK?
WELL, ANYWAY...
...DO YOU HAVE A MINUTE?
I NEED YOUR HELP.
WHAT'S HAPPENED?
INN
SULK
UH... SHE LOOKS REALLY ANGRY.
HER MOOD SEEMS WORSE THAN YESTERDAY...
WHAT HAVE YOU DONE?

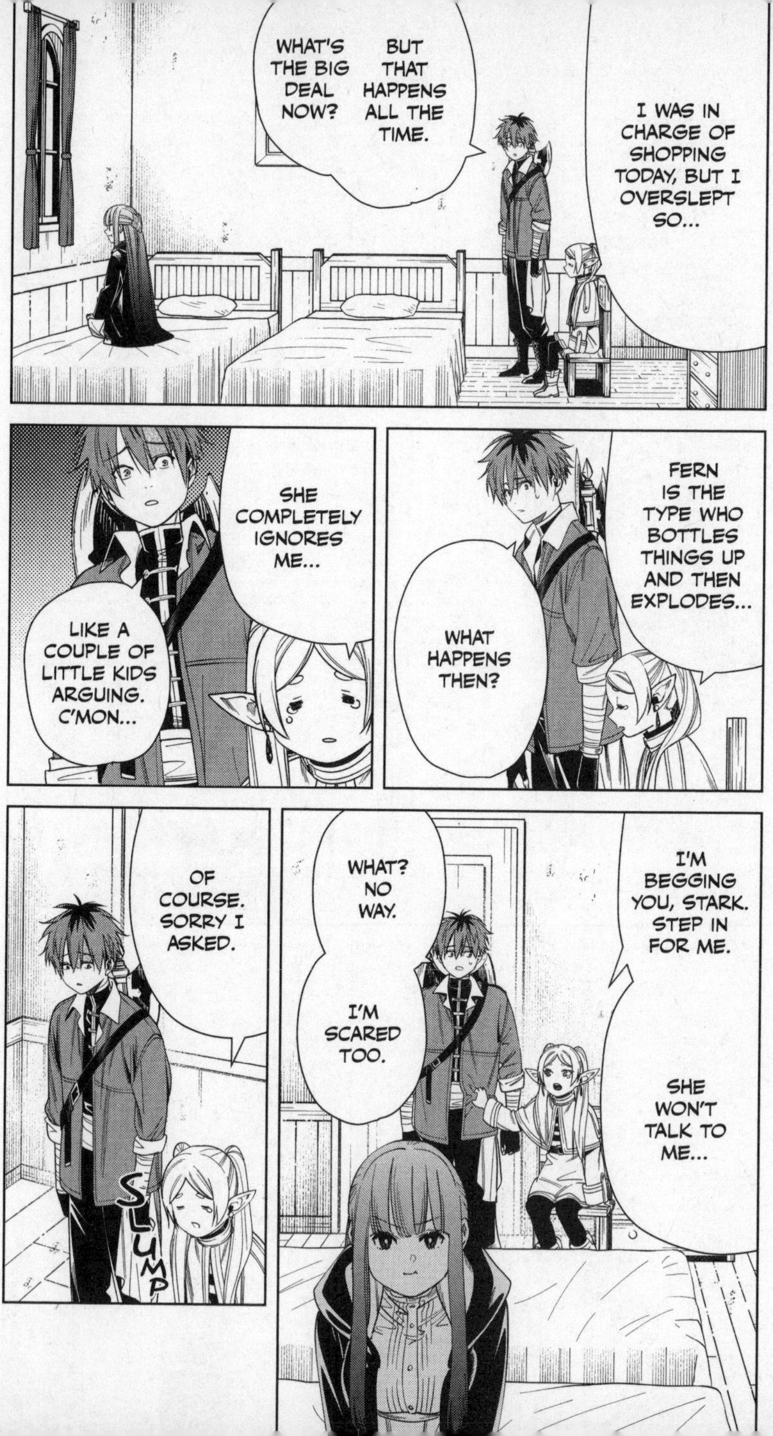
I WAS IN CHARGE OF SHOPPING TODAY, BUT I OVERSLEPT SO...
BUT THAT HAPPENS ALL THE TIME.
WHAT'S THE BIG DEAL NOW?
FERN IS THE TYPE WHO BOTTLES THINGS UP AND THEN EXPLODES...
WHAT HAPPENS THEN?
SHE COMPLETELY IGNORES ME...
LIKE A COUPLE OF LITTLE KIDS ARGUING. C'MON...
I'M BEGGING YOU, STARK. STEP IN FOR ME.
SHE WON'T TALK TO ME...
WHAT? NO WAY.
I'M SCARED TOO.
OF COURSE. SORRY I ASKED.
SLUMP

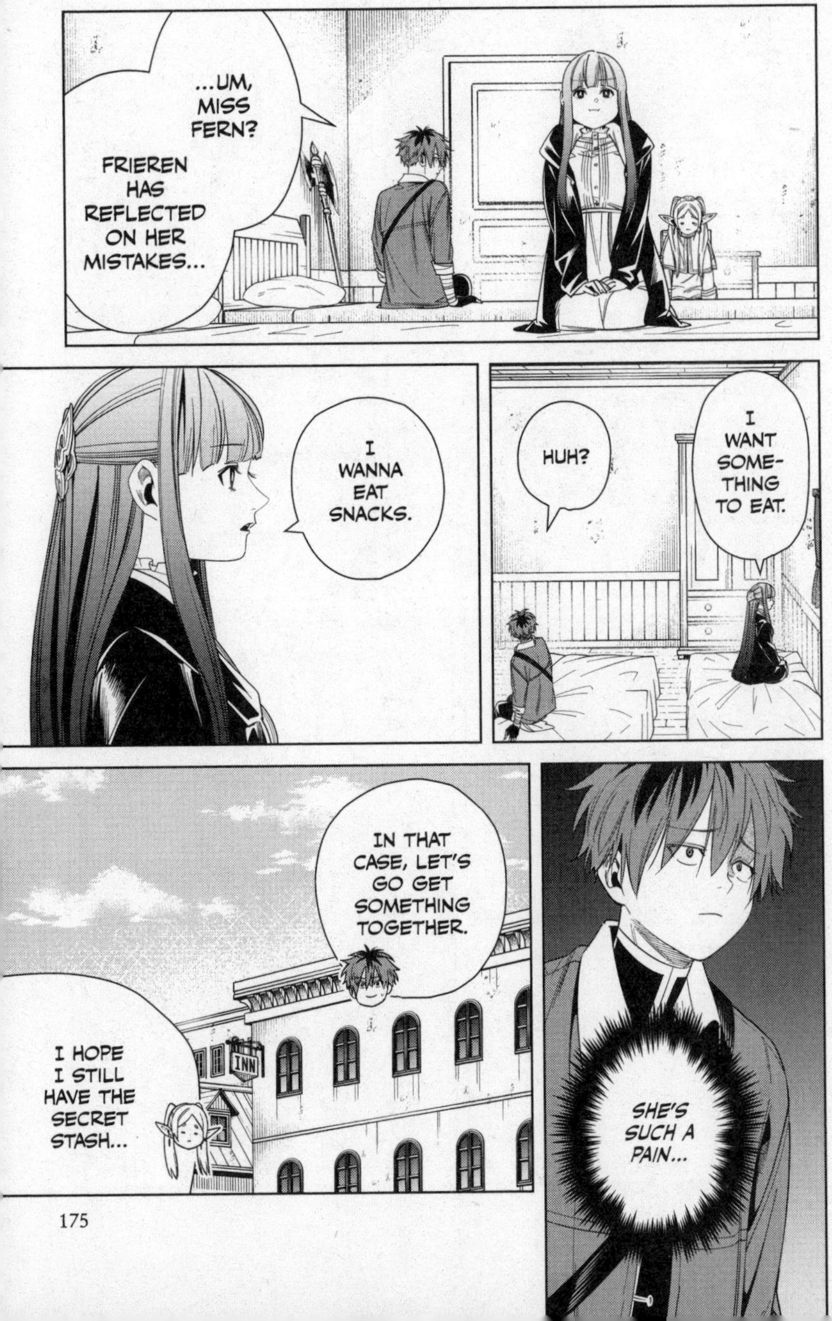
...UM, MISS FERN?
FRIEREN HAS REFLECTED ON HER MISTAKES...
I WANT SOMETHING TO EAT.
HUH?
I WANNA EAT SNACKS.
SHE'S SUCH A PAIN...
IN THAT CASE, LET'S GO GET SOMETHING TOGETHER.
INN
I HOPE I STILL HAVE THE SECRET STASH...

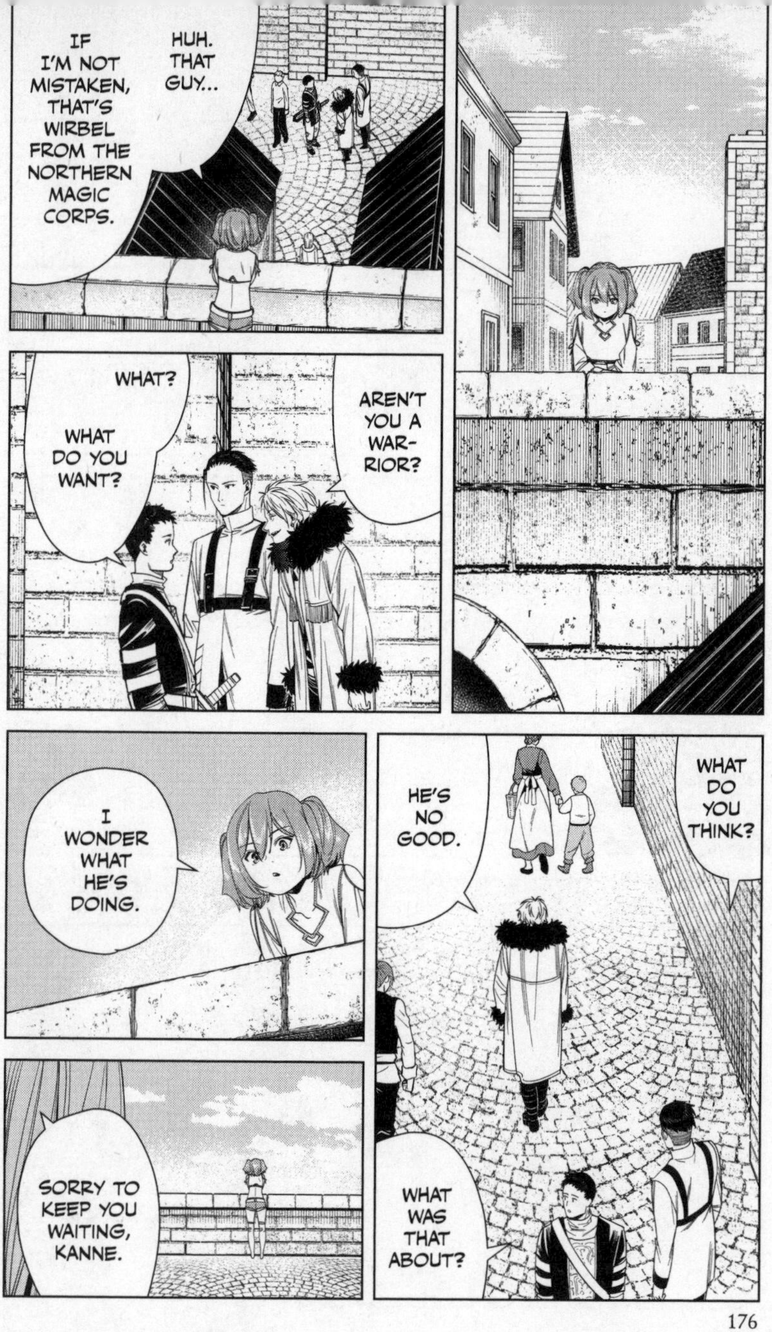
HUH. THAT GUY...
IF I'M NOT MISTAKEN, THAT'S WIRBEL FROM THE NORTHERN MAGIC CORPS.
AREN'T YOU A WAR-RIOR?
WHAT?
WHAT DO YOU WANT?
WHAT DO YOU THINK?
HE'S NO GOOD.
WHAT WAS THAT ABOUT?
I WONDER WHAT HE'S DOING.
SORRY TO KEEP YOU WAITING, KANNE.

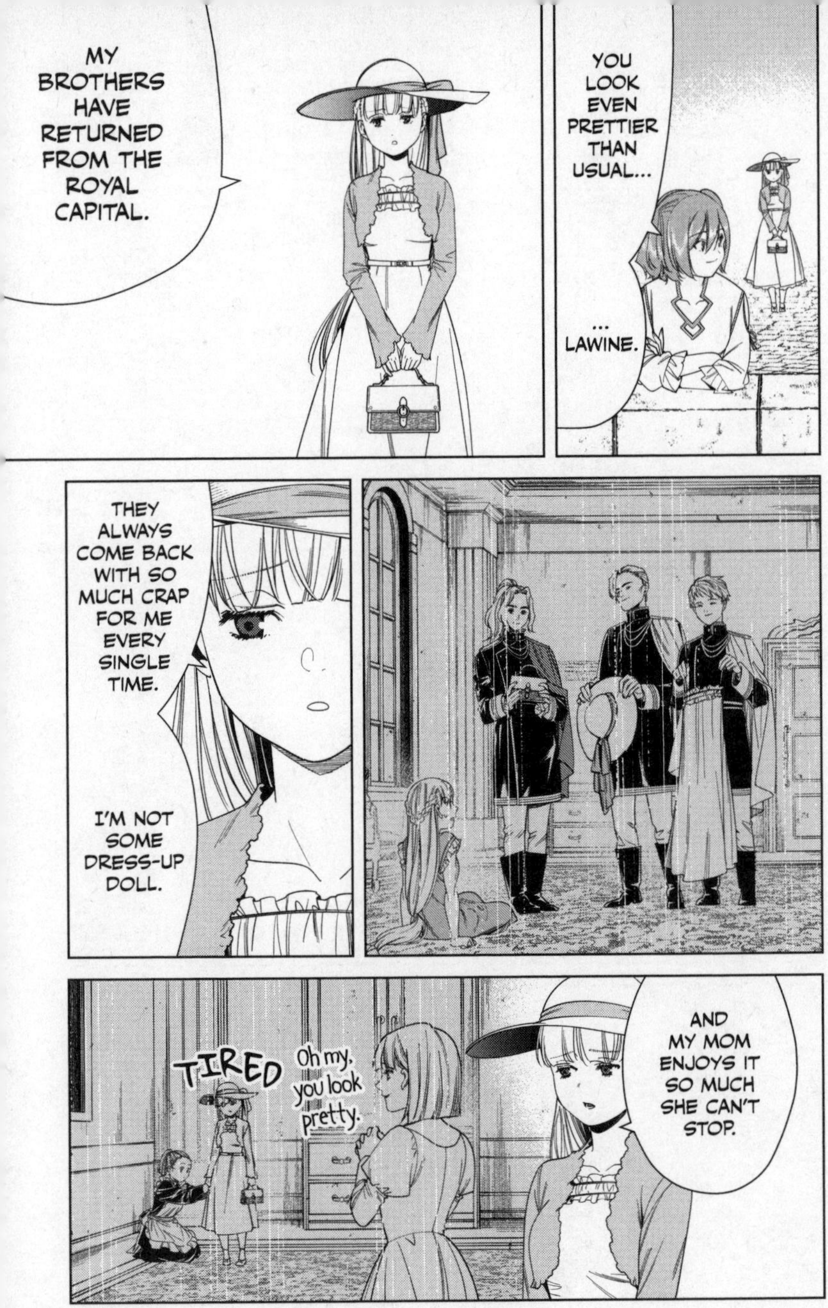
YOU LOOK EVEN PRETTIER THAN USUAL...
... LAWINE.
MY BROTHERS HAVE RETURNED FROM THE ROYAL CAPITAL.
THEY ALWAYS COME BACK WITH SO MUCH CRAP FOR ME EVERY SINGLE TIME.
I'M NOT SOME DRESS-UP DOLL.
AND MY MOM ENJOYS IT SO MUCH SHE CAN'T STOP.
Oh my, you look pretty.
TIRED

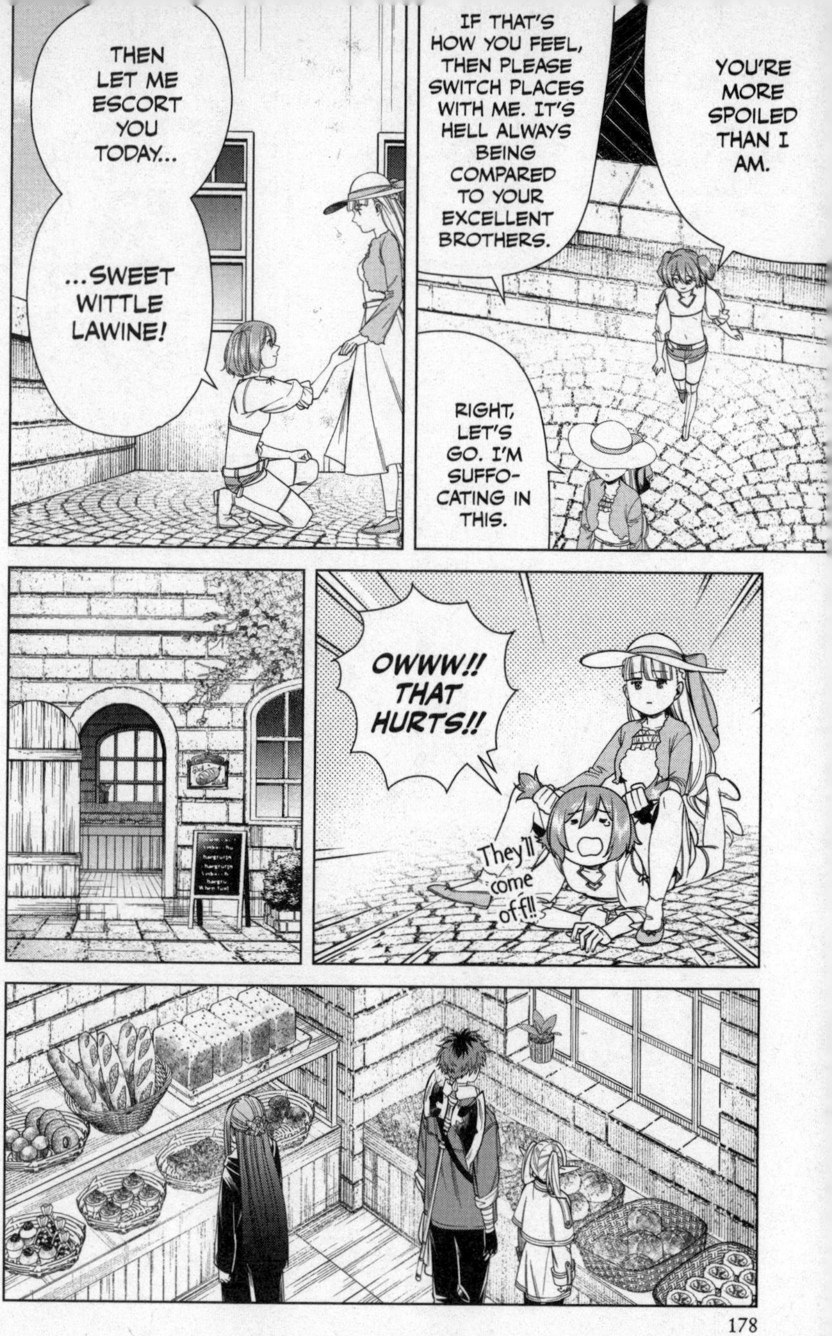
YOU'RE MORE SPOILED THAN I AM.
IF THAT'S HOW YOU FEEL, THEN PLEASE SWITCH PLACES WITH ME. IT'S HELL ALWAYS BEING COMPARED TO YOUR EXCELLENT BROTHERS.
RIGHT, LET'S GO. I'M SUFFO-CATING IN THIS.
THEN LET ME ESCORT YOU TODAY...
...SWEET WITTLE LAWINE!
OWWW!! THAT HURTS!!
They'll come off!!

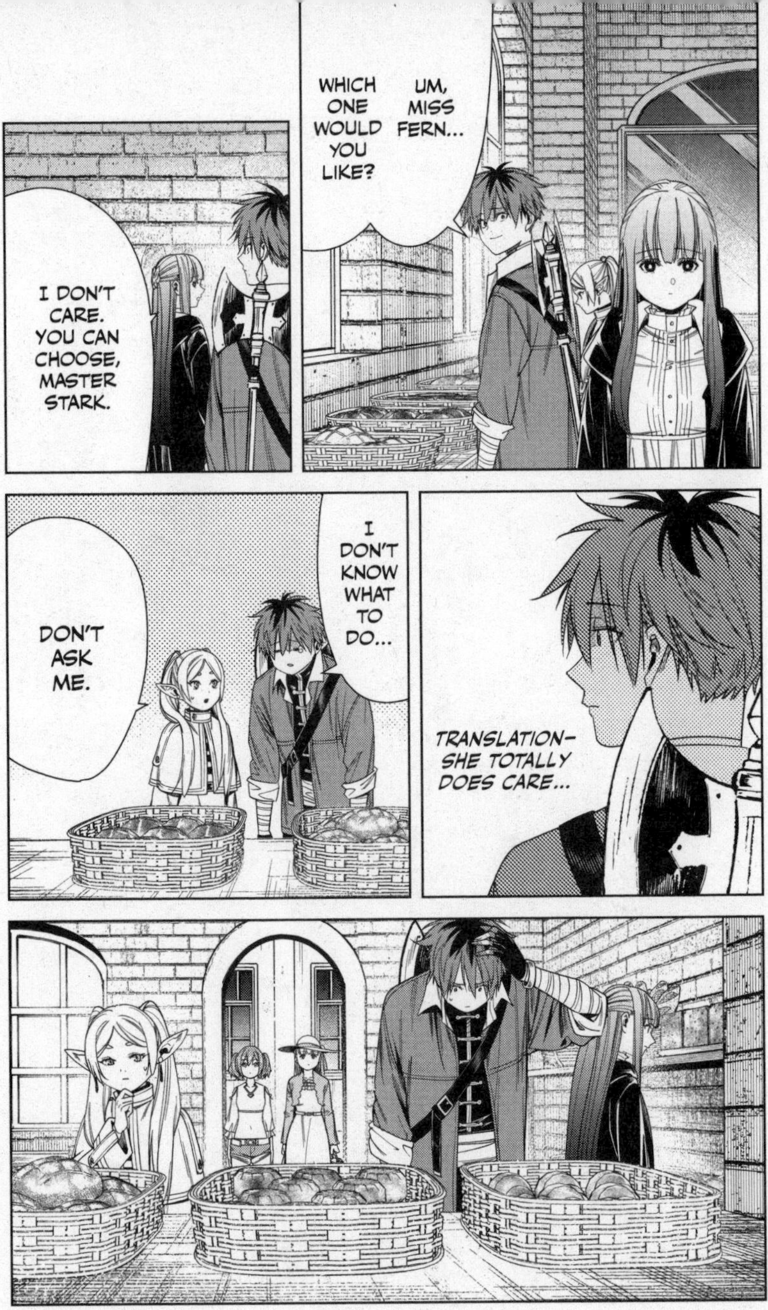
UM, MISS FERN...
WHICH ONE WOULD YOU LIKE?
I DON'T CARE. YOU CAN CHOOSE, MASTER STARK.
TRANSLATION— SHE TOTALLY DOES CARE...
I DON'T KNOW WHAT TO DO...
DON'T ASK ME.

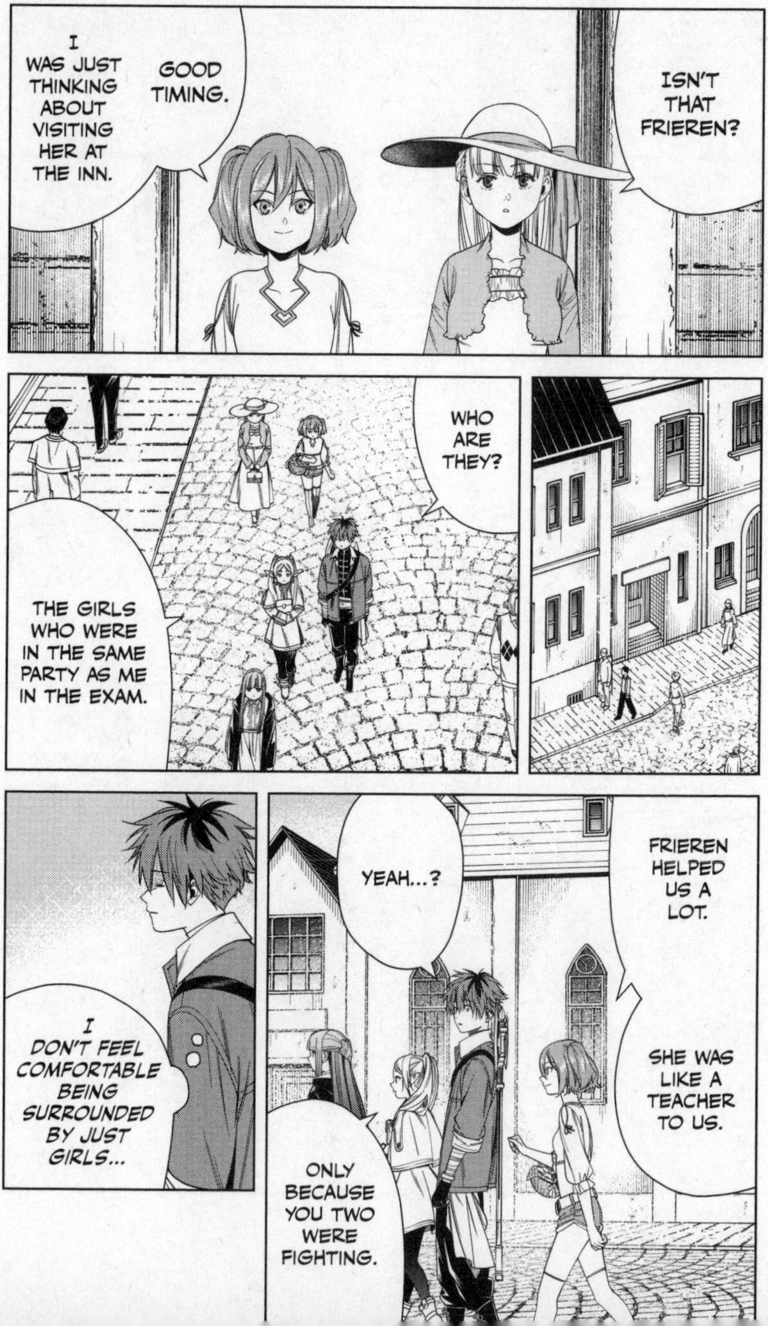
ISN'T THAT FRIEREN?
GOOD TIMING.
I WAS JUST THINKING ABOUT VISITING HER AT THE INN.
WHO ARE THEY?
THE GIRLS WHO WERE IN THE SAME PARTY AS ME IN THE EXAM.
FRIEREN HELPED US A LOT.
SHE WAS LIKE A TEACHER TO US.
YEAH...?
ONLY BECAUSE YOU TWO WERE FIGHTING.
I DON'T FEEL COMFORTABLE BEING SURROUNDED BY JUST GIRLS...

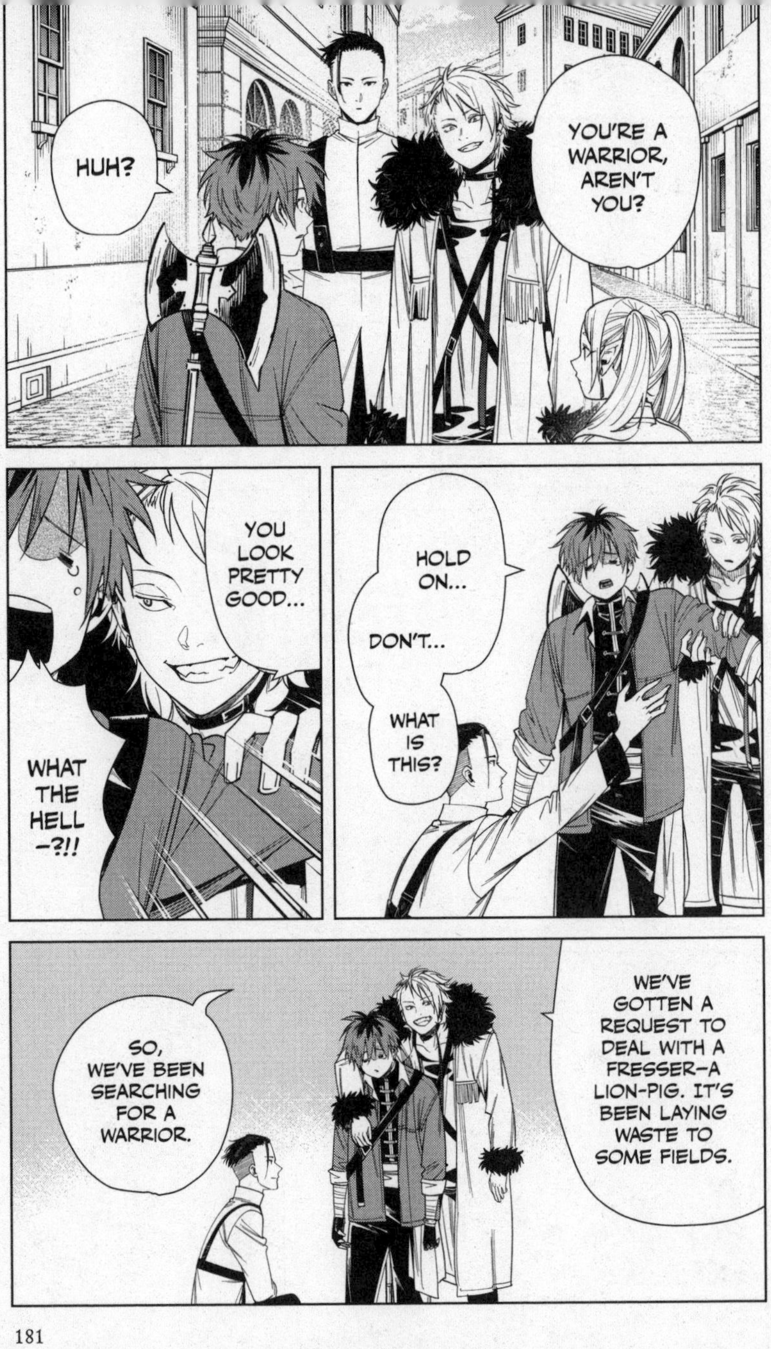
YOU'RE A WARRIOR, AREN'T YOU?
HUH?
HOLD ON...
DON'T...
WHAT IS THIS?
YOU LOOK PRETTY GOOD...
WHAT THE HELL—?!!
WE'VE GOTTEN A REQUEST TO DEAL WITH A FRESSER—A LION-PIG. IT'S BEEN LAYING WASTE TO SOME FIELDS.
SO, WE'VE BEEN SEARCHING FOR A WARRIOR.

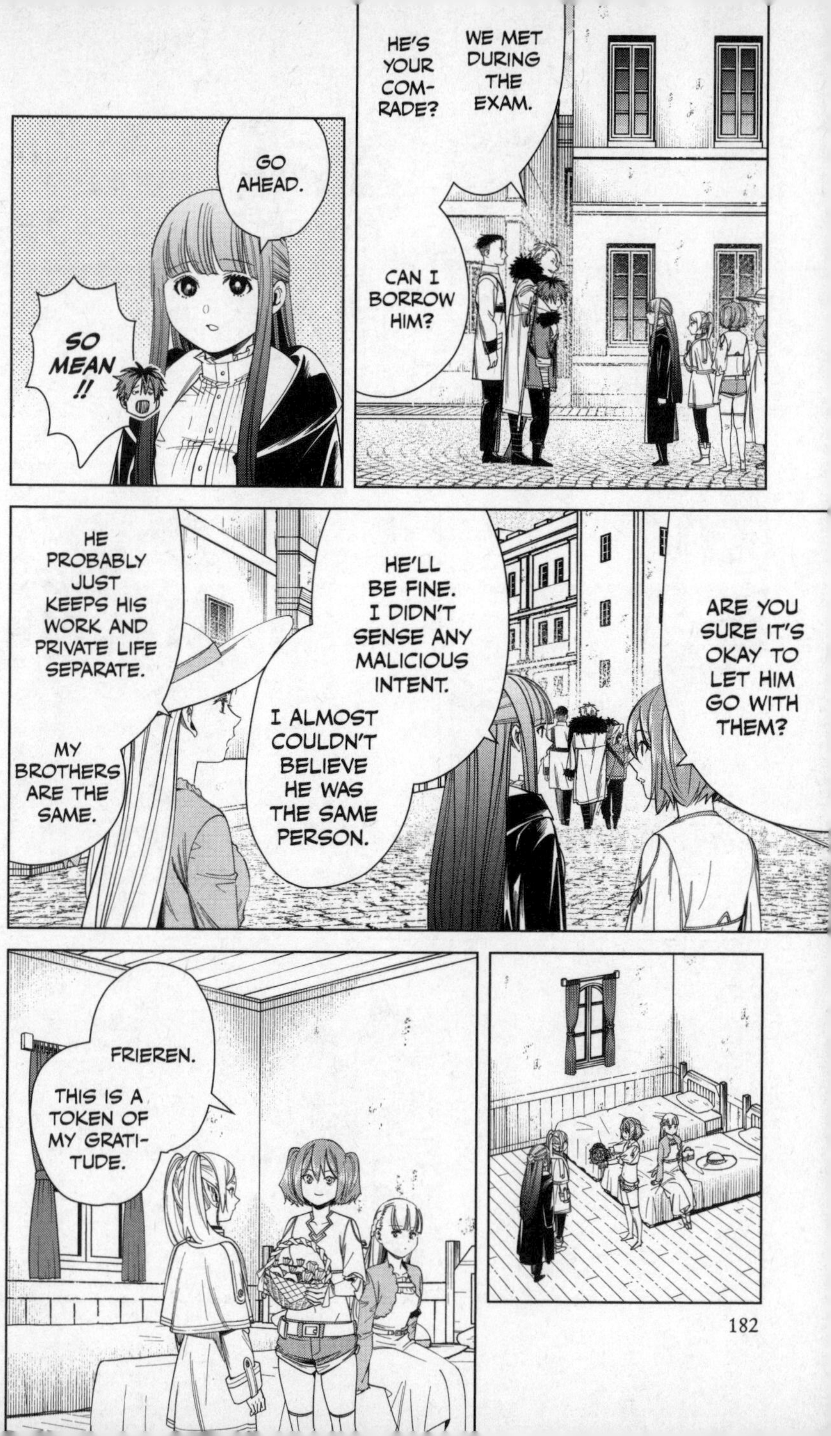
WE MET DURING THE EXAM.
HE'S YOUR COM-RADE?
CAN I BORROW HIM?
GO AHEAD.
SO MEAN!!
ARE YOU SURE IT'S OKAY TO LET HIM GO WITH THEM?
HE'LL BE FINE. I DIDN'T SENSE ANY MALICIOUS INTENT.
I ALMOST COULDN'T BELIEVE HE WAS THE SAME PERSON.
HE PROBABLY JUST KEEPS HIS WORK AND PRIVATE LIFE SEPARATE.
MY BROTHERS ARE THE SAME.
FRIEREN.
THIS IS A TOKEN OF MY GRATI-TUDE.

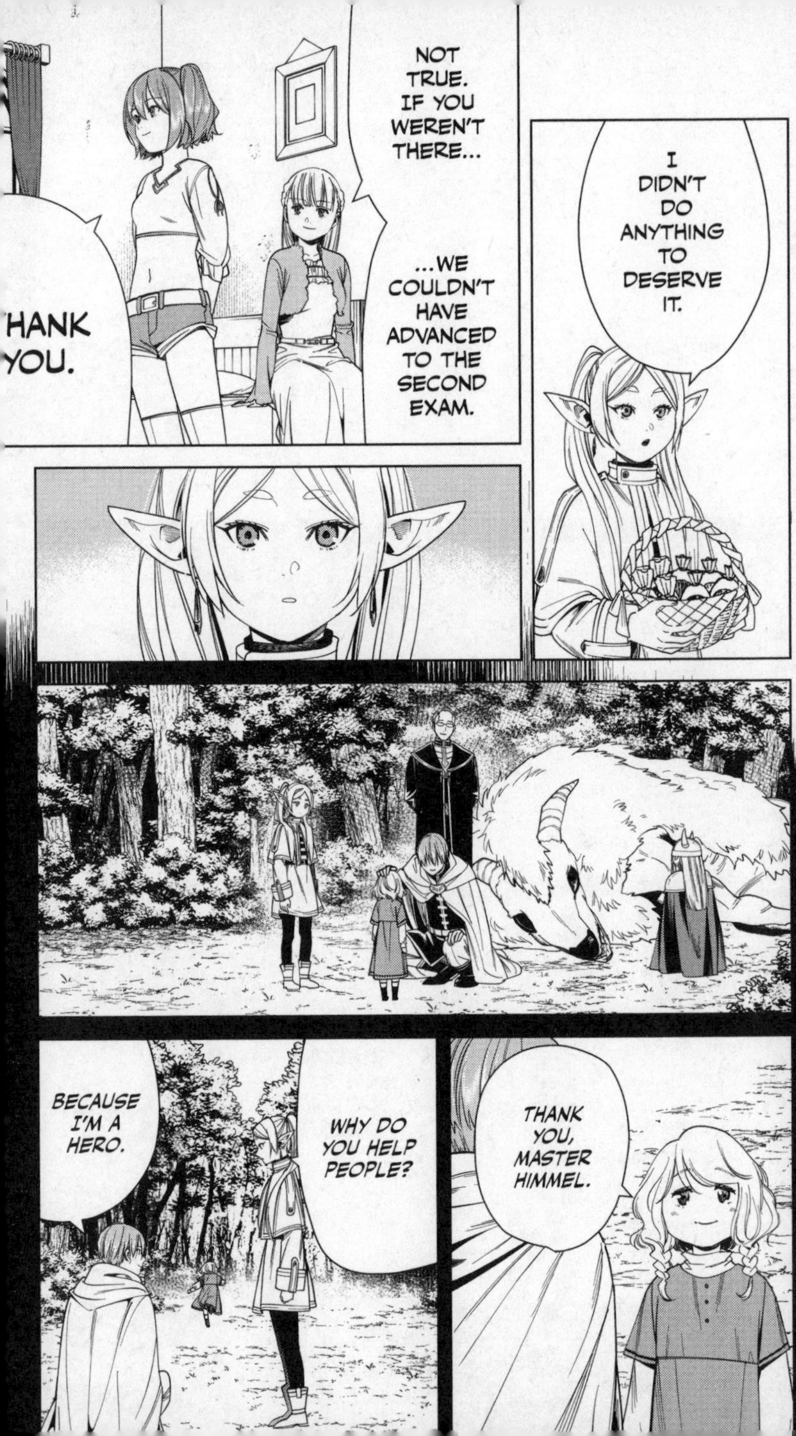
I DIDN'T DO ANYTHING TO DESERVE IT.
NOT TRUE. IF YOU WEREN'T THERE...
...WE COULDN'T HAVE ADVANCED TO THE SECOND EXAM.
THANK YOU.
THANK YOU, MASTER HIMMEL.
WHY DO YOU HELP PEOPLE?
BECAUSE I'M A HERO.

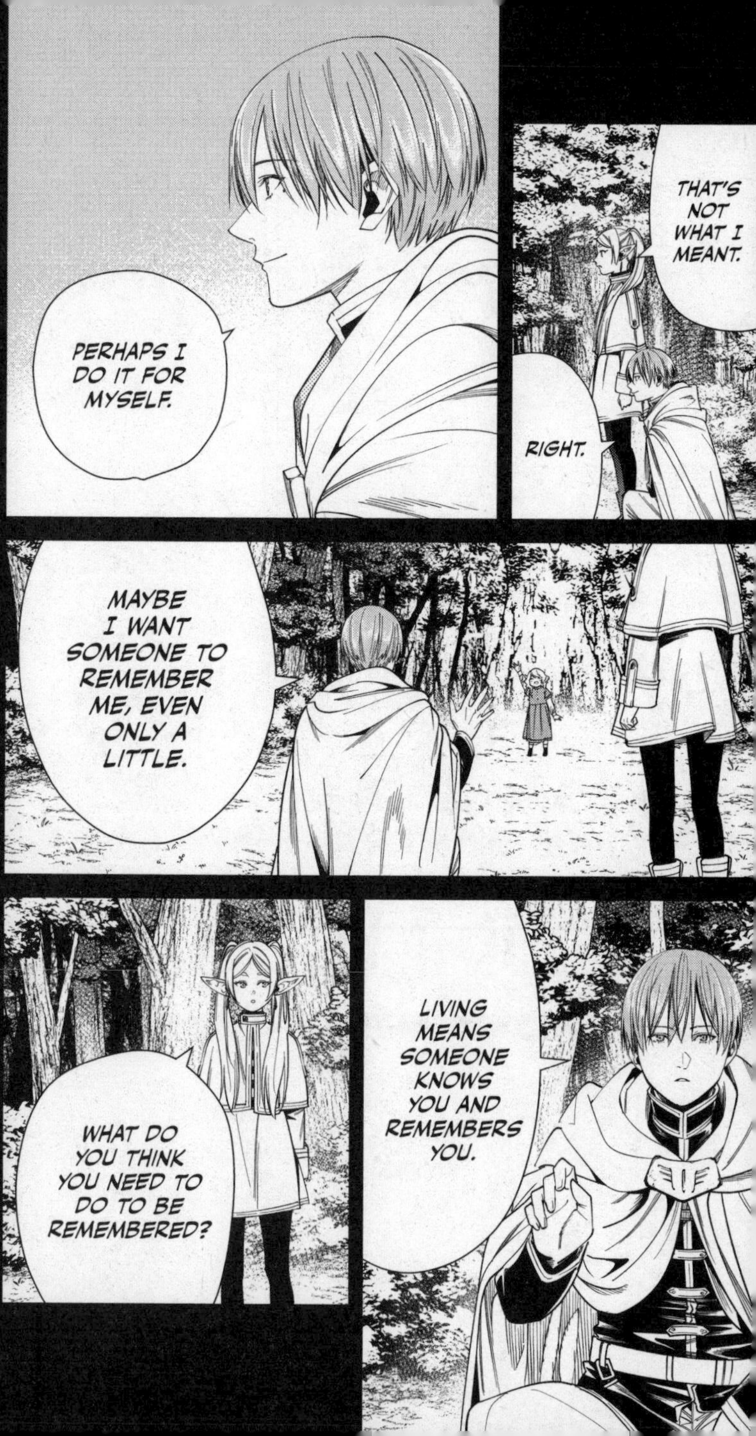
THAT'S NOT WHAT I MEANT.
RIGHT.
PERHAPS I DO IT FOR MYSELF.
MAYBE I WANT SOMEONE TO REMEMBER ME, EVEN ONLY A LITTLE.
LIVING MEANS SOMEONE KNOWS YOU AND REMEMBERS YOU.
WHAT DO YOU THINK YOU NEED TO DO TO BE REMEMBERED?

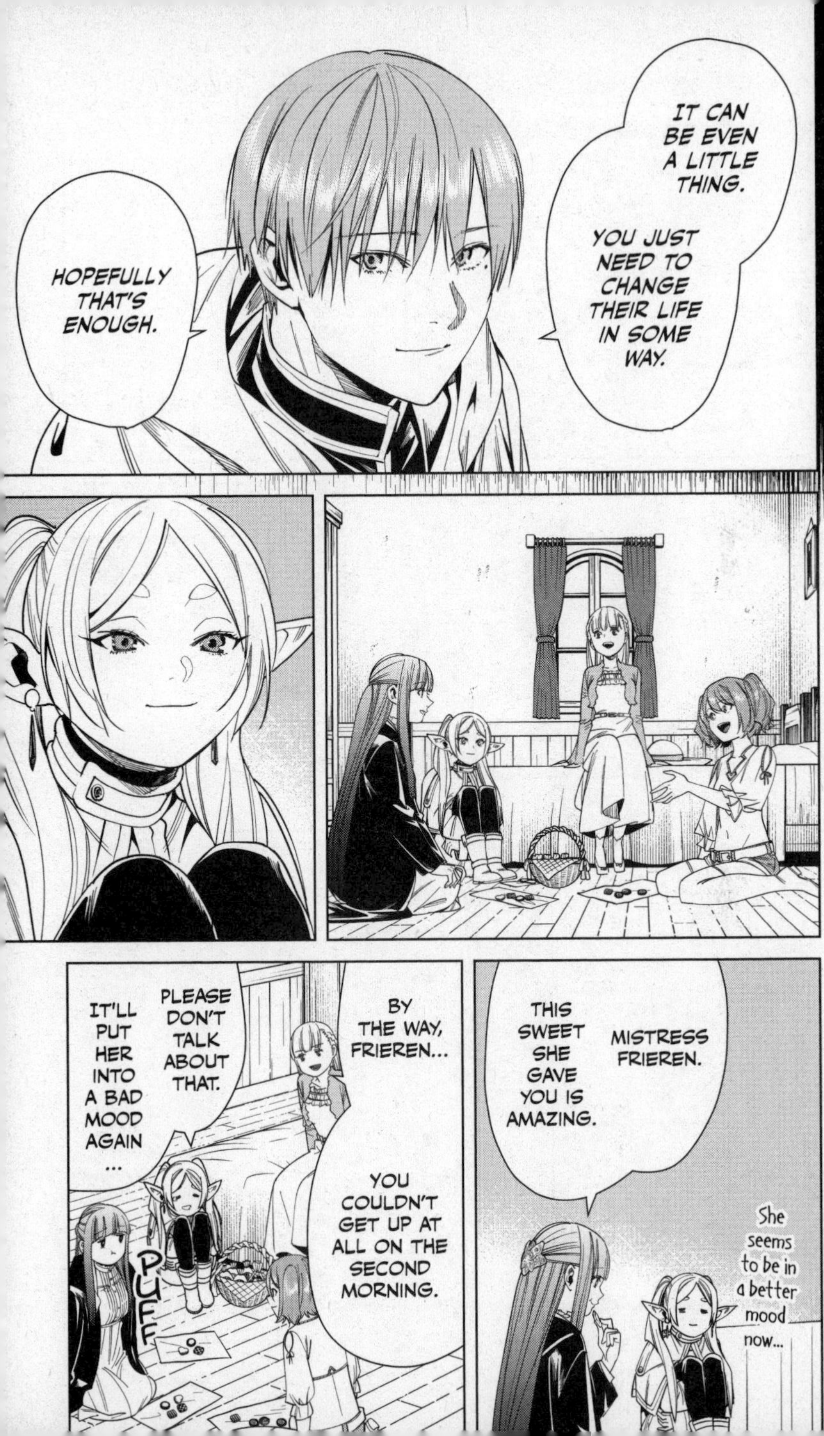
IT CAN BE EVEN A LITTLE THING.
YOU JUST NEED TO CHANGE THEIR LIFE IN SOME WAY.
HOPEFULLY THAT'S ENOUGH.
MISTRESS FRIEREN.
THIS SWEET SHE GAVE YOU IS AMAZING.
She seems to be in a better mood now...
BY THE WAY, FRIEREN...
YOU COULDN'T GET UP AT ALL ON THE SECOND MORNING.
PLEASE DON'T TALK ABOUT THAT.
IT'LL PUT HER INTO A BAD MOOD AGAIN...
PUFF

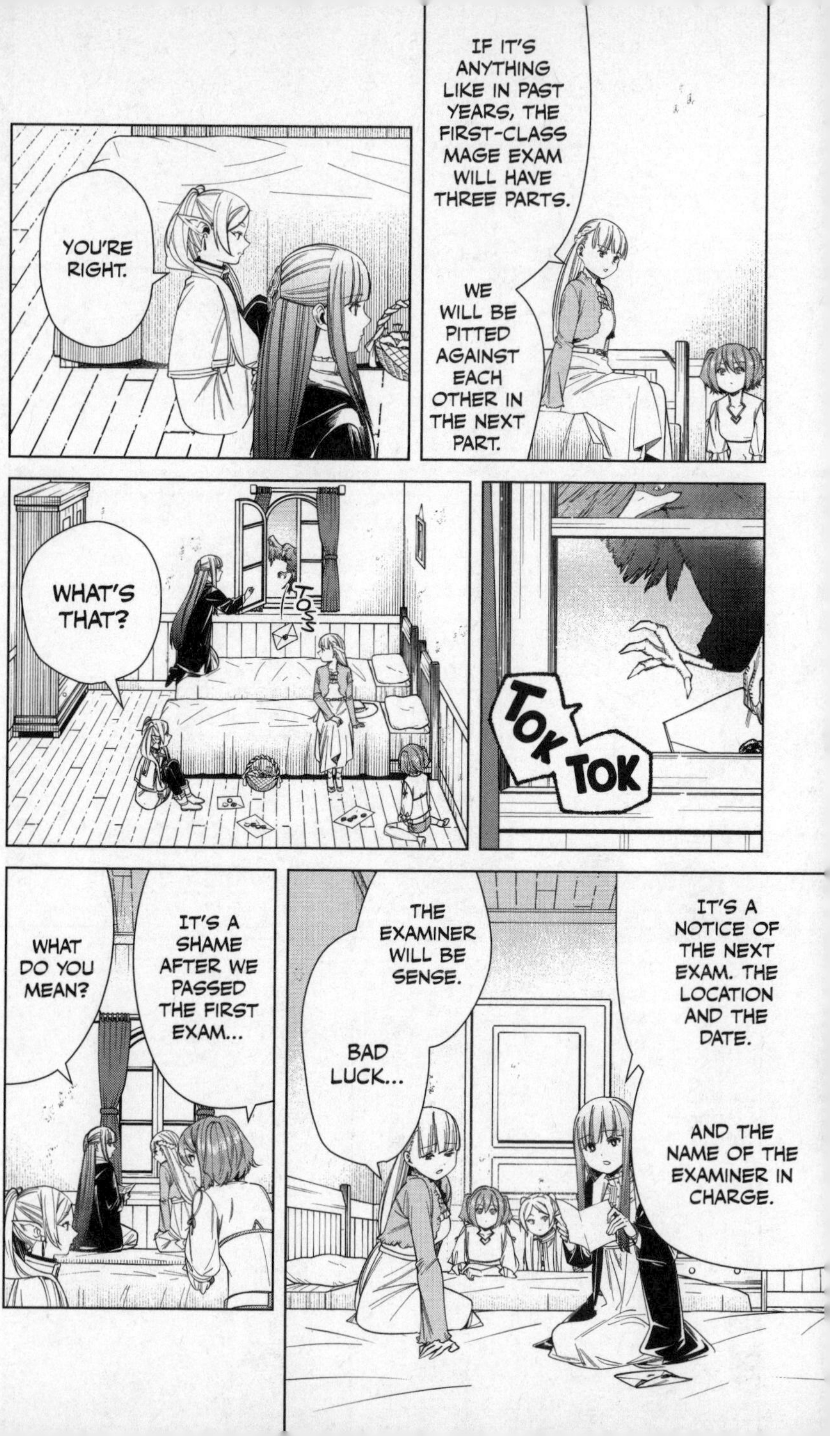
IF IT'S ANYTHING LIKE IN PAST YEARS, THE FIRST-CLASS MAGE EXAM WILL HAVE THREE PARTS.
WE WILL BE PITTED AGAINST EACH OTHER IN THE NEXT PART.
YOU'RE RIGHT.
TOK TOK
TOSS
WHAT'S THAT?
IT'S A NOTICE OF THE NEXT EXAM. THE LOCATION AND THE DATE.
AND THE NAME OF THE EXAMINER IN CHARGE.
THE EXAMINER WILL BE SENSE.
BAD LUCK...
IT'S A SHAME AFTER WE PASSED THE FIRST EXAM...
WHAT DO YOU MEAN?

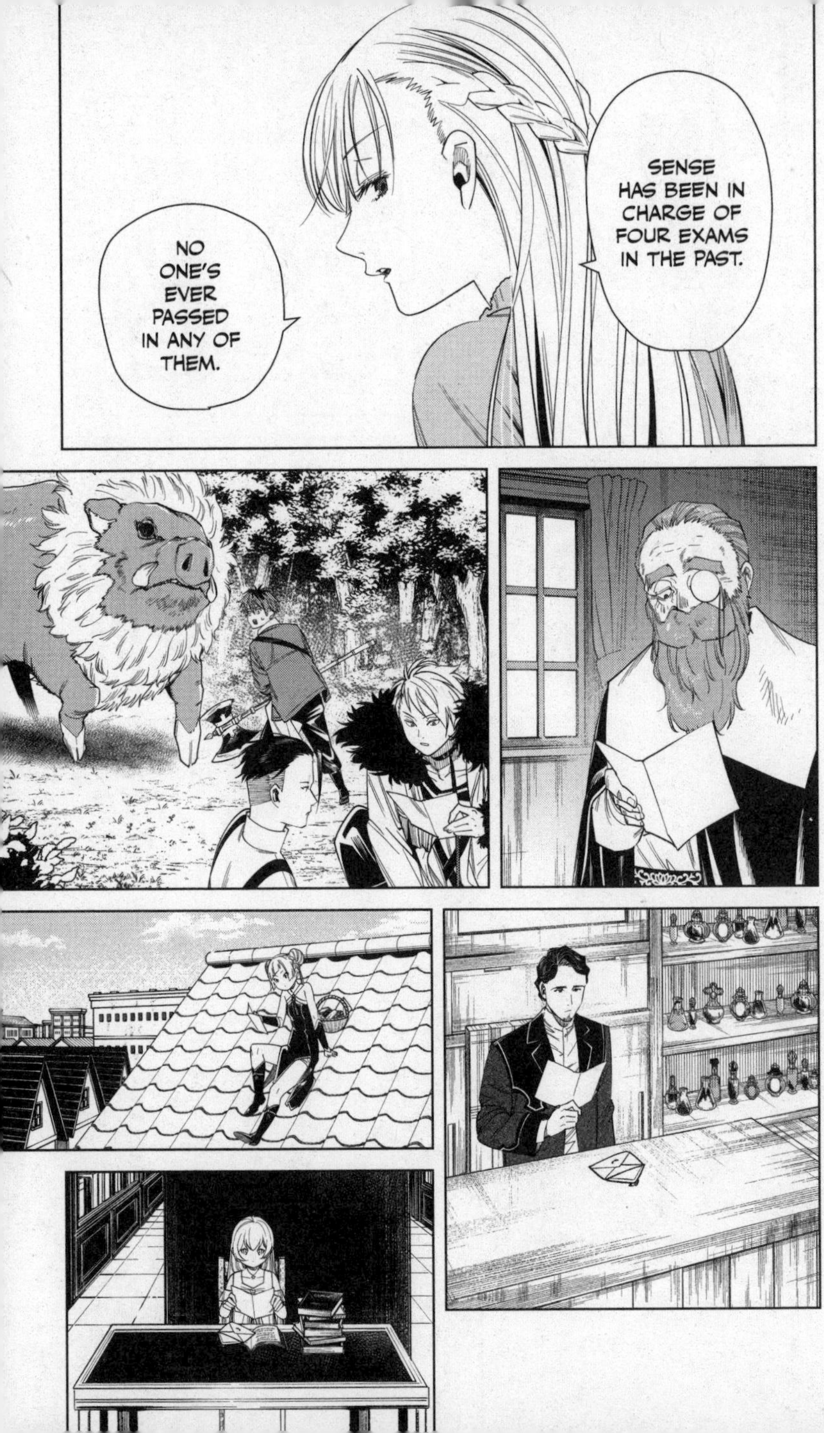
SENSE HAS BEEN IN CHARGE OF FOUR EXAMS IN THE PAST.
NO ONE'S EVER PASSED IN ANY OF THEM.

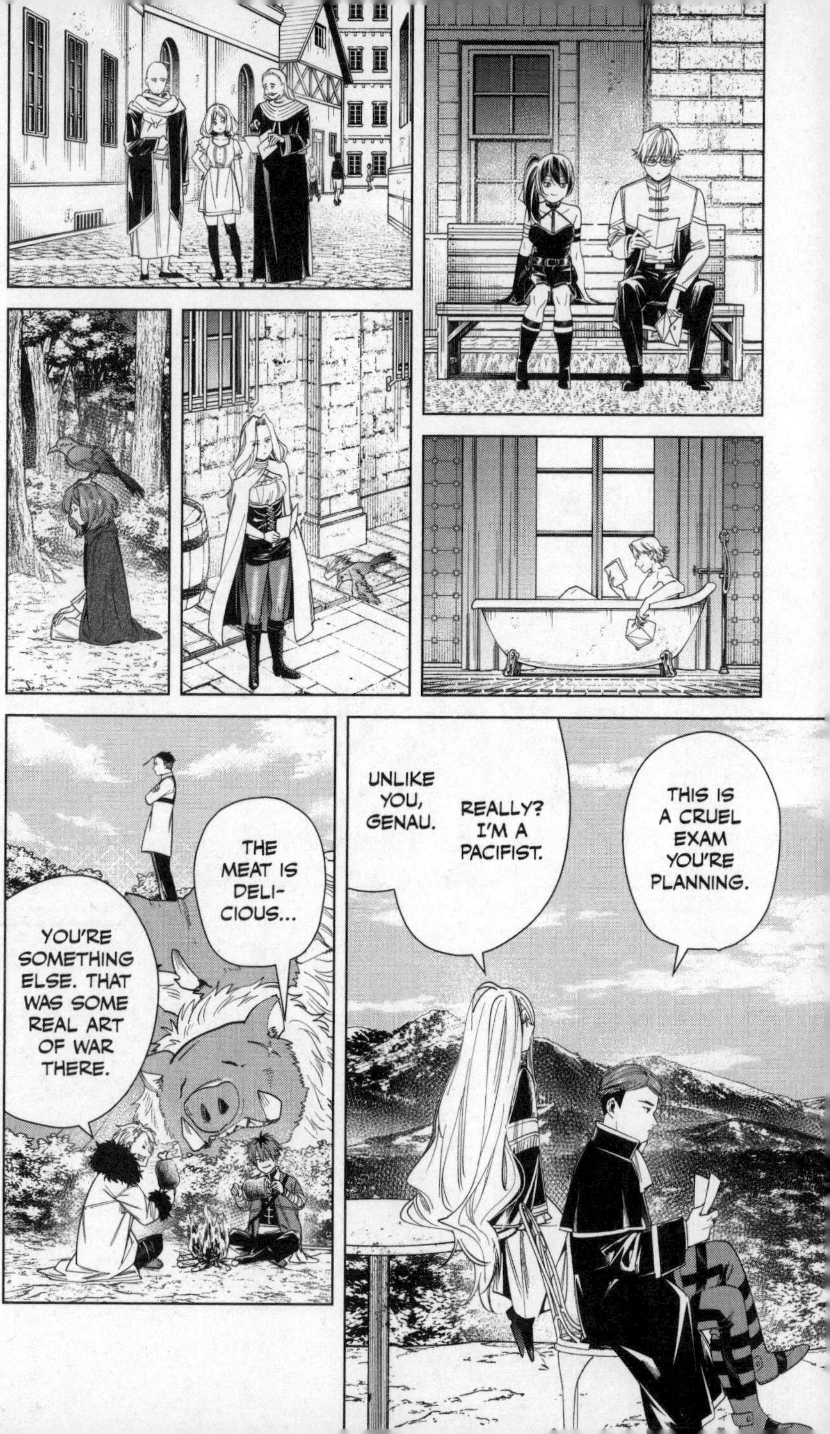
THIS IS A CRUEL EXAM YOU'RE PLANNING.
REALLY? I'M A PACIFIST.
UNLIKE YOU, GENAU.
THE MEAT IS DELI-CIOUS...
YOU'RE SOMETHING ELSE. THAT WAS SOME REAL ART OF WAR THERE.

Frieren: Beyond Journey's End – Vol. 5 - End

Frieren

Beyond Journey's End

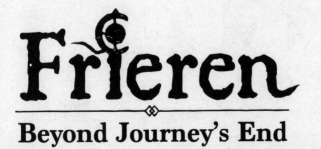

Frieren: Beyond Journey's End

VOLUME 5
Shonen Sunday Edition

STORY BY
KANEHITO YAMADA

ART BY
TSUKASA ABE

SOSO NO FRIEREN Vol. 5
by Kanehito YAMADA, Tsukasa ABE
© 2020 Kanehito YAMADA, Tsukasa ABE
All rights reserved.
Original Japanese edition published by SHOGAKUKAN.
English translation rights in the United States of America, Canada,
the United Kingdom, Ireland, Australia and New Zealand arranged
with SHOGAKUKAN.

Original Cover Design: Masato ISHIZAWA + Bay Bridge Studio

Translation/Misa 'Japanese Ammo'
Touch-Up Art & Lettering/Annaliese "Ace" Christman
Design/Yukiko Whitley
Editor/Mike Montesa

Printed in the U.S.A.

Published by VIZ Media, LLC
P.O. Box 77010
San Francisco, CA 94107

10 9 8 7 6 5 4 3 2 1
First printing, July 2022

PARENTAL ADVISORY
FRIEREN: BEYOND JOURNEY'S END is rated
T for Teen and recommended for ages 13 and
up. This volume contains fantasy violence.

viz.com

shonensunday.com

Kidnapped by the Demon King and imprisoned in his castle, Princess Syalis is...bored.

SLEEPY PRINCESS IN THE DEMON CASTLE

Story & Art by
KAGIJI KUMANOMATA

Captured princess Syalis decides to while away her hours in the Demon Castle by sleeping, but getting a good night's rest turns out to be a lot of work! She begins by fashioning a DIY pillow out of the fur of her Teddy Demon guards and an "air mattress" from the magical Shield of the Wind. Things go from bad to worse—for her captors—when some of Princess Syalis's schemes end in her untimely—if temporary—demise and she chooses the Forbidden Grimoire for her bedtime reading...

Hey! You're Reading in the Wrong Direction!

This is the end of this graphic novel!

To properly enjoy this VIZ graphic novel, please turn it around and begin reading from right to left. Unlike English, Japanese is read right to left, so Japanese comics are read in reverse order from the way English comics are typically read.

This book has been printed in the original Japanese format in order to preserve the orientation of the original artwork. Have fun with it!

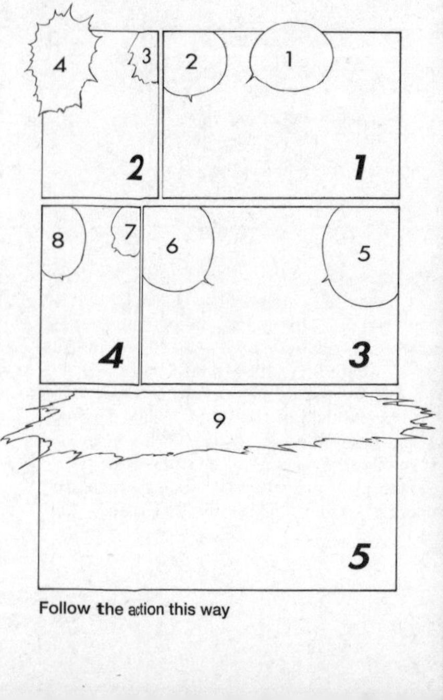
1
2
1
3
4
2
5
6
3
7
8
4
9
5

Follow the action this way

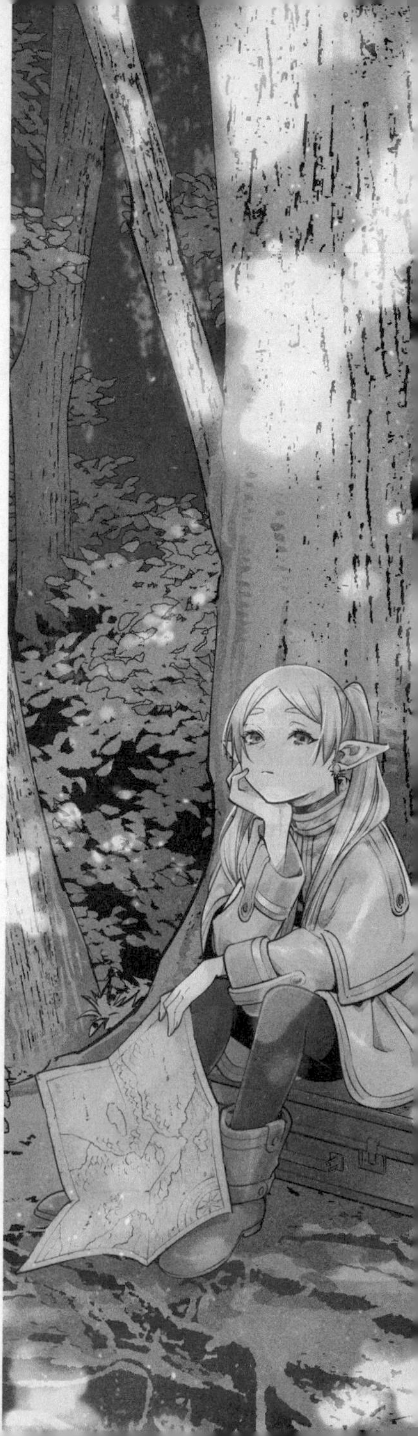